D1358315

Principles of Accounting

Second Custom Edition for Oakland Community College

Taken from:
Accounting: The Financial Chapters, Ninth Edition
by Charles T. Horngren, Walter T. Harrison Jr., and M. Suzanne Oliver

Cover Art: Courtesy of Photodisc/Getty Images.

Taken from:

Accounting: The Financial Chapters, Ninth Edition
by Charles T. Horngren, Walter T. Harrison Jr., and M. Suzanne Oliver
Copyright © 2012, 2009, 2008 by Pearson Education, Inc.
Published by Prentice Hall
Upper Saddle River, New Jersey 07458

This special edition published in cooperation with Pearson Learning Solutions.

All trademarks, service marks, registered trademarks, and registered service marks are the property of their respective owners and are used herein for identification purposes only.

Pearson Learning Solutions, 501 Boylston Street, Suite 900, Boston, MA 02116
A Pearson Education Company
www.pearsoned.com

Printed in the United States of America

4 5 6 7 8 9 10 VOCR 16 15 14 13 12

000200010270791773

KB

ISBN 10: 1-256-36608-0
ISBN 13: 978-1-256-36608-9

About the Authors

Charles T. Horngren is the Edmund W. Littlefield professor of accounting, emeritus, at Stanford University. A graduate of Marquette University, he received his MBA from Harvard University and his PhD from the University of Chicago. He is also the recipient of honorary doctorates from Marquette University and DePaul University.

A CPA, Horngren served on the Accounting Principles Board for six years, the Financial Accounting Standards Board (FASB) Advisory Council for five years, and the Council of the AICPA for three years. For six years he served as a trustee of the Financial Accounting Foundation, which oversees the FASB and the Government Accounting Standards Board.

Horngren is a member of the Accounting Hall of Fame.

A member of the AAA, Horngren has been its president and its director of research. He received its first annual Outstanding Accounting Educator Award.

The California Certified Public Accountants Foundation gave Horngren its Faculty Excellence Award and its Distinguished Professor Award. He is the first person to have received both awards.

The AICPA presented its first Outstanding Educator Award to Horngren.

Horngren was named Accountant of the Year, in Education, by the national professional accounting fraternity, Beta Alpha Psi.

Professor Horngren is also a member of the IMA, from whom he has received its Distinguished Service Award. He was a member of the institute's Board of Regents, which administers the CMA examinations.

Walter T. Harrison, Jr., is professor emeritus of accounting at the Hankamer School of Business, Baylor University. He received his BBA degree from Baylor University, his MS from Oklahoma State University, and his PhD from Michigan State University.

Professor Harrison, recipient of numerous teaching awards from student groups as well as from university administrators, has also taught at Cleveland State Community College, Michigan State University, the University of Texas, and Stanford University.

A member of AAA and the AICPA, Professor Harrison has served as chairman of the Financial Accounting Standards Committee of AAA, on the Teaching/Curriculum Development Award Committee, on the Program Advisory Committee for Accounting Education and Teaching, and on the Notable Contributions to Accounting Literature Committee.

Professor Harrison has lectured in several foreign countries and published articles in numerous journals, including *Journal of Accounting Research*, *Journal of Accountancy*, *Journal of Accounting and Public Policy*, *Economic Consequences of Financial Accounting Standards*, *Accounting Horizons*, *Issues in Accounting Education*, and *Journal of Law and Commerce*.

Professor Harrison has received scholarships, fellowships, and research grants or awards from PriceWaterhouse Coopers, Deloitte & Touche, the Ernst & Young Foundation, and the KPMG Foundation.

M. Suzanne Oliver is an accounting instructor at the University of West Florida in Pensacola, Florida. She received her BA in accounting information systems and her MA in accountancy from the University of West Florida.

Oliver began her career in the tax department of a regional accounting firm, specializing in benefit plan administration. She has served as a software analyst for a national software development firm and as the Oracle fixed assets analyst for Spirit Energy, formerly part of Unocal. A CPA, Oliver is a member of the AAA, AICPA, FICPA, IAAER, IMA, TACTYC, and the Florida Association of Accounting Educators.

Oliver has taught accounting courses of all levels for the University of West Florida, state colleges, community colleges, and to practitioners since 1988. She has developed and instructed online courses using MyAccountingLab, WebCT, D2L, and other proprietary software.

Oliver lives in Niceville, FL, with her husband, Greg, and son, CJ. She especially thanks her husband, Greg, her son, CJ, and her uncle and aunt, Jimmy and Lida Lewis, for their unwavering support and encouragement. Oliver donates a portion of royalties to www.raffieskids.org, a charitable organization that assists children.

Brief Contents

Contents

Changes to This Edition

Students and Instructors will both benefit from a variety of new content and features in the ninth edition of *Accounting*:

NEW and IMPROVED Chapter Openers. All of the chapter openers have been redesigned and rewritten. The financial chapter openers include a visual of a balance sheet, highlighting the specific section of the balance sheet that will be covered within the chapter. As students progress through these chapters, the decision being discussed is highlighted on the first page of the chapter. These visuals help set the stage while providing students with direction as they navigate through the material.

FOCUSED on Student Success. We've made it easy for students to identify what their focal point should be in every chapter:

- **NEW Key Takeaway Feature.** At the end of each main topic throughout the book, we've included a brief takeaway feature. This marginal feature hones in on the key point of that section so students will know exactly what they should have understood before moving on.
- **NEW Translation Guides.** We've included "translation guides" throughout the text, set off by a different font style/treatment, in which accounting terminology is translated into a language students can easily understand. In doing so, we aim to make accounting more approachable (for example: **Assets are resources that provide future economic benefits to a company. An asset is something you own that has value, like your iPod.**).
- **NEW Connect To Boxes.** We've included a marginal "Connect To" box in each chapter that focuses on topics such as IFRS, Ethics, Technology, and Accounting Information Systems. Each contains a subtitle so instructors can easily see what each box features.
- **IMPROVED Stop & Think Boxes.** We've refined many of the existing Stop & Think boxes, making them less technical.

EXTENSIVE REVISION of the End-of-Chapter Materials:

- **NEW End-of-Chapter Student Success Section.** We've added a new half-page, end-of-chapter "Student Success" section that does the following:
  - Lists hints on some common trouble spots/mistakes students make when taking a test on the chapter.
  - Tells students exactly where to go in the chapter and **MyAccountingLab** to get help related to a particular topic covered within that chapter.
- **IMPROVED End-of-Chapter Material.** We've improved the end-of-chapter exercises, while retaining the exercises often used in **MyAccountingLab**.
- **NEW End-of-Chapter Fraud Activity.** We've added a short end-of-chapter activity that asks students to look at a fraud issue related to the chapter.
- **NEW End-of-Chapter Communication Activity.** We've added a short end-of-chapter activity that asks students to restate key chapter content in their own words, encouraging them to learn and use chapter vocabulary.

ACCURACY. To ensure the level of accuracy instructors expect and require, accuracy checkers verified the in-chapter content, figures, and illustrations while additional accuracy checkers worked through the end-of-chapter material.

Students will have more "I Get It!" moments

Students understand (or "get it") right after the instructor does a problem in class. Once they leave the classroom, however, students often struggle to complete the homework on their own. This frustration can cause them to give up on the material altogether and fall behind in the course, resulting in an entire class falling behind as the instructor attempts to keep everyone on the same page.

Text

Study Resources

MyLab

With the *Accounting, Ninth Edition* Student Learning System, all the features of the student textbook, study resources, and online homework system are designed to work together to provide students with the consistency and repetition that will keep both the instructor and students on track by providing more "I Get It!" moments inside and outside the classroom.

Replicating the Classroom Experience with Demo Doc Examples

The Demo Doc Examples, available in chapters 1 through 4 of the text, consist of entire problems, worked through step-by-step and narrated with the kind of comments that instructors would say in class. Demo Docs will aid students when they are trying to solve exercises and problems on their own, duplicating the classroom experience outside of class.

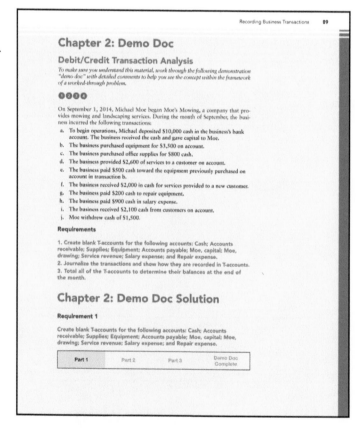

with *Accounting* and MyAccountingLab!

Consistency and Repetition Throughout the Learning Process

The concepts, materials, and practice problems are presented with clarity and consistency across all mediums—textbook, study resources, and online homework system. No matter which platform students use, they will continually experience the same look, feel, and language, minimizing confusion and ensuring clarity.

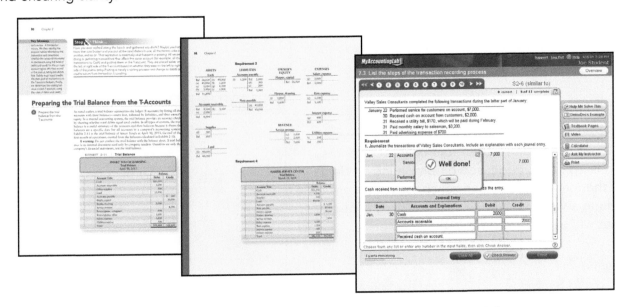

Experiencing the Power of Practice with MyAccountingLab: myaccountinglab.com

MyAccountingLab is an online homework system that gives students more "I Get It!" moments through the power of practice. With **MyAccountingLab** students can:

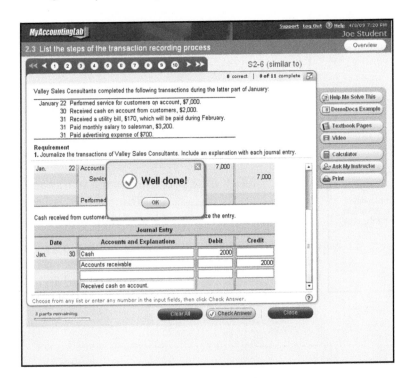

- work on the exact end-of-chapter material and/or similar problems assigned by the instructor.
- use the Study Plan for self-assessment and customized study outlines.
- use the Help Me Solve This tool for a step-by-step tutorial.
- watch a video to see additional information pertaining to the lecture.
- open the etext to the exact section of the book that will provide help on the specific problems.

Accounting...

With its tried-and-true framework and respected author team, Horngren/Harrison/Oliver's *Accounting* is the trusted choice for instructors and students of Introductory Accounting.

The ninth edition preserves the classic, solid foundation of the previous editions, while also including a modern and fresh teaching approach that helps students understand the complexities of accounting and achieve more "I Get It" moments.

NEW *Off to the right start:*
Chapter Openers _____

Redesigned and rewritten, the chapter openers in this edition are focused on preparing students for the reading. The financial chapter openers include a visual of a balance sheet that highlights what will be covered within the chapter.

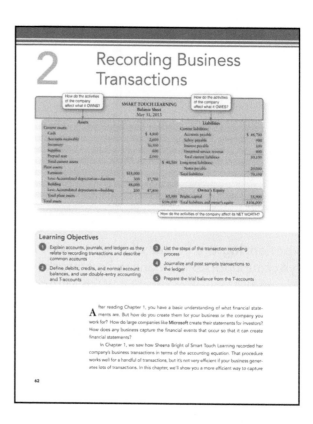

Current Assets

Current assets will be converted to cash, sold, or used up during the next 12 months, or within the business's operating cycle if the cycle is longer than a year. **Current assets are items that will be used up in a year, like your notebook paper for this class or the change in your pocket.** The **operating cycle** is the time span when

1. cash is used to acquire goods and services,

2. these goods and services are sold to customers, and

3. the business collects cash from customers.

NEW *Interpret the terms with ease:*
_____ **Translation Guides**

Translation guides, found throughout the chapters, translate accounting terminology in a way students can understand. For example, **Current assets are items that will be used up in a year, like your notebook paper for this class or the change in your pocket.**

The trusted choice for "I Get It" moments!

NEW *Link today's topics to the fundamentals:* **Connect To** _____

The Connect To marginal boxes in each chapter highlight hot topics such as IFRS, Ethics, and Accounting Information Systems as they pertain to the material being presented.

NEW *Highlight what matters:*
Key Takeaway

At the end of each learning objective, the authors added a new marginal feature that emphasizes the key points covered within the section so students can see what they need to understand before reading further.

> **Connect To: Ethics**
>
> The classification of assets and liabilities as current or long-term affects many key ratios that outsiders use to evaluate the financial health of a company. Many times, the classification of a particular account is very clear—for example, a building is normally a long-term asset. But what if the company must demolish the existing building within six months due to some structural default? It would not be ethical to still show the building as a long-term asset.

IMPROVED *Put the concepts in context:* **Stop & Think Boxes**

Improved Stop & Think boxes relate accounting concepts to students' everyday lives by presenting them with relevant examples of the topic in practice.

Keep it consistent: **Consistent Examples**

Rather than learn about a new company each time an example is presented, this text provides two sets of company data that are carried through all of the in-chapter examples. As a result, students gain a sense of familiarity with the context of these examples and can focus their energy on learning the accounting principles in question.

Illustrate the concepts: **Decision Guidelines**

Decision Guidelines explain why the accounting concepts addressed in the chapter are important in a business setting. The left-hand side of the Decision Guidelines table explains the decision or action asked of the student in simple terms, while the right-hand side shows the accounting topics that will help facilitate those decisions.

Putting "I Get It" moments into practice!

NEW *Help where it's needed:* Destination Student Success

The new Destination Student Success sections at the end of each chapter list hints on some common mistakes in order to prevent students from falling into the same traps. These sections also show students exactly where to go within the chapter and in **MyAccountingLab** to get help related to a particular topic or learning objective.

● Destination: Student Success

Student Success Tips	Getting Help
The following are hints on some common trouble areas for students in this chapter:	If there's a learning objective from the chapter you aren't confident about, try using one or more of the following resources:
● Commit to memory the normal balance of the six main account types. The normal balance is the side of the T-account where the account INCREASES. Assets, Drawing, and Expenses have normal debit balances. Liabilities, Equity, and Revenues have normal credit balances.	● Review the Chapter 2 Demo Doc located on page 89 of the textbook.
● Recall that debits are listed first in every journal entry.	● Practice additional exercises or problems at the end of Chapter 2 that cover the specific learning objective that is challenging you.
● Remember debits ALWAYS EQUAL credits in every journal entry.	● Watch the white board videos for Chapter 2 located at myaccountinglab.com under the Chapter Resources button.
● Keep in mind that posting is just gathering all the journal entries made to an individual T-account so that you can determine the new balance in the account. Journal debit entries are posted on the left side of the T-account. Journal credit entries are posted on the right side of the T-account.	● Go to myaccountinglab.com and select the Study Plan button. Choose Chapter 2 and work the questions covering that specific learning objective until you've mastered it.
● The accounting equation MUST ALWAYS balance after each transaction is posted.	● Work the Chapter 2 pre/post tests in myaccountinglab.com.
● The trial balance lists all accounts with a balance, ordered by assets, liabilities, equity, drawing, revenues, and expenses. Total debits should equal total credits on the trial balance.	● Visit the learning resource center on your campus for tutoring.

NEW *Examine the potential for fraud:* End-of-Chapter Fraud Case

This edition now includes a new end-of-chapter activity that asks students to look at a fraud issue related to the material. This activity helps students make the connection between the concepts and this popular accounting topic.

● Fraud Case 2-1

Roy Akins was the accounting manager at Zelco, a tire manufacturer, and he played golf with Hugh Stallings, the CEO, who was something of a celebrity in the community. The CEO stood to earn a substantial bonus if Zelco increased net income by year-end. Roy was eager to get into Hugh's elite social circle; he boasted to Hugh that he knew some accounting tricks that could increase company income by simply revising a few journal entries for rental payments on storage units. At the end of the year, Roy changed the debits from "rent expense" to "prepaid rent" on several entries. Later, Hugh got his bonus, and the deviations were never discovered.

Requirements

1. How did the change in the journal entries affect the net income of the company at year-end?

2. Who gained and who lost as a result of these actions?

NEW *Speak accounting fluently:* End-of-Chapter Communication Activity

To help students increase their confidence, understanding, and communication of accounting terms, the end-of-chapter Communication Activity asks students to restate, in their own words, what they've learned within the chapter.

● Communication Activity 2-1

In 35 words or fewer, explain the difference between a debit and a credit and explain what the normal balance of the six account types is.

Master the material: Extensive Practice Opportunities

Five Book-Match Sets of Problems and Exercises (A, B, C, D, E):

EXERCISES: Students will have access to exercise set A within the text. Exercise set A along with alternative static exercise sets B, C, D, and E can be assigned by the instructor and completed by students in **MyAccountingLab**.

PROBLEMS: Students will have access to A and B problems within the text. Problem set A and B along with alternative static problem sets C, D, and E can be assigned by the instructor and completed by students in **MyAccountingLab**.

Continuing Exercise:

The unique Continuing Exercise takes a single company and adds transactions or questions in each chapter to the existing fact pattern. As students move through the text, they complete additional steps in this comprehensive exercise. Students are able to see the big picture and learn how the accounting topics build off one another. The Continuing Exercise is also available in **MyAccountingLab**.

Continuing Problem:

For more detailed and in-depth practice, a Continuing Problem is also available. Like the Continuing Exercise, the Continuing Problem takes a single company and adds transactions or questions in each chapter to the existing fact pattern. As students move through the text, they complete additional steps in this comprehensive problem. The Continuing Problem is also available in **MyAccountingLab**.

Unique Practice Set Within Chapters 1–8:

An in-text Practice Set is built into Chapters 1–8 of the student text. Students do not have to purchase any additional material for their practice sets, and instructors no longer have to create their own. Since the same authors of the textbook created the Practice Set, students will once again have consistency. The Practice Set is also available in **MyAccountingLab**.

MyAccountingLab®

End-of-Chapter Material Integrated with MyAccountingLab

myaccountinglab.com

Students need practice and repetition in order to successfully learn the fundamentals. All of the end-of-chapter problems and exercises in *Accounting* can be assigned and graded through **MyAccountingLab**. And learning goes one step further with **MyAccountingLab's** algorithmic versions of the questions that provide students with unlimited practice.

pearsonhighered.com/horngren

Student and Instructor Resources

For Students

MyAccountingLab®

myaccountinglab.com Online Homework and Assessment Manager
MyAccountingLab is Web-based tutorial and assessment software for accounting that gives students more "I Get It!" moments. MyAccountingLab provides students with a personalized interactive learning environment where they can complete their course assignments with immediate tutorial assistance, learn at their own pace, and measure their progress.

In addition to completing assignments and reviewing tutorial help, students have access to the following resources in **MyAccountingLab**:

- Pearson eText
- Data Files
- Videos
- Demo Docs

- Audio and Student PowerPoint® Presentations
- Working Papers in Both Excel and PDF
- MP3 Files with Chapter Objectives and Summaries
- Flash Cards

Student Resource Web site: pearsonhighered.com/horngren
The book's Web site contains the following:
- Data Files: Select end-of-chapter problems have been set up in different software applications, including Peachtree 2010, QuickBooks 2010, and Excel
- Excel Working Papers
- Online Chapter Materials (Special Purpose Journals and Investments)

For Instructors

MyAccountingLab®

myaccountinglab.com Online Homework and Assessment Manager

Instructor Resource Center: pearsonhighered.com/accounting
For the instructor's convenience, the instructor resources are available on CD or can be downloaded from the textbook's catalog page (pearsonhighered.com/horngren) and **MyAccountingLab**. Available resources include the following:

- **Online Instructor's Manual:** Includes chapter summaries, teaching tips provided by reviewers, pitfalls for new students, and "best of" practices from instructors across the country. And, to effectively implement the array of resources available, a Resource Roadmap is provided, giving a description and location of each resource, along with recommendations for classroom applications. Additional resources offered in the instructor's manual include the following:

- Introduction to the Instructor's Manual with a list of resources and a roadmap to help navigate what's available in MyAccountingLab.
- Instructor tips for teaching courses in multiple formats—traditional, hybrid, or online.
- "First Day of Class" student handout that includes tips for success in the course, as well as an additional document that shows students how to register and log on to MyAccountingLab.
- Sample syllabi for 10- and 16-week courses.
- Chapter overview and teaching outline that includes a brief synopsis and overview of each chapter.
- Key topics that walk instructors through what material to cover and what examples to use when addressing certain items within the chapter.
- Student chapter summary handout.
- Assignment grid that outlines all end-of-chapter exercises and problems, the topic being covered in that particular exercise or problem, estimated completion time, level of difficulty, and availability in Excel templates.
- Ten-minute quizzes that quickly assess students' understanding of the chapter material.

- **Instructor's Solutions Manual:** Contains solutions to all end-of-chapter questions, including short exercises, exercises, and problems.
- **TestBank:** Includes more than 3,000 questions and is formatted for use with WebCT, Blackboard, and CourseCompass™. Both objective-based questions and computational problems are available.
- **PowerPoint Presentations:** These presentations help facilitate classroom discussion by demonstrating where the numbers come from and what they mean to the concept at hand.
  - Instructor PowerPoint Presentations—complete with lecture notes
  - Student PowerPoint Presentations
  - Audio Narrated PowerPoint Presentations
  - Clicker Response System (CRS) PowerPoint Presentations

- **Working Papers and Solutions in Excel and PDF Format**
- **Image Library**
- **Data and Solution Files:** Select end-of-chapter problems have been set up in different software applications, including Peachtree 2010, QuickBooks 2010, and Excel. Corresponding solution files are also provided.

Acknowledgments

Acknowledgments for This Edition

The authors and editorial team thank Jodi McPherson for her vision and unwavering support over the past five years. Go SOX!

We would also like to extend a special thank you to the following individuals who were very helpful in the revision of this book:

Contributors:

Marcye Hampton, *University of Central Florida*
Brenda Mattison, *Tri-County Technical College*
Craig Reeder, *Florida Agricultural and Mechanical University*

Advisory Panel:

Lisa Banks, *Mott Community College*
Betty Christopher, *Mission College*
Tracy Corr, *Southeast Community College*
Anthony J. Dellarte, *Luzerne County Community College*
Robert Fahnestock, *University of West Florida*
Charles Fazzi, *Saint Vincent College*
Jaclyn Felder-Strauss, *Kaplan University*
Anita Feller, *University of Illinois at Urbana–Champaign*
Marina Grau, *Houston Community College*
Geoffrey Gurka, *Mesa State College of Colorado*
Geoffrey Heriot, *Greenville Technical College*
Patty Holmes, *Des Moines Area Community College*
Emil Koren, *Saint Leo University*
Suzanne Lay, *Mesa State College of Colorado*
Maria Leach, *Auburn University–Montgomery*

Dorinda Lynn, *Pensacola State College*
Brenda Mattison, *Tri-County Technical College*
Cheryl McKay, *Monroe County Community College*
Audrey Morrison, *Pensacola State College*
Tim Murphy, *Diablo Valley College*
Ed Napravnik, *Metropolitan Community College*
Tracie Nobles, *Austin Community College*
Jamie Payton, *Gadsden State Community College*
Craig Reeder, *Florida Agricultural and Mechanical University*
Carla Rich, *Pensacola State College*
Randy Rinke, *Mercyhurst College*
Dennis Roth, *West Virginia Northern Community College*
Linda Tarrago, *Hillsborough Community College*
Melanie Torborg, *Minnesota School of Business*
Andy Williams, *Edmonds Community College*

Accuracy Checkers:

Nabanita Bhattacharya, *Northwest Florida State College*
Ron Burris, *GEX Publishing Services*
David Doyon, *GEX Publishing Services*
Anita Hope, *Tarrant County College*
Peg Johnson, *Metropolitan Community College*

Dorinda Lynn, *Pensacola State College*
Cynthia Miller, *University of Kentucky*
Noriko Tilley, *Northwest Florida State College*
Greg Yost, *University of West Florida*

Reviewers:

Dave Alldredge, *Salt Lake Community College*
Lee Daniel, *Troy University*
Heidi Hansel, *Kirkwood Community College*
Paige Paulson, *Salt Lake Community College*
Michelle Powell-Dancy, *Holmes Community College–Ridgeland*

Joan Ryan, *Clackamas Community College*
Beverly Strachan, *Troy University*
Rick Turpin, *Troy University*
Susan Wright, *Dekalb Technical College*

Supplements Authors and Reviewers:

Natalie Allen, *Texas A&M University*
Helen Brubeck, *San Jose State University*
Colleen Chung, *Miami Dade College*
Wanda Edwards, *Troy State University*
Shirley Glass, *Macomb Community College*
Rob Hochschild, *Ivy Tech Community College*
Jamie McCracken, *Saint Mary-of-the-Woods College*
Brit McKay, *Georgia Southern University*
Jennie Mitchell, *Saint Mary-of-the-Woods College*

Cathy Nash, *Dekalb Technical College*
Craig Reeder, *Florida Agricultural and Mechanical University*
Rick Street, *Spokane Community College*
Allan Sheets, *International Business College*
John Stancil, *Florida Southern University College*
Noriko Tilley, *Northwest Florida State College*
Robin Turner, *Rowan-Cabarrus Community College*
Susan Wright, *Dekalb Technical College*
Greg Yost, *University of West Florida*

Acknowledgments for Previous Editions

Contributors:

Helen Brubeck, *San Jose State University*
Florence McGovern, *Bergen Community College*
Sherry Mills, *New Mexico State University*

Advisory panel:

David Baglia, *Grove City College*
Joan Cezair, *Fayetteville State University*
Margaret Costello Lambert, *Oakland Community College*
Kathy Crusto-Way, *Tarrant County College*
Jim Ellis, *Bay State College–Boston*
Anita Ellzey, *Harford Community College*

Al Fagan, *University of Richmond*
Todd Jackson, *Northeastern State University*
Donnie Kristof-Nelson, *Edmonds Community College*
Cheryl McKay, *Monroe County Community College*
Mary Ann Swindlehurst, *Carroll Community College*
Andy Williams, *Edmonds Community College*

Reviewers:

Joseph Adamo, *Cazenovia College*
Audrey Agnello, *Niagara County Community College*
William Alexander, *Indian Hills Community College–Ottumwa*
Asokan Anandarajan, *New Jersey Institute of Technology*
Susan Anders, *St. Bonaventure University*
Joe Aubert, *Bemidji State University*
Melody Ashenfelter, *Southwestern Oklahoma State University*

Charles Baird, *University of Wisconsin-Stout*
Dan Bayak, *Northampton Community College*
Richard Bedwell, *Jones County Junior College*
Judy Beebe, *Western Oregon University*
Irene Bembenista, *Davenport University*
Margaret Berezewski, *Robert Morris College*
Lecia Berven, *Iowa Lakes Community College*
Charles Betts, *Delaware Technical and Community College*
Greg Bischoff, *Houston Community College*
Margaret Black, *San Jacinto College*
William Black, *Raritan Valley Community College*
David Bland, *Cape Fear Community College*
Allen Blay, *University of California–Riverside*
Susan Blizzard, *San Antonio College*
Michael Blue, *Bloomsburg University*
Dale Bolduc, *Intercoast College*
Linda Bolduc, *Mount Wachusett Community College*
Donald Bond, *Houston Community College*
John Boyd, *Oklahoma City Community College*
Suzanne Bradford, *Angelina College*
Thomas Branton, *Alvin Community College*
Jerold Braun, *Daytona Beach Community College*
Nat Briscoe, *Northwestern State University*
Julie Browning, *California Baptist University*
Carroll Buck, *San Jose State University*

Jane Calvert, *University of Central Oklahoma*
Vickie Campbell, *Cape Fear Community College*
David Candelaria, *Mount San Jacinto College*

Lee Cannell, *El Paso Community College*
Michelle Cannon, *Ivy Tech Community College*
Greg Carlton, *Davidson County Community College*
Kay Carnes, *Gonzaga University–Spokane*
Brian Carpenter, *University of Scranton*
Thomas Carr, *International College of Naples*
Lloyd Carroll, *Borough Manhattan Community College*
Stanley Carroll, *New York City College of Technology of CUNY*
Roy Carson, *Anne Arundel Community College*
Al Case, *Southern Oregon University*
Gerald Caton, *Yavapai College*
Bea Chiang, *The College of New Jersey*
Catherine Chiang, *North Carolina Central University*
Stephen Christian, *Jackson Community College*
Shifei Chung, *Rowan University of New Jersey*
Toni Clegg, *Palm Beach Atlantic University*
Lynn Clements, *Florida Southern College*
Doug Clouse, *Lakeland Community College*
Cynthia Coleman, *Sandhills Community College*
Christie Comunale, *Long Island University*
Sally Cook, *Texas Lutheran University*
Sue Counte, *St. Louis Community College*
Chris Crosby, *York Technical College*
Ted Crosby, *Montgomery County Community College*
Barbara Crouteau, *Santa Rosa Junior College*
Chris Cusatis, *Gwynedd-Mercy College*

Julie Dailey, *Central Virginia Community College*
DeeDee Daughtry, *Johnston Community College*
Judy Daulton, *Piedmont Technical College*
David L. Davis, *Tallahassee Community College*
Elaine Dessouki, *Virginia Wesleyan College*
Ken Duffe, *Brookdale Community College*

John Eagan, *Erie Community College*
Gene Elrod, *University of Texas–Arlington*
Beth Engle, *Montgomery County Community College*

Harlan Etheridge, *University of Louisiana*
Charles Evans, *Keiser College*

Charles Fazzi, *Saint Vincent College*
Calvin Fink, *Bethune Cookman College*
Phil Fink, *University of Toledo*
Carolyn Fitzmorris, *Hutchinson Community College*
Rebecca Floor, *Greenville Technical College*
Joseph Foley, *Assumption College*
Jeannie Folk, *College of DuPage*
David Forsyth, *Palomar College*

Shelly Gardner, *Augustana College*
Harold Gellis, *York College of CUNY*
Renee Goffinet, *Spokane Community College*
Saturnino (Nino) Gonzales, *El Paso Community College*
Janet Grange, *Chicago State University*
Marina Grau, *Houston Community College*
John Graves, *PCDI*
Gloria Grayless, *Sam Houston State University*
Barbara Gregorio, *Nassau Community College*
Tim Griffin, *Hillsborough Community College*
Judy Grotrian, *Peru State College*

Amy Haas, *Kingsborough Community College*
Betty Habershon, *Prince George's Community College*
Patrick Haggerty, *Lansing Community College*
Penny Hanes, *Mercyhurst College–Erie*
Phil Harder, *Robert Morris University*
Marc Haskell, *Fresno City College*
Clair Helms, *Hinds Community College*
Kathy Heltzel, *Luzerne County Community College*
Sueann Hely, *West Kentucky Community and Technical College*
Geoffrey Heriot, *Greenville Technical College*
Humberto M. Herrera, *Laredo Community College*
Chuck Heuser, *Brookdale Community College*
Matt Hightower, *Three Rivers Community College*

Merrily Hoffman, *San Jacinto College*
Mary Hollars, *Vincennes University*
Patty Holmes, *Des Moines Area Community College–Ankeny*
Bambi Hora, *University of Central Oklahoma*
Maggie Houston, *Wright State University*
William Huffman *Missouri Southern State College*
James Hurat, *National College of Business and Technology*
Larry Huus, *University of Minnesota*
Constance Hylton, *George Mason University*

Verne Ingram, *Red Rocks Community College*

Fred Jex, *Macomb Community College*
Peg Johnson, *Metropolitan Community College*
Becky Jones, *Baylor University*
Jeffrey Jones, *Community College of Southern Nevada*
Christine Jonick, *Gainesville State College*
Paul Juriga, *Richland Community College*

Lolita Keck, *Globe College*
Christopher Kelly, *Community College of Southern Nevada*
James Kelly, *Ft. Lauderdale City College*
Ashraf Khallaf, *University of Southern Indiana*
Randy Kidd, *Longview Community College*
Chula King, *University of West Florida*
Cody King, *Georgia Southwestern State University*
Susan Koepke, *Illinois Valley Community College*
Ken Koerber, *Bucks County Community College*
Dennis Kovach, *Community College of Allegheny County–Allegheny*

Lawrence Leaman, *University of Michigan*
Denise Leggett, *Middle Tennessee State University*
Pamela Legner, *College of DuPage*
Maria Lehoczky, *American Intercontinental University*
Bruce Leung, *City College of San Francisco*
Judy Lewis, *Angelo State University*
Bruce Lindsey, *Genesee Community College*
Elizabeth Lynn Locke, *Northern Virginia Community College*

Michelle Maggio, *Westfield State College*
Bridgette Mahan, *Harold Washington College*
Lori Major, *Luzerne County Community College*
James Makofske, *Fresno City College*
Ken Mark, *Kansas City Kansas Community College*
Ariel Markelevich, *Long Island University*
Hector Martinez, *San Antonio College*
John May, *Southwestern Oklahoma State University*
Nora McCarthy, *Wharton County Junior College*
Bruce McMurrey, *Community College of Denver*

Patrick McNabb, *Ferris State University*
Pam Meyer, *University of Louisiana*
John Miller, *Metropolitan Community College*
Barry Mishra, *University of California–Riverside*
Norma Montague, *Central Carolina Community College*
Tim Murphy, *Diablo Valley College*

Lisa Nash, *Vincennes University*
Lanny Nelms, *Gwinnet Technical College*
Jennifer Niece, *Assumption College*
Deborah Niemer, *Oakland Community College*
Tom Nohl, *Community College of Southern Nevada*
Pat Novak, *Southeast Community College*

Ron O'Brien, *Fayetteville Technical Community College*
Kathleen O'Donnell, *Onondaga Community College*
John Olsavsky, *SUNY at Fredonia*
Liz Ott, *Casper College*
Glenn Owen, *Marymount College*

Carol Pace, *Grayson County College*
Susan Pallas, *Southeast Community College*
Jeffrey Patterson, *Grove City College*
Kathy Pellegrino, *Westfield State College*
Susan Pope, *University of Akron*
Robert Porter, *Cape Fear Community College*
Michelle Powell, *Holmes Community College*
Cheryl Prachyl, *University of Texas–El Paso*
Debra Prendergast, *Northwestern Business College*
Darlene Pulliam, *West Texas A&M University–Canyon*
Karl Putnam, *University of Texas–El Paso*

Margaret Quarles, *Sam Houston State University*
Behnaz Quigley, *Marymount College*

Jim Racic, *Lakeland Community College*
Paulette Ratliff-Miller, *Arkansas State University*
Carla Rich, *Pensacola State College*
Denver Riffe, *National College of Business and Technology*
Michael Robinson, *Baylor University*
Stephen Rockwell, *University of Tulsa*
Patrick Rogan, *Cosumnes River College*
Dennis Roth, *West Virginia Northern Community College*
Karen Russom, *North Harris College*
J.T. Ryan, *Onondaga Community College*

Martin Sabo, *Community College of Denver*
Phillipe Sammour, *Eastern Michigan University*
Richard Savich, *California State University–San Bernardino*
Nancy Schendel, *Iowa Lakes Community College*
Sandra Scheuermann, *University of Louisiana*

Bunney Schmidt, *Keiser College*
Debbie Schmidt, *Cerritos College*
Robert Schoener, *New Mexico State University*
Tony Scott, *Norwalk Community College*
Linda Serres Sweeny, *Sam Houston State University*
Brandi Shay, *Southwestern Community College*
Alice Sineath, *Forsyth Technical Community College*
Lois Slutsky, *Broward Community College South*
Kimberly Smith, *County College of Morris*
Chuck Smith, *Iowa Western Community College*
Ken Snow, *Kaplan Education Centers*
John Stancil, *Florida Southern College*
Lawrence Steiner, *College of Marin*
Sally Stokes, *Wilmington College*
Thomas Stolberg, *Alfred State University*
Joan Stone, *University of Central Oklahoma*
John Stone, *Potomac State College*
Thomas Szczurek, *Delaware County Community College*

Kathy Terrell, *University of Central Oklahoma*
Cynthia Thompson, *Carl Sandburg College–Carthage*

Shafi Ullah, *Broward Community College South*

Peter Van Brunt, *SUNY College of Technology at Delhi*
Kathi Villani, *Queensborough Community College*
Audrey Voyles, *San Diego Miramar College*

Patricia Walczak, *Lansing Community College*
Kay Walker-Hauser, *Beaufort County Community College–Washington*
Scott Wallace, *Blue Mountain College*
Douglas Ward, *Southwestern Community College*
Jeffrey Waybright, *Spokane Community College*
Roberta Wheeler, *Northwest Florida State College*
Bill Whitley, *Athens State University*
Randall Whitmore, *San Jacinto College*
Vicki White, *Ivy Tech Community College*
Idalene Williams, *Metropolitan Community College*
Betsy Willis, *Baylor University*
Tom Wilson, *University of Louisiana*
Joe Woods, *University of Arkansas*
Patty Worsham, *Riverside Community College*
Gloria Worthy, *Southwest Tennessee Community College*

Shi-Mu (Simon) Yang, *Adelphi University*
Lynnette Yerbuy, *Salt Lake Community College*
Laura Young, *University of Central Arkansas*

Tony Zordan, *University of St.Francis*

1

Accounting and the Business Environment

As you'll learn in this chapter, the accounting equation (Assets = Liabilities + Equity) IS the balance sheet.

SMART TOUCH LEARNING
Balance Sheet
May 31, 2013

Assets				Liabilities	
Current assets:				Current liabilities:	
Cash		$ 4,800		Accounts payable	$ 48,700
Accounts receivable		2,600		Salary payable	900
Inventory		30,500		Interest payable	100
Supplies		600		Unearned service revenue	400
Prepaid rent		2,000		Total current liabilities	50,100
Total current assets			$ 40,500	Long-term liabilities:	
Plant assets:				Notes payable	20,000
Furniture	$18,000			Total liabilities	70,100
Less: Accumulated depreciation—furniture	300	17,700			
Building	48,000				
Less: Accumulated depreciation—building	200	47,800		**Owner's Equity**	
Total plant assets			65,500	Bright, capital	35,900
Total assets			$106,000	Total liabilities and owner's equity	$106,000

Learning Objectives

1 Define accounting vocabulary

2 Define the users of financial information

3 Describe the accounting profession and the organizations that govern it

4 Identify the different types of business organizations

5 Delineate the distinguishing characteristics and organization of a proprietorship

6 Apply accounting concepts and principles

7 Describe the accounting equation, and define assets, liabilities, and equity

8 Use the accounting equation to analyze transactions

9 Prepare financial statements

10 Use financial statements to evaluate business performance

Have you ever dreamed of running your own business? If so, where would you begin? How much money would you need? How would you measure its success or failure? Or maybe you're looking to become a manager in an organization. How would you gather the information you need to make strategic decisions? Do you have dreams of retiring early? If so, how do you pick companies to invest in? How can you make smart investment decisions throughout your life? You don't have to be an accountant to make good decisions, but understanding accounting can help you answer these questions and many more.

•   •   •

In this chapter, we'll start our exploration into accounting by looking at two businesses: Smart Touch Learning and Greg's Tunes. We'll see how the owners of these two businesses—Sheena Bright of Smart Touch and Greg Moore of Greg's Tunes—started successful companies by treating people fairly, having realistic expectations, and capitalizing on their general business and accounting savvy. We'll also see how understanding financial statements—like the balance sheet shown on the previous page—is one of the first steps toward business success.

Accounting Vocabulary: The Language of Business

 Define accounting vocabulary

You've heard the term *accounting*, but what exactly is it? **Accounting** is the information system that measures business activity, processes the data into reports, and communicates the results to decision makers. **Accounting is "the language of business."** The better you understand the language of business, the better you can manage your own business. For example, how will you decide whether to borrow money to start up a business? You need to consider your income and whether you will be able to pay back that loan. Understanding what income is and how it's calculated is an accounting concept.

A key product of accounting is a set of reports called financial statements. **Financial statements** report on a business in monetary terms. Is Smart Touch making a profit? Should Greg's Tunes expand? If Greg's Tunes expands, how will it get the funds needed to expand? Where is Smart Touch's cash coming from? Financial statements help managers and owners answer questions like these and many more. We'll discuss financial statements in detail later in the chapter. For now, let's turn our attention to the users of accounting information.

Key Takeaway

Accounting is the language of business. Financial statements report a company's activities in monetary terms.

Decision Makers: The Users of Accounting Information

 Define the users of financial information

We can divide accounting into two fields—financial accounting and managerial accounting.

Financial accounting provides information for external decision makers, such as outside investors and lenders. **Financial accounting provides data for outsiders.**

Managerial accounting focuses on information for internal decision makers, such as the company's managers. **Managerial accounting provides data for insiders.**

Exhibit 1-1 illustrates the difference between financial accounting and managerial accounting. Regardless of whether they are external or internal to the company, all decision makers need information to make the best choices. The bigger the decision, the more information decision makers need. Let's look at some ways in which various people use accounting information to make important decisions.

Individuals

How much cash do you have? How much do you need to save each month to retire at a certain age or pay for your children's college education? Accounting can help you answer questions like these. By using accounting information, you can manage your money, evaluate a new job, and better decide whether you can afford to buy a new computer. Businesses need accounting information to make similar decisions.

EXHIBIT 1-1   Financial Accounting and Managerial Accounting

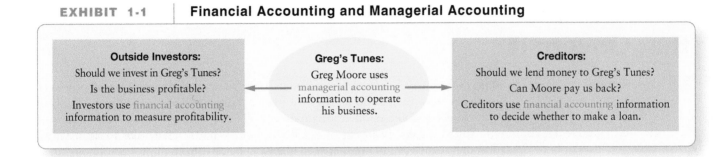

Businesses

Business owners use accounting information to set goals, to measure progress toward those goals, and to make adjustments when needed. The financial statements give owners the information they need to help make those decisions. For example, say Sheena Bright of Smart Touch wants to know whether her business is profitable enough to purchase another computer. Financial statements will help her make that decision.

Investors

Outside investors who have some ownership interest often provide the money to get a business going. For example, Smart Touch may need to raise cash for an expansion. Suppose you're considering investing in Smart Touch. How would you decide whether it is a good investment? In making this decision, you might try to predict the amount of income you would earn on the investment. Also, after making an investment, investors can use a company's financial statements to analyze how their investment is performing.

Every person has the opportunity to invest in their retirement through a company-sponsored retirement plan or IRA contributions. Which investments should you pick? Understanding a company's financial statements will help you decide. (Note that you can view the financial statements of large companies that report to the SEC by logging on to finance.yahoo.com, google.com/finance, or the Security and Exchange Commission's EDGAR database.)

Creditors

Any person or business lending money is a **creditor**. For example, suppose Smart Touch needs $200,000 to buy an office building. Before lending money to Smart Touch, a bank will evaluate the company's ability to make the loan payments by reviewing its financial statements. The same process will apply to you if you need to borrow money for a new car or a house. The bank will review accounting data to determine your ability to make the loan payments. What does your financial position tell the bank about your ability to pay the loan? Are you a good risk for the bank?

Taxing Authorities

Local, state, and federal governments levy taxes. Income tax is figured using accounting information. Good accounting records can help individuals and businesses take advantage of lawful deductions. Without good records, the IRS can disallow tax deductions, resulting in a higher tax bill plus interest and penalties.

Key Takeaway

Different users—including individuals, business owners, managers, investors, creditors, and tax authorities—review a company's financial statements for different reasons. Each user's goal will determine which pieces of the financial statements he or she will find most useful.

The Accounting Profession and the Organizations that Govern It

3 Describe the accounting profession and the organizations that govern it

What do businesses such as Smart Touch, Greg's Tunes, **Walmart**, or the **Coca-Cola Company** have in common? They all need accountants! That is why accounting opens so many doors upon graduation.

You've probably heard of a CPA before. What does it take to be a CPA? Although requirements vary between states, to be certified in a profession, one must meet the educational and/or experience requirements AND pass a qualifying exam. **Certified public accountants**, or **CPAs**, are licensed professional accountants who serve the general public. **Certified management accountants**, or CMAs, are certified professionals who work for a single company.

How much do accountants make? The average starting salary for a 2009 college graduate with a bachelor's degree in accounting was $48,334.[1] A graduate with a master's degree earns about 10% more to start, and CPAs earn another 10%.

Many accounting firms are organized as partnerships, and the partners are the owners. It usually takes 10 to 15 years to rise to the rank of partner. The partners of large accounting firms, such as **Ernst & Young**, earn from $150,000 to $500,000 per year. In private accounting, where accountants work for a single company, such as **Walmart**, the top position is called the chief financial officer (CFO), and a CFO earns about as much as a partner in an accounting firm.

Accountants get to the top of organizations as often as anyone else. Why? Because accountants must deal with every aspect of the company's business in order to record all of its activities. Accountants often have the broadest view of what is going on in the company.

As you move through this book, you will learn to account for everything that affects a business—all the revenue, all the expenses, all the cash, all the inventory, all the debts, and all the owner's accounts. Accounting requires you to consider everything, and that is why it is so valuable to an organization. Ultimately, accounting affects everyone, which is why it is important to you.

All professions have regulations. Let's look at the organizations that govern the accounting profession.

Governing Organizations

In the United States, the **Financial Accounting Standards Board (FASB)**, a privately funded organization, formulates accounting standards. The FASB works with governmental regulatory agencies like the Securities and Exchange Commission (SEC). The SEC is the U.S. governmental agency that oversees U.S. financial markets. It also oversees those organizations that set standards (like the FASB). The FASB also works with congressionally created groups like the Public Companies Accounting Oversight Board (PCAOB) and private groups like the American Institute of Certified Public Accountants (AICPA) and the Institute of Management Accountants (IMA).

The guidelines for public information are called **generally accepted accounting principles (GAAP)**. GAAP is the main U.S. accounting rule book. Some of these guidelines are described later in this chapter. Currently, the SEC has indicated that U.S. GAAP will move to converge with **international financial reporting standards (IFRS)** published by the **International Accounting Standards Board (IASB)** as early as 2012 for some companies. Whereas U.S. GAAP is more specific in its regulation, IFRS is

---

[1] http://www.employmentwebsites.org/salary-offers-college-class-2009-are-flat

less specific and based more on general principles, leaving more room for professional judgment. **IFRS is the international accounting rule book.**

Ethics in Accounting and Business

Ethical considerations affect accounting. Investors and creditors need relevant and reliable information about a company such as **Amazon.com** or **Walmart**. Companies want to be profitable and financially strong to attract investors, so there is a conflict of interest here. To provide reliable information, the SEC requires companies to have their financial statements audited by independent accountants. An **audit** is an examination of a company's financial records. The independent accountants then issue an opinion that states whether or not the financial statements give a fair picture of the company's financial situation.

The vast majority of accountants do their jobs professionally and ethically, but we never hear about them. Unfortunately, only those who cheat make the headlines. In recent years we have seen many accounting scandals.

In response to the **Enron** and **WorldCom** reporting scandals, the U.S. government took swift action. It passed the Sarbanes-Oxley Act, which made it a criminal offense to falsify financial statements. It also created a new watchdog agency, the PCAOB, to monitor the work of independent accountants who audit public companies. More recent scandals, such as the Bernie Madoff scandal, have further undermined the public's faith in financial reporting. This may result in more legislation for future reporting.

Standards of Professional Conduct

The AICPA's Code of Professional Conduct for Accountants provides guidance to CPAs in their work. Ethical standards are designed to produce relevant and reliable information for decision making. The preamble to the Code states the following:

> "[A] certified public accountant assumes an obligation of self-discipline above and beyond the requirements of laws and regulations ... [and] an unswerving commitment to honorable behavior... ."

The opening paragraph of the Standards of Ethical Conduct of the Institute of Management Accountants (IMA) states the following:

> "Management accountants have an obligation to the organizations they serve, their profession, the public, and themselves to maintain the highest standards of ethical conduct."

Most companies also set standards of ethical conduct for employees. For example, Greg's Tunes must comply with copyright laws in order to serve customers ethically. **Microsoft** has a highly developed set of business conduct guidelines. For example, **Microsoft** states that "it is not enough to intend to do things right, we must also do them in the right way."[2] A business's or an individual's reputation is often hard earned and can easily be lost. As one chief executive has stated, "Ethical practice is simply good business." Truth is always better than dishonesty—in accounting, in business, and in life.

Key Takeaway
Most U.S. businesses follow generally accepted accounting principles (GAAP). If the company is publicly traded, then it must also follow SEC guidelines. If the company operates internationally, then international financial reporting standards (IFRS) will apply. The goal is that, eventually, all public U.S. companies will report using IFRS rules.

Types of Business Organizations

A business can be organized as one of the following:

- Proprietorship
- Partnership

 Identify the different types of business organizations

[2]Excerpt from http://www.microsoft.com/about/legal/en/us/Compliance/Buscond/Default.aspx

- Corporation
- Limited-liability partnership (LLP) and limited-liability company (LLC)
- Not-for-profit

Let's look at the differences among the five types of business organizations.

Proprietorships

A **proprietorship** has a single owner, called the proprietor, who often manages the business. Proprietorships tend to be small retail stores or professional businesses, such as attorneys and accountants. From an accounting perspective, every proprietorship is distinct from its owner: The accounting records of the proprietorship do *not* include the proprietor's personal records. However, from a legal perspective, the business *is* the proprietor. **A proprietorship has one owner called a proprietor.** Smart Touch Learning is a proprietorship.

Partnerships

A **partnership** joins two or more individuals as co-owners. Each owner is a partner and can commit the partnership in a binding contract. This is called **mutual agency**. Mutual agency means that one partner can make all partners mutually liable. Many retail stores and professional organizations of physicians, attorneys, and accountants are partnerships. Most partnerships are small or medium-sized, but some are gigantic, with thousands of partners. For accounting purposes, the partnership is a separate organization, distinct from the partners. **A partnership has two or more owners called partners.**

Corporations

A **corporation** is a business owned by **stockholders,** or **shareholders.** These are the people who own shares of stock in the business. **Stock** is a certificate representing ownership interest in a corporation. A business becomes a corporation when the state grants a **charter** to the company, and the state approves its articles of incorporation and the first stock share is issued. The **articles of incorporation** are the rules approved by the state that govern the management of the corporation. Unlike a proprietorship and a partnership, a corporation is a legal entity distinct from its owners. This legal distinction between corporations and traditional proprietorships and partnerships can be very important for the following reason: If a proprietorship or a partnership cannot pay its debts, lenders can take the owners' personal assets to satisfy the obligations. But if a corporation goes bankrupt, lenders *cannot* take the personal assets of the stockholders. The largest businesses in the United States and in other countries are corporations. The **Coca-Cola Company,** for example, has billions of shares of stock owned by many stockholders. **A corporation has one or more owners called shareholders.**

Limited-Liability Partnerships (LLPs) and Limited-Liability Companies (LLCs)

In a **limited-liability partnership,** each member/partner is liable (obligated) only for his or her own actions and those under his or her control. Similarly, a business can be organized as a **limited-liability company.** In an LLC, the business—and not the members of the LLC—is liable for the company's debts. This arrangement prevents an unethical partner from creating a large liability for the other partners, much like the protection a corporation has. Today most proprietorships and partnerships are organized as LLCs and LLPs. **An LLC has one or more owners called members.**

Not-for-Profits

A **not-for-profit** is an organization that has been approved by the Internal Revenue Service to operate for a religious, charitable, or educational purpose. A board, usually composed of volunteers, makes the decisions for the not-for-profit organization.

Board members have **fiduciary responsibility**, which is an ethical and legal obligation to perform their duties in a trustworthy manner. Their goal is to raise cash to fund their operations. Examples of not-for-profit organizations are the **United Way**, churches, and schools. **A not-for-profit has no owners.** Exhibit 1-2 summarizes the differences among the five types of business organization.

EXHIBIT 1-2 | **Comparison of the Five Forms of Business Organization**

	Proprietorship	Partnership	Corporation	LLP/LLC	Not-for-Profit
1. Owner(s)	Proprietor—only one owner	Partners—two or more owners	Stockholders—generally many owners	Members	None
2. Life of the organization	Limited by the owner's choice, or death	Limited by the owners' choice, or death	Indefinite	Indefinite	Indefinite
3. Personal liability of the owner(s) for the business's debts	Proprietor is personally liable	Partners are personally liable*	Stockholders are not personally liable	Members are not personally liable	Fiduciary liability of board members

*unless it is a limited-liability partnership (LLP)

Stop & Think...

How does a company pick the best type of organization? Deciding on the type of business organization that best meets a company's needs and objectives should be a well-thought-out decision. Small businesses should consult a CPA to consider the tax implications and an attorney to discuss the legal implications of the form of business.

Key Takeaway

There are five main forms of business organizations: proprietorships, partnerships, corporations, LLPs/LLCs, and not-for-profits. Each is unique in its formation, ownership, life, and liability exposure.

Distinguishing Characteristics and Organization of a Proprietorship

There are several features that distinguish a proprietorship from other types of business organizations. Let's look at them now.

5 Delineate the distinguishing characteristics and organization of a proprietorship

Separate Legal Entity

As we noted earlier, a *corporation* is a business entity formed under state law. The state grants a charter (articles of incorporation), which is the document that gives the state's permission to form a corporation. This is called **authorization** because the state "authorizes" or approves the establishment of the corporate entity.

A proprietorship is a business entity that is not formally "created" by registering with a state agency. It is formed when one individual decides to create a business. It is an entity that exists apart from its owner. However, the proprietorship has many of the rights that a person has. For example, a proprietorship may buy, own, and sell property; enter into contracts; sue; and be sued. Items that the business owns (its assets) and those items that the business has to pay later (its liabilities) belong to the business.

The ownership interest of a proprietorship is recognized in the capital account, which is part of owner's equity. This is listed in the company's books as "Name of owner, capital." So, for example, Sheena Bright is the owner of Smart Touch. Her capital account in the accounting records of Smart Touch would be named Bright, capital.

No Continuous Life or Transferability of Ownership

The life of a proprietorship business is limited by either the owner's choice or the owner's death, whichever comes first. Thus, there is no transferability of ownership in a proprietorship.

Unlimited Liability of Owner

A proprietor has unlimited liability for the business's debts. General partners in partnerships have the same liability; however, stockholders in corporations have limited liability. This unlimited liability makes owning a proprietorship unattractive due to the owner's real fear of losing his or her personal wealth if the proprietorship fails.

Unification of Ownership and Management

The owners of a proprietorship also manage the business. This unification between owners and management is beneficial to the proprietorship and its sole owner because their goals are the same.

Conversely, the separation that exists between stockholders (owners of the corporation) and management in a corporation may create problems. Corporate officers may decide to run the business for their own benefit rather than for the benefit of the company. Stockholders may find it difficult to lodge an effective protest against management because of the distance between them and the top managers.

Business Taxation

Proprietorships are not separate taxable entities. The income earned by the business flows directly to the sole owner. The owner pays tax on the business income on his or her personal tax return. Additionally, the owner must pay self-employment tax for both the employee and employer portions (discussed in Chapter 10).

Government Regulation

Government regulation is an advantage for the proprietorship. There are no stockholders to notify nor are there articles of incorporation to file. Decisions can easily be made by the sole owner/manager.

Organization of a Corporation

As noted earlier, creation of a corporation begins when its organizers, called the incorporators, obtain a charter from the state. The charter includes the authorization for the corporation to issue a certain number of shares of stock, which represent the ownership in the corporation. The incorporators pay fees, sign the charter, and file the required documents with the state. Once the first share of stock is issued, the corporation comes into existence. The incorporators agree to a set of bylaws, which act as the constitution for governing the corporation. Bylaws are the rule book that guides the corporation.

The ultimate control of the corporation rests with the stockholders, who normally receive one vote for each share of stock they own. The stockholders elect the members of the board of directors, which sets policy for the corporation and appoints the officers. The board elects a chairperson, who usually is the most powerful person in the corporation. The board also designates the president, who as chief operating officer manages day-to-day operations. Most corporations also have vice-presidents in charge of sales, operations, accounting and finance, and other key areas. Exhibit 1-3 shows the authority structure in a corporation. In the next section, we'll cover the concepts and principles behind financial statements.

> **Key Takeaway**
>
> Proprietorships are formed when one person creates a business. One person owns the proprietorship. Although the proprietorship is a separate entity, it has no continuous life and the owner has unlimited liability for the business's debts. Proprietorships have a more difficult time raising capital but have the advantage of reduced regulation and less taxes than the corporate form of business.

EXHIBIT 1-3 | **Structure of a Corporation**

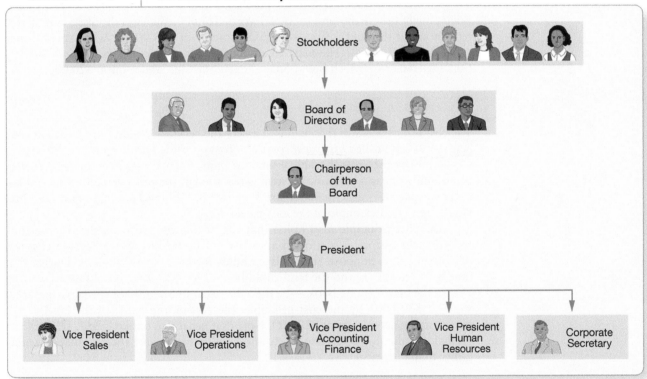

Accounting Concepts and Principles

As mentioned earlier in the chapter, the guidelines that govern accounting fall under GAAP, which stands for generally accepted accounting principles. GAAP rests on a conceptual framework. The primary objective of financial reporting is to provide information useful for making investment and lending decisions. To be useful, information must be relevant, reliable, and comparable. These basic accounting concepts and principles are part of the foundation for the financial reports that companies present.

6 Apply accounting concepts and principles

The Entity Concept

The most basic concept in accounting is that of the **entity**. An accounting entity is an organization that stands apart as a separate economic unit. We draw boundaries around each entity to keep its affairs distinct from those of other entities. **An entity refers to one business, separate from its owners.**

Consider Smart Touch. Assume Sheena Bright started the business by investing capital of $30,000. Following the entity concept, Smart Touch accounted for the $30,000 separately from Sheena's personal assets, such as her clothing and car. To mix the $30,000 of business cash with her personal assets would make it difficult to measure the success or failure of Smart Touch. Thus, *the entity concept applies to any economic unit that needs to be evaluated separately*.

The Faithful Representation Principle

Accounting information is based on the fact that the data faithfully represents the measurement or description of that data. This guideline is the **faithful representation principle**. Faithfully represented data are complete, neutral, and free from material error. For example, a promissory note outlines the details of a bank loan. This note is a faithful representation (evidence) of the loan.

For example, say Smart Touch purchased land for $20,000. The owner, Sheena Bright, might believe the land is instead worth $25,000. Which is the more faithful representation of the land's value—Sheena's estimate of $25,000 or what Smart Touch actually paid, $20,000? The $20,000 amount paid is more complete, neutral, and free from material error, which is why Smart Touch listed the land value at $20,000.

The Cost Principle

The **cost principle** states that acquired assets and services should be recorded at their actual cost (also called *historical cost*). **The cost principle means we list at the amount shown on the receipt—the actual amount paid.** Even though the purchaser may believe the price is a bargain, the item is recorded at the price actually paid and not at the "expected" cost. Again, Smart Touch's $20,000 land purchase discussed previously is a good example of the cost principle.

The cost principle also holds that the accounting records should continue reporting the historical cost of an asset over its useful life. Why? Because cost is a reliable measure. Suppose Smart Touch holds the land for six months. During that time land prices rise, and the land could be sold for $30,000. Should its accounting value—the figure on the books—be the actual cost of $20,000 or the current market value of $30,000? By the cost principle, the accounting value of the land would remain at the actual cost of $20,000. Note that generally, unlike GAAP, IFRS allows periodic revaluation of certain assets and liabilities to restate them to market value, rather than historical cost.

The Going-Concern Concept

Another reason for measuring assets at historical cost is the **going-concern concept**. This concept assumes that the entity will remain in operation for the foreseeable future. Under the going-concern concept, accountants assume that the business will remain in operation long enough to use existing resources for their intended purpose. **The going-concern principle assumes the business won't close soon.**

To understand the going-concern concept better, consider the alternative—which is to go out of business. A store that is closing intends to cease future operations. In that case, the relevant measure is current market value. But going out of business is the exception rather than the rule, which is why we use historical cost.

The Stable Monetary Unit Concept

In the United States, we record transactions in dollars because the dollar is the medium of exchange. The value of a dollar changes over time, and a rise in the price level is called inflation. During periods of inflation, a dollar will purchase less. But accountants assume that the dollar's purchasing power is stable. This assumption is the basis of the **stable monetary unit concept. The stable monetary unit concept means stable currency buying power.**

Now that we've reviewed some of the basic concepts/assumptions underlying financial statements, we'll cover the accounting equation.

Key Takeaway

The accounting concepts are the underlying assumptions used when recording financial information for a business. Think of the concepts like rules of a game. You have to play by the rules.

The Accounting Equation

The basic tool of accounting is the **accounting equation**. It measures the resources of a business and the claims to those resources.

7 Describe the accounting equation, and define assets, liabilities, and equity

Assets and Liabilities

Assets are economic resources that are expected to benefit the business in the future. **Assets are something the business owns that has value.** Cash, merchandise inventory, furniture, and land are examples of assets.

Claims to those assets come from two sources. **Liabilities** are debts payable to outsiders who are known as creditors. **Liabilities are something the business owes.** For example, a creditor who has loaned money to Smart Touch has a claim to some of the business's assets until the business pays the debt. Many liabilities have the word *payable* in their titles. Examples include Accounts payable, Notes payable, and Salary payable.

The owner's claims to the assets of the business are called **equity** (also called **owner's, stockholders'**, or **shareholders' equity**, depending on how the company is organized). **Equity equals what is owned (assets) minus what is owed (liabilities). It is the company's net worth.** These insider claims begin when an owner, such as Sheena Bright, invests assets in the business and receives capital.

The accounting equation shows how assets, liabilities, and owner's equity are related. Assets appear on the left side of the equation, and the liabilities and owner's equity appear on the right side. **The accounting equation is an equation—so the left side of the equation always equals the right side of the equation.**

Exhibit 1-4 diagrams how the two sides must always be equal (amounts are assumed for this illustration):

(Economic Resources)		(Claims to Economic Resources)
ASSETS	=	LIABILITIES + EQUITY
$5,000	=	$2,000 + $3,000

EXHIBIT 1-4 | **The Accounting Equation**

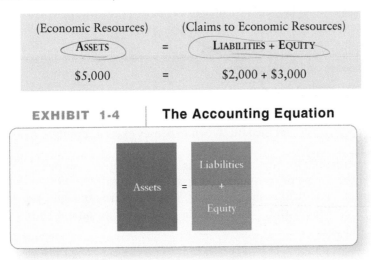

Equity

The equity of a sole proprietorship is called owner's equity. For a proprietorship, the accounting equation can be written as

$$\text{ASSETS} = \text{LIABILITIES} + \overbrace{\underset{\text{CAPITAL}}{\text{OWNER'S EQUITY}}}$$

$$\text{ASSETS} = \text{LIABILITIES} + \text{CAPITAL}$$

- **Capital** is the net amount invested in the business by the owner. An owner can contribute cash or other net assets to the business and receive capital.
- Capital contains the amount earned by income-producing activities and kept (retained) for use in the business. Two types of events that affect capital are revenues and expenses. **Revenues** are increases in capital from delivering goods or services to customers. Revenues are earnings. For example, if Smart Touch provided e-learning services and earned $5,500 of revenue, the business's capital increased by $5,500.

There are relatively few types of revenue, including the following:

- **Sales revenue.** Greg's Tunes earns sales revenue by selling CDs to customers.
- **Service revenue.** Smart Touch earns service revenue by providing e-learning services.
- **Interest revenue.** Interest revenue is earned on bank deposits and on money lent out to others.
- **Dividend revenue.** Dividend revenue is earned on investments in the stock of other corporations.

Expenses are the decreases in capital that result from operations. Expenses are incurred costs that you will have to pay for, either now or later. For example, Smart Touch paid salaries of $1,200 to its employees and that is an expense that decreases capital. Expenses are the opposite of revenues.

Unfortunately, businesses have lots of expenses. Some common expenses are as follows:

- Store (or office) rent expense
- Salary expense for employees
- Advertising expense
- Utilities expense for water, electricity, and gas
- Insurance expense
- Supplies expense for supplies used up
- Interest expense on loans payable
- Property tax expense

Businesses strive for net income. When revenues exceed expenses, the result of operations is a profit or **net income**. When expenses exceed revenues, the result is a **net loss**.

After earning net income, the business may distribute cash or other assets to the owner, a third type of transaction that affects capital. **Drawings** are distributions of capital (usually of cash) to owners. Drawings are not expenses. An owner may or may not make withdrawals from the business. Exhibit 1-5 shows the components of capital.

EXHIBIT 1-5 | **Components of Capital**

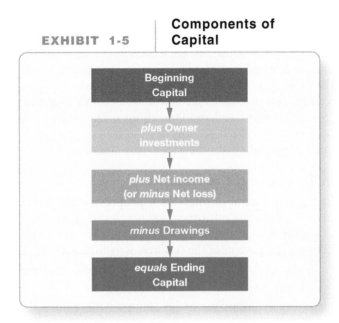

The owners' equity of partnerships is similar. The main difference is there are separate capital accounts for each partner. For example, a partnership of Joan Pratt and Simon Nagle would have accounts for Pratt, capital and Nagle, capital. The owners' equity (or shareholders' or stockholders' equity) of a corporation is also different. Stockholders' equity has two components: Paid-in capital and Retained earnings. **Paid-in capital, or contributed capital,** is the amount invested in the corporation by its owners, the stockholders. The basic component of paid-in capital is stock, which the corporation issues to the stockholders as evidence of their ownership. **Common stock** represents the basic ownership of every corporation. **Retained earnings** of a corporation represent the net earnings retained by the corporation.

Stop & Think...

The accounting equation is important to a business, but it is also important to the individual. Consider your "personal" accounting equation. Are you content with your current net worth (equity) or do you want to increase it? Do you think your education will help you to increase your net worth?

Students enroll in education programs for many reasons. However, underneath all the reasons is a basic desire to increase net worth through knowledge, higher paying job skills, or a better understanding of business.

Accounting for Business Transactions

Accounting is based on actual transactions, not opinions or desires. A **transaction** is any event that affects the financial position of the business *and* can be measured reliably. **Transactions affect what the company owns, owes, or its net worth.** Many events affect a company, including economic booms and recessions. Accountants, however, do not record the effects of those events. An accountant records only those events that have dollar amounts that can be measured reliably, such as the purchase of a building, a sale of merchandise, and the payment of rent.

What are some of your personal transactions? You may have bought a car. Your purchase was a transaction. If you are making payments on an auto loan, your payments are also transactions. You need to record all your business transactions—just as Smart Touch does—in order to manage your business affairs.

8 Use the accounting equation to analyze transactions

Transaction Analysis for Smart Touch Learning

To illustrate accounting for a business, we'll use Smart Touch Learning, an e-learning agency organized as a proprietorship. Online customers can access and pay for training through the business's Web site. The Web site offers courses in accounting, economics, marketing, and management, in addition to software training on specific applications, like Microsoft Excel and QuickBooks. The Web site allows the agency to transact more business. We'll account for the transactions of Smart Touch and show how each transaction affects the accounting equation.

Transaction 1: Starting the Business

Sheena Bright starts the new business as a proprietorship named Smart Touch Learning. In April 2013, the e-learning agency receives $30,000 cash from the owner, Sheena Bright, and the business gave capital to her. The effect of this transaction on the accounting equation of the business is as follows:

ASSETS		LIABILITIES	+	OWNER'S EQUITY (OE)	TYPE OF OE TRANSACTION
Cash	=			Bright, capital	
(1) +30,000				+30,000	*Owner investment*

For each transaction, the amount on the left side of the equation must equal the amount on the right side. The first transaction increases both the assets (in this case, Cash) and the owner's equity (Bright, capital) of the business. To the right of the transaction, we write "Owner investment" to keep track of the source of the equity.

BE SURE TO START ON THE RIGHT TRACK—Keep in mind that we are doing the accounting for Smart Touch Learning, the business. We are *not* accounting for Sheena Bright, the person.

View all transactions, and do all the accounting, from the perspective of the business—not from the viewpoint of the owner. This is the entity concept we reviewed earlier in the chapter.

Transaction 2: Purchase of Land

The business purchases land for an office location, paying cash of $20,000. This transaction affects the accounting equation of Smart Touch as follows:

	ASSETS			LIABILITIES	+	OWNER'S EQUITY
	Cash	+	Land			Bright, capital
(1)	30,000			=		30,000
(2)	−20,000		+20,000			
Bal	10,000		20,000			30,000
		30,000				30,000

The cash purchase of land increases one asset, Land, and decreases another asset, Cash. After the transaction is completed, the business has cash of $10,000, land of $20,000, no liabilities, and owner's equity of $30,000. Note that the total balances (abbreviated Bal) on both sides of the equation must always be equal—in this case $30,000.

Transaction 3: Purchase of Office Supplies

The e-learning agency buys office supplies on account (credit), agreeing to pay $500 within 30 days. The company will use the supplies in the future, so they are an asset to the business. This transaction increases both the assets and the liabilities of the business, as follows:

			ASSETS						LIABILITIES	+	OWNER'S EQUITY
			Office						Accounts		Bright,
	Cash	+	supplies	+	Land				payable	+	capital
Bal	10,000				20,000		=				30,000
(3)	___		+500		___				+500		___
Bal	10,000		500		20,000				500		30,000
			30,500							30,500	

Office supplies is an asset, not an expense, because the supplies aren't used up now, but will be in the future. The liability created by purchasing "on account" is an **Account payable**, which is a short-term liability that will be paid in the future. A payable is always a liability.

Transaction 4: Earning of Service Revenue

Smart Touch earns service revenue by providing training services for clients. The business earns $5,500 of revenue and collects this amount in cash. The effect on the accounting equation is an increase in Cash and an increase in Bright, capital as follows:

			ASSETS					LIABILITIES +	OWNER'S EQUITY	TYPE OF OE TRANSACTION
			Office					Accounts	Bright,	
	Cash	+	supplies	+	Land			payable +	capital	
Bal	10,000		500		20,000	=		500	30,000	
(4)	+5,500		___		___			___	+5,500	*Service revenue*
Bal	15,500		500		20,000			500	35,500	
			36,000						36,000	

A revenue transaction grows the business, as shown by the increases in assets and owner's equity (Bright, capital).

Transaction 5: Earning of Service Revenue on Account

Smart Touch performs a service for clients who do not pay immediately. The business receives the clients' promise to pay $3,000 within one month. This promise is an asset, an **Account receivable**, because the agency expects to collect the cash in the future. In accounting, we say that Smart Touch performed this service *on account*. It is in performing the service (doing the work), not collecting the cash, that the company *earns* the revenue. As in transaction 4, increasing earnings increases Bright, capital. Smart Touch records the earning of $3,000 of revenue on account, as follows:

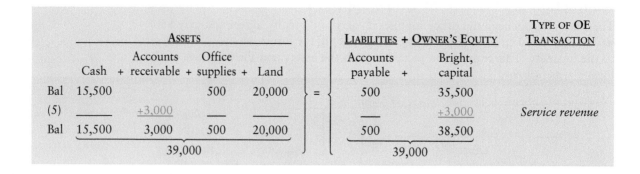

Transaction 6: Payment of Expenses

During the month, the business pays $3,300 in cash expenses: rent expense on a computer, $600; office rent, $1,100; employee salary, $1,200; and utilities, $400. The effects on the accounting equation are as follows:

		ASSETS				LIABILITIES +	OWNER'S EQUITY	TYPE OF OE TRANSACTION
	Cash +	Accounts receivable +	Office supplies +	Land		Accounts payable +	Bright, capital	
Bal	15,500	3,000	500	20,000		500	38,500	
(6)	−600						−600	Rent expense, computer
(6)	−1,100						−1,100	Rent expense, office
(6)	−1,200						−1,200	Salary expense
(6)	−400						−400	Utilities expense
Bal	12,200	3,000	500	20,000		500	35,200	
		35,700			=		35,700	

Expenses have the opposite effect of revenues. Expenses shrink the business, as shown by the decreased balances of assets and owner's equity (Bright, capital).

Each expense can be recorded separately. The expenses are listed as one transaction here for simplicity. We could record the cash payment in a single amount for the sum of the four expenses: $3,300 ($600 + $1,100 + $1,200 + $400). However the expenses are recorded, the accounting equation must balance. (Notice that each side totals to $35,700.)

Transaction 7: Payment on Account

The business pays $300 to the store from which it purchased supplies in transaction 3. In accounting, we say that the business pays $300 *on account*. The effect on the accounting equation is a decrease in Cash and a decrease in Accounts payable, as shown here:

	ASSETS					LIABILITIES + OWNER'S EQUITY	
	Cash +	Accounts receivable +	Office supplies +	Land		Accounts payable +	Bright, capital
Bal	12,200	3,000	500	20,000	=	500	35,200
(7)	−300					−300	
Bal	11,900	3,000	500	20,000		200	35,200
		35,400				35,400	

The payment of cash on account has no effect on the amount of office supplies (asset) Smart Touch has nor on the amount of office supplies it uses (expense). Smart Touch was paying off a liability (accounts payable decreased $300), with cash (Cash decreased $300).

Transaction 8: Personal Transaction

Sheena Bright buys groceries at a cost of $200, paying cash from personal funds. This event is *not* a transaction of Smart Touch. It has no effect on the e-learning agency and, therefore, is not recorded by the business. It is a transaction of the Sheena Bright *personal* entity, not the e-learning agency. This transaction illustrates the *entity concept*.

Transaction 9: Collection on Account

In transaction 5, the business performed services for a client on account. The business now collects $1,000 from the client. We say that Smart Touch collects the cash *on account*. The business will record an increase in the asset Cash. Should it also record an increase in service revenue? No, because the business already recorded the revenue when it earned the revenue in transaction 5. The phrase "collect cash on account" means to record an increase in Cash and a decrease in Accounts receivable. Accounts receivable is decreased because the $1,000 that the business was to collect at some point in the future is being collected today. The effect on the accounting equation is as follows:

	ASSETS					LIABILITIES + OWNER'S EQUITY	
	Cash +	Accounts receivable +	Office supplies +	Land		Accounts payable +	Bright, capital
Bal	11,900	3,000	500	20,000	=	200	35,200
(9)	+1,000	−1,000					
Bal	12,900	2,000	500	20,000		200	35,200
		35,400				35,400	

Total assets are unchanged from the preceding total. Why? Because Smart Touch exchanged one asset (Cash) for another (Accounts receivable).

Transaction 10: Sale of Land

The business sells some land owned by the e-learning agency. The sale price of $9,000 is equal to the cost of the land, so Smart Touch didn't gain or lose anything extra from the land sale. The business receives $9,000 cash, and the effect on the accounting equation follows:

		ASSETS				LIABILITIES +	OWNER'S EQUITY
	Cash +	Accounts receivable +	Office supplies +	Land		Accounts payable +	Bright, capital
Bal	12,900	2,000	500	20,000	=	200	35,200
(10)	+9,000			−9,000			
Bal	21,900	2,000	500	11,000		200	35,200
		35,400				35,400	

Transaction 11: Owner Drawing of Cash

Sheena Bright withdraws $2,000 cash from the business. The effect on the accounting equation is:

		ASSETS				LIABILITIES +	OWNER'S EQUITY	TYPE OF OE TRANSACTION
	Cash +	Accounts receivable +	Office supplies +	Land		Accounts payable +	Bright, capital	
Bal	21,900	2,000	500	11,000	=	200	35,200	
(11)	−2,000						−2,000	Owner withdrawal
Bal	19,900	2,000	500	11,000		200	33,200	
		33,400				33,400		

> **Key Takeaway**
>
> The accounting equation is Assets = Liabilities + Equity. Every business transaction affects various parts of the equation, but after each transaction is recorded, the equation must ALWAYS balance (equal).

The owner withdrawal decreases the business's Cash and owner's equity (Bright, capital). *Drawings do not represent an expense because they are not related to the earning of revenue. Therefore, drawings do not affect the business's net income or net loss.* The double underlines below each column indicate a final total after the last transaction.

Preparing the Financial Statements—The User Perspective of Accounting

 Prepare financial statements

We have now recorded Smart Touch's transactions, and they are summarized in Exhibit 1-6. Notice how total assets equals total liabilities plus owner's equity.

But a basic question remains: How will people actually use this information? The mass of data in Exhibit 1-6 will not tell a lender whether Smart Touch can pay off a loan. The data in the exhibit do not tell whether the business is profitable.

To address these important questions, we need financial statements. As noted earlier, *financial statements* are business documents that report on a business in

EXHIBIT 1-6 | **Analysis of Transactions, Smart Touch Learning**

PANEL A—Details of Transactions

1. The e-learning agency received $30,000 cash and gave capital to Sheena Bright.
2. Paid $20,000 cash for land.
3. Bought $500 of office supplies on account.
4. Received $5,500 cash from clients for service revenue earned.
5. Performed services for clients on account, $3,000.
6. Paid cash expenses: computer rent, $600; office rent, $1,100; employee salary, $1,200; utilities, $400.
7. Paid $300 on the account payable created in transaction 3.
8. Bright buys $200 of groceries. This is *not* a transaction of the business.
9. Collected $1,000 on the account receivable created in transaction 5.
10. Sold land for cash at its cost of $9,000.
11. Owner withdrew cash of $2,000.

PANEL B—Analysis of Transactions

	Cash	+	Accounts receivable	+	Office supplies	+	Land	=	Accounts payable	+	Bright, capital	Type of OE Transaction
1.	+ 30,000										+ 30,000	Owner investment
Bal	30,000		0		0		0		0		30,000	
2.	− 20,000						+ 20,000					
Bal	10,000		0		0		20,000		0		30,000	
3.					+ 500				+ 500			
Bal	10,000		0		500		20,000		500		30,000	
4.	+ 5,500										+ 5,500	Service revenue
Bal	15,500		0		500		20,000		500		35,500	
5.			+ 3,000								+ 3,000	Service revenue
Bal	15,500		3,000		500		20,000		500		38,500	
6.	− 600										− 600	Rent expense, computer
6.	− 1,100										− 1,100	Rent expense, office
6.	− 1,200										− 1,200	Salary expense
6.	− 400										− 400	Utilities expense
Bal	12,200		3,000		500		20,000		500		35,200	
7.	− 300								− 300			
Bal	11,900		3,000		500		20,000		200		35,200	
8.	Not a transaction of the business											
9.	+ 1,000		− 1,000									
Bal	12,900		2,000		500		20,000		200		35,200	
10.	+ 9,000						− 9,000					
Bal	21,900		2,000		500		11,000		200		35,200	
11.	− 2,000										− 2,000	Owner withdrawal
Bal	19,900		2,000		500		11,000		200		33,200	

Assets = 33,400   Liabilities + Owner's Equity = 33,400 monetary terms. People use financial statements to make business decisions. Consider the following examples:

- Sheena Bright wants to know whether the business is profitable. Is the business earning a net income, or is it experiencing a net loss? The **income statement** answers this question by reporting the net income or net loss of the business.
- The banker asks what the business did with any profits earned. Did Bright withdraw the earnings or did she keep the earnings in the training agency? The **statement of owner's equity** answers this question. Suppose the business needs $200,000 to buy an office building. The banker will want to know how much in assets the e-learning company has and how much it already owes. The **balance sheet** answers this question by reporting the business's assets and liabilities.
- The banker wants to know if the agency generates enough cash to pay its bills. The **statement of cash flows** answers this question by reporting cash receipts and cash payments and whether cash increased or decreased.
- Outside investors also use financial statements. Smart Touch may need to raise cash for an expansion. Suppose you are considering investing in the training agency. In making this decision, you would ask the same questions that Sheena Bright and the banker have been asking.

In summary, the main users of financial statements are

- business owners and managers,
- lenders, and
- outside investors.

Others also use the financial statements, but the three user groups listed above are paramount, and we will be referring to them throughout this book. Now let's examine the financial statements in detail.

The Financial Statements

After analyzing transactions, we want to see the overall results. The financial statements summarize the transaction data into a form that is useful for decision making. As we discussed the financial statements are the

- income statement,
- statement of owner's equity,
- balance sheet, and
- statement of cash flows.

Headings

Each financial statement (and every other financial document you'll probably see or use) has a heading that provides three pieces of data:

- Name of the business (such as Smart Touch Learning)
- Name of the financial statement (income statement, balance sheet, or other financial statement)
- Date or time period covered by the statement (April 30, 2013, for the balance sheet; month ended April 30, 2013, for the other statements)

Financial statements that show activity, like an income statement that covers a year that ended in December 2013, are dated "Year Ended December 31, 2013." A monthly income statement (or statement of owner's equity) for September 2013 shows "Month Ended September 30, 2013." A quarterly income statement (or statement of owner's equity) for the three months ending June 30, 2013, shows "Quarter Ended June 30, 2013." The dateline describes the period covered by the statement. Let's look at each of these financial statements in a bit more detail.

Income Statement

The income statement (also called the **statement of earnings** or **statement of operations**) presents a summary of a business entity's revenues and expenses for a period of time, such as a month, quarter, or year. The income statement is like a video—a moving picture of operations during the period. It displays one of the most important pieces of information about a business: Did the business make a profit? The income statement tells us whether the business enjoyed net income or suffered a net loss. Remember,

- **net income** means total revenues are greater than total expenses.
- **net loss** means total expenses are greater than total revenues.

Net income is good news, net loss is bad news. What was the result of Smart Touch's operations during April? Good news—the business earned net income of $5,200 (see the first part of Exhibit 1-7 on the next page).

Statement of Owner's Equity

The statement of owner's equity (shown in the first overlay of Exhibit 1-7) shows the changes in capital for a business entity during a time period, such as a month, quarter, or year.

Capital increases when the business has

- owner contributions of capital, or
- a net income (revenues exceed expenses).

Capital decreases when the business has

- a net loss (expenses exceed revenues), or
- owner withdrawals of cash or other assets.

What changes occurred in Smart Touch's capital during April? Capital increased by the $30,000 of capital contributed by Sheena Bright and by the amount of net income of $5,200. Capital decreased $2,000 for the drawing made by Sheena Bright (see Exhibit 1-7).

Balance Sheet

The balance sheet lists a business entity's assets, liabilities, and owner's equity as of a specific date, usually the end of a month, quarter, or year. The balance sheet is like a snapshot of the entity. It is also called the **statement of financial position** (see the second overlay showing the middle of Exhibit 1-7.) The balance sheet mirrors the accounting equation.

Statement of Cash Flows

The statement of cash flows reports the cash coming in (positive amounts) and the cash going out (negative amounts) during a period. Business activities result in a net cash inflow or a net cash outflow. The statement of cash flows reports the net increase or decrease in cash during the period and the ending cash balance. (See the final overlay of Exhibit 1-7.)

In the first part of this book, we focus on the

- income statement,
- statement of owner's equity, and
- balance sheet.

In Chapter 14 we cover the statement of cash flows in detail.

Key Takeaway

Financial statements are prepared from the ending balances of each account. Each financial statement shows a different view of the company's overall results.

EXHIBIT 1-7 | **Financial Statements of Smart Touch Learning**

SMART TOUCH LEARNING
Income Statement
Month Ended April 30, 2013

Revenue:		
Service revenue		$8,500
Expenses:		
Salary expense	$1,200	
Rent expense, office	1,100	
Rent expense, computer	600	
Utilities expense	400	
Total expenses		3,300
Net income		$5,200

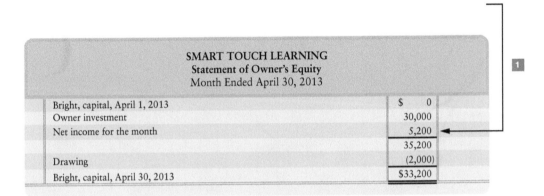

SMART TOUCH LEARNING
Statement of Owner's Equity
Month Ended April 30, 2013

Bright, capital, April 1, 2013	$ 0
Owner investment	30,000
Net income for the month	5,200
	35,200
Drawing	(2,000)
Bright, capital, April 30, 2013	$33,200

1

SMART TOUCH LEARNING
Balance Sheet
April 30, 2013

Assets		Liabilities	
Cash	$19,900	Accounts payable	$ 200
Accounts receivable	2,000		
Office supplies	500	**Owner's Equity**	
Land	11,000	Bright, capital	33,200
Total assets	$33,400	Total liabilities and owner's equity	$33,400

2

SMART TOUCH LEARNING
Statement of Cash Flows*
Month Ended April 30, 2013

Cash flows from operating activities:		
Receipts:		
Collections from customers ($5,500 + $1,000)		$ 6,500
Payments:		
To suppliers ($600 + $1,100 + $400 + $300)	$ (2,400)	
To employees	(1,200)	(3,600)
Net cash provided by operating activities		$ 2,900
Cash flows from investing activities:		
Acquisition of land	$(20,000)	
Sale of land	9,000	
Net cash used for investing activities		(11,000)
Cash flows from financing activities:		
Owner investment	$ 30,000	
Owner drawing	(2,000)	
Net cash provided by financing activities		28,000
Net increase in cash		$19,900
Cash balance, April 1, 2013		0
Cash balance, April 30, 2013		$19,900

*Chapter 14 shows how to prepare this statement.

Using Financial Statements to Evaluate Business Performance

Exhibit 1-7 illustrates all four financial statements in the order that we prepare them. The data come from the transaction analysis in Exhibit 1-6 that covers the month of April 2013. Study the exhibit carefully. Then, observe the following in Exhibit 1-7:

10 Use financial statements to evaluate business performance

1. The *income statement* for the month ended April 30, 2013,
    a. reports April's revenues and expenses.
    b. lists expenses in order of largest to smallest expense.
    c. calculates and lists total expenses.
    d. reports *net income* of the period if total revenues exceed total expenses. If total expenses exceed total revenues, a *net loss* is reported instead.

2. The *statement of owner's equity* for the month ended April 30, 2013,
    a. opens with the capital balance at the beginning of the period (zero for a new entity).
    b. adds *owner contributions* made during the month.
    c. adds *net income* directly from the income statement (see arrow 1 in Exhibit 1-7).
    d. subtracts *drawings* (and net loss, if applicable). Parentheses indicate a subtraction.
    e. ends with the capital balance at the end of the period.

3. The *balance sheet* at April 30, 2013,
    a. reports all *assets*, all *liabilities*, and *owner's equity* at the end of the period.
    b. lists assets in the order of their liquidity (closeness to cash) with cash coming first because it is the most liquid asset.
    c. reports liabilities similarly. That is, the liability that must be paid first is listed first, usually Accounts payable.
    d. reports that total assets equal total liabilities plus total equity (the accounting equation).
    e. reports the ending capital balance, taken directly from the statement of owner's equity (see arrow 2).

4. The *statement of cash flows* for the month ended April 30, 2013,
    a. reports cash flows from three types of business activities (*operating*, *investing*, and *financing activities*) during the month. Each category of cash-flow activities includes both cash receipts (positive amounts), and cash payments (negative amounts denoted by parentheses).
    b. reports a net increase (or decrease) in cash during the month and ends with the cash balance at April 30, 2013. This is the amount of cash to report on the balance sheet (see arrow 3).

Each of the statements identified in Exhibit 1-7 provides different information about the company to the users of the financial statements.

*   The income statement provides information about profitability for a particular period for the company. Recall that expenses are listed in this statement from largest to smallest. This ordering shows users which expenses are consuming the largest part of the revenues.

- The statement of owner's equity informs users about how much of the earnings were kept and reinvested in the company. Recall from Exhibit 1-7 that three main items appear in this statement that explain the change in the capital balance:

1. Owner contributions

2. Net income or net loss

3. Drawings by the owner

If the owner drawings were larger than income for the period, this could signal concern to financial statement users.

The balance sheet in Exhibit 1-7 provides valuable information to financial statement users about economic resources the company owns (assets) as well as debts the company owes (liabilities). Thus, the balance sheet presents the overall financial position of the company on a specific date. This allows decision makers to determine their opinion about the financial status of the company.

The cash flow statement is covered in detail in a later chapter in the textbook. Briefly, its purpose and value to users is to explain why the net income number on the income statement does not equal the change in the cash balance for the period.

As we conclude this chapter, we return to our opening question: Have you ever thought of having your own business? The Decision Guidelines feature on the next page shows how to make some of the decisions that you will face if you start a business. Decision Guidelines appear in each chapter.

Key Takeaway

Financial statements are prepared from the transaction analyses (summary of events) reported in each account (Exhibit 1-6) in the order shown in Exhibit 1-7. No one financial statement shows everything about a company. It is the financial statements AND the relationships the statements show that give users the overall picture for a specific company.

Decision Guidelines 1-1

MAJOR BUSINESS DECISIONS

Suppose you open a business to take photos at parties at your school. You hire a professional photographer and line up suppliers for party favors and photo albums. Here are some factors you must consider if you expect to be profitable.

Decision	Guidelines
• How to organize the business?	If a single owner—a *proprietorship*.
	If two or more owners, but not incorporated— a *partnership* or *limited liability company*.
	If the business issues stock to stockholders—a *corporation*.
	If the motives are religious, charitable, or educational—a *not-for-profit*.
• What to account for?	Account for the business, a separate entity apart from its owner (*entity concept*).
	Account for transactions and events that affect the business's accounting equation and can be measured reliably.
• How much to record for assets and liabilities?	U.S. GAAP—Actual historical amount (*cost principle*).
	IFRS—Market value.
• How to analyze a transaction?	The accounting equation:

$$\text{(own)} = \text{(owe)} + \text{(net worth)}$$
$$\text{Assets} = \text{Liabilities} + \text{Owner's Equity}$$

• How to measure profits and losses?	Income statement:

$$\text{Revenues} - \text{Expenses} = \text{Net Income (or Net Loss)}$$

• Did owner's equity increase or decrease?	Statement of owner's equity:

Beginning capital
+ Owner investments
+ Net income (or – Net loss)
– Drawings
= Ending capital

• Where does the business stand financially?	Balance sheet (accounting equation):

$$\text{Assets} = \text{Liabilities} + \text{Owner's Equity}$$

Summary Problem 1-1

Ron Smith opens an apartment-locator business near a college campus. The company will be named Campus Apartment Locators. During the first month of operations, July 2013, the business completes the following transactions:

a. Smith invests $35,000. The business receives $35,000 cash and gives capital to Smith.
b. Purchases $350 of office supplies on account.
c. Pays cash of $30,000 to acquire a lot next to the campus. Smith intends to use the land as a future building site for the business office.
d. Locates apartments for clients and receives cash of $1,900.
e. Pays $100 on the account payable he created in transaction b.
f. Pays $2,000 of personal funds for a vacation.
g. Pays cash expenses for office rent, $400, and utilities, $100.
h. Returns office supplies of $150 from transaction b.
i. Smith withdrew cash of $1,200.

Requirements

1. Analyze the preceding transactions in terms of their effects on the accounting equation of Campus Apartment Locators. Use Exhibit 1-6 as a guide, but show balances only after the last transaction.
2. Prepare the income statement, statement of owner's equity, and balance sheet of the business after recording the transactions. Use Exhibit 1-7 as a guide.

Solution

Requirement 1

Analysis of transactions

	ASSETS				LIABILITIES +	OWNER'S EQUITY	TYPE OF OE TRANSACTION
	Cash	+	Office supplies	+ Land	Accounts payable +	Smith, capital	
(a)	+35,000					+35,000	Owner investment
(b)			+350		+350		
(c)	−30,000			+30,000			
(d)	+1,900					+1,900	Service revenue
(e)	−100				−100		
(f)	Not a transaction of the business						
(g)	−400					−400	Rent expense
	−100					−100	Utilities expense
(h)			−150		−150		
(i)	−1,200					−1,200	Owner withdrawal
Bal	5,100		200	30,000	100	35,200	

$$= $$

35,300   35,300

Requirement 2

Financial Statements of Campus Apartment Locators.

CAMPUS APARTMENT LOCATORS
Income Statement
Month Ended July 31, 2013

Revenue:		
Service revenue		$1,900
Expenses:		
Rent expense	$400	
Utilities expense	100	
Total expenses		500
Net income		$1,400

CAMPUS APARTMENT LOCATORS
Statement of Owner's Equity
Month Ended July 31, 2013

Smith, capital, July 1, 2013	$ 0
Owner investment	35,000
Net income for the month	1,400
	36,400
Drawing	(1,200)
Smith, capital, July 31, 2013	$35,200

CAMPUS APARTMENT LOCATORS
Balance Sheet
July 31, 2013

Assets		Liabilities	
Cash	$ 5,100	Accounts payable	$ 100
Office supplies	200		
Land	30,000		
		Owner's Equity	
		Smith, capital	35,200
Total assets	$35,300	Total liabilities and owner's equity	$35,300

Chapter 1: Demo Doc

Transaction Analysis Using Accounting Equation/Financial Statement Preparation

To make sure you understand this material, work through the following demonstration "demo doc" with detailed comments to help you see the concept within the framework of a worked-through problem.

7 **8** **9**

On March 1, 2014, David Richardson started a painting business near a historical housing district. David was the sole proprietor of the company, which he named DR Painting. During March 2014, DR Painting engaged in the following transactions:

a.   DR Painting received cash of $40,000 from David Richardson and gave capital to Richardson.

b.   The business paid $20,000 cash to acquire a truck.

c.   The business purchased supplies costing $1,800 on account.

d.   The business painted a house for a client and received $3,000 cash.

e.   The business painted a house for a client for $4,000. The client agreed to pay next week.

f.   The business paid $800 cash toward the supplies purchased in transaction c.

g.   The business paid employee salaries of $1,000 in cash.

h.   Richardson withdrew cash of $1,500.

i.   The business collected $2,600 from the client in transaction e.

j.   David paid $100 cash for personal groceries.

Requirements

1. Analyze the preceding transactions in terms of their effects on the accounting equation of DR Painting. Use Exhibit 1-6 as a guide, but show balances only after the last transaction.

2. Prepare the income statement, statement of owner's equity, and balance sheet of the business after recording the transactions. Use Exhibit 1-7 in the text as a guide.

Chapter 1: Demo Doc Solution

Requirement 1

Analyze the preceding transactions in terms of their effects on the accounting equation of DR Painting. Use Exhibit 1-6 as a guide, but show balances only after the last transaction.

Part 1	Part 2	Part 3	Part 4	Demo Doc Complete

a.   DR Painting received $40,000 cash from David Richardson and gave capital to Richardson.

     The business is receiving cash from the owner, so this is a recordable transaction for DR Painting.

     The business's Cash (an asset) is increased by $40,000 and Richardson, capital (owner's equity) is also increased by $40,000.

The effect of this transaction on the accounting equation is as follows:

	ASSETS	= LIABILITIES +	OWNER'S EQUITY (OE)	TYPE OF OE TRANSACTION
	Cash =		Richardson, capital	
a.	+40,000		+40,000	*Owner investment*
	40,000 =		40,000	

To record this in the table, we add $40,000 under Assets (Cash) and add $40,000 under Owner's Equity (Richardson, capital). To the right of the transaction, we write "Owner investment" to help us keep track of changes in the equity of the business. Before we move on, we should double-check to see that the left side of the equation equals the right side. It is important to remember that the equation must always balance after each transaction is recorded.

b. **The business paid $20,000 cash to acquire a truck.**

The Truck (an asset) is increased by $20,000, while Cash (an asset) decreases by $20,000.

The effect of this transaction on the accounting equation is as follows:

	ASSETS		= LIABILITIES +	OWNER'S EQUITY	TYPE OF OE TRANSACTION
	Cash +	Truck =		Richardson, capital	
Bal	40,000	=		40,000	
b.	−20,000	+20,000		_____	
Bal	20,000	20,000 =		40,000	
		40,000 =	40,000		

Note that transactions do not have to affect both sides of the equation. However, the accounting equation *always* equals, so *both sides must always balance*. It helps to check that this is true after every transaction.

c. **The business purchased supplies costing $1,800 on account.**

The supplies are an asset that is increased by $1,800. However, the supplies were not paid for in cash, but instead *on account*. This relates to accounts *pay*able (because it will have to be *paid* later). Because we now owe *more* money that has to be paid later, it is an increase to Accounts payable (a liability) of $1,800.

The effect of this transaction on the accounting equation is as follows:

	ASSETS			= LIABILITIES +	OWNER'S EQUITY	TYPE OF OE TRANSACTION
	Cash +	Supplies +	Truck =	Accounts payable +	Richardson, capital	
Bal	20,000		20,000		40,000	
c.	_____	+1,800	_____	+1,800	_____	
Bal	20,000	1,800	20,000 =	1,800	40,000	
			41,800 =	41,800		

Remember that the supplies will be recorded as an asset until the time that they are used by the business (the adjustment will be addressed in a later chapter). The obligation to pay the $1,800 will remain in Accounts payable until it is paid.

d. **The business painted a house for a client and received cash of $3,000.**

When the business paints houses, it means that it is doing work, or performing services for clients, which is the way that the business makes money. By performing services, the business is earning service revenues.

This means that there is an increase in Service revenue (which increases Richardson, capital) of $3,000. Because the clients paid in cash, there is also an increase in Cash (an asset) of $3,000.

Remember: Revenues *increase* net income, which increases owner's equity (Richardson, capital).

The effect of this transaction on the accounting equation is as follows:

	ASSETS			=	LIABILITIES	+	OWNER'S EQUITY	TYPE OF OE TRANSACTION
	Cash	+ Supplies	+ Truck	=	Accounts payable	+	Richardson, capital	
Bal	20,000	1,800	20,000	=	1,800		40,000	
d.	+3,000						+3,000	*Service revenue*
Bal	23,000	1,800	20,000	=	1,800		43,000	
			44,800	=	44,800			

Note that we write "Service revenue" to the right of the Richardson, capital column to record the type of transaction.

e. **The business painted a house for a client for $4,000. The client agreed to pay next month.**

This transaction is similar to transaction **d**, except that the business is not receiving the cash immediately. Does this mean that we should wait to record the revenue until the cash is received? No, DR Painting should recognize the revenue when the service is performed, regardless of whether it has received the cash.

Again, the business is performing services for clients, which means that it is earning service revenues. This results in an increase to Service revenue (Richardson, capital) of $4,000.

However, this time the client did not pay in cash but instead agreed to pay later. This is the same as charging the services *on account*. This is money that the business will *receive* in the future (when the customers eventually pay), so it is called accounts *receivable*. Accounts receivable (an asset) is increasing by $4,000. Accounts receivable represents amounts owed to the business and decreases when a customer pays.

The effect of this transaction on the accounting equation is as follows:

	ASSETS				=	LIABILITIES	+	OWNER'S EQUITY	TYPE OF OE TRANSACTION
	Cash	+ Accounts receivable	+ Supplies	+ Truck	=	Accounts payable	+	Richardson, capital	
Bal	23,000		1,800	20,000		1,800		43,000	
e.		+4,000						+4,000	*Service revenue*
Bal	23,000	4,000	1,800	20,000	=	1,800		47,000	
				48,800	=	48,800			

f. **The business paid $800 cash toward the supplies purchased in transaction c.**

Think of Accounts payable (a liability) as a list of companies to which the business will *pay* money at some point in the future. In this particular problem, the business owes money to the company from which it purchased supplies on account in transaction c. When the business *pays* the money in full, it can cross this company off of the list. Right now, the business is paying only *part* of the money owed.

This is a decrease to Accounts payable (a liability) of $800 and a decrease to Cash (an asset) of $800. Because the business is only paying part of the money it owes to the supply store, the balance of Accounts payable is $1,800 – $800 = $1,000.

You should note that this transaction does not affect Supplies because we are not buying more supplies. We are simply paying off a liability, not acquiring more assets or incurring a new expense.

The effect of this transaction on the accounting equation is as follows:

		ASSETS			=	LIABILITIES	+	OWNER'S EQUITY	TYPE OF OE TRANSACTION
	Cash	+ Accounts receivable	+ Supplies	+ Truck	=	Accounts payable	+	Richardson, capital	
Bal	23,000	4,000	1,800	20,000		1,800		47,000	
f.	–800	___	___	___		–800		___	
Bal	22,200	4,000	1,800	20,000	=	1,000		47,000	
				48,000	=	48,000			

g. **The business paid employee salaries of $1,000 cash.**

The work the employees have given to the business has *already been used*. By the end of March, DR Painting has had the employees working and painting for customers for the entire month. This means that the *benefit* of the work has already been received. This means that it is a salary *expense*. So, Salary expense would increase by $1,000, which is a decrease to owner's equity.

Remember: Expenses *decrease* net income, which decreases Richardson, capital.

The salaries were paid in cash, so Cash (an asset) is also decreased by $1,000.

The effect of this transaction on the accounting equation is as follows:

		ASSETS			=	LIABILITIES	+	OWNER'S EQUITY	TYPE OF OE TRANSACTION
	Cash	+ Accounts receivable	+ Supplies	+ Truck	=	Accounts payable	+	Richardson, capital	
Bal	22,200	4,000	1,800	20,000		1,000		47,000	
g.	–1,000	___	___	___		___		–1,000	Salary expense
Bal	21,200	4,000	1,800	20,000	=	1,000		46,000	
				47,000	=	47,000			

h. **Richardson withdrew cash of $1,500.**

When the business pays cash, it is a recordable transaction. In this case, there is a decrease of $1,500 to Cash (an asset). David is the owner of the proprietorship and is being given some of his value/ownership in cash. In other words, some of the *earnings* that were *retained* by the business are now being distributed to the owner. This results in a decrease of $1,500 to owner's equity, because Richardson, capital is decreasing.

You should note that *drawings are not an expense* because the cash is not used for operations. The cash drawings are for the owner's personal use rather than to earn revenue for the business.

The effect of this transaction on the accounting equation is as follows:

	ASSETS				= LIABILITIES +	OWNER'S EQUITY	TYPE OF OE TRANSACTION
	Cash +	Accounts receivable +	Supplies +	Truck =	Accounts payable +	Richardson, capital	
Bal	21,200	4,000	1,800	20,000	1,000	46,000	
h.	−1,500					−1,500	*Owner withdrawal*
Bal	19,700	4,000	1,800	20,000 =	1,000	44,500	
				45,500 =	45,500		

i. **The business collected $2,600 from the client in transaction e.**

Think of Accounts receivable (an asset) as a list of clients from whom the business will *receive* money at some point in the future. Later, when the business collects (*receives*) the cash in full from any particular customer, it can cross that customer off the list.

In transaction e, DR Painting performed services for a client on account. Now, DR is receiving part of that money. This is a collection that decreases Accounts receivable (an asset) by $2,600.

Because the cash is received, this is an increase to Cash (an asset) of $2,600.

The effect of this transaction on the accounting equation is as follows:

	ASSETS				= LIABILITIES +	OWNER'S EQUITY	TYPE OF OE TRANSACTION
	Cash +	Accounts receivable +	Supplies +	Truck =	Accounts payable +	Richardson, capital	
Bal	19,700	4,000	1,800	20,000	1,000	44,500	
i.	+2,600	−2,600					
Bal	22,300	1,400	1,800	20,000 =	1,000	44,500	
				45,500 =	45,500		

j. **David paid $100 cash for personal groceries.**

David is using $100 of *his own cash* for groceries. This is a *personal* expense for David's *personal* use that does not relate to the business and therefore is not a recordable transaction for the business. This transaction has no effect on the business's accounting equation. Had David used the *business's* cash to purchase groceries, *then* the business would record the transaction.

	ASSETS			=	LIABILITIES +	OWNER'S EQUITY (OE)	TYPE OF OE TRANSACTION
	Cash +	Accounts receivable + Supplies +	Truck =		Accounts payable +	Richardson, capital	
a.	+$40,000					+40,000	*Owner investment*
b.	−$20,000		+$20,000				
c.		+$1,800			+$1,800		
d.	+$3,000					+$ 3,000	*Service revenue*
e.		+$4,000				+4,000	*Service revenue*
f.	−$800				−$800		
g.	−$1,000					−$ 1,000	*Salary expense*
h.	−$1,500					−$ 1,500	*Owner withdrawal*
i.	+$2,600	−$2,600					
j.	Not a transaction of business						
Bal	$22,300	$1,400	$1,800	$20,000 =	$1,000	$44,500	
				$45,500 =	$45,500		

Requirement 2

Prepare the income statement, statement of owner's equity, and balance sheet of the business after recording the transactions. Use Exhibit 1-7 in the text as a guide.

Part 1	**Part 2**	Part 3	Part 4	Demo Doc Complete

Income Statement

The income statement is the first statement that can be prepared because the other financial statements rely upon the net income number calculated on the income statement.

The income statement reports the profitability of the business. To prepare an income statement, begin with the proper heading. A proper heading includes the name of the company (DR Painting), the name of the statement (Income Statement), and the time period covered (Month Ended March 31, 2014). Notice that we are reporting income for a period of time, rather than a single date.

The income statement lists all revenues and expenses. It uses the following formula to calculate net income:

Revenues − Expenses = Net Income

First, you should list revenues. Second, list the expenses. Having trouble finding the revenues and expenses? Look in the equity column of the accounting equation. After you have listed and totaled the revenues and expenses, you subtract the total expenses from total revenues to determine net income or net loss. If you have a positive number, then you will record net income. A negative number indicates that expenses exceeded revenues, and you will record this as a net loss.

In the case of DR Painting, transactions **d** and **e** increased Service revenue (by $3,000 and $4,000, respectively). This means that total Service revenue for the month was $3,000 + $4,000 = $7,000.

The only expenses that were incurred were in transaction **g**, which resulted in a Salary expense of $1,000. On the income statement, these would be recorded as follows:

DR PAINTING Income Statement Month Ended March 31, 2014		
Revenue:		
Service revenue		$7,000
Expenses:		
Salary expense	$1,000	
Total expenses		1,000
Net income		$6,000

Note the result is a net income of $6,000 ($7,000 − $1,000 = $6,000). You will use this amount on the statement of owner's equity.

Part 1	Part 2	**Part 3**	Part 4	Demo Doc Complete

Statement of Owner's Equity

The statement of owner's equity shows the changes in the owner's capital for a period of time. To prepare a statement of owner's equity, begin with the proper heading. A proper heading includes the name of the company (DR Painting), the name of the statement (Statement of Owner's Equity), and the time period covered (Month Ended March 31, 2014). As with the income statement, we are reporting capital for a period of time, rather than a single date.

Net income is used on the statement of owner's equity to calculate the new balance in the owner's capital account. This calculation uses the following formula:

> Beginning Capital
> + Owner investment
> + Net Income (or − Net Loss)
> − Drawing
> Ending Capital

Start the body of the statement of owner's equity with the Richardson, capital account balance at the beginning of the period (March 1). In this case, because this is a new company, the beginning Richardson, capital is zero. Next, add the owner investment during March of $40,000. Then, add net income as reported on the income statement, $6,000. Following net income, you will add the amounts on the statement so far, $46,000. Then, list the drawing by the owner of $1,500 from transaction **h**, which reduces capital. Finally, total all amounts and compute the balance at the end of the period. The statement of owner's equity follows:

DR PAINTING Statement of Owner's Equity Month Ended March 31, 2014	
Richardson, capital, March 1, 2014	$ 0
Owner investment	40,000
Net income for the month	6,000
	46,000
Drawing	(1,500)
Richardson, capital, March 31, 2014	$ 44,500

Note the result is a balance of $44,500 ($40,000 + $6,000 − $1,500 = $44,500) for Richardson, capital. You will use this amount on the balance sheet.

Part 1	Part 2	Part 3	**Part 4**	Demo Doc Complete

Balance Sheet

The balance sheet reports the financial position of the business. To prepare a balance sheet, begin with the proper heading. A proper heading includes the name of the company (DR Painting), the name of the statement (Balance Sheet), and the specific date (March 31, 2014). Unlike the income statement and statement of owner's equity, we are reporting the financial position of the company for a specific date rather than a period of time.

The balance sheet is a listing of all assets, liabilities, and equity, with the accounting equation verified at the bottom.

To prepare the body of the statement, begin by listing assets. Then you will record liabilities and owner's equity. Notice that the balance sheet is organized in the same order as the accounting equation. You should note that the amount of Richardson, capital comes directly from the ending Richardson, capital on the statement of owner's equity. You should then total both sides to make sure that they are equal. If they are not equal, then you will need to look for an error.

In this case, assets include the cash balance of $22,300, accounts receivable of $1,400, $1,800 worth of supplies, and the truck's cost of $20,000, for a total of $45,500 in assets. Liabilities total $1,000, the balance of the Accounts payable account. The figures for assets and liabilities come directly from the accounting equation worksheet. From the statement of owner's equity, we have ending Richardson, capital of $44,500. This gives us a total for liabilities and equity of $1,000 + $44,500 = $45,500, confirming that assets = liabilities + equity.

DR PAINTING
Balance Sheet
March 31, 2014

Assets		Liabilities	
Cash	$22,300	Accounts payable	$ 1,000
Accounts receivable	1,400		
Supplies	1,800	**Owner's Equity**	
Truck	20,000	Richardson, capital	44,500
Total assets	$45,500	Total liabilities and owner's equity	$45,500

Part 1	Part 2	Part 3	Part 4	**Demo Doc Complete**

Review *Accounting and the Business Environment*

● Accounting Vocabulary

Account Payable (p. 15)
A liability backed by the general reputation and credit standing of the debtor.

Account Receivable (p. 15)
The right to receive cash in the future from customers to whom the business has sold goods or for whom the business has performed services.

Accounting (p. 2)
The information system that measures business activities, processes that information into reports, and communicates the results to decision makers.

Accounting Equation (p. 11)
The basic tool of accounting, measuring the resources of the business and the claims to those resources: Assets = Liabilities + Equity.

Articles of Incorporation (p. 6)
The rules approved by the state that govern the management of the corporation.

Asset (p. 11)
An economic resource that is expected to be of benefit in the future.

Audit (p. 5)
An examination of a company's financial records.

Authorization (p. 7)
The acceptance by the state of the Corporate by-laws.

Balance Sheet (p. 20)
An entity's assets, liabilities, and owner's equity as of a specific date. Also called the **statement of financial position**.

Capital (p. 12)
The net amount invested in the business by the owner.

Certified Management Accountant (CMA) (p. 4)
A certified accountant who works for a single company.

Certified Public Accountants (CPAs) (p. 4)
Licensed accountants who serve the general public rather than one particular company.

Charter (p. 6)
Document that gives the state's permission to form a corporation.

Common Stock (p. 13)
Represents the basic ownership of every corporation.

Contributed Capital (p. 13)
The amount invested in a corporation by its owners, the stockholders. Also called **paid-in capital**.

Corporation (p. 6)
A business owned by stockholders. A corporation begins when the state approves its articles of incorporation and the first share of stock is issued. It is a legal entity, an "artificial person," in the eyes of the law.

Cost Principle (p. 10)
A principle that states that acquired assets and services should be recorded at their actual cost.

Creditors (p. 3)
Those to whom a business owes money.

Drawing (p. 12)
Distributions of capital by a company to its owner.

Entity (p. 10)
An organization or a section of an organization that, for accounting purposes, stands apart from other organizations and individuals as a separate economic unit.

Equity (p. 11)
The claim of a company's owners to the assets of the business. Also called **owner's equity** for proprietorships and partnerships and called **shareholders' equity** or **stockholders' equity** for a corporation.

Expenses (p. 12)
Decrease in equity that occurs from using assets or increasing liabilities in the course of delivering goods or services to customers.

Faithful Representation Principle (p. 10)
Principle that asserts accounting information is based on the fact that the data faithfully represents the measurement or description of that data. Faithfully represented data are complete, neutral, and free from material error.

Fiduciary Responsibility (p. 7)
An ethical and legal obligation to perform a person's duties in a trustworthy manner.

Financial Accounting (p. 2)
The branch of accounting that focuses on information for people outside the firm.

Financial Accounting Standards Board (FASB) (p. 4)
The private organization that determines how accounting is practiced in the United States.

Financial Statements (p. 2)
Documents that report on a business in monetary amounts, providing information to help people make informed business decisions.

Generally Accepted Accounting Principles (GAAP) (p. 4)
Accounting guidelines, formulated by the Financial Accounting Standards Board, that govern how accountants measure, process, and communicate financial information.

Going-Concern Concept (p. 10)
This concept assumes that the entity will remain in operation for the foreseeable future.

Income Statement (p. 20)
Summary of an entity's revenues, expenses, and net income or net loss for a specific period. Also called the **statement of earnings** or the **statement of operations**.

International Accounting Standards Board (p. 4)
The organization that determines how accounting is practiced internationally.

International Financial Reporting Standards (IFRS) (p. 4)
Accounting guidelines, formulated by the International Accounting Standards Board, that govern how accountants measure, process, and communicate financial information.

Liabilities (p. 11)
Economic obligations (debts) payable to an individual or an organization outside the business.

Limited-Liability Company (p. 6)
Company in which each member is only liable for his or her own actions or those under his or her control.

Limited-Liability Partnership (p. 6)
Company in which each partner is only liable for his or her own actions or those under his or her control.

Managerial Accounting (p. 2)
The branch of accounting that focuses on information for internal decision makers of a business.

Mutual Agency (p. 6)
The ability of partners in a partnership to commit other partners and the business to a contract.

Net Income (p. 12)
Excess of total revenues over total expenses. Also called **net earnings** or **net profit**.

Net Loss (p. 12)
Excess of total expenses over total revenues.

Not-for-Profit (p. 6)
Organization that has been approved by the Internal Revenue Service to operate for a religious, charitable, or educational purpose.

Owner's Equity (p. 11)
The claim of a company's owners to the assets of the business. For a corporation, owner's equity is called **shareholders'** or **stockholders' equity**.

Paid-In Capital (p. 13)
The amount invested in a corporation by its owners, the stockholders. Also called **contributed capital**.

Partnership (p. 6)
A business with two or more owners and not organized as a corporation.

Proprietorship (p. 6)
A business with a single owner.

Retained Earnings (p. 13)
The amount earned over the life of a business by income-producing activities and kept (retained) for use in the business.

Revenue (p. 12)
Amounts earned by delivering goods or services to customers. Revenues increase capital.

Shareholder (p. 6)
A person who owns stock in a corporation. Also called a **stockholder**.

Shareholders' Equity (p. 11)
The claim of a corporation's owners to the assets of the business. Also called **stockholders' equity**.

Stable Monetary Unit Concept (p. 11)
The concept that says that accountants assume that the dollar's purchasing power is stable.

Statement of Cash Flows (p. 20)
Report of cash receipts and cash payments during a period.

Statement of Earnings (p. 21)
Summary of an entity's revenues, expenses, and net income or net loss for a specific period. Also called the **income statement** or the **statement of operations**.

Statement of Financial Position (p. 21)
An entity's assets, liabilities, and owner's equity as of a specific date. Also called the **balance sheet**.

Statement of Operations (p. 21)
Summary of an entity's revenues, expenses, and net income or net loss for a specific period. Also called the **income statement** or **statement of earnings**.

Statement of Owner's Equity (p. 20)
Summary of the changes in an owner's capital account during a specific period.

Stock (p. 6)
A certificate representing ownership interest in a corporation. The holders of stock are called **stockholders** or **shareholders**.

Stockholder (p. 6)
A person who owns stock in a corporation. Also called a **shareholder**.

Stockholders' Equity (p. 11)
The claim of a corporation's owners to the assets of the business. Also called **shareholders' equity**.

Transaction (p. 13)
An event that affects the financial position of a particular entity and can be measured and recorded reliably.

● Destination: Student Success

Student Success Tips

The following are hints on some common trouble areas for students in this chapter:

- The four financial statements are prepared in this order: Income statement, statement of owner's equity, balance sheet, statement of cash flows.

- The accounting equation contains the same accounts as the balance sheet: Assets = Liabilities + Equity.

- Business forms vary, but the goal of accounting is to provide information to users of financial information.

- The accounting concepts are guidelines that help us record business activities.

Getting Help

If there's a learning objective from the chapter you aren't confident about, try using one or more of the following resources:

- Review the Chapter 1 Demo Doc located on page 28 of the textbook.

- Practice additional exercises or problems at the end of Chapter 1 that cover the specific learning objective you are working on.

- Watch the white board videos for Chapter 1, located at myaccountinglab.com under the Chapter Resources button.

- Go to myaccountinglab.com and select the Study Plan button. Choose Chapter 1 and work the questions covering that specific learning objective until you've mastered it.

- Work the Chapter 1 pre/post tests in myaccountinglab.com.

- Consult the Check Figures for End of Chapter starters, exercises, and problems, located at myaccountinglab.com.

- Visit the learning resource center on your campus for tutoring.

● Quick Check

1. Generally accepted accounting principles (GAAP) are formulated by the
   a. Financial Accounting Standards Board (FASB).
   b. Securities and Exchange Commission (SEC).
   c. Institute of Management Accountants (IMA).
   d. American Institute of Certified Public Accountants (AICPA).

2. Which type of business organization is owned by one owner?
   a. Corporation   c. Proprietorship
   b. Partnership   d. Items a, b, and c are all correct.

3. Which accounting concept or principle specifically states that we should record transactions at amounts that can be verified?
   a. Faithful representation   c. Entity concept
   b. Cost principle   d. Going-concern concept

4. **Fossil** is famous for fashion wristwatches and leather goods. At the end of a recent year, **Fossil's** total assets added up to $363,000,000, and equity was $228,000,000. How much were **Fossil's** liabilities?
   a. Cannot determine from the data given   c. $135,000,000
   b. $363,000,000   d. $228,000,000

5. Assume that **Fossil** sold watches to a department store on account for $48,000. How would this transaction affect **Fossil's** accounting equation?
   a. Increase both assets and liabilities by $48,000
   b. Increase both assets and equity by $48,000
   c. Increase both liabilities and equity by $48,000
   d. No effect on the accounting equation because the effects cancel out

6. Accounting is the information system that
   a. measures business activity.
   b. communicates the results to decision makers.
   c. processes data into reports.
   d. All of the above

7. Which of the following is least likely to be a user of a business's financial information?
   a. Taxing authorities   c. Creditors
   b. Customers   d. Investors

8. Consider the overall effects on **Fossil** of selling watches on account for $64,000 and paying expenses totaling $25,000. What is **Fossil's** net income or net loss?
   a. Net income of $39,000
   b. Net loss of $39,000
   c. Net income of $64,000
   d. Cannot determine from the data given

9. The balance sheet reports
   a. financial position on a specific date.
   b. results of operations on a specific date.
   c. financial position for a specific period.
   d. results of operations for a specific period.

10. Which of the following characteristics best describes a corporation?
    a. Mutual agency
    b. A board of investors
    c. Limited liability of stockholders
    d. Not for profit

Answers are given after Apply Your Knowledge (p. 61).

Assess Your Progress

● Short Exercises

S1-1   ❶ **Explaining revenues and expenses [5 min]**
Sherman Lawn Service has been open for one year, and Hannah Sherman, the owner, wants to know whether the business earned a net income or a net loss for the year. First, she must identify the revenues earned and the expenses incurred during the year.

Requirements

1. What are *revenues* and *expenses*?
2. If revenues increase, what would be the effect, if any, on equity?

S1-2   ❷ **Users of financial information [5 min]**
Suppose you are the manager of Greg's Tunes. The company needs a bank loan in order to purchase music equipment. In evaluating the loan request, the banker asks about the assets and liabilities of the business. In particular, the banker wants to know the amount of the business's owner's equity.

Requirements

1. Is the banker considered an internal or external user of financial information?
2. Which financial statement would provide the best information to answer the banker's questions?

S1-3   ❸ **Organizations that govern CPAs [5–10 min]**
Suppose you are starting a business, Wholly Shirts, to imprint logos on T-shirts. In organizing the business and setting up its accounting records, you take your information to a CPA to prepare financial statements for the bank. You state to the CPA, "I really need to get this loan, so be sure you make my financial statements look great."

Requirement

1. Name the organization that governs the majority of the guidelines that the CPA will use to prepare financial statements for Wholly Shirts.

S1-4   ❹ **Types of business organizations [5–10 min]**
Chloe Michaels plans on opening Chloe Michaels Floral Designs. She is considering the various types of business organizations and wishes to organize her business with unlimited life and limited liability features. Additionally, Chloe wants the option to raise additional equity easily in the future.

Requirement

1. Which type of business organization will meet Chloe's needs best?

MyAccountingLab

S1-5 ⑤ **Organizing a proprietorship [5–10 min]**

You begin No Limits Cell Service by investing $10,000 of your own money in a business bank account. You receive capital. Then the business borrows $5,000 cash by signing a note payable to Summit Bank.

Requirement

1. Identify the advantages and disadvantages of owning a proprietorship.

S1-6 ⑥ **Applying accounting concepts and principles [5–10 min]**

Michael McNamee is the proprietor of a property management company near the campus of Pensacola State College. The business has cash of $8,000 and furniture that cost $9,000 and has a market value of $13,000. Debts include accounts payable of $6,000. Michael's personal home is valued at $400,000 and his personal bank account has a balance of $1,200.

Requirements

1. Consider the accounting principles discussed in the chapter and define the principle that best matches the situation:
   a. Michael's personal assets are not recorded on the property management company's balance sheet.
   b. Michael records furniture at its cost of $9,000, not its market value of $13,000.
   c. Michael does not make adjustments for inflation.
   d. The account payable of $6,000 is documented by a statement from the furniture company showing the business still owes $6,000 on the furniture. Michael's friend thinks he should only owe about $5,000. The account payable is recorded at $6,000.
2. How much equity is in the business?

S1-7 ⑦ **Using the accounting equation [5 min]**

Turtle Creek Kennel earns service revenue by caring for the pets of customers. Turtle Creek's main expense is the salary paid to an employee.

Requirement

1. Write the accounting equation for the following transactions:
   a. Received $320 cash for service revenue earned.
   b. Paid $125 cash for salary expense.
   c. Earned $440 for service revenue, but the customer has not paid Turtle Creek Kennel yet.
   d. Received utility bill of $65, which will be paid next month.

S1-8 ⑧ **Analyzing transactions [5 min]**

Monte Hall Gaming paid $26,000 cash to purchase land.

Requirement

1. Identify which accounts were affected by this transaction and the amount of the change.

S1-9   ⑧ **Analyzing transactions [5 min]**
Getaway Travel recorded revenues of $2,800 earned on account by providing travel service for clients.

Requirements

1. How much are the business's cash and total assets after the transaction?
2. Name the business's asset which was increased as a result of the transaction.

S1-10   ⑧ **Analyzing transactions [5 min]**
Bob Martin Deliveries collected cash on account from a client for whom the business had provided delivery services one month earlier.

Requirements

1. Why didn't the business record revenue when it collected the cash on account?
2. Write two accounting equations to show the effects of
   a. receiving cash of $500 for service revenue earned.
   b. receiving cash of $500 from a customer on account.

S1-11   ⑨ **Prepare the balance sheet [10 min]**
Examine Exhibit 1-6. The exhibit summarizes the transactions of Smart Touch Learning for the month of April 2013. Suppose the business has completed only the first seven transactions and needs a bank loan on April 21. The vice president of the bank requires financial statements to support all loan requests.

Requirement

1. Prepare the balance sheet that the business would present to the banker *after completing the first seven transactions* on April 21, 2013. Exhibit 1-7 shows the format of the balance sheet.

S1-12   ⑨ **Prepare the income statement [10 min]**
Elegant Arrangements has just completed operations for the year ended December 31, 2012. This is the third year of operations for the company. As the owner, you want to know how well the business performed during the year. To address this question, you have assembled the following data:

Insurance expense	$ 4,000	Salary expense	$42,000
Service revenue	74,000	Accounts payable	6,800
Supplies expense	1,100	Supplies	2,100
Rent expense	13,000	Rose, drawing	3,900

Requirement

1. Prepare the income statement of Elegant Arrangements for the year ended December 31, 2012.

Note: Short Exercise 1-13 should be attempted only after completing Short Exercise 1-12.

S1-13   ⑩ **Evaluating business performance [10 min]**
Consider the facts presented in S1-12 for Elegant Arrangements.

Requirements

1. Review the income statement prepared in S1-12. Evaluate the results of 2012 operations for Elegant Arrangements. Was the year good or bad?
2. If the company's service revenue was 20% less than reported in S1-12, how will the net income (loss) change?
3. If the company's salary expense was 20% more than reported in S1-12, how will the net income (loss) change?

● Exercises

MyAccountingLab **E1-14** **1 5 6** **Using accounting vocabulary [10–15 min]**
Consider the following accounting terms and definitions:

TERMS:	DEFINITIONS:
1. Accounting Equation ~~e~~	A. An economic resource that is expected to be of benefit in the future
2. Asset used up becomes a cost	B. An economic obligation (a debt) payable to an individual or an organization outside the business
3. Balance Sheet I	
4. Expense F expired asset	C. Excess of total expenses over total revenues
5. Income Statement J	D. Excess of total revenues over total expenses
6. Liability B	E. The basic tool of accounting, stated as Assets = Liabilities + Equity
7. Net Income D	F. Decrease in equity that occurs from using assets or increasing liabilities in the course of delivering goods or services to customers
8. Net Loss C	
9. Revenue G	G. Amounts earned by delivering goods or services to customers
10. Statement of Cash Flows H	H. Report of cash receipts and cash payments during a period
11. Statement of Owner's Equity K	I. Report of an entity's assets, liabilities, and equity as of a specific date
	J. Report of an entity's revenues, expenses and net income/net loss for the period
	K. Report that shows the changes in capital for a period of time

Requirement

1. Match the term to the correct definition.

E1-15 **2 3 4 9** **Users of financial information; the accounting profession, types of business organizations, and preparing the financial statements [15–20 min]**
Evan O'Brien publishes a travel magazine. In need of cash, the business applies for a loan with National Bank. The bank requires borrowers to submit financial statements. With little knowledge of accounting, Evan O'Brien, the proprietor, does not know how to proceed.

Requirements

1. Explain how to prepare the balance sheet and the income statement.
2. Which organization is the privately funded body of accountants that defines pronouncements that guide how the financial statements will be prepared?
3. Indicate why a lender would require this information.
4. What type of organization is Evan O'Brien?
5. If Evan wanted to attract outside investors, which form of business would best enable that option?

E1-16 **5 6 7** **Characteristics of a proprietorship, accounting concepts, and using the accounting equation [5–10 min]**
Select financial information for three companies follows:

	Assets =	Liabilities +	Owner's Equity
New Rock Gas	$ 243,000	$24,000	$50,000
DJ Video Rentals	75,000	? 43,000	32,000
Corner Grocery	100,000	53,000	? 47,000

Requirements

1. Compute the missing amount in the accounting equation for each entity.
2. List the main characteristics of a proprietorship.
3. Which accounting concept tells us that the previous three proprietorships will continue to exist in the future?

E1-17   ⑥ **Comparing U.S. GAAP to IFRS [5–10 min]**
Winged Wheel Garage purchased a parcel of land on January 3, 2012, for $50,000. Its market value at the end of 2012 was $55,000.

Requirements

1. Using the U.S. GAAP cost principle, at what value would the land be reported on the balance sheet as of January 3, 2012? What value would the land be reported at on the December 31, 2012, balance sheet?
2. Using IFRS, at what value would the land be reported on the balance sheet as of January 3, 2012? What value would the land be reported at on the December 31, 2012, balance sheet?

E1-18   ⑦⑧ **Using the accounting equation to analyze business transactions [5–10 min]**
Great City Builders balance sheet data at May 31, 2012, and June 30, 2012, follow:

	May 31, 2012	June 30, 2012
Total assets	$177,000	$213,000
Total liabilities	122,000	144,000

Requirement

1. Following are three situations about owner's investments and drawings of the business during June. For each situation, compute the amount of net income or net loss during June 2012.

   a. The owner invested $6,000 in the business and made no withdrawals.
   b. The owner made no investments. The owner withdrew cash of $10,000.
   c. The company owner made investments of $18,000 and withdrew cash of $20,000.

E1-19   ⑦⑧ **Using the accounting equation to analyze transactions [5–10 min]**
As the manager of a Papa Sam's restaurant, you must deal with a variety of business transactions.

Requirement

1. Give an example of a transaction that has each of the following effects on the accounting equation:

   a. Increase one asset and decrease another asset.
   b. Decrease an asset and decrease owner's equity.
   c. Decrease an asset and decrease a liability.
   d. Increase an asset and increase owner's equity.
   e. Increase an asset and increase a liability.

E1-20 ⑦ ⑧ **Using the accounting equation to analyze transactions [10–20 min]**

Requirement

1. Indicate the effects of the following business transactions on the accounting equation of a Viviani Video store. Transaction (a) is answered as a guide.

   a. Received cash of $8,000 and gave capital.
      Answer: Increase asset (Cash)
                   Increase capital (Viviani, capital)
   b. Earned video rental revenue on account, $1,800.
   c. Purchased office furniture on account, $400.
   d. Received cash on account, $600.
   e. Paid cash on account, $100.
   f. Sold land for $15,000, which was the cost of the land.
   g. Rented videos and received cash of $300.
   h. Paid monthly office rent of $900.
   i. Paid $200 cash to purchase supplies that will be used in the future.

E1-21 ⑦ ⑧ **Using the accounting equation to analyze transactions [10–20 min]**
Caren Smith opened a medical practice. During July, the first month of operation, the business, titled Caren Smith, M.D., experienced the following events:

Jul 6	Smith invested $55,000 in the business by opening a bank account in the name of C. Smith, M.D. The business gave capital to Smith.
9	Paid $46,000 cash for land.
12	Purchased medical supplies for $1,800 on account.
15	Officially opened for business.
15–31	During the rest of the month, Smith treated patients and earned service revenue of $8,000, receiving cash.
29	Paid cash expenses: employees' salaries, $1,600; office rent, $900; utilities, $100.
30	Returned supplies purchased on the 12th for the cost of those supplies, $700.
31	Paid $1,100 on account.

Requirement

1. Analyze the effects of these events on the accounting equation of the medical practice of Caren Smith, M.D. Use a format similar to that of Exhibit 1-6, with headings for Cash; Medical supplies; Land; Accounts payable; and Smith, capital.

E1-22 ⑦ ⑧ ⑨ **Using the accounting equation to analyze transactions and calculate net income or net loss [10–15 min]**
The analysis of the first eight transactions of All-in-one Accounting Service follows. The owner made only one investment and there were no owner drawings.

		Cash	+	Accounts receivable	+	Equipment	=	Accounts payable	+	Larrison, capital
I	1	+ 31,000								+31,000
R	2			+ 3,800						+ 3,800
	3					+ 13,400		+ 13,400		
	4	+ 190		– 190						
	5	– 410				+ 410				
	6	– 8,000						– 8,000		
R	7	+ 790								+790
E	8	– 1,500								– 1,500

Requirements

1. Describe each transaction.
2. If these transactions fully describe the operations of All-in-one Accounting Service during the month, what was the amount of net income or net loss?

E1-23 **7** **10** **Using the accounting equation and evaluating business performance [10 min]**

Bob Auto Repairs started 2012 with total assets of $19,000 and total liabilities of $9,000. At the end of 2012, Bob's total assets stood at $27,000, and total liabilities were $13,000.

Requirements

1. Did the owner's equity of Bob Auto Repairs increase or decrease during 2012? By how much?
2. Identify three possible reasons for the change in owner's equity during the year.

E1-24 **7** **9** **10** **Using the accounting equation, preparing financial statements, and evaluating business performance [10–15 min]**

The 2012 annual report of American Express Services (AES) reported revenue of $21,000,000,000. Total expenses for the year were $14,000,000,000. AES ended the year with total assets of $30,000,000,000, and it owed debts totaling $14,000,000,000. At year-end 2011, the business reported total assets of $23,000,000,000 and total liabilities of $14,000,000,000.

Requirements

1. Compute AES's net income for 2012.
2. Did AES's owner's equity increase or decrease during 2012? By how much?
3. Assume you are a creditor of AES. Would the company's 2012 performance be good or bad for you, as a creditor?

E1-25 **7** **9** **10** **Using the accounting equation, preparing financial statements, and evaluating business performance [30–40 min]**

Compute the missing amount for Felix Company. You will need to work through total owner's equity.

Beginning:		Owner's Equity:	
Assets	$45,000	Owner investments	$ 0
Liabilities	29,000	Owner drawings	19,000
Ending:		Income Statement:	
Assets	$55,000	Revenues	$242,000
Liabilities	38,000	Expenses	223,000

Requirements

1. Did Felix earn a net income or suffer a net loss for the year? Compute the amount.
2. Would you consider Felix's performance for the year to be good or bad? Give your reason.

E1-26 ❽ **Analyzing business transactions [10–15 min]**
Shane's Roasted Peanuts supplies snack foods. The business experienced the following events.

   a. Shane's Roasted Peanuts received cash from the owner and gave capital to Shane.
   b. Cash purchase of land for a building site.
   c. Paid cash on accounts payable.
   d. Purchased equipment; signed a note payable.
   e. Performed service for a customer on account.
   f. Employees worked for the week but will be paid next Tuesday.
   g. Received cash from a customer on account receivable.
   h. Borrowed money from the bank.
   i. Owner withdrew cash.
   j. Incurred utility expense on account.

Requirement

   1. State whether each event (1) increased, (2) decreased, or (3) had no effect on the *total assets* of the business. Identify any specific asset affected.

E1-27 ❾ ❿ **Preparing financial statements and evaluating business performance [10–20 min]**
The account balances of Wilson Towing Service at June 30, 2012, follow:

Equipment	$13,600	Service revenue	$11,200
Supplies	900	Accounts receivable	6,200
Note payable	6,900	Accounts payable	3,000
Rent expense	550	Wilson, capital, Jun 1, 2012	4,950
Cash	2,900	Salary expense	1,900
Wilson, drawing	0		

Requirements

   1. Prepare the balance sheet of the business at June 30, 2012.
   2. What does the balance sheet report—financial position or operating results?
   3. Which financial statement reports the other accounts listed for the business?

E1-28 ❾ ❿ **Preparing financial statements and evaluating business performance [10–15 min]**
The assets, liabilities, owner's equity, revenues, and expenses of Davis Design Studio have the following balances at December 31, 2012, the end of its first year of operation. During the year, the owner invested $15,000.

Note payable	$ 42,000	Office furniture	$ 49,000
Rent expense	23,000	Utilities expense	6,900
Cash	3,600	Accounts payable	3,200
Office supplies	4,500	Davis, capital	33,300
Salary expense	65,000	Service revenue	158,300
Salaries payable	2,200	Accounts receivable	8,600
Property tax expense	1,500	Supplies expense	4,200

Requirements

   1. Prepare the income statement of Davis Design Studio for the year ended December 31, 2012. What is the result of operations for 2012?
   2. What was the amount of the owner drawing during the year?

● Problems (Group A)

P1-29A ① ② ③ ④ ⑤ ⑥ **Accounting vocabulary, financial statement users, accounting profession, types of business organizations, proprietorship characteristics, and accounting concepts [15–20 min]**   *MyAccountingLab*
Consider the following terms and definitions:

TERMS:	DEFINITIONS:
1. Proprietorship	A. Feature that enables a corporation to raise more money than proprietorships and partnerships
2. Faithful representation	B. Holds that fair market value should not be used over actual costs
3. Partnership	C. Stands for Financial Accounting Standards Board
4. Stock	D. Owner is referred to as a proprietor
5. Limited liability	E. Asserts that data are complete, neutral, and free from material error
6. Limited Liability Company	F. Revenues of $70,000 and expenses of $85,000
7. Cost principle	G. Has unlimited liability
8. FASB	H. Represents ownership in a corporation
9. Net loss of $15,000	I. Type of entity that is designed to limit personal liability exposure
10. Creditors	J. Person or business lending money

Requirement

1. Match the terms with their correct definitions.

P1-30A ⑤ ⑥ ⑨ **Proprietorship attributes, applying the entity concept, and preparing financial statements [20–25 min]**
Andrea Scarlett is a realtor. She organized her business as a proprietorship, Andrea Scarlett, Realtor, by investing $19,000 cash. The business gave capital to her. Consider the following facts at September 30, 2012.

   a. The business owes $61,000 on a note payable for land that the business acquired for a total price of $83,000.
   b. The business spent $23,000 for a Zinka Banker real estate franchise, which entitles the business to represent itself as a Zinka Banker office. This franchise is a business asset.
   c. Scarlett owes $80,000 on a personal mortgage for her personal residence, which she acquired in 2012 for a total price of $160,000.
   d. Scarlett has $5,000 in her personal bank account, and the business has $9,000 in its bank account.
   e. Scarlett owes $4,000 on a personal charge account with Chico's.
   f. The office acquired business furniture for $15,000 on September 25. Of this amount, the business owes $2,000 on account at September 30.
   g. Office supplies on hand at the real estate office total $1,300.

Requirements

1. Scarlett was concerned about taxes. Which proprietorship feature limits Scarlett's business taxes?
2. Prepare the balance sheet of the real estate business of Andrea Scarlett, Realtor, at September 30, 2012.
3. Identify the personal items that would not be reported on the business records.

P1-31A ⑥ ⑦ ⑧ ⑨ **Applying the entity concept, using the accounting equation for transaction analysis, and preparing financial statements [20–30 min]**
Alex Shore practiced accounting with a partnership for five years. Recently he opened his own accounting firm, which he operates as a proprietorship. The name of the new entity is Alex Shore, CPA. Shore experienced the following

events during the organizing phase of the new business and its first month of operations. Some of the events were personal and did not affect the business.

Feb	4	Shore received $27,000 cash from former accounting partners.*
	5	Deposited $50,000 in a new business bank account titled Alex Shore, CPA. The business gave capital to Shore.
	6	Paid $100 cash for letterhead stationery for the new office.
	7	Purchased office furniture for the office. The business will pay the account payable, $9,700, within three months.
	10	Shore sold personal investment in Amazing.com stock, which he had owned for several years, receiving $50,000 cash.*
	11	Shore deposited the $50,000 cash from sale of the Amazing.com stock in his personal bank account.*
	12	A representative of a large company telephoned Shore and told him of the company's intention to transfer its accounting business to Shore.
	18	Finished tax hearings on behalf of a client and submitted a bill for accounting services, $17,000. Shore expected to collect from this client within two weeks.
	25	Paid office rent, $1,500.
	28	Shore withdrew cash of $1,000.

*Personal transaction of Alex Shore.

Requirements

1. Analyze the effects of the events on the accounting equation of the proprietorship of Alex Shore, CPA. Use a format similar to Exhibit 1-6.
2. As of February 28, compute Alex Shore's
   a. total assets.
   b. total liabilities.
   c. total owner's equity.
   d. net income or net loss for February.

P1-32A ⑥ ⑦ ⑧ ⑨ ⑩ **Applying the entity concept, using the accounting equation for transaction analysis, preparing financial statements, and evaluating business performance [20–30 min]**

Angela Peters practiced law with a partnership for 10 years. Recently she opened her own law office, which she operates as a proprietorship. The name of the new entity is Angela Peters, Attorney. Peters experienced the following events during the organizing phase of the new business and its first month of operation. Some of the events were personal and did not affect the law practice. Others were business transactions and should be accounted for by the business.

Mar	1	Sold personal investment in **eBay** stock, which she had owned for several years, receiving $31,000 cash.
	2	Deposited the $31,000 cash from sales of the **eBay** stock in her personal bank account.
	3	Received $139,000 cash from former law partners.
	5	Deposited $89,000 cash in a new business bank account titled Angela Peters, Attorney. The business gave capital to Peters.
	7	Paid $400 cash for ink cartridges for the printer.
	9	Purchased computer for the law office, agreeing to pay the account, $9,300, within three months.
	23	Finished court hearings on behalf of a client and submitted a bill for legal services, $13,500, on account.
	30	Paid utilities, $1,200.
	31	Peters withdrew cash of $2,000.

Requirements

1. Analyze the effects of the preceding events on the accounting equation of the proprietorship of Angela Peters, Attorney. Use a format similar to Exhibit 1-6.
2. At March 31, compute the business's
   a. total assets.   c. total owner's equity.
   b. total liabilities.   d. net income or net loss for the month.

3. Evaluate Angela Peters, Attorney's first month of operations. Were the results good or bad?

P1-33A **7 8** **Using the accounting equation for transaction analysis [20–25 min]**
Zelinsky Electronics was recently formed as a proprietorship. The balance of each item in the company's accounting equation is shown for October 1 and for each of the following business days.

	Cash	Accounts receivable	Supplies	Land	Accounts payable	Zelinsky, capital
Oct 1	$4,000	$7,300	$1,200	$12,800	$4,000	$21,300
4	9,000	7,300	1,200	12,800	4,000	26,300
9	5,000	7,300	1,200	16,800	4,000	26,300
13	5,000	7,300	1,600	16,800	4,400	26,300
16	3,500	7,300	1,600	16,800	2,900	26,300
19	4,800	6,000	1,600	16,800	2,900	26,300
22	9,800	6,000	1,600	16,800	2,900	31,300
25	9,200	6,000	1,600	16,800	2,300	31,300
27	8,400	6,000	2,400	16,800	2,300	31,300
30	2,700	6,000	2,400	16,800	2,300	25,600

Requirement

1. A single transaction took place on each day. Briefly describe the transaction that most likely occurred on each day, beginning with October 4. Indicate which accounts were increased or decreased and by what amounts. Assume that no revenue or expense transactions occurred during the month.

P1-34A **7 8** **Using the accounting equation for transaction analysis [15–25 min]**
Matilda Crone owns and operates a public relations firm called Dance Fever. The following amounts summarize her business on August 31, 2012:

		Assets						=	Liabilities	+	Owner's equity
Date	Cash	+	Accounts receivable	+	Supplies	+	Land	=	Accounts payable	+	Crone, capital
Bal	2,300		1,800		0		14,000		8,000		10,100

During September 2012, the business completed the following transactions:

a. Gave capital to Crone and received cash of $13,000.
b. Performed service for a client and received cash of $900.
c. Paid off the beginning balance of accounts payable.
d. Purchased supplies from **OfficeMax** on account, $600.
e. Collected cash from a customer on account, $700.
f. Received cash of $1,600 and gave capital to owner.
g. Consulted for a new band and billed the client for services rendered, $5,500.
h. Recorded the following business expenses for the month:
   1. Paid office rent, $1,200.
   2. Paid advertising, $600.
i. Returned supplies to **OfficeMax** for $110 from item d, which was the cost of the supplies.
j. Crone withdrew cash of $2,000.

Requirement

1. Analyze the effects of the preceding transactions on the accounting equation of Dance Fever. Adapt the format to that of Exhibit 1-6.

P1-35A   ⑨ ⑩ **Preparing financial statements and evaluating business performance [20–30 min]**

Presented here are the accounts of Gate City Answering Service for the year ended December 31, 2012.

Land	$ 8,000	Owner investment, 2012	$ 28,000
Note payable	32,000	Accounts payable	11,000
Property tax expense	2,600	Accounts receivable	1,000
Wayne, drawing	30,000	Advertising expense	15,000
Rent expense	13,000	Building	145,200
Salary expense	65,000	Cash	3,000
Salary payable	1,300	Equipment	16,000
Service revenue	192,000	Insurance expense	2,500
Supplies	10,000	Interest expense	7,000
Wayne, capital, 12/31/2011	54,000		

Requirements

1. Prepare Gate City Answering Service's income statement.
2. Prepare the statement of owner's equity.
3. Prepare the balance sheet.
4. Answer these questions about the company:
   a. Was the result of operations for the year a profit or a loss? How much?
   b. How much in total economic resources does the company have as it moves into the new year?
   c. How much does the company owe to creditors?
   d. What is the dollar amount of the owner's equity in the business at the end of the year?

P1-36A   ⑨ **Preparing financial statements [20–30 min]**

Studio Photography works weddings and prom-type parties. The balance of Ansel, capital was $16,000 at December 31, 2011. At December 31, 2012, the business's accounting records show these balances:

Insurance expense	$ 8,000	Accounts receivable	$ 8,000
Cash	37,000	Note payable	12,000
Accounts payable	7,000	Ansel, capital, Dec 31, 2012	?
Advertising expense	3,000	Salary expense	25,000
Service revenue	80,000	Equipment	50,000
Ansel, drawing	13,000	Owner investment, 2012	29,000

Requirement

1. Prepare the following financial statements for Studio Photography for the year ended December 31, 2012:
   a. Income statement
   b. Statement of owner's equity
   c. Balance sheet

P1-37A   ⑨ ⑩ **Preparing financial statements and evaluating business performance [20–30 min]**

The bookkeeper of Greener Landscaping prepared the company's balance sheet while the accountant was ill. The balance sheet contains numerous errors. In particular, the bookkeeper knew that the balance sheet should balance, so he plugged in the owner's equity amount needed to achieve this balance. The owner's equity is incorrect. All other amounts are right, but some are out of place.

GREENER LANDSCAPING					
Balance Sheet					
Month Ended November 30, 2012					
Assets			**Liabilities**		
Cash	$	4,900	Accounts receivable	$	2,200
Office supplies		600	Tum, drawing		10,000
Land		34,200	Service revenue		39,000
Salary expense		2,800	Property tax expense		2,600
Office furniture		6,100	Accounts payable		2,700
Note payable		24,200			
Rent expense		300	**Owner's Equity**		
			Tum, capital		16,600
Total assets	$	73,100	Total liabilities	$	73,100

Requirements

1. Prepare a corrected balance sheet.
2. Consider the original balance sheet as presented and the corrected balance sheet you prepared for Requirement 1. Did total assets as presented in your corrected balance sheet increase, decrease, or stay the same from the original balance sheet? Why?

● Problems (Group B)

P1-38B ① ② ③ ④ ⑤ ⑥ **Accounting vocabulary, financial statement users, accounting profession, types of business organizations, proprietorship characteristics, and accounting concepts [15–20 min]**   *MyAccountingLab*

Consider the following terms and definitions:

TERMS:	DEFINITIONS:
1. Proprietorship	A. Feature that sets the maximum amount of financial loss by a stockholder to the cost of the investment
2. Faithful representation	B. Reason why accountants should not write up the value of equipment due to an increase in its fair value
3. Partnership	C. Is composed of accountants
4. Stock	D. An entity that has fewer than two owners
5. Limited liability	E. Principle that does not accept incomplete or bias data
6. Limited Liability Company	F. Revenues of $40,000 and expenses of $25,000
7. Cost principle	G. Possess mutual agency
8. FASB	H. The corporate charter specifies how much of this a corporation can sell
9. Net income of $15,000	I. Entity where the business, and not the proprietor, is liable for the company's debts
10. Business owners	J. Use accounting information to set goals, to measure progress toward those goals, and to make adjustments when needed

Requirement

1. Match the terms with their correct definitions.

P1-39B ⑤ ⑥ ⑨ **Proprietorship attributes, applying the entity concept, and preparing financial statements [20–25 min]**

Sandy White is a realtor. She organized her business as a proprietorship, Sandy White, Realtor, by investing $27,000 cash.

The business gave capital to her. Consider the following facts at May 31, 2012:

a. The business owes $62,000 on a note payable for land that the business acquired for a total price of $80,000.

b. The business spent $26,000 for a Minko Banker real estate franchise, which entitles the business to represent itself as a Minko Banker office. This franchise is a business asset.

c. White owes $70,000 on a personal mortgage for her personal residence, which she acquired in 2012 for a total price of $130,000.

d. White has $4,000 in her personal bank account, and the business has $13,000 in its bank account.

e. White owes $3,000 on a personal charge account with **Chico's**.

f. The office acquired business furniture for $20,000 on May 25. Of this amount, the business owes $5,000 on account at May 31.

g. Office supplies on hand at the real estate office total $1,100.

Requirements

1. White was concerned about taxes. Which propriertorship feature limits White's business taxes?

2. Prepare the balance sheet of the real estate business of Sandy White, Realtor at May 31, 2012.

3. Identify the personal items that would not be reported on the business records.

P1-40B ⑥ ⑦ ⑧ ⑨ **Applying the entity concept, using the accounting equation for transaction analysis, and preparing financial statements [20–30 min]**

Arron Woody practiced accounting with a partnership for five years. Recently he opened his own accounting firm, which he operates as a proprietorship. The name of the new entity is Arron Woody, CPA. Woody experienced the following events during the organizing phase of the new business and its first month of operations. Some of the events were personal and did not affect the business.

Feb	4	Woody received $31,000 cash from former accounting partners.*
	5	Deposited $40,000 in a new business bank account titled Arron Woody, CPA. The business gave capital to Woody.
	6	Paid $200 cash for letterhead stationery for the new office.
	7	Purchased office furniture for the office. The business will pay the account payable, $9,500, within three months.
	10	Woody sold personal investment in Amazing.com stock, which he had owned for several years, receiving $51,000 cash.*
	11	Woody deposited the $51,000 cash from sale of the Amazing.com stock in his personal bank account.*
	12	A representative of a large company telephoned Woody and told him of the company's intention to transfer its accounting business to Woody.
	18	Finished tax hearings on behalf of a client and submitted a bill for accounting services, $14,000. Woody expected to collect from this client within two weeks.
	25	Paid office rent, $1,900.
	28	Woody withdrew cash of $8,000.

*Personal transaction of Arron Woody.

Requirements

1. Analyze the effects of the events on the accounting equation of the proprietorship of Arron Woody, CPA. Use a format similar to Exhibit 1-6.

2. As of February 28, compute Arron Woody's
   a. total assets.
   b. total liabilities.
   c. total owner's equity.
   d. net income or net loss for February.

P1-41B ⑥ ⑦ ⑧ ⑨ ⑩ **Applying the entity concept, using the accounting equation for transaction analysis, preparing financial statements, and evaluating business performance [20–30 min]**

Aimee Griffin practiced law with a partnership for 10 years. Recently she opened her own law office, which she operates as a proprietorship. The name of the new entity is Aimee Griffin, Attorney. Griffin experienced the following events during the organizing phase of the new business and its first month of operation. Some of the events were personal and did not affect the law practice. Others were business transactions and should be accounted for by the business.

Dec 1	Sold personal investment in **eBay** stock, which she had owned for several years, receiving $33,000 cash.
2	Deposited the $33,000 cash from sales of the **eBay** stock in her personal bank account.
3	Received $159,000 cash from former law partners.
5	Deposited $109,000 cash in a new business bank account titled Aimee Griffin, Attorney. The business gave capital to Griffin.
7	Paid $900 cash for ink cartridges for the printer.
9	Purchased a computer for the law office, agreeing to pay the account, $9,200, within three months.
23	Finished court hearings on behalf of a client and submitted a bill for legal services, $17,000, on account.
30	Paid utilities, $1,900.
31	Griffin withdrew cash of $5,000.

Requirements

1. Analyze the effects of the preceding events on the accounting equation of the propriertorship of Aimee Griffin, Attorney. Use a format similar to Exhibit 1-6.

2. At December 31, compute the business's
   a. total assets.
   b. total liabilities.
   c. total owner's equity.
   d. net income or net loss for the month.

3. Evaluate Aimee Griffin, Attorney's first month of operations. Were the results good or bad?

P1-42B ⑦ ⑧ **Using the accounting equation for transaction analysis [20–25 min]**

Alterri Mechanical was recently formed as a proprietorship. The balance of each item in the company's accounting equation is shown for November 1 and for each of the following business days:

	Cash	Accounts receivable	Supplies	Land	Accounts payable	Alterri, capital
Nov 1	$3,000	$7,300	$ 1,100	$12,000	$4,300	$19,100
4	6,000	7,300	1,100	12,000	4,300	22,100
9	3,000	7,300	1,100	15,000	4,300	22,100
13	3,000	7,300	1,300	15,000	4,500	22,100
16	1,300	7,300	1,300	15,000	2,800	22,100
19	2,200	6,400	1,300	15,000	2,800	22,100
22	10,200	6,400	1,300	15,000	2,800	30,100
25	9,700	6,400	1,300	15,000	2,300	30,100
27	9,100	6,400	1,900	15,000	2,300	30,100
30	3,600	6,400	1,900	15,000	2,300	24,600

Requirement

1. A single transaction took place on each day. Briefly describe the transaction that most likely occurred on each day, beginning with November 4. Indicate which accounts were increased or decreased and by what amounts. Assume that no revenue or expense transactions occurred during the month.

P1-43B 7 8 9 10 **Using the accounting equation for transaction analysis [60–75 min]**
Missy Crone owns and operates a public relations firm called Top 40. The following amounts summarize her business on August 31, 2012:

			Assets						=	Liabilities	+	Owner's equity
Date	Cash	+	Accounts receivable	+	Supplies	+	Land	=		Accounts payable	+	Crone, capital
Bal	2,100	+	2,000	+	0	+	10,000	=		6,000	+	8,100

During September 2012, the business completed the following transactions:

a. Gave capital to Crone and received cash of $10,000.
b. Performed service for a client and received cash of $1,000.
c. Paid off the beginning balance of accounts payable.
d. Purchased supplies from **OfficeMax** on account, $700.
e. Collected cash from a customer on account, $500.
f. Received cash of $1,900 and gave capital to owner.
g. Consulted for a new band and billed the client for services rendered, $5,800.
h. Recorded the following business expenses for the month:
   1. Paid office rent, $900.
   2. Paid advertising, $400.
i. Returned supplies to **OfficeMax** for $80 from item d, which was the cost of the supplies.
j. Crone withdrew cash of $2,700.

Requirement

1. Analyze the effects of the preceding transactions on the accounting equation of Top 40. Adapt the format to that of Exhibit 1-6.

P1-44B 9 10 **Preparing financial statements and evaluating business performance [20–30 min]**
Presented here are the accounts of Quick and EZ Delivery for the year ended December 31, 2012.

Land	$ 7,000	Owner investment, 2012	$ 32,000
Note payable	30,000	Accounts payable	14,000
Property tax expense	2,900	Accounts receivable	1,700
Trott, drawing	32,000	Advertising expense	17,000
Rent expense	13,000	Building	137,900
Salary expense	69,000	Cash	6,000
Salary payable	500	Equipment	17,000
Service revenue	192,000	Insurance expense	2,000
Supplies	8,000	Interest expense	6,000
Trott, capital, 12/31/2011	51,000		

Requirements

1. Prepare Quick and EZ Delivery's income statement.
2. Prepare the statement of owner's equity.
3. Prepare the balance sheet.
4. Answer these questions about the company:
   a. Was the result of operations for the year a profit or a loss? How much?
   b. How much in total economic resources does the company have as it moves into the new year?
   c. How much does the company owe to creditors?
   d. What is the dollar amount of the owner's equity in the business at the end of the year?

P1-45B ⑨ **Preparing financial statements [20–30 min]**

Photo Gallery works weddings and prom-type parties. The balance of Leibovitz, capital was $17,000 at December 31, 2011. At December 31, 2012, the business's accounting records show these balances:

Insurance expense	$ 9,000	Accounts receivable	$ 6,000
Cash	26,000	Note payable	14,000
Accounts payable	4,000	Leibovitz, capital, Dec 31, 2012	?
Advertising expense	2,000	Salary expense	21,000
Service revenue	78,000	Equipment	70,000
Leibovitz, drawing	14,000	Owner investment, 2012	35,000

Requirement

1. Prepare the following financial statements for Photo Gallery for the year ended December 31, 2012:
   a. Income statement
   b. Statement of owner's equity
   c. Balance sheet

P1-46B ⑨ ⑩ **Preparing financial statements and evaluating business performance [20–30 min]**

The bookkeeper of Outdoor Life Landscaping prepared the company's balance sheet while the accountant was ill. The balance sheet contains numerous errors. In particular, the bookkeeper knew that the balance sheet should balance, so he plugged in the owner's equity amount needed to achieve this balance. The owner's equity is incorrect. All other amounts are right, but some are out of place.

OUTDOOR LIFE LANDSCAPING			
Balance Sheet			
Month Ended July 31, 2012			
Assets		**Liabilities**	
Cash	$ 5,000	Accounts receivable	$ 2,300
Office supplies	800	Kamp, drawing	8,000
Land	28,400	Service revenue	39,200
Salary expense	3,500	Property tax expense	2,000
Office furniture	5,200	Accounts payable	2,800
Note payable	26,400		
Rent expense	700	**Owner's Equity**	
		Kamp, capital	15,700
Total assets	$ 70,000	Total liabilities	$ 70,000

Requirements

1. Prepare a corrected balance sheet.
2. Consider the original balance sheet as presented and the corrected balance sheet you prepared for Requirement 1. Did total assets as presented in your corrected balance sheet increase, decrease, or stay the same from the original balance sheet? Why?

● Continuing Exercise

Exercise 1-47 is the first exercise in a sequence that begins an accounting cycle. The cycle is continued in Chapter 2 and completed in Chapter 5.

E1-47 ❽ Analyzing transactions [10–15 min]

Lawlor Lawn Service began operations and completed the following transactions during May 2012:

May	1	Received $1,700 and gave capital to Lawlor. Deposited this amount in bank account titled Lawlor Lawn Service.
	3	Purchased on account a mower, $1,200, and weed whacker, $240. The equipment is expected to remain in service for four years.
	5	Purchased $30 of gas. Wrote check #1 from the new bank account.
	6	Performed lawn services for client on account, $150.
	8	Purchased $150 of fertilizer that will be used on future jobs. Wrote check #2 from the new bank account.
	17	Completed landscaping job for client, received cash $800.
	31	Received $100 on account from May 6 sale.

Requirement

1. Analyze the effects of Lawlor Lawn Service transactions on the accounting equation. Use the format of Exhibit 1-6, and include these headings: Cash; Accounts receivable; Lawn supplies; Equipment; Accounts payable; and Lawlor, capital.

In Chapter 2, we will account for these same transactions a different way—as the accounting is actually performed in practice.

● Continuing Problem

Problem 1-48 is the first problem in a sequence that begins an accounting cycle. The cycle is continued in Chapter 2 and completed in Chapter 5.

P1-48 ❽ ❾ Analyzing transactions and preparing financial statements [20–25 min]

Draper Consulting began operations and completed the following transactions during the first half of December:

Dec	2	Received $18,000 cash and gave capital to Draper.
	2	Paid monthly office rent, $550.
	3	Paid cash for a **Dell** computer, $1,800. This equipment is expected to remain in service for five years.
	4	Purchased office furniture on account, $4,200. The furniture should last for five years.
	5	Purchased supplies on account, $900.
	9	Performed consulting service for a client on account, $1,500.
	12	Paid utility expenses, $250.
	18	Performed service for a client and received cash of $1,100.

Requirements

1. Analyze the effects of Draper Consulting's transactions on the accounting equation. Use the format of Exhibit 1-6, and include these headings: Cash; Accounts receivable; Supplies; Equipment; Furniture; Accounts payable; and Draper, capital.
2. Prepare the income statement of Draper Consulting for the month ended December 31, 2012.
3. Prepare the statement of owner's equity for the month ended December 31, 2012.
4. Prepare the balance sheet at December 31, 2012.

In Chapter 2, we will account for these same transactions a different way—as the accounting is actually performed in practice.

● Practice Set

⑧ Analyzing transactions [10–15 min] Consider the following transactional data for the first month of operations of Shine King Cleaning.

Nov 1: Evan Hudson deposited $35,000 in the business account. Also on this date, Evan transferred his truck title, worth $8,000, to the business. Evan received capital in return.

Nov 2: Wrote a check for $2,000 to Pleasant Properties. In the "for" area of the the check, it states "November through February Rent." (Debit Prepaid rent)

Nov 3: Purchased business insurance policy for $2,400 for the term November 1, 2012, through October 31, 2013 and paid cash. (Debit Prepaid insurance)

Nov 4: Evan went to the Cleaning Supply Company and purchased $270 of cleaning supplies on account. The invoice is due 20 days from the date of purchase.

Nov 5: Purchased on account an industrial vacuum cleaner from Penny Purchase costing $1,000. The invoice is payable on or before November 25.

Nov 7: Purchased a computer and printer costing a total of $1,200. A check for the same amount to the computer store was written on the same date.

Nov 9: Performed cleaning services on account for Pierre's Wig Stand in the amount of $3,000.

Nov 10: Deposited Pierre's check for $100 in the bank.

Nov 15: Wrote check payable to Eric Ryder for $500 for contract labor.

Nov 16: Received $3,600 for 1-year contract beginning November 16 for cleaning services to be provided to the Sea Side Restaurant. Contract begins November 16, 2012, and ends November 15, 2013. (Credit Unearned service revenue)

Nov 17: Provided cleaning services for Tip Top Solutions for $800. Tip Top paid with a check.

Nov 18: Received water and electric bill for $175 with due date of December 4, 2012.

Nov 20: Borrowed $40,000 from bank with interest rate of 9% per year.

Nov 21: Deposited check from Pierre's Wig Stand for $900 paid on account.

Nov 25: Wrote check to Penny Purchase for invoice #1035 in the amount of $500.

Nov 29: Wrote check payable to St. Petersburg News for $100 for advertising.

Nov 30: Evan withdrew cash of $600.

Requirement

1. Prepare an analysis of the November activity using the format displayed in Exhibit 1-6 as a guide. Include the following headings: Cash; Accounts receivable, Supplies; Prepaid rent; Prepaid insurance; Truck; Equipment; Accounts payable; Unearned service revenue; Notes payable; and Hudson, capital.

Apply Your Knowledge

● Decision Cases

Decision Case 1-1 Let's examine a case using Greg's Tunes and another company, Sal's Silly Songs. It is now the end of the first year of operations, and both owners—Sally Siegman and Greg Moore—want to know how well they came out at the end of the year. Neither business kept complete accounting records and neither owner made any drawings. Moore and Siegman throw together the following data at year end:

Sal's Silly Songs:	
Total assets	$23,000
Siegman, capital	8,000
Total revenues	35,000
Total expenses	22,000
Greg's Tunes:	
Total liabilities	$10,000
Moore, capital	6,000
Total expenses	44,000
Net income	9,000

Working in the music business, Moore has forgotten all the accounting he learned in college. Siegman majored in English literature, so she never learned any accounting. To gain information for evaluating their businesses, they ask you several questions. For each answer, you must show your work to convince Moore and Siegman that you know what you are talking about.

1. Which business has more assets?
2. Which business owes more to creditors?
3. Which business has more owner's equity at the end of the year?
4. Which business brought in more revenue?
5. Which business is more profitable?
6. Which of the foregoing questions do you think is most important for evaluating these two businesses? Why? (Challenge)
7. Which business looks better from a financial standpoint? (Challenge)

Decision Case 1-2 Dave and Reba Guerrera saved all their married life to open a bed and breakfast (B&B) named Tres Amigos. They invested $100,000 of their own money and the company gave capital to them. The business then got a $100,000 bank loan for the $200,000 needed to get started. The company bought a run-down old Spanish colonial home in Tucson for $80,000. It cost another $50,000 to renovate. They found most of the furniture at antique shops and flea markets—total cost was $20,000. Kitchen equipment cost $10,000, and a **Dell** computer set cost $2,000.

Prior to the grand opening, the banker requests a report on their activities thus far. Tres Amigos' bank statement shows a cash balance of $38,000. Dave and Reba believe that the $38,000 represents net income for the period, and they feel pretty good about the results of their business. To better understand how well they are doing, they prepare the following income statement for presentation to the bank:

TRES AMIGOS BED AND BREAKFAST
Income Statement
Six Months Ended June 30, 2013

Revenues:	
Investments by owner	$100,000
Bank loan	100,000
Total revenues	200,000
Expenses:	
Cost of the house	$ 80,000
Renovation to the house	50,000
Furniture expense	20,000
Kitchen equipment expense	10,000
Computer expense	2,000
Total expenses	162,000
Net income	38,000

1. Suppose you are the Guerreras' banker, and they have given you this income statement. Would you congratulate them on their net income? If so, explain why. If not, how would you advise them to measure the net income of the business? Does the amount of cash in the bank measure net income? Explain.
2. Prepare Tres Amigos' balance sheet from their data. There is no net income or loss yet.

● Ethical Issues

Ethical Issue 1-1 The board of directors of Xiaping Trading Company is meeting to discuss the past year's results before releasing financial statements to the bank. The discussion includes this exchange:

Wai Lee, company owner: "This has not been a good year! Revenue is down and expenses are way up. If we are not careful, we will report a loss for the third year in a row. I can temporarily transfer some land that I own into the company's name, and that will beef up our balance sheet. Brent, can you shave $500,000 from expenses? Then we can probably get the bank loan that we need."

Brent Ray, company chief accountant: "Wai Lee, you are asking too much. Generally accepted accounting principles are designed to keep this sort of thing from happening."

Requirements
1. What is the fundamental ethical issue in this situation?
2. How do the two suggestions of the company owner differ?

Ethical Issue 1-2 The tobacco companies have paid billions because of smoking-related illnesses. In particular, **Philip Morris**, a leading cigarette manufacturer, paid over $3,000,000,000 in one year.

Requirements
1. Suppose you are the chief financial officer (CFO) responsible for the financial statements of **Philip Morris**. What ethical issue would you face as you consider what to report in your company's annual report about the cash payments? What is the ethical course of action for you to take in this situation?
2. What are some of the negative consequences to **Philip Morris** for not telling the truth? What are some of the negative consequences to **Philip Morris** for telling the truth?

• Fraud Case 1-1

Exeter is a building contractor on the Gulf Coast. After losing a number of big lawsuits, it was facing its first annual net loss as the end of the year approached. The owner, Hank Snow, was under intense pressure from the company's creditors to report positive net income for the year. However, he knew that the controller, Alice Li, had arranged a short-term bank loan of $10,000 to cover a temporary shortfall of cash. He told Alice to record the incoming cash as "construction revenue" instead of a loan. That would nudge the company's income into positive territory for the year, and then, he said, the entry could be corrected in January when the loan was repaid.

Requirements

1. How would this action affect the year-end income statement? How would it affect the year-end balance sheet?
2. If you were one of the company's creditors, how would this fraudulent action affect you?

• Financial Statement Case 1-1

This and similar cases in later chapters focus on the financial statement of a real company—**Amazon.com, Inc.**, the Internet shopping leader. As you work each case, you will gain confidence in your ability to use the financial statements of real companies.

Refer to **Amazon.com's** financial statements in Appendix A at the end of the book.

Requirements

1. How much in cash (including cash equivalents) did **Amazon.com** have on December 31, 2009?
2. What were the company's total assets at December 31, 2009? At December 31, 2008?
3. Write the company's accounting equation at December 31, 2009, by filling in the dollar amounts:

> ASSETS = LIABILITIES + EQUITY

4. Identify net sales (revenue) for the year ended December 31, 2009. How much did total revenue increase or decrease from 2008 to 2009?
5. How much net income or net loss did **Amazon** earn for 2009 and for 2008? Based on net income, was 2009 better or worse than 2008?

• Team Projects

Team Project 1-1 You are opening Quail Creek Pet Kennel. Your purpose is to earn a profit, and you organize as a proprietorship.

1. Make a detailed list of 10 factors you must consider to establish the business.
2. Identify 10 or more transactions that your business will undertake to open and operate the kennel.
3. Prepare the Quail Creek Pet Kennel income statement, statement of owner's equity, and balance sheet at the end of the first month of operations. Use made-up figures and include a complete heading for each financial statement. Date the balance sheet as of January 31, 20XX.
4. Discuss how you will evaluate the success of your business and how you will decide whether to continue its operation.

Team Project 1-2 You are promoting a rock concert in your area. Your purpose is to earn a profit, and you organize Concert Enterprises as a proprietorship.

Requirements

1. Make a detailed list of 10 factors you must consider to establish the business.

2. Describe 10 of the items your business must arrange in order to promote and stage the rock concert.

3. Prepare your business's income statement, statement of owner's equity, and balance sheet on June 30, 20XX, immediately after the rock concert. Use made-up amounts, and include a complete heading for each financial statement. For the income statement and the statement of owner's equity, assume the period is the three months ended June 30, 20XX.

4. Assume that you will continue to promote rock concerts if the venture is successful. If it is unsuccessful, you will terminate the business within three months after the concert. Discuss how you will evaluate the success of your venture and how you will decide whether to continue in business.

● Communication Activity 1-1

In 25 words or fewer, illustrate the accounting equation and explain each part of the accounting equation.

Quick Check Answers

1. *a* 2. *c* 3. *a* 4. *c* 5. *b* 6. *d* 7. *b* 8. *a* 9. *a* 10. *c*

For online homework, exercises, and problems that provide you immediate feedback, please visit myaccountinglab.com.

2 Recording Business Transactions

How do the activities of the company affect what it OWNS?

How do the activities of the company affect what it OWES?

SMART TOUCH LEARNING
Balance Sheet
May 31, 2013

Assets				Liabilities	
Current assets:				Current liabilities:	
Cash		$ 4,800		Accounts payable	$ 48,700
Accounts receivable		2,600		Salary payable	900
Inventory		30,500		Interest payable	100
Supplies		600		Unearned service revenue	400
Prepaid rent		2,000		Total current liabilities	50,100
Total current assets			$ 40,500	Long-term liabilities:	
Plant assets:				Notes payable	20,000
Furniture	$18,000			Total liabilities	70,100
Less: Accumulated depreciation—furniture	300	17,700			
Building	48,000			**Owner's Equity**	
Less: Accumulated depreciation—building	200	47,800			
Total plant assets			65,500	Bright, capital	35,900
Total assets			$106,000	Total liabilities and owner's equity	$106,000

How do the activities of the company affect its NET WORTH?

Learning Objectives

1 Explain accounts, journals, and ledgers as they relate to recording transactions and describe common accounts

2 Define debits, credits, and normal account balances, and use double-entry accounting and T-accounts

3 List the steps of the transaction recording process

4 Journalize and post sample transactions to the ledger

5 Prepare the trial balance from the T-accounts

After reading Chapter 1, you have a basic understanding of what financial statements are. But how do you create them for your business or the company you work for? How do large companies like **Microsoft** create their statements for investors? How does any business capture the financial events that occur so that it can create financial statements?

In Chapter 1, we saw how Sheena Bright of Smart Touch Learning recorded her company's business transactions in terms of the accounting equation. That procedure works well for a handful of transactions, but it's not very efficient if your business generates lots of transactions. In this chapter, we'll show you a more efficient way to capture business transactions. As you'll see, this chapter is a critical foundation for learning accounting.

The Account, the Journal, and the Ledger

The basic summary device of accounting is the account. An **account** is the detailed record of all the changes that have occurred in an individual asset, liability, or owner's equity (or stockholders' equity for a corporation) during a specified period. As we saw in Chapter 1, business transactions cause the changes.

Accountants record transactions first in a **journal**, which is the chronological record of transactions. Accountants then post (copy) the data to the book of accounts called the **ledger**. A list of all the ledger accounts and their balances is called a **trial balance**.

The following diagram summarizes the accounting process covered in this chapter. Take a moment to become familiar with these important terms. You will be using them over and over again.

1 Explain accounts, journals, and ledgers as they relate to recording transactions and describe common accounts

- **Account**—the detailed record of all the changes that have occurred in a particular asset, liability, or owner's equity
- **Journal**—the chronological record of transactions
- **Ledger**—the book holding all the accounts with their balances
- **Trial balance**—the list of all the ledger accounts with their balances

Accounts are grouped in three broad categories, according to the accounting equation:

$$\text{Assets} = \text{Liabilities} + \text{Owner's Equity}$$

Assets

Assets are economic resources that will benefit the business in the future, **or simply, something the business owns that has value.** Most firms use the following asset accounts:

Cash

The Cash account is a record of the cash effects of transactions. Cash includes money, such as a bank balance, paper currency, coins, and checks. Cash is the most pressing need of start-up businesses, such as Smart Touch Learning and Greg's Tunes.

Accounts Receivable

Most businesses sell goods or services in exchange for a promise of future cash receipts. Such sales are made on credit ("on account"), and Accounts receivable is the account that holds these amounts. **Accounts receivable is the right to receive cash in the near future.** Most sales in the United States and in other developed countries are made on account.

Notes Receivable

A business may sell goods or services and receive a **note receivable** or *promissory note*. A note receivable is a written pledge that the customer will pay a fixed amount of money and interest by a certain date. **A note receivable is the right to receive cash and interest in the future.**

Prepaid Expenses

A business often pays certain expenses, such as rent and insurance, in advance. A **prepaid expense** is considered an asset because the prepayment provides a future bene-fit. **With a prepaid expense, the company pays for the expense before it is used.** Prepaid rent, Prepaid insurance, and Office supplies are separate prepaid expense accounts. Your college tuition that you paid at the beginning of the term is an asset to you.

Land

The Land account shows the cost of land a business holds for use in operations. Land held for sale is different. Its cost is an investment.

Building

The cost of buildings—an office or a warehouse—appears in the Buildings account. **Frito-Lay** and **The Coca-Cola Company** own buildings around the world where they make chips and drinks.

Equipment, Furniture, and Fixtures

A business has a separate asset account for each type of equipment—Computer equipment, Office equipment, and Store equipment, for example. The Furniture account shows the cost of this asset. Similarly, the Fixtures account shows the cost of light fixtures and shelving, for example.

Liabilities

Recall that a *liability* is a debt—that is, something you owe. A business generally has fewer liability accounts than asset accounts.

Accounts Payable

Accounts payable is the opposite of Accounts receivable. The promise to pay a debt arising from a credit purchase is an Account payable. Such a purchase is said to be made on account. **An account payable is an obligation to pay cash in the near future.** All companies, from Smart Touch and Greg's Tunes to **Coca-Cola** to **eBay**, have Accounts payable.

Notes Payable

Notes payable is the opposite of Notes receivable. A note payable is an obligation to pay, whereas a note receivable is a right to receive. Notes payable represents debts the business owes because it signed promissory notes to borrow money or to purchase something. **Notes payable is an obligation to pay cash and interest in the future.**

Accrued Liabilities

An **accrued liability** is a liability for which the business knows the amount owed, but the bill has not been paid. Taxes payable, Interest payable, and Salary payable are examples of accrued liability accounts.

Owner's Equity

The owner's claim to the assets of the business is called *owner's equity*. A company has separate accounts for the various elements of owner's equity.

Capital

The capital account represents the net investment of the owner in the business. It holds the accumulation of owner investment, withdrawals, and net income (loss) of the business over the life of the business. In other words, capital is the net worth invested in the business by the owner.

Drawing

The owner may withdraw cash or other assets at any time from the company. This represents a return of his or her capital investment, as well as a distribution of earnings from the company. **Owner drawings mean less earnings retained by the company for future growth.**

Revenues

The increase in equity created by delivering goods or services to customers is called *revenue*. **Revenues refer to earnings for work done or goods delivered by the company, regardless of when the cash is received.** The ledger contains as many revenue accounts as needed. Smart Touch, for example, needs a Service revenue account for amounts earned by providing e-learning services. If Smart Touch lends money to an outsider, it needs an Interest revenue account for the interest earned on the loan. If the business rents out a building to a tenant, it needs a Rent revenue account.

Expenses

Expenses use up assets or create liabilities in the course of operating a business. Expenses have the opposite effect of revenues. Expenses *decrease* equity. **Expenses are present or future payments of cash that are incurred to help the company earn revenues.** A business needs a separate account for each type of expense, such as Salary expense, Rent expense, Advertising expense, and Utilities expense. Businesses strive to minimize their expenses in order to maximize net income—whether that business is **General Electric**, Smart Touch, or Greg's Tunes.

Exhibit 2-1 shows how asset, liability, and owner's equity accounts can be grouped in the ledger.

Chart of Accounts

The ledger contains the accounts grouped under these headings:

- Assets, Liabilities, and Owner's Equity
- Revenues and Expenses

Companies use a **chart of accounts** to list all their accounts along with the account numbers. The chart of accounts for Smart Touch appears in Exhibit 2-2. Account numbers are just shorthand versions of the account names. One account number equals one account name—just like your Social Security number is unique to you.

Account numbers usually have two or more digits. Assets are often numbered beginning with 1, liabilities with 2, owner's equity with 3, revenues with 4, and expenses with 5. The second and third digits in an account number indicate where the account fits within the category. For example, if Sheena Bright is using three-digit

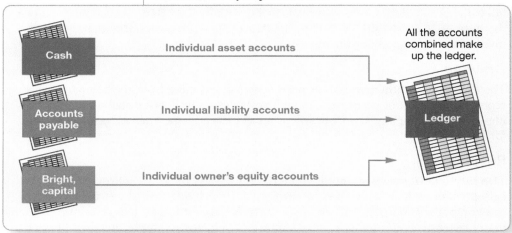

EXHIBIT 2-1 | **The Ledger—Asset, Liability, and Owner's Equity Accounts**

account numbers, Cash may be account number 101, the first asset account. Accounts receivable may be account number 111, the second asset. Accounts payable may be number 201, the first liability. When numbers are used, all accounts are numbered by this system. However, each company chooses its own account numbering system.

Notice in Exhibit 2-2 the gap in account numbers between 121 and 141. Sheena Bright of Smart Touch may need to add another asset account in the future. For example, she may start selling some type of inventory and want to use account number 131 for Inventory. So, the chart of accounts will change as the business evolves.

EXHIBIT 2-2 | **Chart of Accounts— Smart Touch Learning**

Balance Sheet Accounts

Assets	Liabilities	Owner's Equity
101 Cash	201 Accounts payable	301 Bright, capital
111 Accounts receivable	211 Salary payable	311 Bright, drawing
121 Notes receivable	221 Interest payable	
141 Supplies	231 Notes payable	
151 Furniture		
171 Building		
191 Land		

Income Statement Accounts
(Part of Owner's Equity)

Revenues	Expenses
401 Service revenue	501 Rent expense, computer
411 Interest revenue	502 Rent expense, office
	505 Salary expense
	510 Depreciation expense
	520 Utilities expense
	530 Advertising expense
	540 Supplies expense

Charts of accounts vary from business to business, though many account names are common to all companies' charts of accounts. For example, you will find Cash on every company's chart of accounts. **The chart of accounts contains the list of account names you might use to record a transaction to.**

Debits, Credits, and Double-Entry Accounting

As we saw in Chapter 1, accounting is based on transaction data, not on mere whim or opinion. Each business transaction has dual effects:

- The receiving side
- The giving side

For example, in the $30,000 cash receipt by Smart Touch in Chapter 1, the business

- received cash of $30,000.
- gave or issued $30,000 of capital to Bright.

Accounting uses the **double-entry system,** which means that we record the dual effects of each transaction. As a result, every transaction affects at least two accounts. It would be incomplete to record only the giving side, or only the receiving side, of a transaction.

Consider a cash purchase of supplies. What are the dual effects? A cash purchase of supplies

1. increases supplies (you received supplies).

2. decreases cash (you gave cash).

Similarly, a credit purchase of equipment (a purchase on account)

1. increases equipment (you received equipment).

2. increases accounts payable (you gave your promise to pay in the future).

② Define debits, credits, and normal account balances, and use double-entry accounting and T-accounts

The T-Account

A shortened form of the general ledger account is called the **T-account** because it takes the form of the capital letter *T*. The vertical line divides the account into its left and right sides, with the title at the top. For example, the Cash account appears as follows.

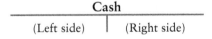

The left side of the account is called the **Debit** side, and the right side is called the **Credit** side. To become comfortable using these terms, remember the following:

Debits go on the left; credits go on the right. The terms *debit* and *credit* are deeply entrenched in business.[1] They are abbreviated as follows:

DR = Debit	CR = Credit

Increases and Decreases in the Accounts

The account category (asset, liability, equity) governs how we record increases and decreases. For any given account, increases are recorded on one side, and decreases are recorded on the opposite side. The following T-accounts provide a summary:

Assets		Liabilities and Owner's Equity	
Increase = Debit	Decrease = Credit	Decrease = Debit	Increase = Credit

These are the *rules of debit and credit*. **Whether an account is increased or decreased by a debit or a credit depends on the type of account.** Debits are not "good" or "bad." Neither are credits. Debits are not always increases or always decreases—neither are credits.

In a computerized accounting information system, the computer interprets debits and credits as increases or decreases, based on the account type. For example, a computer reads a debit to Cash as an increase, because it is an asset account. The computer reads a debit to Accounts payable as a decrease, because it is a liability account.

Exhibit 2-3 shows the relationship between the accounting equation and the rules of debit and credit.

EXHIBIT 2-3 | **The Accounting Equation and the Rules of Debit and Credit**

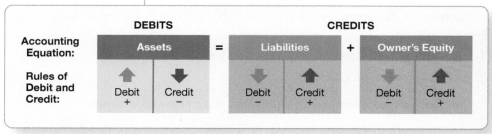

To illustrate the ideas diagrammed in Exhibit 2-3, let's look at the first transaction from Chapter 1 again. Smart Touch received $30,000 cash and gave capital to Bright. Which accounts of the business are affected?

The answer: The business's assets and equity would increase by $30,000, as the T-accounts show.

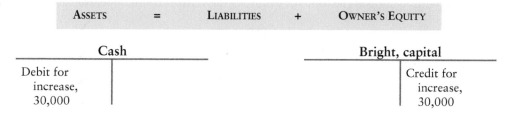

ASSETS	=	LIABILITIES	+	OWNER'S EQUITY

Cash			Bright, capital	
Debit for increase, 30,000				Credit for increase, 30,000

---

[1]The words *debit* and *credit* abbreviate the Latin terms *debitum* and *creditum*. Luca Pacioli, the Italian monk who wrote about accounting in the fifteenth century, popularized these terms.

The amount remaining in an account is called its *balance*. The first transaction gives Cash a $30,000 debit balance and Bright, capital a $30,000 credit balance.

The second transaction is a $20,000 purchase of land. Exhibit 2-4 illustrates the accounting equation after Smart Touch Learning's first two transactions. After transaction 2, Cash has a $10,000 debit balance, Land has a debit balance of $20,000, and Bright, capital has a $30,000 credit balance.

We create accounts as needed. The process of creating a new account is called *opening the account*. For transaction 1, we opened the Cash account and the Bright, capital account. For transaction 2, we opened the Land account.

> **Key Takeaway**
>
> The accounting equation MUST ALWAYS BALANCE after each transaction is recorded. To achieve this balance, we record transactions using a double-entry accounting system. In that system, debits are on the left and credits are on the right. Debits ALWAYS equal credits.

EXHIBIT 2-4 | **The Accounting Equation After the First Two Transactions of Smart Touch Learning**

Transaction 1
Received $30,000 cash and gave capital to Bright

DEBITS		CREDITS
Cash $30,000	=	Bright, capital $30,000

Transaction 2
Paid $20,000 cash to purchase land

DEBITS		CREDITS
Cash $10,000		
Land $20,000	=	Bright, capital $30,000

List the Steps of the Transaction Recording Process

In practice, accountants record transactions in a *journal*. The journalizing process has three steps:

3 List the steps of the transaction recording process

1. Identify each account affected and its type (asset, liability, or owner's equity).

2. Determine whether each account is increased or decreased. Use the rules of debit and credit.

3. Record the transaction in the journal, including a brief explanation. The debit side of the entry is entered first. The credit side is indented. Total debits should always equal total credits. This step is also called "making the journal entry" or "journalizing the transaction."

These steps are the same whether done by computer or manually.

Let's journalize the first transaction of Smart Touch—the receipt of $30,000 cash and investment of capital by Bright.

STEP 1: The accounts affected by the receipt of cash and issuance of stock are *Cash* and *Bright, capital*. Cash is an asset. Bright, capital is equity.

STEP 2: Both accounts increase by $30,000. Assets increase with debits. Therefore, we debit Cash because it is an asset. Equity increases in the business because capital investment by the owner increased. To increase equity, we credit. Therefore, we credit the Bright, capital account.

STEP 3: The journal entry is as follows:

Journal				Page 1
Date	Accounts and Explanation		Debit	Credit
Apr 1[a]	Cash[b] (A+)		30,000[b]	
	Bright, capital[c] (Q+)			30,000[c]
	Owner investment.[d]			

Footnotes a, b, c, and d are explained as follows. The journal entry includes four parts:

a. Date of the transaction

b. Title of the account debited, along with the dollar amount

c. Indented title of the account credited, along with the dollar amount

d. Brief explanation of the transaction

Dollar signs are omitted because it is understood that the amounts are in dollars.

The journal entry presents the full story for each transaction. To help reinforce your learning of the account types and how they increase or decrease, we will indicate after each account in the journal what type of account it is and whether it is increasing or decreasing. For example, Assets increasing will be shown as (A+), Capital (Equity) increasing will be shown as (Q+), and so on. These notations would not normally show up in a journal, but we have included them here to reinforce the rules of debit and credit. Exhibit 2-5 shows how Journal Page 1 looks after the business has recorded the first transaction.

EXHIBIT 2-5 | **The Journal Page**

Journal				Page 1
Date	Accounts and Explanation		Debit	Credit
Apr 1	Cash (A+)		30,000	
	Bright, capital (Q+)			30,000
	Owner investment.			

Posting (Copying Information) from the Journal to the Ledger

Journalizing a transaction records the data only in the journal—but not in the ledger. The data must also be copied to the ledger. The process of copying from the journal to the ledger is called **posting.** We *post* from the journal to the ledger.

Debits in the journal are posted as debits in the ledger and credits as credits—no exceptions. The first transaction of Smart Touch is posted to the ledger in Exhibit 2-6.

		Making a Journal Entry and Posting
EXHIBIT 2-6		**to the Ledger in T-Account Form**

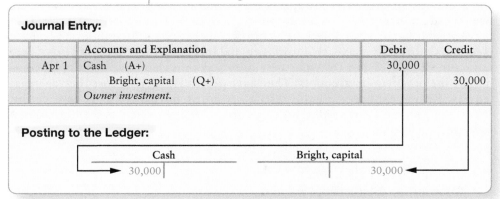

Journal Entry:

	Accounts and Explanation	Debit	Credit
Apr 1	Cash (A+)	30,000	
	Bright, capital (Q+)		30,000
	Owner investment.		

Posting to the Ledger:

Cash	Bright, capital
30,000	30,000

Expanding the Rules of Debit and Credit: Revenues and Expenses

As we have noted, *revenues* are increases in equity that result from providing goods or services for customers. *Expenses* are decreases in equity that result from using up assets or increasing liabilities in the course of operations. **Revenues are earned. Expenses are incurred.** Therefore, we must expand the accounting equation to include revenues and expenses. There are several elements of owner's equity.

Exhibit 2-7 shows revenues and expenses under owner's equity because they directly affect equity.

	The Accounting Equation
EXHIBIT 2-7	**Includes Revenues and Expenses**

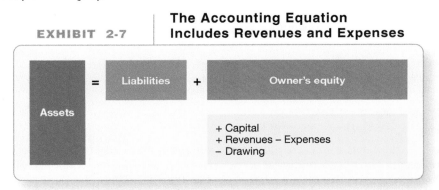

We can now express the rules of debit and credit in complete form as shown in Exhibit 2-8. Note that the accounting equation now includes revenues and expenses.

EXHIBIT 2-8	**Complete Rules of Debit and Credit**

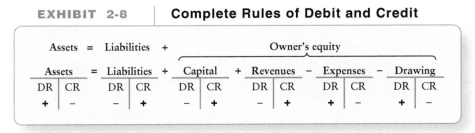

The Normal Balance of an Account

An account's **normal balance** appears on the side—either debit or credit—where we record an *increase* (+) in the account's balance. For example, assets normally have a debit balance, so assets are *debit-balance accounts*. Liabilities and equity accounts normally have the opposite balance, so they are *credit-balance accounts*. Expenses and Drawing are equity accounts that have debit balances—unlike the other equity accounts. They have debit balances because they decrease equity. Revenues increase equity, so a revenue's normal balance is a credit. Notice in Exhibit 2-8 that all the + signs are bolded because + is the normal balance for all accounts.

As we have seen, owner's equity includes the following:

Capital—a credit-balance account

Drawing—a debit-balance account

Revenues—a credit balance account

Expenses—a debit balance account

An account with a normal debit balance may occasionally have a credit balance. That indicates a negative amount of the item. For example, Cash will have a credit balance if the business overdraws its bank account. Also, the liability Accounts payable—a credit balance account—could have a debit balance if the company overpays its accounts payable. In other cases, a non-normal account balance indicates an error. For example, a credit balance in Office supplies, Furniture, or Buildings is an error because negative amounts of these assets make no sense. In each journal entry, we will indicate the type of account and whether it increased (+) or decreased (−). We'll use A for Assets, L for Liabilities, Q for Equity, D for Drawing, R for Revenues, and E for Expenses.

> Normal Balance Tip: Assets, Expenses, and Drawing: left Debits.
> Liabilities, Equity, and Revenues: right Credits.

Stop & Think...

The terms debit and credit really just mean left and right. A way to remember what normal account balance a particular account has is to associate the accounts with the accounting equation. Assets are on the LEFT so they have a normal Debit balance. Liabilities and Equity accounts are on the RIGHT so they have a normal Credit balance. So think of debit as left and credit as right when remembering normal balance of accounts.

Now let's put your new learning into practice and account for the early transactions of Smart Touch.

Exhibit 2-9 summarizes the flow of data through the accounting system. In the pages that follow, we record Smart Touch's early transactions. Keep in mind that we are accounting for the e-learning business. We are *not* accounting for Sheena Bright's personal transactions because of the entity concept we learned in Chapter 1.

EXHIBIT 2-9 | **Flow of Accounting Data from the Journal to the Ledger**

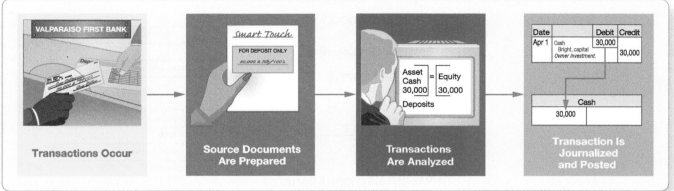

Source Documents—The Origin of the Steps

Accounting data come from source documents, as shown in the second segment of Exhibit 2-9. In that exhibit, Smart Touch received $30,000 and gave capital to Sheena Bright. The *bank deposit ticket* is the document that shows the amount of cash received by the business, and the capital account shows the net investment of the owner, Sheena Bright. Based on these documents, Bright can determine how to record this transaction in the journal.

When the business buys supplies on account, the vendor sends Smart Touch an invoice requesting payment. The *purchase invoice* is the source document that tells the business how much and when to pay the vendor. The invoice shows what Smart Touch purchased and how much it cost—indicating to the business how to record the transaction.

Smart Touch may pay the account payable with a *bank check*, another source document. The check and the purchase invoice give the business the information it needs to record the cash payment accurately.

When Smart Touch provides education services for a client, the business e-mails a sales invoice to the client. Smart Touch's *sales invoice* is the source document that tells the business how much revenue to record.

There are many different types of source documents in business. In the transactions that follow, we illustrate some of the more common types of documents that Smart Touch uses in its business.

> **Key Takeaway**
>
> A transaction occurs and is recorded on a source document. Then, we identify the account names affected by the transaction and determine whether the accounts increased or decreased using the rules of debit and credit for the six main account types. We then record the transaction in the journal, listing the debits first. Debits must equal credits. We then post all transactions to the ledger (T-account).

Journalizing Transactions and Posting to the Ledger

Practice Journalizing with Specific Examples

4 Journalize and post sample transactions to the ledger

Transaction 1

Smart Touch received $30,000 cash on April 1 from Sheena Bright and gave her capital in the business. The business deposited the money in its bank account, as shown by the following deposit ticket:

```
    ──┤ DEPOSIT TICKET ├──

    Smart Touch Learning
    281 Wave Ave
    Niceville, FL 32578


    DATE _____April 1_____ , 2013


    VALPARAISO FIRST BANK
    John Sims Pkwy
    Valparaiso, FL


    ⑆122000661⑆1400⑈03857
```

CASH	CURRENCY		
	COIN		
LIST CHECKS SEPARATELY		30,000	00
TOTAL FROM OTHER SIDE			
TOTAL		30,000	00
LESS CASH RECEIVED			
NET DEPOSIT		30,000	00

The business increased cash, which is an asset, so we debit Cash. The business also increased owner's equity, so we credit Bright, capital.

Journal Entry	Apr 1	Cash (A+)		30,000	
		Bright, capital (Q+)			30,000
		Owner investment.			

Ledger Accounts	Cash		Bright, capital	
	Apr 1 30,000			Apr 1 30,000

Transaction 2

On April 2, Smart Touch paid $20,000 cash for land. The purchase decreased cash. Therefore, we credit Cash. The asset, land, increased, so we debit the Land account.

Journal Entry	Apr 2	Land (A+)		20,000	
		Cash (A–)			20,000
		Paid cash for land.			

Ledger Accounts	Cash		Land	
	Apr 1 30,000	Apr 2 20,000	Apr 2 20,000	

Transaction 3

Smart Touch purchased $500 of office supplies on account on April 3, as shown on this purchase invoice.

INVOICE (purchase)

WHOLESALE OFFICE SUPPLY, INC.
500 HENDERSON ROAD
DESTIN, FL 32540

Date: April 3, 2013
Invoice No.   487
Terms: 30 days
Sold To: **Smart Touch Learning**
                281 Wave Ave
                Niceville, FL 32578

Quantity	Item	Price	Total
38	Reams of paper	$10	$380.00
8	Desk calendars	15	120.00

Total amount due: **$500.00**

The supplies will benefit Smart Touch in future periods, so they are an asset to the company until they are used. (We will talk about accounting for using the supplies in Chapter 3.)

The asset office supplies increased, so we debit Office supplies. The liability accounts payable increased, so we credit Accounts payable.

Journal Entry	Apr 3	Office supplies (A+)		500	
		Accounts payable (L+)			500
		Purchased supplies on account.			

Ledger Accounts

Office supplies			Accounts payable		
Apr 3	500			Apr 3	500

Transaction 4

On April 8, Smart Touch collected cash of $5,500 for service revenue that the business earned by providing e-learning services for clients. The source document is Smart Touch's sales invoice on the following page.

```
┌─────────────────────────────────────────────────────────────┐
│                                                             │
│  ┌───────────────────────────────────────────────────────┐  │
│  │                                                       │  │
│  │              INVOICE  (sale)                          │  │
│  │                                                       │  │
│  │              Smart Touch Learning                     │  │
│  │                 281 Wave Ave.                         │  │
│  │               Niceville, FL 32578                     │  │
│  │                                                       │  │
│  │                                                       │  │
│  │   Date:          April 8, 2013                        │  │
│  │   Sold to:       Allied Energy, Inc.                  │  │
│  │                  325 Brooks Street                    │  │
│  │                                                       │  │
│  │   Invoice No:    15                                   │  │
│  │   Service:       1000 DVD0503                         │  │
│  │                                                       │  │
│  │   Total amount due: $5,500                            │  │
│  │                                                       │  │
│  │   All accounts are due and payable within 30 days.    │  │
│  │                                                       │  │
│  └───────────────────────────────────────────────────────┘  │
│                                                             │
└─────────────────────────────────────────────────────────────┘
```

The asset cash increased, so we debit Cash. Revenue increased, so we credit Service revenue.

Journal Entry				
Apr 8	Cash (A+)		5,500	
	Service revenue (R+)			5,500
	Performed service and received cash.			

Ledger Accounts	Cash			Service revenue	
	Apr 1 30,000	Apr 2 20,000			Apr 8 5,500
	Apr 8 5,500				

In Chapter 1 we listed service revenue and expenses under Bright, capital. Here we record the revenues and the expenses directly in their own accounts. You will see in Chapter 4 how the revenue and expense accounts ultimately get into the Bright, capital account.

Transaction 5

On April 10, Smart Touch performed services for clients, for which the clients will pay the company later. The business earned $3,000 of service revenue on account.

This transaction increased Accounts receivable, so we debit this asset. Service revenue is increased with a credit.

Journal Entry				
Apr 10	Accounts receivable (A+)		3,000	
	Service revenue (R+)			3,000
	Performed service on account.			

Ledger Accounts	Accounts receivable		Service revenue	
	Apr 10 3,000		Apr 8 5,500	
			Apr 10 3,000	

Notice the differences and the similarities between transactions 4 and 5. In both transactions, Service revenue was increased (credited) because in both cases the company had earned revenue. However, in transaction 4, the company was paid at the time of service. In transaction 5, on the other hand, the company will receive cash later (Accounts receivable). This difference is key, because the amount of earnings is not determined by when the company receives cash. Earnings (Revenue) are recorded when the company does the work or provides the service.

Transaction 6

Smart Touch paid the following cash expenses on April 15: Rent expense on a computer, $600; Office rent, $1,000; Salary expense, $1,200; Utilities expense, $400. We need to debit each expense account to record its increase and credit Cash for the total decrease.

Journal Entry	Apr 15	Rent expense, computer (E+)	600	
		Rent expense, office (E+)	1,000	
		Salary expense (E+)	1,200	
		Utilities expense (E+)	400	
		Cash (A–)		3,200
		Paid cash expenses.		

Note: In practice, the business would record these expenses in four separate journal entries. Here we show them together to illustrate a **compound journal entry**. A compound journal entry (like transaction 6) has more than two accounts, but total debits still must equal total credits.

Ledger Accounts

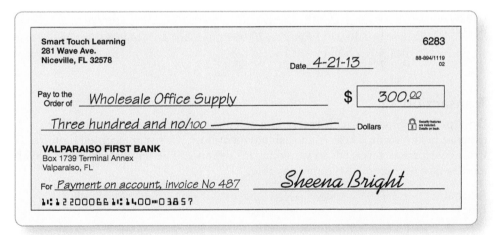

	Cash				Rent expense, computer			Rent expense, office	
Apr 1	30,000	Apr 2	20,000	Apr 15	600		Apr 15	1,000	
Apr 8	5,500	Apr 15	3,200						

	Salary expense			Utilities expense	
Apr 15	1,200		Apr 15	400	

Transaction 7

On April 21, Smart Touch paid $300 on the account payable created in transaction 3. The paid check is Smart Touch's source document, or proof, for this transaction.

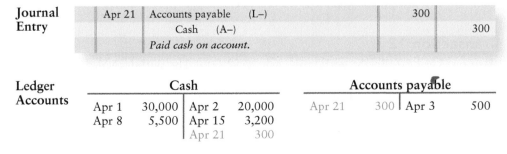

Smart Touch Learning
281 Wave Ave.
Niceville, FL 32578

6283
88-894/1119 02

Date *4-21-13*

Pay to the Order of *Wholesale Office Supply* $ 300.00

Three hundred and no/100 —————————— Dollars

VALPARAISO FIRST BANK
Box 1739 Terminal Annex
Valparaiso, FL

For *Payment on account, invoice No 487*   *Sheena Bright*

⑆ 1 2 2 0 0 0 6 6 ⑆ 1 4 0 0 ⑈ 0 3 8 5 7

The payment decreased cash, so we credit Cash. The payment decreased Accounts payable, so we debit that liability.

Journal Entry	Apr 21	Accounts payable (L–)	300	
		Cash (A–)		300
		Paid cash on account.		

Ledger Accounts

	Cash				Accounts payable			
Apr 1	30,000	Apr 2	20,000	Apr 21	300	Apr 3	500	
Apr 8	5,500	Apr 15	3,200					
		Apr 21	300					

Transaction 8

Sheena Bright remodeled her home with personal funds. This is not a transaction of the business, so there is no entry on the business's books (based on the entity concept).

Transaction 9

On April 22, Smart Touch collected $2,000 cash from the client in transaction 5. Cash is increased, so we debit Cash. Accounts receivable is decreased, so we credit Accounts receivable.

Journal Entry				
Apr 22	Cash (A+)		2,000	
	Accounts receivable (A–)			2,000
	Received cash on account.			

Note: This transaction has no effect on revenue; the related revenue was recorded in transaction 5.

Ledger Accounts

Cash					Accounts receivable			
Apr 1	30,000	Apr 2	20,000		Apr 10	3,000	Apr 22	2,000
Apr 8	5,500	Apr 15	3,200					
Apr 22	2,000	Apr 21	300					

Transaction 10

On April 24, Smart Touch sold a parcel of land owned by the business. The sale price, $9,000, equaled the cost. Cash increased, so we debit Cash. Land decreased, so we credit Land.

Journal Entry				
Apr 24	Cash (A+)		9,000	
	Land (A–)			9,000
	Sold land at cost.			

Ledger Accounts

Cash					Land			
Apr 1	30,000	Apr 2	20,000		Apr 2	20,000	Apr 24	9,000
Apr 8	5,500	Apr 15	3,200					
Apr 22	2,000	Apr 21	300					
Apr 24	9,000							

Transaction 11

On April 30, Smart Touch received a telephone bill for $100 and will pay this expense next month. There is no cash payment now. This is an accrued liability. The Utilities expense increased, so we debit this expense. The liability accounts payable increased, so we credit Accounts payable.

Journal Entry				
Apr 30	Utilities expense (E+)		100	
	Accounts payable (L+)			100
	Received utility bill.			

Ledger Accounts

Accounts payable					Utilities expense		
		Apr 21	300	Apr 3	500	Apr 15	400
				Apr 30	100	Apr 30	100

Transaction 12

Also on April 30, Bright withdrew cash of $2,000. The withdrawal decreased the entity's cash, so we credit Cash. The drawing also decreased total owner's equity. Decreases in equity that result from owner withdrawals are debited to the owner's drawing account, so we debit Bright, drawing.

Journal Entry	Apr 30	Bright, drawing (D+)	2,000	
		Cash (A–)		2,000
		Owner withdrawal.		

Ledger Accounts		Cash				Bright, drawing	
	Apr 1	30,000	Apr 2	20,000	Apr 30	2,000	
	Apr 8	5,500	Apr 15	3,200			
	Apr 22	2,000	Apr 21	300			
	Apr 24	9,000	Apr 30	2,000			

Each journal entry posted to the ledger is keyed by date or by transaction number. In this way, any transaction can be traced back and forth between the journal and the ledger. This helps you locate any information you may need.

The Ledger Accounts After Posting

We next show the accounts of Smart Touch after posting. The accounts are grouped under their headings in Exhibit 2-10.

Each account has a balance. An account balance is the difference between the account's total debits and its total credits. For example, the $21,000 balance in the Cash account is the difference between the following:

- Total debits, $46,500 ($30,000 + $5,500 + $2,000 + $9,000)
- Total credits, $25,500 ($20,000 + $3,200 + $300 + $2,000)

We set a balance apart from the transaction amounts by a horizontal line. The final figure, below the horizontal line, is denoted as the balance (Bal).

Connect To: Accounting Information Systems

The journals you've seen are called general journals because all types of transactions may be posted in them. There are also special purpose journals, used for posting large volumes of similar transactions. Special purpose journals are mostly used with computer software programs, such as QuickBooks and Peachtree. Many of the icons used in these software programs represent a specific type of transaction. For example, in QuickBooks, the Write Check icon is used to print checks. Refer to Transaction 7. It's the same kind of transaction: We wrote a check to pay a vendor. This would be called a "cash payments special purpose journal." In this chapter and in this text, we will focus on general journals only.

EXHIBIT 2-10 | **Smart Touch Learning's Ledger Accounts After Posting April's Transactions**

ASSETS

Cash

Apr 1	30,000	Apr 2	20,000
Apr 8	5,500	Apr 15	3,200
Apr 22	2,000	Apr 21	300
Apr 24	9,000	Apr 30	2,000
Bal	21,000		

Accounts receivable

Apr 10	3,000	Apr 22	2,000[†]
Bal	1,000		

Office supplies

Apr 3	500		
Bal	500		

Land

Apr 2	20,000	Apr 24	9,000
Bal	11,000		

LIABILITIES

Accounts payable

Apr 21	300	Apr 3	500
		Apr 30	100
		Bal	300

OWNER'S EQUITY

Bright, capital

		Apr 1	30,000
		Bal	30,000

Bright, drawing

Apr 30	2,000		
Bal	2,000		

REVENUE

Service revenue

		Apr 8	5,500
		Apr 10	3,000
		Bal	8,500

EXPENSES

Rent expense, computer

Apr 15	600		
Bal	600		

Rent expense, office

Apr 15	1,000[†]		
Bal	1,000		

Salary expense

Apr 15	1,200		
Bal	1,200		

Utilities expense

Apr 15	400		
Apr 30	100		
Bal	500[†]		

[†]These values are intentionally different than those presented in Chapter 1.

 **Think...**

Have you ever walked along the beach and gathered sea shells? Maybe you had more than one bucket and you put all the sand dollars in one, all the hermit crabs in another, and so on. That separation is essentially what happens in posting. All we are doing is gathering transactions that affect the same account (for example, all the transactions to Cash) and putting them in the T-account. They are placed either on the left or right side of the T-account based on whether they were on the left or right side of the journal entry. Posting is merely a sorting process—no change to debits or credits occurs from transaction to posting.

Preparing the Trial Balance from the T-Accounts

 Prepare the trial balance from the T-accounts

As noted earlier, a trial balance summarizes the ledger (T-accounts) by listing all the accounts with their balances—assets first, followed by liabilities, and then owner's equity. In a manual accounting system, the trial balance provides an accuracy check by showing whether total debits equal total credits. In all types of systems, the trial balance is a useful summary of the accounts and their balances because it shows the balances on a specific date for all accounts in a company's accounting system. Exhibit 2-11 is the trial balance of Smart Touch at April 30, 2013, the end of the first month of operations, created from the balances calculated in Exhibit 2-10.

A warning: Do not confuse the trial balance with the balance sheet. A trial balance is an internal document used only by company insiders. Outsiders see only the company's financial statements, not the trial balance.

EXHIBIT 2-11 | **Trial Balance**

		Account Title	Balance	
			Debit	Credit
		Cash	$21,000	
		Accounts receivable	1,000	
		Office supplies	500	
		Land	11,000	
		Accounts payable		$ 300
		Bright, capital		30,000
		Bright, drawing	2,000	
		Service revenue		8,500
		Rent expense, computer	600	
		Rent expense, office	1,000	
		Salary expense	1,200	
		Utilities expense	500	
		Total	$38,800	$38,800

SMART TOUCH LEARNING
Trial Balance
April 30, 2013

Correcting Trial Balance Errors

Throughout the accounting process, total debits should always equal total credits. If they do not, there is an error. Computerized accounting systems eliminate many errors because most software will not let you make a journal entry that does not balance. But computers cannot *eliminate* all errors because humans can input the wrong data.

Balancing errors can be detected by computing the difference between total debits and total credits on the trial balance. Then perform one or more of the following actions:

1. Search the trial balance for a missing account. For example, suppose the accountant omitted Bright, drawing from the trial balance in Exhibit 2-11. Total debits would then be $36,800 ($38,800 – $2,000). Trace each account from the ledger to the trial balance, and you will locate the missing account.

2. Divide the difference between total debits and total credits by 2. A debit treated as a credit, or vice versa, doubles the amount of error. Suppose the accountant posted a $500 credit as a debit. Total debits contain the $500, and total credits omit the $500. The out-of-balance amount is $1,000. Dividing the difference by 2 identifies the $500 amount of the transaction. Then search the trial balance for a $500 transaction and trace it to the account affected.

3. Divide the out-of-balance amount by 9. If the result is evenly divisible by 9, the error may be a *slide* (example: writing $1,000 as $100 or writing $100 as $1,000) or a *transposition* (example: listing $1,200 as $2,100). Suppose, for example, that the accountant printed the $2,000 Bright, drawing as $20,000 on the trial balance. This is a slide-type error. Total debits would differ from total credits by $18,000 ($20,000 – $2,000 = $18,000). Dividing $18,000 by 9 yields $2,000, the correct amount of drawing. Trace $2,000 through the ledger until you reach the Bright, drawing account. You have then found the error.

Total debits can equal total credits on the trial balance; however, there still could be errors in individual account balances because an incorrect account might have been selected in an individual journal entry.

Details of Journals and Ledgers

In practice, the journal and the ledger provide details to create a "trail" through the records. Suppose a supplier bills us twice for an item that we purchased. To show we have already paid the bill, we must prove our payment. That requires us to use the journal and the ledger to get to the source document (cancelled check).

Details in the Journal

Exhibit 2-12 illustrates recording a transaction in a journal with these details:

- The *transaction date*, April 1, 2013
- The *accounts* debited and credited, along with their dollar amounts
- The *posting reference*, abbreviated Post. Ref.

EXHIBIT 2-12 | Details of Journalizing and Posting

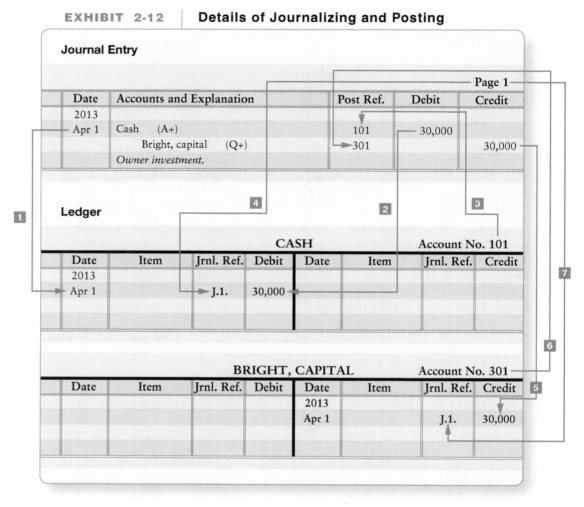

Details in the Ledger

As noted earlier, posting means copying information from the journal to the ledger. But how do we handle the details? Exhibit 2-12 illustrates the steps, denoted by arrows:

Arrow **1**—Post the transaction **date** from the journal to the ledger.

Arrow **2**—Post the debit, **$30,000**, from the journal as a debit to the Cash account in the ledger.

Arrow **3**—Post the account number **(101)** from the ledger back to the journal. This step shows that the debit has been posted to the ledger. **Post. Ref.** is the abbreviation for Posting Reference.

Arrow **4**—Post the page number from the journal to the ledger. **Jrnl. Ref.** means Journal Reference, and **J.1** refers to Journal Page **1**. This step shows where the data came from, in this case Journal Page 1. Arrows **5**, **6**, and **7** repeat steps 2, 3, and 4 to post the credit, **$30,000**, from the journal to the Bright, capital account in the ledger. Now the ledger accounts have correct amounts.

The Four-Column Account: An Alternative to the T-Account

The ledger accounts illustrated thus far appear as T-accounts, with the debits on the left and the credits on the right. The T-account clearly separates debits from credits and is used for teaching. Another account format has four amount columns, as illustrated in Exhibit 2-13.

EXHIBIT 2-13 | **Account in Four-Column Format**

CASH   Account No. 101

Date	Item	Jrnl. Ref.	Debit	Credit	Balance Debit	Balance Credit
2013						
Apr 1		J.1	30,000		30,000	
Apr 2		J.1		20,000	10,000	
Apr 8		J.1	5,500		15,500	
Apr 15		J.1		3,200	12,300	
Apr 21		J.1		300	12,000	
Apr 22		J.1	2,000		14,000	
Apr 24		J.1	9,000		23,000	
Apr 30		J.1		2,000	21,000	

The first pair of Debit/Credit columns is for transaction amounts posted to the account from the journal, such as the $30,000 debit. The second pair of Debit/Credit columns shows the balance of the account as of each date. Because the four-column format provides more information, it is used more often in practice than the T-account. In Exhibit 2-13, Cash has a debit balance of $30,000 after the first transaction and a $10,000 balance after the second transaction. Notice that the balance after the last transaction on April 30 is $21,000, which is the same balance calculated in the T-account in Exhibit 2-10.

Key Takeaway

Once the ledger (T-account) balances are calculated, the ending balance for each account is transferred to the trial balance. Recall that the trial balance is a listing of all accounts and their balances on a specific date. Total debits must ALWAYS equal total credits on the trial balance. If they do not, then review the correcting trial balance errors section on page 81.

Decision Guidelines 2-1

ANALYZING AND RECORDING TRANSACTIONS

Suppose Greg Moore, the owner of Greg's Tunes, opens a small office and needs an accountant to keep his books. Moore interviews you for the job. The pay is good. Can you answer Moore's questions, which are outlined in the Decision Guidelines? If so, you may get the job.

Decision	Guidelines
• What determines if a transaction has occurred?	If the event affects the entity's financial position and can be recorded
• Where would a business record the transaction?	In the *journal*, the chronological record of transactions
• What does a business record for each transaction?	Increases and/or decreases in all the accounts affected by the transaction
• How do we record an increase/decrease in accounts?	Rules of debit and credit:

	Debit	Credit
Asset	+	−
Liability	−	+
Owner's Equity	−	+
Drawing	+	−
Revenue	−	+
Expense	+	−

Decision	Guidelines
• Where is all the information for each account's transactions and ending balance stored?	In the *ledger* (T-account), the record holding all the accounts
• What statement lists all the accounts and their balances for a business?	The *trial balance*

Summary Problem 2-1

The trial balance of Harper Service Center on March 1, 2014, lists the entity's assets, liabilities, and equity on that date.

			Balance	
	Account Title		Debit	Credit
	Cash		$26,000	
	Accounts receivable		4,500	
	Accounts payable			$ 2,000
	Harper, capital			28,500
	Total		$30,500	$30,500

During March, the business engaged in the following transactions:

    a. Borrowed $45,000 from the bank and signed a note payable in the name of the business.
    b. Paid cash of $40,000 to acquire land.
    c. Performed service for a customer and received cash of $5,000.
    d. Purchased supplies on account, $300.
    e. Performed customer service and earned revenue on account, $2,600.
    f. Paid $1,200 on account.
    g. Paid the following cash expenses: salaries, $3,000; rent, $1,500; and interest, $400.
    h. Received $3,100 on account.
    i. Received a $200 utility bill that will be paid next week.
    j. Harper withdrew cash of $1,800.

Requirements

1. Open the following accounts, with the balances indicated, in the ledger of Harper Service Center. Use the T-account format.

    • **Assets**—Cash, $26,000; Accounts receivable, $4,500; Supplies, no balance; Land, no balance

    • **Liabilities**—Accounts payable, $2,000; Note payable, no balance

    • **Owner's equity**—Harper, capital, $28,500; Harper, drawing, no balance

    • **Revenue**—Service revenue, no balance

    • **Expenses**—(none have balances) Salary expense, Rent expense, Utilities expense, Interest expense

2. Journalize each transaction. Key journal entries by transaction letter.
3. Post to the ledger.
4. Prepare the trial balance of Harper Service Center at March 31, 2014.

Solution

Requirement 1

ASSETS	LIABILITIES	OWNER'S EQUITY	EXPENSES

ASSETS

Cash	
Bal 26,000	

Accounts receivable	
Bal 4,500	

Supplies	

Land	

LIABILITIES

Accounts payable	
	Bal 2,000

Note payable	

OWNER'S EQUITY

Harper, capital	
	Bal 28,500

Harper, drawing	

REVENUE

Service revenue	

EXPENSES

Salary expense	

Rent expense	

Utilities expense	

Interest expense	

Requirement 2

a. Journal Entry		Cash (A+)	45,000	
		Note payable (L+)		45,000
		Borrowed cash on note payable.		
b. Journal Entry		Land (A+)	40,000	
		Cash (A–)		40,000
		Purchased land.		
c. Journal Entry		Cash (A+)	5,000	
		Service revenue (R+)		5,000
		Performed service and received cash.		
d. Journal Entry		Supplies (A+)	300	
		Accounts payable (L+)		300
		Purchased supplies on account.		
e. Journal Entry		Accounts receivable (A+)	2,600	
		Service revenue (R+)		2,600
		Performed service on account.		
f. Journal Entry		Accounts payable (L–)	1,200	
		Cash (A–)		1,200
		Paid on account.		
g. Journal Entry		Salary expense (E+)	3,000	
		Rent expense (E+)	1,500	
		Interest expense (E+)	400	
		Cash (A–)		4,900
		Paid expenses.		
h. Journal Entry		Cash (A+)	3,100	
		Accounts receivable (A–)		3,100
		Received cash on account.		
i. Journal Entry		Utilities expense (E+)	200	
		Accounts payable (L+)		200
		Received utility bill.		
j. Journal Entry		Harper, drawing (D+)	1,800	
		Cash (A–)		1,800
		Owner withdrawal.		

Requirement 3

ASSETS			
Cash			
Bal	26,000	(b)	40,000
(a)	45,000	(f)	1,200
(c)	5,000	(g)	4,900
(h)	3,100	(j)	1,800
Bal	31,200		

Accounts receivable			
Bal	4,500	(h)	3,100
(e)	2,600		
Bal	4,000		

Supplies		
(d)	300	
Bal	300	

Land		
(b)	40,000	
Bal	40,000	

LIABILITIES			
Accounts payable			
(f)	1,200	Bal	2,000
		(d)	300
		(i)	200
		Bal	1,300

Note payable			
		(a)	45,000
		Bal	45,000

OWNER'S EQUITY			
Harper, capital			
		Bal	28,500

Harper, drawing		
(j)	1,800	
Bal	1,800	

REVENUE			
Service revenue			
		(c)	5,000
		(e)	2,600
		Bal	7,600

EXPENSES		
Salary expense		
(g)	3,000	
Bal	3,000	

Rent expense		
(g)	1,500	
Bal	1,500	

Interest expense		
(g)	400	
Bal	400	

Utilities expense		
(i)	200	
Bal	200	

Requirement 4

HARPER SERVICE CENTER
Trial Balance
March 31, 2014

Account Title	Balance	
	Debit	Credit
Cash	$31,200	
Accounts receivable	4,000	
Supplies	300	
Land	40,000	
Accounts payable		$ 1,300
Note payable		45,000
Harper, capital		28,500
Harper, drawing	1,800	
Service revenue		7,600
Salary expense	3,000	
Rent expense	1,500	
Interest expense	400	
Utilities expense	200	
Total	$82,400	$82,400

Chapter 2: Demo Doc

Debit/Credit Transaction Analysis

To make sure you understand this material, work through the following demonstration "demo doc" with detailed comments to help you see the concept within the framework of a worked-through problem.

① ② ③ ④

On September 1, 2014, Michael Moe began Moe's Mowing, a company that provides mowing and landscaping services. During the month of September, the business incurred the following transactions:

a. To begin operations, Michael deposited $10,000 cash in the business's bank account. The business received the cash and gave capital to Moe.

b. The business purchased equipment for $3,500 on account.

c. The business purchased office supplies for $800 cash.

d. The business provided $2,600 of services to a customer on account.

e. The business paid $500 cash toward the equipment previously purchased on account in transaction b.

f. The business received $2,000 in cash for services provided to a new customer.

g. The business paid $200 cash to repair equipment.

h. The business paid $900 cash in salary expense.

i. The business received $2,100 cash from customers on account.

j. Moe withdrew cash of $1,500.

Requirements

1. Create blank T-accounts for the following accounts: Cash; Accounts receivable; Supplies; Equipment; Accounts payable; Moe, capital; Moe, drawing; Service revenue; Salary expense; and Repair expense.

2. Journalize the transactions and show how they are recorded in T-accounts.

3. Total all of the T-accounts to determine their balances at the end of the month.

Chapter 2: Demo Doc Solution

Requirement 1

Create blank T-accounts for the following accounts: Cash; Accounts receivable; Supplies; Equipment; Accounts payable; Moe, capital; Moe, drawing; Service revenue; Salary expense; and Repair expense.

Part 1	Part 2	Part 3	Demo Doc Complete

Opening a T-account means drawing a blank account that looks like a capital "T" and putting the account title across the top. T-accounts give you a diagram of the additions and subtractions made to the accounts. For easy reference, they are usually organized into assets, liabilities, owner's equity, revenue, and expenses (in that order).

ASSETS   =   LIABILITIES   +   OWNER'S EQUITY

Cash   Supplies   Accounts payable   Moe, capital

                                                                            Moe, drawing

                                                                            Service revenue

Accounts receivable   Equipment

                                                                            Salary expense

                                                                            Repair expense

Requirement 2

Journalize the transactions and show how they are recorded in T-accounts.

Part 1	**Part 2**	Part 3	Demo Doc Complete

a. **To begin operations, Moe deposited $10,000 cash in the business's bank account. The business received the cash and gave capital to Moe.**

First, we must determine which accounts are affected.

The business received $10,000 cash from its owner (Michael Moe). In exchange, the business gave capital to Moe. So, the accounts involved are Cash and Moe, capital.

The next step is to determine what type of accounts these are. Cash is an asset and Moe, capital is part of equity.

Next, we must determine if these accounts increased or decreased. From *the business's* point of view, Cash (an asset) has increased. Moe, capital (equity) has also increased.

Now we must determine if these accounts should be debited or credited. According to the rules of debit and credit, an increase in assets is a debit, while an increase in equity is a credit.

So, Cash (an asset) increases, which is a debit. Moe, capital (equity) also increases, which is a credit.

The journal entry would be as follows:

a.	Cash (A+)		10,000	
	Moe, capital (Q+)			10,000
	Owner investment.			

Note that the total dollar amounts of debits will equal the total dollar amounts of credits.

Remember to use the transaction letters as references. This will help as we post this entry to the T-accounts.

Each T-account has two sides for recording debits and credits. To record the transaction to the T-account, simply transfer the amount of the debit(s) to the correct account(s) as a debit (left-side) entry, and transfer the amount of the credit(s) to the correct account(s) as a credit (right-side) entry.

For this transaction, there is a debit of $10,000 to cash. This means that $10,000 is entered on the left side of the Cash T-account. There is also a credit of $10,000 to Moe, capital. This means that $10,000 is entered on the right side of the Moe, capital account.

Cash		Moe, capital	
a. 10,000			a. 10,000

b. **The business purchased equipment for $3,500 on account.**

The business received equipment in exchange for a promise to pay for the $3,500 cost at a future date. So the accounts involved in the transaction are Equipment and Accounts payable.

Equipment is an asset and Accounts payable is a liability.

The asset Equipment has increased. The liability Accounts payable has also increased.

Looking at Exhibit 2-8, an increase in assets (in this case, the increase in Equipment) is a debit, while an increase in liabilities (in this case, Accounts payable) is a credit.

The journal entry would be as follows:

b.	Equipment (A+)		3,500	
	Accounts payable (L+)			3,500
	Purchase of equipment on account.			

$3,500 is entered on the debit (left) side of the Equipment T-account. $3,500 is entered on the credit (right) side of the Accounts payable account.

Equipment		Accounts payable	
b. 3,500			b. 3,500

c. **The business purchased office supplies for $800 cash.**

The business purchased supplies in exchange for $800 cash. So the accounts involved in the transaction are Supplies and Cash.

Supplies and Cash are both assets.

Supplies (an asset) has increased. Cash (an asset) has decreased.

Looking at Exhibit 2-8, an increase in assets is a debit, while a decrease in assets is a credit.

So the increase to Supplies (an asset) is a debit, while the decrease to Cash (an asset) is a credit.

The journal entry would be as follows:

c.	Supplies (A+)	800	
	Cash (A–)		800
	Purchase of supplies for cash.		

$800 is entered on the debit (left) side of the Supplies T-account. $800 is entered on the credit (right) side of the Cash account.

Cash			Supplies		
a.	10,000	c. 800	c. 800		

Notice the $10,000 already on the debit side of the Cash account. This is from transaction **a.**

d. **The business provided $2,600 of services to a customer on account.**

The business received promises from customers to send $2,600 cash next month in exchange for services rendered. So the accounts involved in the transaction are Accounts receivable and Service revenue.

Accounts receivable is an asset and Service revenue is revenue.

Accounts receivable (an asset) has increased. Service revenue (revenue) has also increased.

Looking at Exhibit 2-8, an increase in assets is a debit, while an increase in revenue is a credit.

So the increase to Accounts receivable (an asset) is a debit, while the increase to Service revenue (revenue) is a credit.

The journal entry is as follows:

d.	Accounts receivable (A+)	2,600	
	Service revenue (R+)		2,600
	Provided services on account.		

$2,600 is entered on the debit (left) side of the Accounts receivable T-account. $2,600 is entered on the credit (right) side of the Service revenue account.

Accounts receivable			Service revenue		
d.	2,600			d.	2,600

e. **The business paid $500 cash toward the equipment previously purchased on account in transaction b.**

The business paid *some* of the money that was owed on the purchase of equipment in transaction b. The accounts involved in the transaction are Accounts payable and Cash.

Accounts payable is a liability that has decreased. Cash is an asset that has also decreased.

Remember, the Accounts payable account is a list of creditors to whom the business will have to make payments in the future (a liability). When the business makes these payments to the creditors, the amount of this account decreases, because the business now owes less (in this case, it reduces from $3,500—in transaction **b**—to $3,000).

Looking at Exhibit 2-8, a decrease in liabilities is a debit, while a decrease in assets is a credit.

So Accounts payable (a liability) decreases, which is a debit. Cash (an asset) decreases, which is a credit.

e.			
	Accounts payable (L–)		500	
	Cash (A–)			500
	Partial payment on Accounts payable.		

$500 is entered on the debit (left) side of the Accounts payable T-account. $500 is entered on the credit (right) side of the Cash account.

	Cash					Accounts payable		
a.	10,000						b.	3,500
		c.	800		e.	500		
		e.	500					

Again notice the amounts already in the T-accounts from previous transactions. We can tell which transaction caused each amount to appear by looking at the reference letter next to each number.

f. **The business received $2,000 in cash for services provided to a new customer.**

The business received $2,000 cash in exchange for mowing and landscaping services rendered to clients. The accounts involved in the transaction are Cash and Service revenue.

Cash is an asset that has increased and Service revenue is revenue, which has also increased.

Looking at Exhibit 2-8, an increase in assets is a debit, while an increase in revenue is a credit.

So the increase to Cash (an asset) is a debit. The increase to Service revenue (revenue) is a credit.

f.			
	Cash (A+)		2,000	
	Service revenue (R+)			2,000
	Provided services for cash.		

$2,000 is entered on the debit (left) side of the Cash T-account. $2,000 is entered on the credit (right) side of the Service revenue account.

	Cash				Service revenue	
a.	10,000				d.	2,600
		c.	800		f.	2,000
		e.	500			
f.	2,000					

Notice how we keep adding onto the T-accounts. The values from previous transactions are already in place.

g.   **The business paid $200 cash to repair equipment.**

The business paid $200 cash to repair equipment. Because the benefit of the repairs has already been used, the repairs are recorded as Repair expense. Because the repairs were paid in cash, the Cash account is also involved.

Repair expense is an expense that has increased and Cash is an asset that has decreased.

Looking at Exhibit 2-8, an increase in expenses is a debit, while a decrease in an asset is a credit.

So Repair expense (an expense) increases, which is debit. Cash (an asset) decreases, which is a credit.

g.	Repair expense (E+)		200	
	Cash (A–)			200
	Payment for repairs.			

$200 is entered on the debit (left) side of the Repair expense T-account. $200 is entered on the credit (right) side of the Cash account.

	Cash				Repair expense	
a.	10,000				g.	200
		c.	800			
		e.	500			
f.	2,000					
		g.	200			

h.   **The business paid $900 cash for salary expense.**

The business paid employees $900 in cash. Because the benefit of the employees' work has already been used, their salaries are recorded as Salary expense. Because the salaries were paid in cash, the Cash account is also involved.

Salary expense is an expense that has increased and Cash is an asset that has decreased.

Looking at Exhibit 2-8, an increase in expenses is a debit, while a decrease in an asset is a credit.

In this case, Salary expense (an expense) increases, which is a debit. Cash (an asset) decreases, which is a credit.

h.	Salary expense (E+)		900	
	Cash (A–)			900
	Payment of salary.			

$900 is entered on the debit (left) side of the Salary expense T-account. $900 is entered on the credit (right) side of the Cash account.

	Cash				Salary expense	
a.	10,000			h.	900	
		c.	800			
		e.	500			
f.	2,000					
		g.	200			
		h.	900			

i. **The business received $2,100 cash from customers on account.**

The business received $2,100 from customers for services previously provided in transaction d. The accounts involved in this transaction are Cash and Accounts receivable.

Cash and Accounts receivable are both assets.

The asset Cash has increased, and the asset Accounts receivable has decreased.

Remember, Accounts receivable is a list of customers from whom the business will receive money. When the business receives these payments from its customers, the amount of this account decreases, because the business now has less to receive in the future (in this case, it reduces from $2,600—in transaction d—to $500).

Looking at Exhibit 2-8, an increase in assets is a debit, while a decrease in assets is a credit.

So Cash (an asset) increases, which is a debit. Accounts receivable (an asset) decreases, which is a credit.

i.	Cash (A+)		2,100	
	Accounts receivable (A–)			2,100
	Receipt of payment from customer.			

$2,100 is entered on the debit (left) side of the Cash T-account. $2,100 is entered on the credit (right) side of the Accounts receivable account.

	Cash				Accounts receivable		
a.	10,000			d.	2,600		
		c.	800			i.	2,100
		e.	500				
f.	2,000						
		g.	200				
		h.	900				
i.	2,100						

j. **Moe withdrew cash of $1,500.**

Moe withdrew cash from the business. This caused Moe's ownership interest (equity) to decrease. The accounts involved in this transaction are Moe, drawing and Cash.

Moe, drawing has increased and Cash is an asset that has decreased.

Looking at Exhibit 2-8, an increase in drawing is a debit, while a decrease in an asset is a credit.

Remember that Drawing is a negative element of owner's equity. Therefore, when Drawing increases, owner's equity decreases. So in this case, Moe, drawing decreases equity with a debit. Cash (an asset) decreases with a credit.

j.	Moe, drawing (D+)		1,500	
	Cash (A–)			1,500
	Owner withdrawal.			

$1,500 is entered on the debit (left) side of the Moe, drawing T-account. $1,500 is entered on the credit (right) side of the Cash account.

Cash					Moe, drawing		
a.	10,000				j.	1,500	
		c.	800				
		e.	500				
f.	2.000						
		g.	200				
		h.	900				
i.	2,100						
		j.	1,500				

Now we will summarize all of the journal entries during the month:

Ref.		Accounts and Explanation	Debit	Credit
a.		Cash	10,000	
		Moe, capital		10,000
		Owner investment.		
b.		Equipment	3,500	
		Accounts payable		3,500
		Purchase of equipment on account.		
c.		Supplies	800	
		Cash		800
		Purchase of supplies for cash.		
d.		Accounts receivable	2,600	
		Service revenue		2,600
		Provided services on credit.		
e.		Accounts payable	500	
		Cash		500
		Partial payment on account.		
f.		Cash	2,000	
		Service revenue		2,000
		Provided services for cash.		
g.		Repair expense	200	
		Cash		200
		Payment for repairs.		
h.		Salary expense	900	
		Cash		900
		Payment of salary.		
i.		Cash	2,100	
		Accounts receivable		2,100
		Receipt of cash on account.		
j.		Moe, drawing	1,500	
		Cash		1,500
		Owner withdrawal.		

Requirement 3

Total all of the T-accounts to determine their balances at the end of the month.

Part 1	Part 2	**Part 3**	Demo Doc Complete

To compute the balance in a T-account (total the T-account), add up the numbers on the debit/left side of the account and (separately) the credit/right side of the account. The difference between the total debits and total credits is the account's balance, which is placed on the side of the larger number (that is, the side with a balance). This gives the balance in the T-account (the net total of both sides combined).

For example, for the Cash account, the numbers on the debit/left side total $10,000 + $2,000 + $2,100 = $14,100. The credit/right side = $800 + $500 + $200 + $900 + $1,500 = $3,900. The difference is $14,100 – $3,900 = $10,200. We put the $10,200 on the debit side because that was the side of the bigger number of $14,100. This is called a debit balance.

Following is an easy way to think of totaling T-accounts:

> Beginning balance in T-account
> \+ Increases to T-account
> – Decreases to T-account
> T-account balance (total)

T-accounts after posting all transactions and totaling each account:

ASSETS   =   LIABILITIES   +   OWNER'S EQUITY

Cash

a.	10,000		
		c.	800
		e.	500
f.	2,000		
		g.	200
		h.	900
i.	2,100		
		j.	1,500
Bal	10,200		

Accounts receivable

d.	2,600		
		i.	2,100
Bal	500		

Supplies

| c. | 800 | | |
| Bal | 800 | | |

Equipment

| b. | 3,500 | | |
| Bal | 3,500 | | |

Accounts payable

		b.	3,500
e.	500		
		Bal	3,000

Moe, capital

| | | a. | 10,000 |
| | | Bal | 10,000 |

Moe, drawing

| j. | 1,500 | | |
| Bal | 1,500 | | |

Service revenue

		d.	2,600
		f.	2,000
		Bal	4,600

Salary expense

| h. | 900 | | |
| Bal | 900 | | |

Repair expense

| g. | 200 | | |
| Bal | 200 | | |

Part 1	Part 2	Part 3	**Demo Doc Complete**

Review *Recording Business Transactions*

● Accounting Vocabulary

Account (p. 63)
The detailed record of all the changes that have occurred in a particular asset, liability, or owner's equity (stockholders' equity) during a period. The basic summary device of accounting.

Accrued Liability (p. 64)
A liability for which the business knows the amount owed but the bill has not been paid.

Chart of Accounts (p. 65)
A list of all a company's accounts with their account numbers.

Compound Journal Entry (p. 77)
Same as a journal entry, except this entry is characterized by having multiple debits and/or multiple credits. The total debits still equal the total credits in the compound journal.

Credit (p. 67)
The right side of an account.

Debit (p. 67)
The left side of an account.

Double-Entry System (p. 67)
A system of accounting where every transaction affects at least two accounts.

Journal (p. 63)
The chronological accounting record of an entity's transactions.

Ledger (p. 63)
The record holding all the accounts and amounts.

Normal Balance (p. 72)
The balance that appears on the side of an account—debit or credit—where we record increases.

Note Receivable (p. 64)
A written promise for future collection of cash.

Notes Payable (p. 64)
Represents debts the business owes because it signed promissory notes to borrow money or to purchase something.

Posting (p. 70)
Copying amounts from the journal to the ledger.

Prepaid Expenses (p. 64)
Expenses paid in advance of their use.

T-account (p. 67)
Summary device that is shaped like a capital "T" with debits posted on the left side of the vertical line and credits on the right side of the vertical line. A "shorthand" version of a ledger.

Trial Balance (p. 63)
A list of all the ledger accounts with their balances at a point in time.

● Destination: Student Success

Student Success Tips

The following are hints on some common trouble areas for students in this chapter:

● Commit to memory the normal balance of the six main account types. The normal balance is the side of the T-account where the account INCREASES. Assets, Drawing, and Expenses have normal debit balances. Liabilities, Equity, and Revenues have normal credit balances.

● Recall that debits are listed first in every journal entry.

● Remember debits ALWAYS EQUAL credits in every journal entry.

● Keep in mind that posting is just gathering all the journal entries made to an individual T-account so that you can determine the new balance in the account. Journal debit entries are posted on the left side of the T-account. Journal credit entries are posted on the right side of the T-account.

● The accounting equation MUST ALWAYS balance after each transaction is posted.

● The trial balance lists all accounts with a balance, ordered by assets, liabilities, equity, drawing, revenues, and expenses. Total debits should equal total credits on the trial balance.

Getting Help

If there's a learning objective from the chapter you aren't confident about, try using one or more of the following resources:

● Review the Chapter 2 Demo Doc located on page 89 of the textbook.

● Practice additional exercises or problems at the end of Chapter 2 that cover the specific learning objective that is challenging you.

● Watch the white board videos for Chapter 2 located at myaccountinglab.com under the Chapter Resources button.

● Go to myaccountinglab.com and select the Study Plan button. Choose Chapter 2 and work the questions covering that specific learning objective until you've mastered it.

● Work the Chapter 2 pre/post tests in myaccountinglab.com.

● Visit the learning resource center on your campus for tutoring.

● Quick Check

1. Which sequence correctly summarizes the accounting process?

   a. Journalize transactions, post to the accounts, prepare a trial balance

   b. Journalize transactions, prepare a trial balance, post to the accounts

   c. Post to the accounts, journalize transactions, prepare a trial balance

   d. Prepare a trial balance, journalize transactions, post to the accounts

2. The left side of an account is used to record which of the following?

   a. Debit or credit, depending on the type of account

   b. Increases

   c. Credits

   d. Debits

3. Suppose Hunt Company has receivables of $65,000, furniture totaling $205,000, and cash of $52,000. The business has a $109,000 note payable and owes $81,000 on account. How much is Hunt's owner's equity?

   a. $28,000

   b. $132,000

   c. $190,000

   d. $322,000

4. Your business purchased supplies of $2,500 on account. The journal entry to record this transaction is as follows:

   a.

Supplies	2,500	
Accounts receivable		2,500

   b.

Supplies	2,500	
Accounts payable		2,500

   c.

Accounts payable	2,500	
Supplies		2,500

   d.

Inventory	2,500	
Accounts payable		2,500

5. Which journal entry records your payment for the supplies purchase described in Quick Check question 4?

   a.

Accounts payable	2,500	
Accounts receivable		2,500

   b.

Accounts payable	2,500	
Cash		2,500

   c.

Cash	2,500	
Accounts payable		2,500

   d.

Supplies	2,500	
Cash		2,500

Experience the Power of Practice!

As denoted by the logo, all of these questions, as well as additional practice materials, can be found in *MyAccountingLab*.

Please visit myaccountinglab.com

6. Posting a $2,500 purchase of supplies on account appears as follows:

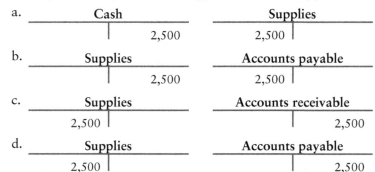

a.

Cash	
	2,500

Supplies	
2,500	

b.

Supplies	
	2,500

Accounts payable	
2,500	

c.

Supplies	
2,500	

Accounts receivable	
	2,500

d.

Supplies	
2,500	

Accounts payable	
	2,500

7. The detailed record of the changes in a particular asset, liability, or owner's equity is called

a. an account.

b. a journal.

c. a ledger.

d. a trial balance.

8. Pixel Copies recorded a cash collection on account by debiting Cash and crediting Accounts payable. What will the trial balance show for this error?

a. Too much for cash

b. Too much for liabilities

c. Too much for expenses

d. The trial balance will not balance

9. Timothy McGreggor, Attorney, began the year with total assets of $129,000, liabilities of $77,000, and owner's equity of $52,000. During the year the business earned revenue of $113,000 and paid expenses of $34,000. McGreggor also withdrew cash of $63,000. How much is the business's equity at year-end?

a. $68,000

b. $97,000

c. $131,000

d. $165,000

10. Michael Barry, Attorney, began the year with total assets of $126,000, liabilities of $74,000, and owner's equity of $52,000. During the year the business earned revenue of $110,000 and paid expenses of $33,000. Barry also withdrew cash of $69,000. How would Michael Barry record expenses paid of $33,000?

a.

Cash	33,000	
Expenses		33,000

b.

Accounts payable	33,000	
Cash		33,000

c.

Expenses	33,000	
Accounts payable		33,000

d.

Expenses	33,000	
Cash		33,000

Answers are given after Apply Your Knowledge (p. 129).

Assess Your Progress

● Short Exercises

S2-1   **❶ Using accounting vocabulary [10 min]**
Accounting has its own vocabulary and basic relationships.

Requirement

1. Match the accounting terms on the left with the corresponding definitions on the right.

————— 1. Posting

————— 2. Receivable

————— 3. Debit

————— 4. Journal

————— 5. Expense

————— 6. Net income

————— 7. Normal balance

————— 8. Ledger

————— 9. Payable

————— 10. Equity

A. Using up assets in the course of operating a business

B. Book of accounts

C. An asset

D. Record of transactions

E. Left side of an account

F. Side of an account where increases are recorded

G. Copying data from the journal to the ledger

H. Always a liability

I. Revenues – Expenses = _____

J. Assets – Liabilities = _____

S2-2   **❷ Explaining accounts and the rules of debit and credit [5 min]**
Margaret Alves is tutoring Timothy Johnson, who is taking introductory accounting. Margaret explains to Timothy that *debits* are used to record increases in accounts and *credits* record decreases. Timothy is confused and seeks your advice.

Requirements

1. When are debits increases? When are debits decreases?
2. When are credits increases? When are credits decreases?

S2-3   **❷ Normal account balances [5 min]**
The accounting equation includes three basic types of accounts: assets, liabilities, and owner's equity. In turn, owner's equity holds the following types: capital, drawing, revenues, and expenses.

Requirement

1. Identify which types of accounts have a normal debit balance and which types have a normal credit balance.

S2-4   **❸ Steps of the transaction recording process [5 min]**
Data Integrity Company performed $1,000 of services on account for a customer on January 5. The same customer paid $600 of the January 5 bill on January 28.

Requirement

1. Identify the three steps to record a transaction and perform the three steps to record the transactions for Data Integrity Company.

S2-5   **❹ Journalizing transactions [10 min]**
Ned Brown opened a medical practice in San Diego, California.

Jan 1	The business received $29,000 cash and gave capital to Brown.
2	Purchased medical supplies on account, $14,000.
2	Paid monthly office rent of $2,600.
3	Recorded $8,000 revenue for service rendered to patients on account.

Requirement

1. Record the preceding transactions in the journal of Ned Brown, M.D. Include an explanation with each entry.

S2-6 ④ **Journalizing transactions [10 min]**
Texas Sales Consultants completed the following transactions during the latter part of January:

Jan 22	Performed service for customers on account, $8,000.
30	Received cash on account from customers, $7,000.
31	Received a utility bill, $180, which will be paid during February.
31	Paid monthly salary to salesman, $2,000.
31	Paid advertising expense of $700.

Requirement

1. Journalize the transactions of Texas Sales Consultants. Include an explanation with each journal entry.

S2-7 ④ **Journalizing transactions and posting to T-accounts [10–15 min]**
Kenneth Dolkart Optical Dispensary purchased supplies on account for $3,400. Two weeks later, the business paid half on account.

Requirements

1. Journalize the two transactions for Kenneth Dolkart Optical Dispensary. Include an explanation for each entry.
2. Open the Accounts payable T-account and post to Accounts payable. Compute the balance, and denote it as *Bal*.

S2-8 ④ **Journalizing transactions and posting [10–15 min]**
Washington Law Firm performed legal services for a client who could not pay immediately. The business expected to collect the $16,000 the following month. Later, the business received $9,600 cash from the client.

Requirements

1. Record the two transactions for Washington Law Firm. Include an explanation for each transaction.
2. Open these T-accounts: Cash; Accounts receivable; Service revenue. Post to all three accounts. Compute each T-account's balance, and denote as *Bal*.
3. Answer these questions based on your analysis:
   a. How much did the business earn? Which account shows this amount?
   b. How much in total assets did the business acquire as a result of the two transactions? Identify each asset and show its balance.

Note: Short Exercise 2-9 should be used only after completing Short Exercise 2-5.

S2-9 ④ ⑤ **Posting, balancing T-accounts, and preparing a trial balance [10–15 min]**
Use the January transaction data for Ned Brown, M.D., given in Short Exercise 2-5.

Requirements

1. Open the following T-accounts: Cash; Accounts receivable; Medical supplies; Accounts payable; Brown, capital; Service revenue; and Rent expense.
2. After making the journal entries in Short Exercise 2-5, post to the T-accounts. No dates or posting references are required. Compute the balance of each account, and denote it as *Bal*.
3. Prepare the trial balance, complete with a proper heading, at January 3, 2012.

S2-10   ⑤ **Preparing a trial balance [10 min]**
Oakland Floor Coverings reported the following summarized data at December 31, 2012. Accounts appear in no particular order.

Revenues	$34,000	Other liabilities	$18,000
Equipment	45,000	Cash	12,000
Accounts payable	2,000	Expenses	19,000
Oakland, capital	22,000		

Requirement

1. Prepare the trial balance of Oakland Floor Coverings at December 31, 2012.

S2-11   ⑤ **Correcting a trial balance [10 min]**
Brenda Longval Travel Design prepared its trial balance. Suppose Longval made an error: She erroneously listed capital of $30,600 as a debit rather than a credit.

BRENDA LONGVAL TRAVEL DESIGN		
Trial Balance		
April 30, 2012		
	Balance	
Account Title	**Debit**	**Credit**
Cash	$ 18,000	
Accounts receivable	1,000	
Office supplies	500	
Land	14,000	
Accounts payable		$ 400
Longval, capital	30,600	
Longval, drawing	3,000	
Service revenue		8,800
Rent expense, computer	700	
Rent expense, office	900	
Salary expense	1,100	
Utilities expense	600	
Total		

Requirement

1. Compute the incorrect trial balance totals for debits and credits. Then show how to correct this error.

S2-12 ⑤ **Correcting a trial balance [10 min]**
Review Francis Nangle Travel Design's trial balance. Assume that Nangle accidentally listed drawing as $300 instead of the correct amount of $3,000.

	FRANCIS NANGLE TRAVEL DESIGN Trial Balance January 31, 2012		
		Balance	
Account Title		**Debit**	**Credit**
Cash		$ 20,000	
Accounts receivable		1,000	
Office supplies		500	
Land		12,000	
Accounts payable			$ 100
Nangle, capital			31,000
Nangle, drawing		300	
Service revenue			8,700
Rent expense, computer		700	
Rent expense, office		1,200	
Salary expense		1,200	
Utilities expense		200	
Total			

Requirement

1. Compute the incorrect trial balance totals for debits and credits. Then show how to correct this error, which is called a *slide*.

● Exercises

E2-13 ① **Using accounting vocabulary [10 min]**
Review basic accounting definitions by completing the following crossword puzzle.

Down:
1. Right side of an account
4. The basic summary device of accounting
6. Book of accounts
7. An economic resource
8. Record of transactions
9. Normal balance of a revenue

Across:
2. Records a decrease in a liability
3. List of accounts with their balances
5. Another word for liability

E2-14   ① **Using accounting vocabulary [10–15 min]**

Sharpen your use of accounting terms by working this crossword puzzle.

Down:

1. Records a decrease in a liability
4. Bottom line of an income statement
7. Revenue – net income = _____

Across:

2. Amount collectible from a customer
3. Statement of financial position
5. Copy data from the journal to the ledger
6. Records a decrease in an asset

E2-15   ① ② **Using debits and credits with the accounting equation [10–15 min]**

Link Back to Chapter 1 (Accounting Equation). John's Cream Soda makes specialty soft drinks. At the end of 2012, John's had total assets of $390,000 and liabilities totaling $260,000.

Requirements

1. Write the company's accounting equation, and label each amount as a debit or a credit.
2. The business's total revenues for 2012 were $480,000, and total expenses for the year were $350,000. How much was the business's net income (or net loss) for 2012? Write the equation to compute the company's net income, and indicate which element is a debit and which is a credit. Does net income represent a net debit or a net credit?

E2-16   ③ ④ **Analyzing and journalizing transactions [10–15 min]**

The following transactions occurred for London Engineering:

Jul	2	Paid utilities expense of $400.
	5	Purchased equipment on account, $2,100.
	10	Performed service for a client on account, $2,000.
	12	Borrowed $7,000 cash, signing a note payable.
	19	Sold for $29,000 land that had cost this same amount.
	21	Purchased supplies for $800 and paid cash.
	27	Paid the liability from July 5.

Requirement

1. Identify and perform the three steps to record the previously described transactions.

E2-17   ② ③ ④ ⑤ **Describing transactions, posting to T-accounts, and preparing a trial balance [20–30 min]**

The journal of Ward Technology Solutions includes the following entries for May, 2012:

May	1	The business received cash of $75,000 and gave capital to the owner.
	2	Purchased supplies of $500 on account.
	4	Paid $53,000 cash for a building.
	6	Performed service for customers and received cash, $2,600.
	9	Paid $400 on accounts payable.
	17	Performed service for customers on account, $2,500.
	23	Received $1,900 cash on account from a customer.
	31	Paid the following expenses: salary, $1,100; rent, $900.

Requirements

1. Describe each transaction. For example, the May 4 transaction description could be "Paid cash for building."
2. Open T-accounts using the following account numbers: Cash, 110; Accounts receivable, 120; Supplies, 130; Building, 140; Accounts payable, 210; Ward, capital, 310; Service revenue, 410; Rent expense, 510; Salary expense, 520.
3. Post to the accounts. Write dates and journal references (use account numbers) in the accounts. Compute the balance of each account after posting.
4. Prepare the trial balance of Ward Technology Solutions at May 31, 2012.

E2-18 ② ③ ④ ⑤ **Analyzing accounting errors [20–30 min]**
Danielle Neylon has trouble keeping her debits and credits equal. During a recent month, Danielle made the following accounting errors:

a. In preparing the trial balance, Danielle omitted a $7,000 note payable.
b. Danielle posted a $90 utility expense as $900. The credit to Cash was correct.
c. In recording an $800 payment on account, Danielle debited Furniture instead of Accounts payable.
d. In journalizing a receipt of cash for service revenue, Danielle debited Cash for $1,200 instead of the correct amount of $120. The credit was correct.
e. Danielle recorded a $540 purchase of supplies on account by debiting Supplies and crediting Accounts payable for $450.

Requirements

1. For each of these errors, state whether total debits equal total credits on the trial balance.
2. Identify each account that has an incorrect balance, and indicate the amount and direction of the error (such as "Accounts receivable $500 too high").

Note: Exercise 2-19 should be used only after completing Exercise 2-16.

E2-19 ② ④ ⑤ **Applying the rules of debit and credit, posting, and preparing a trial balance [15–25 min]**
Refer to the transactions of London Engineering in Exercise 2-16.

Requirements

1. Open the following T-accounts with their July 1 balances: Cash, debit balance $4,000; Accounts receivable $0; Equipment $0; Land, debit balance $29,000; Supplies $0; Accounts payable $0; Notes payable $0; London, capital, credit balance $33,000; Service revenue $0; Utilities expense $0.
2. Post the transactions of Exercise 2-16 to the T-accounts. Use the dates as posting references. Start with July 2.
3. Compute the July 31, 2012, balance for each account, and prove that total debits equal total credits by preparing a trial balance.

E2-20 ② ③ ④ ⑤ **Journalizing transactions, posting, and preparing a trial balance [10 min]**
In December, 2012, the first five transactions of Adams' Lawn Care Company have been posted to the accounts as follows:

Cash				Supplies		Equipment		Building	
(1)	53,000	(3)	40,000	(2) 700		(5) 4,700		(3) 40,000	
(4)	50,000	(5)	4,700						

Accounts payable		Note payable		Adams, capital	
	(2) 700		(4) 50,000		(1) 53,000

Requirements

1. Prepare the journal entries that served as the sources for the five transactions. Include an explanation for each entry as illustrated on page 87.

2. Prepare the trial balance of Adams' Lawn Care Company at December 31, 2012.

E2-21 ❹ **Using actual business documents [10 min]**

Suppose your name is Thomas Sell, and Best Automotive repaired your car. You settled the bill as noted on the following invoice. To you this is a purchase invoice. To Best Automotive, it is a sales invoice.

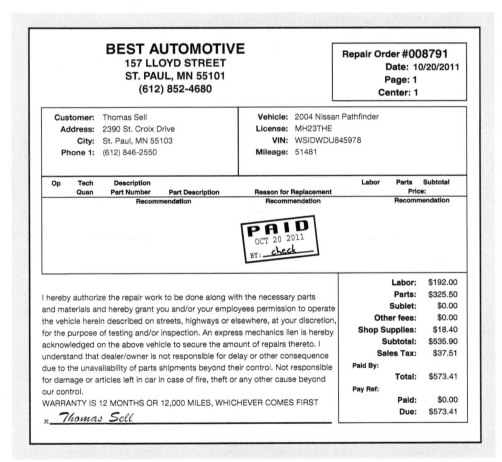

Requirements

1. Journalize your repair expense transaction.

2. Journalize Best Automotive's service revenue transaction.

E2-22 ④⑤ **Recording transactions, using four-column ledger accounts, and preparing a trial balance [20–25 min]**

The following transactions occurred during the month for Teresa Parker, CPA:

a. Parker opened an accounting firm by investing $14,100 cash and office furniture valued at $5,200. The business issued $19,300 of capital to Parker.

b. Paid monthly rent of $1,500.

c. Purchased office supplies on account, $900.

d. Paid employee's salary, $1,700.

e. Paid $700 of the account payable created in transaction (c).

f. Performed accounting service on account, $5,900.

g. Owner withdrew cash of $6,700.

Requirements

1. Open the following four-column accounts of Teresa Parker, CPA: Cash; Accounts receivable; Office supplies; Office furniture; Accounts payable; Parker, capital; Parker, drawing; Service revenue; Salary expense; Rent expense.

2. Journalize the transactions and then post to the four-column accounts. Use the letters to identify the transactions. Keep a running balance in each account.

3. Prepare the trial balance at December 31, 2012.

E2-23 ④ **Journalizing transactions [10–20 min]**

Principe Technology Solutions completed the following transactions during August 2012, its first month of operations:

Aug	1	Received cash of $48,000 and gave capital to the owner.
	2	Purchased supplies of $500 on account.
	4	Paid $47,000 cash for a building.
	6	Performed service for customers and received cash, $4,400.
	9	Paid $200 on accounts payable.
	17	Performed service for customers on account, $2,200.
	23	Received $1,600 cash from a customer on account.
	31	Paid the following expenses: salary, $1,900; rent, $700.

Requirement

1. Record the preceding transactions in the journal of Principe Technology Solutions. Include an explanation for each entry, as illustrated in the chapter. Use the following accounts: Cash; Accounts receivable; Supplies; Building; Accounts payable; Principe, capital; Service revenue; Salary expense; and Rent expense.

Note: Exercise 2-24 should be used only after completing Exercise 2-23.

E2-24 ④⑤ **Posting to the ledger and preparing a trial balance [15–20 min]**

Refer to Exercise 2-23 for the transactions of Principe Technology Solutions.

Requirements

1. After journalizing the transactions of Exercise 2-23, post to the ledger using the T-account format. Date the ending balance of each account Aug 31.

2. Prepare the trial balance of Principe Technology Solutions at August 31, 2012.

E2-25 ⑤ **Preparing a trial balance [10 min]**

The accounts of Atkins Moving Company follow with their normal balances at August 31, 2012. The accounts are listed in no particular order.

Atkins, capital	$ 72,000	Trucks	$ 132,000
Insurance expense	600	Fuel expense	3,000
Accounts payable	4,000	Atkins, drawing	5,400
Service revenue	80,000	Utilities expense	500
Building	48,000	Accounts receivable	8,800
Supplies expense	400	Note payable	54,000
Cash	4,000	Supplies	300
Salary expense	7,000		

Requirement

1. Prepare Atkins' trial balance at August 31, 2012.

E2-26   (5) **Correcting errors in a trial balance [15–20 min]**

The following trial balance of Joy McDowell Tutoring Service at May 31, 2012, does not balance:

Account	Debit	Credit
JOY MCDOWELL TUTORING SERVICE		
Trial Balance		
May 31, 2012		
Cash	$ 3,000	
Accounts receivable	2,000	
Supplies	600	
Computer equipment	25,800	
Accounts payable		$ 11,400
McDowell, capital		11,600
Service revenue		9,800
Salary expense	1,700	
Rent expense	700	
Utilities expense	500	
Total	$ 34,300	$ 32,800

Investigation of the accounting records reveals that the bookkeeper:

a. Recorded a $500 cash revenue transaction by debiting Accounts receivable. The credit entry was correct.
b. Posted a $1,000 credit to Accounts payable as $100.
c. Did not record utilities expense or the related account payable in the amount of $400.
d. Understated McDowell, capital by $600.

Requirement

1. Prepare the corrected trial balance at May 31, 2012, complete with a heading; journal entries are not required.

● Problems (Group A)

P2-27A   (1) (2) **Identifying common accounts and normal account balances [10–15 min]**   *MyAccountingLab*

Showtime Amusements Company owns movie theaters. Showtime engaged in the following business transactions in 2012:

Sep	1	Don Cougliato invested $370,000 personal cash in the business by depositing that amount in a bank account titled Showtime Amusements. The business gave capital to Cougliato.
	2	Paid $360,000 cash to purchase a theater building.
	5	Borrowed $260,000 from the bank. Cougliato signed a note payable to the bank in the name of Showtime.
	10	Purchased theater supplies on account, $1,400.
	15	Paid $1,200 on account.
	15	Paid property tax expense on theater building, $1,500.
	16	Paid employees' salaries $2,500, and rent on equipment $1,400. Make a single compound entry.
	28	Cougliato withdrew cash of $7,000.
	30	Received $21,000 cash from service revenue and deposited that amount in the bank.

Requirements

1. Create the list of accounts that Showtime Amusements will use to record these transactions.

2. Identify the account type and normal balance of each account identified in Requirement 1.

Note: Problem 2-27A must be completed before attempting Problem 2-28A.

P2-28A ③④ **Analyzing and journalizing transactions, posting, and preparing a trial balance [40–50 min]**
Review the facts given in P2-27A.

Requirements

1. Journalize each transaction of Showtime as shown for September 1. Explanations are not required.

Sep 1	Cash	370,000	
	Cougliato, capital		370,000

2. Post the transactions to the T-accounts, using transaction dates as posting references in the ledger accounts. Label the balance of each account *Bal*, as shown in the chapter.

P2-29A ②③④⑤ **Analyzing and journalizing transactions, posting, and preparing a trial balance [45–60 min]**
Vernon Yung practices medicine under the business title Vernon Yung, M.D. During July, the medical practice completed the following transactions:

Jul 1	Yung deposited $68,000 cash in the business bank account. The business gave capital to Yung.
5	Paid monthly rent on medical equipment, $560.
9	Paid $16,000 cash to purchase land for an office site.
10	Purchased supplies on account, $1,600.
19	Borrowed $23,000 from the bank for business use. Yung signed a note payable to the bank in the name of the business.
22	Paid $1,300 on account.
31	Revenues earned during the month included $6,500 cash and $5,800 on account.
31	Paid employees' salaries $2,500, office rent $1,100, and utilities $400. Make a single compound entry.
31	Yung withdrew cash of $7,000.

The business uses the following accounts: Cash; Accounts receivable; Supplies; Land; Accounts payable; Notes payable; Yung, capital; Yung, drawing; Service revenue; Salary expense; Rent expense; and Utilities expense.

Requirements

1. Journalize each transaction, as shown for July 1. Explanations are not required.

Jul 1	Cash	68,000	
	Yung, capital		68,000

2. Post the transactions to the T-accounts, using transaction dates as posting references in the ledger accounts. Label the balance of each account *Bal*, as shown in the chapter.

3. Prepare the trial balance of Vernon Yung, M.D. at July 31, 2012.

P2-30A ③④⑤ **Journalizing transactions, posting to T-accounts, and preparing a trial balance [45–60 min]**

Doris Stewart started her practice as a design consultant on September 1, 2012. During the first month of operations, the business completed the following transactions:

Sep	1	Received $42,000 cash and gave capital to Stewart.
	4	Purchased supplies, $700, and furniture, $1,900, on account.
	6	Performed services for a law firm and received $1,400 cash.
	7	Paid $24,000 cash to acquire land for a future office site.
	10	Performed service for a hotel and received its promise to pay the $1,000 within one week.
	14	Paid for the furniture purchased September 4 on account.
	15	Paid secretary's bi-monthly salary, $490.
	17	Received cash on account, $400.
	20	Prepared a design for a school on account, $700.
	28	Received $2,100 cash for consulting with Plummer & Gorden.
	30	Paid secretary's bi-monthly salary, $490.
	30	Paid rent expense, $650.
	30	Stewart withdrew cash of $3,000.

Requirements

1. Open the following T-accounts: Cash; Accounts receivable; Supplies; Furniture; Land; Accounts payable; Stewart, capital; Stewart, drawing; Service revenue; Salary expense; and Rent expense.

2. Record each transaction in the journal, using the account titles given. Key each transaction by date. Explanations are not required.

3. Post the transactions to the T-accounts, using transaction dates as posting references in the ledger accounts. Label the balance of each account *Bal*, as shown in the chapter.

4. Prepare the trial balance of Doris Stewart, Designer, at September 30, 2012.

P2-31A ④⑤ **Journalizing transactions, posting to accounts in four-column format, and preparing a trial balance [45–60 min]**

Trevor Moore opened a law office on September 2, 2012. During the first month of operations, the business completed the following transactions:

Sep	2	Moore deposited $39,000 cash in the business bank account Trevor Moore, Attorney. The business gave capital to Moore.
	3	Purchased supplies, $600, and furniture, $2,000, on account.
	4	Performed legal service for a client and received cash, $1,300.
	7	Paid cash to acquire land for a future office site, $26,000.
	11	Prepared legal documents for a client on account, $700.
	15	Paid secretary's bi-monthly salary, $590.
	16	Paid for the supplies purchased September 3 on account.
	18	Received $2,400 cash for helping a client sell real estate.
	19	Defended a client in court and billed the client for $800.
	29	Received cash on account, $700.
	30	Paid secretary's bi-monthly salary, $590.
	30	Paid rent expense, $670.
	30	Moore withdrew cash of $2,400.

Requirements

1. Open the following T-accounts: Cash; Accounts receivable; Supplies; Furniture; Land; Accounts payable; Moore, capital; Moore, drawing; Service revenue; Salary expense; and Rent expense.

2. Record each transaction in the journal, using the account titles given. Key each transaction by date. Explanations are not required.

3. Post the transactions to T-accounts, using transaction dates as posting references in the ledger. Label the balance of each account *Bal*, as shown in the chapter.

4. Prepare the trial balance of Trevor Moore, Attorney, at September 30, 2012.

P2-32A ④⑤ **Journalizing transactions, posting to accounts in four-column format, and preparing a trial balance [45–60 min]**

The trial balance of Sam Mitchell, CPA, is dated January 31, 2012:

	SAM MITCHELL, CPA Trial Balance January 31, 2012		
Account No.	Account	Debit	Credit
11	Cash	$ 7,000	
12	Accounts receivable	10,500	
13	Supplies	600	
14	Land	17,000	
21	Accounts payable		$ 4,700
31	Mitchell, capital		30,400
32	Mitchell, drawing		
41	Service revenue		
51	Salary expense		
52	Rent expense		
	Total	$ 35,100	$ 35,100

During February, Mitchell or his business completed the following transactions:

Feb 4 Collected $4,000 cash from a client on account.
      8 Performed tax services for a client on account, $4,600.
    13 Paid business debt on account, $2,400.
    18 Purchased office supplies on account, $900.
    20 Mitchell withdrew cash of $2,200.
    21 Mitchell paid for a deck for his private residence using personal funds, $8,000.
    22 Received $2,300 cash for consulting work just completed.
    27 Paid office rent, $500.
    29 Paid employee salary, $1,600.

Requirements

1. Record the February transactions in the journal. Include an explanation for each entry.

2. Post the transactions to four-column accounts in the ledger, using dates, account numbers, journal references, and posting references. Open the ledger accounts listed in the trial balance, together with their balances at January 31.

3. Prepare the trial balance of Sam Mitchell, CPA, at February 29, 2012.

P2-33A ④ ⑤ **Journalizing transactions, posting to accounts in four-column format, and preparing a trial balance [45–60 min]**

The trial balance of Sharon Silver, Registered Dietician, at June 30, 2012, follows.

	SHARON SILVER, REGISTERED DIETICIAN		
	Trial Balance		
	June 30, 2012		
Account No.	Account	Debit	Credit
11	Cash	$ 7,000	
12	Accounts receivable	8,500	
13	Supplies	800	
14	Equipment	13,000	
21	Accounts payable		$ 4,800
31	Silver, capital		24,500
32	Silver, drawing		
41	Service revenue		
51	Salary expense		
52	Rent expense		
	Total	$ 29,300	$ 29,300

During July, Silver or her business completed the following transactions:

Jul 4 Collected $6,000 cash from a client on account.

7 Performed a nutritional analysis for a hospital on account, $6,600.

12 Silver used personal funds to pay for the renovation of her private residence, $55,000.

16 Purchased supplies on account, $1,000.

19 Silver withdrew cash of $2,300.

20 Paid business debt on account, $2,500.

24 Received $2,200 cash for consulting with Natural Foods.

25 Paid rent, $500.

31 Paid employee salary, $1,700.

Requirements

1. Record the July transactions in the business's journal. Include an explanation for each entry.

2. Post the transactions to four-column accounts in the ledger, using dates, account numbers, journal references, and posting references.

3. Prepare the trial balance of Sharon Silver, Registered Dietician, at July 31, 2012.

P2-34A ④ ⑤ **Recording transactions, using four-column accounts, posting, and preparing a trial balance [45–60 min]**

Maurey Wills started an environmental consulting company and during the first month of operations (February 2012), the business completed the following transactions:

a. Wills began the business with an investment of $48,000 cash and a building at $30,000. The business gave $78,000 of capital to Wills.

b. Purchased office supplies on account, $2,000.

c. Paid $14,000 for office furniture.

d. Paid employee's salary, $2,200.

e. Performed consulting services on account, $3,700.

f. Paid $900 of the account payable created in transaction (b).

g. Received a $600 bill for advertising expense that will be paid in the near future.

h. Performed consulting service for cash, $1,100.

i. Received cash on account, $1,100.

j. Paid the following cash expenses:
   (1) Rent on equipment, $1,000.
   (2) Utilities, $900.

k. Wills withdrew cash of $2,300.

Requirements

1. Open the following four-column accounts: Cash; Accounts receivable; Office supplies; Office furniture; Building; Accounts payable; Wills, capital; Wills, drawing; Service revenue; Salary expense; Rent expense; Advertising expense; and Utilities expense.

2. Record each transaction in the journal. Use the letters to identify the transactions.

3. Post to the accounts and keep a running balance for each account.

4. Prepare the trial balance of Wills Environmental Consulting Company at February 29, 2012.

P2-35A ② ⑤ **Correcting errors in a trial balance [15–25 min]**
The trial balance of Smart Tots Child Care does not balance.

SMART TOTS CHILD CARE Trial Balance August 31, 2012		
Account	Debit	Credit
Cash	$ 6,700	
Accounts receivable	7,000	
Supplies	700	
Equipment	87,000	
Accounts payable		$ 53,000
Tilley, capital		50,500
Tilley, drawing	2,400	
Service revenue		4,700
Salary expense	3,600	
Rent expense	500	
Total	$ 107,900	$ 108,200

The following errors are detected:

a. Cash is understated by $1,000.

b. A $4,000 debit to Accounts receivable was posted as a credit.

c. A $1,000 purchase of supplies on account was neither journalized nor posted.

d. Equipment's cost is $78,500, not $87,000.

e. Salary expense is overstated by $200.

Requirement

1. Prepare the corrected trial balance at August 31, 2012. Journal entries are not required.

P2-36A ② ⑤ **Correcting errors in a trial balance [15–25 min]**
The trial balance for Treasure Hunt Exploration Company does not balance.

Account	Debit	Credit
TREASURE HUNT EXPLORATION COMPANY		
Trial Balance		
February 29, 2012		
Cash	$ 6,300	
Accounts receivable	6,000	
Supplies	400	
Exploration equipment	22,300	
Computers	49,000	
Accounts payable		$ 2,800
Note payable		18,500
Jones, capital		50,000
Jones, drawing	4,000	
Service revenue		4,100
Salary expense	1,400	
Rent expense	800	
Advertising expense	900	
Utilities expense	800	
Total	$ 91,900	$ 75,400

The following errors were detected:

a. The cash balance is overstated by $5,000.
b. Rent expense of $340 was erroneously posted as a credit rather than a debit.
c. A $6,800 credit to Service revenue was not posted.
d. A $400 debit to Accounts receivable was posted as $40.
e. The balance of Utilities expense is understated by $70.
f. A $900 purchase of supplies on account was neither journalized nor posted.
g. Exploration equipment should be $16,490.

Requirement

1. Prepare the corrected trial balance at February 29, 2012. Journal entries are not required.

P2-37A ⑤ **Preparing financial statements from the trial balance [20–30 min]**
Link Back to Chapter 1 (Income Statement, Statement of Owner's Equity, Balance Sheet). Refer to Problem 2-28A. After completing the ledger in Problem 2-28A, prepare the following financial statements for Showtime Amusements Company:

Requirements

1. Income statement for the month ended September 30, 2012.
2. Statement of owner's equity for the month ended September 30, 2012. The beginning balance of capital was $0.
3. Balance sheet at September 30, 2012.

P2-38A ⑤ **Preparing financial statements from the trial balance [20–30 min]**
Link Back to Chapter 1 (Income Statement, Statement of Owner's Equity, Balance Sheet). Refer to Problem 2-29A. After completing the trial balance in Problem 2-29A, prepare the following financial statements for Vernon Yung, M.D.:

Requirements

1. Income statement for the month ended July 31, 2012.
2. Statement of owner's equity for the month ended July 31, 2012. The beginning balance of capital was $0.
3. Balance sheet at July 31, 2012.

P2-39A ⑤ **Preparing financial statements from the trial balance [20–30 min]**
Link Back to Chapter 1 (Income Statement, Statement of Owner's Equity, Balance Sheet). Refer to Problem 2-30A. After completing the trial balance in Problem 2-30A, prepare the following financial statements for Doris Stewart, Designer:

Requirements

1. Income statement for the month ended September 30, 2012.
2. Statement of owner's equity for the month ended September 30, 2012. The beginning balance of capital was $0.
3. Balance sheet at September 30, 2012.

P2-40A ⑤ **Preparing financial statements from the trial balance. [20–30 min]**
Link Back to Chapter 1 (Income Statement, Statement of Owner's Equity, Balance Sheet). Refer to Problem 2-31A. After completing the trial balance in Problem 2-31A, prepare the following financial statements for Trevor Moore, Attorney:

Requirements

1. Income statement for the month ended September 30, 2012.
2. Statement of owner's equity for the month ended September 30, 2012. The beginning balance of capital was $0.
3. Balance sheet at September 30, 2012.

P2-41A ⑤ **Preparing financial statements from the trial balance [20–30 min]**
Link Back to Chapter 1 (Income Statement, Statement of Owner's Equity, Balance Sheet). Refer to Problem 2-32A. After completing the trial balance in Problem 2-32A, prepare the following financial statements for Sam Mitchell, CPA:

Requirements

1. Income statement for the month ended February 29, 2012.
2. Statement of owner's equity for the month ended February 29, 2012. The beginning balance of capital was $0.
3. Balance sheet at February 29, 2012.

P2-42A ⑤ **Preparing financial statements from the trial balance [20–30 min]**
Link Back to Chapter 1 (Income Statement, Statement of Owner's Equity, Balance Sheet). Refer to Problem 2-33A. After completing the trial balance in Problem 2-33A, prepare the following financial statements for Sharon Silver, Registered Dietician:

Requirements

1. Income statement for the month ended July 31, 2012.
2. Statement of owner's equity for the month ended July 31, 2012. The beginning balance of capital was $0.
3. Balance sheet at July 31, 2012.

P2-43A ⑤ **Preparing financial statements from the trial balance [20–30 min]**
Link Back to Chapter 1 (Income Statement, Statement of Owner's Equity, Balance Sheet). Refer to Problem 2-34A. After completing the trial balance in Problem 2-34A, prepare the following financial statements for Wills Environmental Consulting Company:

Requirements

1. Income statement for the month ended February 29, 2012.
2. Statement of owner's equity for the month ended February 29, 2012. The beginning balance of capital was $0.
3. Balance sheet at February 29, 2012.

● Problems (Group B)

P2-44B ① ② **Identifying common accounts and normal account balances [10–15 min]**   MyAccountingLab
Party Time Amusements Company owns movie theaters. Party Time engaged in the following business transactions in 2012:

Aug	1	Daniel Smith invested $400,000 personal cash in the business by depositing that amount in a bank account titled Party Time Amusements. The business gave capital to Smith.
	2	Paid $350,000 cash to purchase a theater building.
	5	Borrowed $200,000 from the bank. Smith signed a note payable to the bank in the name of Party Time.
	10	Purchased theater supplies on account, $1,300.
	15	Paid $1,000 on account.
	15	Paid property tax expense on theater building, $1,200.
	16	Paid employees' salaries $2,700, and rent on equipment $1,700. Make a single compound entry.
	28	Smith withdrew cash of $8,000.
	31	Received $25,000 cash from service revenue and deposited that amount in the bank.

Requirements

1. Create the list of accounts that Party Time Amusements will use to record these transactions.
2. Identify the account type and normal balance of each account identified in Requirement 1.

Note: Problem 2-44B must be completed before attempting Problem 2-45B.

P2-45B ③ ④ **Analyzing and journalizing transactions, posting, and preparing a trial balance [40–50 min]**
Review the facts given in P2-44B.

Requirements

1. Journalize each transaction of Party Time as shown for August 1. Explanations are not required.

Aug 1	Cash	400,000	
	Smith, capital		400,000

2. Post the transactions to the T-accounts, using transaction dates as posting references in the ledger accounts. Label the balance of each account *Bal*, as shown in the chapter.

P2-46B ③ ④ ⑤ **Analyzing and journalizing transactions, posting, and preparing a trial balance [45–60 min]**

Vince Rockford practices medicine under the business title Vince Rockford, M.D. During March, the medical practice completed the following transactions:

Mar	1	Rockford deposited $74,000 cash in the business bank account. The business gave capital to Rockford.
	5	Paid monthly rent on medical equipment, $560.
	9	Paid $24,000 cash to purchase land for an office site.
	10	Purchased supplies on account, $1,300.
	19	Borrowed $19,000 from the bank for business use. Rockford signed a note payable to the bank in the name of the business.
	22	Paid $900 on account.
	31	Revenues earned during the month included $7,100 cash and $4,700 on account.
	31	Paid employees' salaries $2,000, office rent $1,600, and utilities $320. Make a single compound entry.
	31	Rockford withdrew cash of $8,000.

The business uses the following accounts: Cash; Accounts receivable; Supplies; Land; Accounts payable; Notes payable; Rockford, capital; Rockford, drawing; Service revenue; Salary expense; Rent expense; and Utilities expense.

Requirements

1. Journalize each transaction, as shown for March 1. Explanations are not required.

Mar 1	Cash	74,000	
	Rockford, capital		74,000

2. Post the transactions to the T-accounts, using transaction dates as posting references in the ledger accounts. Label the balance of each account *Bal*, as shown in the chapter.

3. Prepare the trial balance of Vince Rockford, M.D., at March 31, 2012.

P2-47B ④ ⑤ **Journalizing transactions, posting to T-accounts, and preparing a trial balance [45–60 min]**

Beth Yung started her practice as a design consultant on November 1, 2012. During the first month of operations, the business completed the following transactions:

Nov	1	Received $34,000 cash and issued capital to Yung.
	4	Purchased supplies, $500, and furniture, $1,900, on account.
	6	Performed services for a law firm and received $1,200 cash.
	7	Paid $25,000 cash to acquire land for a future office site.
	10	Performed service for a hotel and received its promise to pay the $1,200 within one week.
	14	Paid for the furniture purchased November 4 on account.
	15	Paid secretary's bi-monthly salary, $540.
	17	Received cash on account, $500.
	20	Prepared a design for a school on account, $800.
	28	Received $2,200 cash for consulting with Plummer & Gorden.
	30	Paid secretary's bi-monthly salary, $540.
	30	Paid rent expense, $830.
	30	Yung withdrew cash of $2,700.

Requirements

1. Open the following T-accounts: Cash; Accounts receivable; Supplies; Furniture; Land; Accounts payable; Yung, capital; Yung, drawing; Service revenue; Salary expense; and Rent expense.

2. Record each transaction in the journal, using the account titles given. Key each transaction by date. Explanations are not required.

3. Post the transactions to the T-accounts, using transaction dates as posting references in the ledger accounts. Label the balance of each account *Bal*, as shown in the chapter.

4. Prepare the trial balance of Beth Yung, Designer, at November 30, 2012.

P2-48B ④ ⑤ **Journalizing transactions, posting to accounts in four-column format, and preparing a trial balance [45–60 min]**
Vince Smith opened a law office on April 2, 2012. During the first month of operations, the business completed the following transactions:

Apr	2	Smith deposited $32,000 cash in the business bank account Vince Smith, Attorney. The business gave Smith capital.
	3	Purchased supplies, $500, and furniture, $2,000, on account.
	4	Performed legal service for a client and received cash, $1,900.
	7	Paid cash to acquire land for a future office site, $24,000.
	11	Prepared legal documents for a client on account, $1,100.
	15	Paid secretary's bi-monthly salary, $460.
	16	Paid for the supplies purchased April 3 on account.
	18	Received $1,700 cash for helping a client sell real estate.
	19	Defended a client in court and billed the client for $700.
	29	Received cash on account, $800.
	30	Paid secretary's bi-monthly salary, $460.
	30	Paid rent expense, $730.
	30	Smith withdrew cash of $2,700.

Requirements

1. Open the following T-accounts: Cash; Accounts receivable; Supplies; Furniture; Land; Accounts payable; Smith, capital; Smith, drawing; Service revenue; Salary expense; and Rent expense.

2. Record each transaction in the journal, using the account titles given. Key each transaction by date. Explanations are not required.

3. Post the transactions to T-accounts, using transaction dates as posting references in the ledger. Label the balance of each account *Bal*, as shown in the chapter.

4. Prepare the trial balance of Vince Smith, Attorney, at April 30, 2012.

P2-49B ④⑤ **Journalizing transactions, posting to accounts in four-column format, and preparing a trial balance [45–60 min]**

The trial balance of John Hilton, CPA, is dated March 31, 2012:

Account No.	Account	Debit	Credit
	JOHN HILTON, CPA		
	Trial Balance		
	March 31, 2012		
11	Cash	$ 5,000	
12	Accounts receivable	8,100	
13	Supplies	800	
14	Land	14,000	
21	Accounts payable		$ 4,200
31	Hilton, capital		23,700
32	Hilton, drawing		
41	Service revenue		
51	Salary expense		
52	Rent expense		
	Total	$27,900	$27,900

During April, Hilton or his business completed the following transactions:

Apr	4	Collected $7,000 cash from a client on account.
	8	Performed tax services for a client on account, $5,000.
	13	Paid business debt on account, $2,500.
	18	Purchased office supplies on account, $600.
	20	Hilton withdrew cash of $2,300.
	21	Hilton paid for a deck for his private residence, using personal funds, $12,000.
	22	Received $2,100 cash for consulting work just completed.
	27	Paid office rent, $300.
	28	Paid employee salary, $1,300.

Requirements

1. Record the April transactions in the journal. Include an explanation for each entry.
2. Post the transactions to four-column accounts in the ledger, using dates, account numbers, journal references, and posting references. Open the ledger accounts listed in the trial balance, together with their balances at March 31.
3. Prepare the trial balance of John Hilton, CPA, at April 30, 2012.

P2-50B ④ ⑤ **Journalizing transactions, posting to accounts in four-column format, and preparing a trial balance [45–60 min]**

The trial balance of Shermana Peters, Registered Dietician, at June 30, 2012, follows:

	SHERMANA PETERS, REGISTERED DIETICIAN Trial Balance June 30, 2012		
Account No.	**Account**	**Debit**	**Credit**
11	Cash	$ 4,000	
12	Accounts receivable	7,600	
13	Supplies	600	
14	Equipment	16,000	
21	Accounts payable		$ 5,200
31	Peters, capital		23,000
32	Peters, drawing		
41	Service revenue		
51	Salary expense		
52	Rent expense		
	Total	$28,200	$28,200

During July, Peters or her business completed the following transactions:

Jul	4	Collected $7,000 cash from a client on account.
	7	Performed a nutritional analysis for a hospital on account, $4,900.
	12	Peters used personal funds to pay for the renovation of her private residence, $53,000.
	16	Purchased supplies on account, $800.
	19	Peters withdrew cash of $2,200.
	20	Paid business debt on account, $2,300.
	24	Received $2,100 cash for consulting with Bountiful Foods.
	25	Paid rent, $300.
	31	Paid employee salary, $1,500.

Requirements

1. Record the July transactions in the business's journal. Include an explanation for each entry.
2. Post the transactions to four-column accounts in the ledger, using dates, account numbers, journal references, and posting references.
3. Prepare the trial balance of Shermana Peters, Registered Dietician, at July 31, 2012.

P2-51B ④ ⑤ **Recording transactions, using four-column accounts, posting, and preparing a trial balance [45–60 min]**

Van Stubbs started an environmental consulting company and during the first month of operations (October 2012), the business completed the following transactions:

---

a. Stubbs began the business with an investment of $40,000 cash and a building at $26,000. The business gave $66,000 of capital to Stubbs.

b. Purchased office supplies on account, $2,400.

c. Paid $18,000 for office furniture.

d. Paid employee's salary, $1,900.

e. Performed consulting services on account, $3,600.

f. Paid $500 of the account payable created in transaction (b).

g. Received a $300 bill for advertising expense that will be paid in the near future.

h. Performed consulting service for cash, $800.

i. Received cash on account, $1,400.

j. Paid the following cash expenses:
   (1) Rent on equipment, $700.
   (2) Utilities, $500.

k. Stubbs withdrew cash of $2,400.

Requirements

1. Open the following four-column accounts: Cash; Accounts receivable; Office supplies; Office furniture; Building; Accounts payable; Stubbs, capital; Stubbs, drawing; Service revenue; Salary expense; Rent expense; Advertising expense; and Utilities expense.

2. Record each transaction in the journal. Use the letters to identify the transactions.

3. Post to the accounts and keep a running balance for each account.

4. Prepare the trial balance of Stubbs Environmental Consulting Company at October 31, 2012.

P2-52B ② ⑤ **Correcting errors in a trial balance [15–25 min]**
The trial balance of Building Blocks Child Care does not balance.

BUILDING BLOCKS CHILD CARE Trial Balance May 31, 2012		
Account	Debit	Credit
Cash	$ 6,300	
Accounts receivable	3,000	
Supplies	700	
Equipment	88,000	
Accounts payable		$ 57,000
Estella, capital		50,400
Estella, drawing	2,600	
Service revenue		4,700
Salary expense	3,200	
Rent expense	700	
Total	$ 104,500	$ 112,100

The following errors are detected:

a. Cash is understated by $4,000.

b. A $2,000 debit to Accounts receivable was posted as a credit.

c. A $1,200 purchase of supplies on account was neither journalized nor posted.

d. Equipment's cost is $87,700, not $88,000.

e. Salary expense is overstated by $100.

Requirement

1. Prepare the corrected trial balance at May 31, 2012. Journal entries are not required.

P2-53B ② ⑤ **Correcting errors in a trial balance [15–25 min]**

The trial balance for Treasure Hunt Exploration Company does not balance.

TREASURE HUNT EXPLORATION COMPANY Trial Balance July 31, 2012		
Account	Debit	Credit
Cash	$ 6,600	
Accounts receivable	9,000	
Supplies	200	
Exploration equipment	22,600	
Computers	46,000	
Accounts payable		$ 2,900
Note payable		18,900
Indiana, capital		50,100
Indiana, drawing	1,000	
Service revenue		4,900
Salary expense	1,800	
Rent expense	100	
Advertising expense	100	
Utilities expense	700	
Total	$ 88,100	$ 76,800

The following errors were detected:

a. The cash balance is overstated by $1,000.

b. Rent expense of $300 was erroneously posted as a credit rather than a debit.

c. A $6,000 credit to Service revenue was not posted.

d. A $500 debit to Accounts receivable was posted as $50.

e. The balance of Utilities expense is understated by $90.

f. A $600 purchase of supplies on account was neither journalized nor posted.

g. Exploration equipment should be $17,160.

Requirement

1. Prepare the corrected trial balance at July 31, 2012. Journal entries are not required.

P2-54B ⑤ **Preparing financial statements from the trial balance [20–30 min]**

Link Back to Chapter 1 (Income Statement, Statement of Owner's Equity, Balance Sheet). Refer to Problem 2-45B. After completing the ledger in Problem 2-45B, prepare the following financial statements for Party Time Amusements Company:

Requirements

1. Income statement for the month ended August 31, 2012.

2. Statement of owner's equity for the month ended August 31, 2012. The beginning balance of capital was $0.

3. Balance sheet at August 31, 2012.

P2-55B ⑤ **Preparing financial statements from the trial balance [20–30 min]**

Link Back to Chapter 1 (Income Statement, Statement of Owner's Equity, Balance Sheet). Refer to Problem 2-46B. After completing the trial balance in Problem 2-46B, prepare the following financial statements for Vince Rockford, M.D.:

Requirements

1. Income statement for the month ended March 31, 2012.
2. Statement of owner's equity for the month ended March 31, 2012. The beginning balance of capital was $0.
3. Balance sheet at March 31, 2012.

P2-56B ⑤ **Preparing preparing financial statements from the trial balance. [20–30 min]**
Link Back to Chapter 1 (Income Statement, Statement of Owner's Equity, Balance Sheet). Refer to Problem 2-47B. After completing the trial balance in Problem 2-47B, prepare the following financial statements for Beth Yung, Designer:

Requirements

1. Income statement for the month ended November 30, 2012.
2. Statement of owner's equity for the month ended November 30, 2012. The beginning balance of capital was $0.
3. Balance sheet at November 30, 2012.

P2-57B ⑤ **Preparing financial statements from the trial balance. [20–30 min]**
Link Back to Chapter 1 (Income Statement, Statement of Owner's Equity, Balance Sheet). Refer to Problem 2-48B. After completing the trial balance in Problem 2-48B, prepare the following financial statements for Vince Smith, Attorney:

Requirements

1. Income statement for the month ended April 30, 2012.
2. Statement of owner's equity for the month ended April 30, 2012. The beginning balance of capital was $0.
3. Balance sheet at April 30, 2012.

P2-58B ⑤ **Preparing financial statements from the trial balance [20–30 min]**
Link Back to Chapter 1 (Income Statement, Statement of Owner's Equity, Balance Sheet). Refer to Problem 2-49B. After completing the trial balance in Problem 2-49B, prepare the following financial statements for John Hilton, CPA:

Requirements

1. Income statement for the month ended April 30, 2012.
2. Statement of owner's equity for the month ended April 30, 2012. The beginning balance of capital was $0.
3. Balance sheet at April 30, 2012.

P2-59B ⑤ **Preparing financial statements from the trial balance [20–30 min]**
Link Back to Chapter 1 (Income Statement, Statement of Owner's Equity, Balance Sheet). Refer to Problem 2-50B. After completing the trial balance in Problem 2-50B, prepare the following financial statements for Shermana Peters, Registered Dietician:

Requirements

1. Income statement for the month ended July 31, 2012.
2. Statement of owner's equity for the month ended July 31, 2012. The beginning balance of capital was 0.
3. Balance sheet at July 31, 2012.

P2-60B ⑤ **Preparing financial statements from the trial balance [20–30 min]**
Link Back to Chapter 1 (Income Statement, Statement of Owner's Equity, Balance Sheet). Refer to Problem 2-51B. After completing the trial balance in Problem 2-51B, prepare the following financial statements for Stubbs Environmental Consulting Company:

Requirements

1. Income statement for the month ended October 31, 2012.
2. Statement of owner's equity for the month ended October 31, 2012. The beginning balance of capital was $0.
3. Balance sheet at October 31, 2012.

● Continuing Exercise

② ③ ④ ⑤ **Journalizing transactions, posting to T-accounts, and preparing a trial balance [30–45 min]** Exercise 2-61 continues with the consulting business of Lawlor Lawn Service begun in Exercise 1-47. Here you will account for Lawlor Lawn Service's transactions as it is actually done in practice.

MyAccountingLab

E2-61 Lawlor Lawn Service completed the following transactions during May:

May	1	Received $1,700 and gave capital to Lawlor. Opened bank account titled Lawlor Lawn Service.
	3	Purchased on account a mower, $1,200, and weed whacker, $240. The equipment is expected to remain in service for four years.
	5	Purchased $30 of gas. Wrote check #1 from the new bank account.
	6	Performed lawn services for client on account, $150.
	8	Purchased $150 of fertilizer supplies from the lawn store that will be used on future jobs. Wrote check #2 from the new bank account.
	17	Completed landscaping job for client, received cash $800.
	31	Received $100 on account from May 6 sale.

Requirements

1. Open T-accounts: Cash; Accounts receivable; Lawn supplies; Equipment; Accounts payable; Lawlor, capital; Lawlor, drawing; Service revenue; and Fuel expense.
2. Journalize the transactions. Explanations are not required.
3. Post to the T-accounts. Key all items by date, and denote an account balance as *Bal.* Formal posting references are not required.
4. Prepare a trial balance at May 31, 2012.

• Continuing Problem

❷❸❹❺ **Journalizing transactions, posting to T-accounts, and preparing a trial balance [40–50 min]** Problem 2-62 continues with the consulting business of Carl Draper, begun in Problem 1-48. Here you will account for Draper Consulting's transactions as it is actually done in practice.

P2-62 Draper Consulting completed the following transactions during the first half of December, 2012:

Dec	2	Received $18,000 cash and gave capital to Draper.
	2	Paid monthly office rent, $550.
	3	Paid cash for a **Dell** computer, $1,800. This equipment is expected to remain in service for five years.
	4	Purchased office furniture on account, $4,200. The furniture should last for five years.
	5	Purchased supplies on account, $900.
	9	Performed consulting service for a client on account, $1,500.
	12	Paid utility expenses, $250.
	18	Performed service for a client and received cash of $1,100.

Requirements

1. Open T-accounts: Cash; Accounts receivable; Supplies; Equipment; Furniture; Accounts payable; Draper, capital; Draper, drawing; Service revenue; Rent expense; and Utilities expense.

2. Journalize the transactions. Explanations are not required.

3. Post to the T-accounts. Key all items by date, and denote an account balance as *Bal.* Formal posting references are not required.

4. Prepare a trial balance at December 18. In the Continuing Problem of Chapter 3, we will add transactions for the remainder of December and prepare a trial balance at December 31.

• Practice Set

② ③ ④ ⑤ **Journalizing transactions, posting to T-accounts, and preparing a trial** **balance [45–60 min]** Use the chart of accounts you created in Chapter 1 (and add accounts where necessary). All of the first month's activity for Shine King Cleaning is as follows.

Nov	1	Evan Hudson deposited $35,000 in the business account. Also on this date, Evan transferred his truck title, worth $8,000, to the business. Evan received $43,000 of capital.
	2	Wrote a check for $2,000 to Pleasant Properties. In the "for" area of the check, it states "November through February Rent." (Debit Prepaid rent)
	3	Purchased business insurance policy for $2,400 for the term November 1, 2012, through October 31, 2013, and paid cash. (Debit Prepaid insurance)
	4	Evan went to the Cleaning Supply Company and purchased $270 of cleaning supplies on account. The invoice is due 20 days from the date of purchase.
	5	Purchased on account an industrial vacuum cleaner from Penny Purchase costing $1,000. The invoice is payable on or before November 25.
	7	Purchased a computer and printer costing a total of $1,200. A check for the same amount to the computer store was written on the same date.
	9	Performed cleaning services on account for Pierre's Wig Stand in the amount of $3,000.
	10	Deposited Pierre's check for $100 in the bank.
	15	Wrote check payable to Eric Ryder for $500 for contract labor.
	16	Received $3,600 for 1 year contract beginning November 16 for cleaning services to be provided to the Sea Side Restaurant. Contract begins November 16, 2012, and ends November 15, 2013. (Credit Unearned service revenue)
	17	Provided cleaning services for Tip Top Solutions for $800. Tip Top paid with a check.
	18	Received water and electric bill for $175 with due date of December 4, 2012.
	20	Borrowed $40,000 from bank with interest at rate of 9% per year.
	21	Deposited check from Pierre's Wig Stand for $900, with the notation "on account."
	25	Wrote check to Penny Purchase for invoice #1035 in the amount of $500.
	29	Wrote check payable to **St. Petersburg News** for $100 for advertising.
	30	Hudson withdrew cash of $600.

Requirements

1. Journalize transactions as required from the activity data.
2. Post journal entries to T-accounts and calculate account balances.
3. Prepare the trial balance at November 30.

Apply Your Knowledge

• Decision Cases

Decision Case 2-1 You have been requested by a friend named Dean McChesney to advise him on the effects that certain transactions will have on his business. Time is short, so you cannot journalize the transactions. Instead, you must analyze the transactions without a journal. McChesney will continue the business only if he can expect to earn monthly net income of $6,000. The business completed the following transactions during June:

a.	McChesney deposited $10,000 cash in a business bank account to start the company. The company gave capital to McChesney.
b.	Paid $300 cash for supplies.
c.	Incurred advertising expense on account, $700.
d.	Paid the following cash expenses: secretary's salary, $1,400; office rent, $1,100.
e.	Earned service revenue on account, $8,800.
f.	Collected cash from customers on account, $1,200.

Requirements

1. Open the following T-accounts: Cash; Accounts receivable; Supplies; Accounts payable; McChesney, capital; Service revenue; Salary expense; Rent expense; and Advertising expense.

2. Post the transactions directly to the accounts without using a journal. Key each transaction by letter. Follow the format illustrated here for the first transaction.

Cash	McChesney, capital
(a) 10,000	(a) 10,000

3. Prepare a trial balance at June 30, 2014. List the largest expense first, the next largest second, and so on. The business name is A-Plus Travel Planners.

4. Compute the amount of net income or net loss for this first month of operations. Would you recommend that McChesney continue in business?

Decision Case 2-2 Answer the following questions. Consider each question separately.

Requirements

1. Explain the advantages of double-entry bookkeeping instead of recording transactions in terms of the accounting equation to a friend who is opening a used book store.

2. When you deposit money in your bank account, the bank credits your account. Is the bank misusing the word *credit* in this context? Why does the bank use the term *credit* to refer to your deposit, instead of *debit*?

● Ethical Issue 2-1

Better Days Ahead, a charitable organization, has a standing agreement with First National Bank. The agreement allows Better Days Ahead to overdraw its cash balance at the bank when donations are running low. In the past, Better Days Ahead managed funds wisely, and rarely used this privilege. Jacob Henson has recently become the president of Better Days. To expand operations, Henson acquired office equipment and spent large amounts on fundraising. During Henson's presidency, Better Days Ahead has maintained a negative bank balance of approximately $10,000.

Requirement

1. What is the ethical issue in this situation, if any? State why you approve or disapprove of Henson's management of Better Days Ahead's funds.

● Fraud Case 2-1

Roy Akins was the accounting manager at Zelco, a tire manufacturer, and he played golf with Hugh Stallings, the CEO, who was something of a celebrity in the community. The CEO stood to earn a substantial bonus if Zelco increased net income by year-end. Roy was eager to get into Hugh's elite social circle; he boasted to Hugh that he knew some accounting tricks that could increase company income by simply revising a few journal entries for rental payments on storage units. At the end of the year, Roy changed the debits from "rent expense" to "prepaid rent" on several entries. Later, Hugh got his bonus, and the deviations were never discovered.

Requirements

1. How did the change in the journal entries affect the net income of the company at year-end?

2. Who gained and who lost as a result of these actions?

● Financial Statement Case 2-1

This problem helps you develop skill in recording transactions by using a company's actual account titles. Refer to the **Amazon.com** financial statements in Appendix A. Note that large companies like **Amazon.com** use summary account titles in their financials, rather than listing each individual account by name. Assume that **Amazon.com** completed the following selected transactions during December 2009:

Dec	1	Earned sales revenue and collected cash, $60,000 ("Net sales").
	9	Borrowed $200,000 by signing a note payable ("Long-term debt").
	12	Purchased equipment on account, $10,000 ("Fixed assets").
	22	Paid half the account payable from December 12.
	28	Paid electricity bill for $3,000 ("General and administrative expense").
	31	Paid $100,000 of the note payable, plus interest expense of $1,000.

Requirement

1. Journalize these transactions, using the following account headings taken from the **Amazon.com** financial statements: Cash and cash equivalents, Equipment, Fixed assets, Accounts payable, Long-term debt, Net sales, General and administrative expense, and Interest expense. Explanations are not required.

● Team Project 2-1

Contact a local business and arrange with the owner to learn what accounts the business uses.

Requirements

1. Obtain a copy of the business's chart of accounts.

2. Prepare the company's financial statements for the most recent month, quarter, or year. (You may omit the statement of cash flows.) You may use either made-up account balances or balances supplied by the owner.

If the business has a large number of accounts within a category, combine related accounts and report a single amount on the financial statements. For example, the company may have several cash accounts. Combine all cash amounts and report a single Cash amount on the balance sheet.

 You will probably encounter numerous accounts that you have not yet learned. Deal with these as best you can.

 Keep in mind that the financial statements report the balances of the accounts listed in the company's chart of accounts, either by individual account or in summarized categories. Therefore, the financial statements must be consistent with the chart of accounts.

● Communication Activity 2-1

In 35 words or fewer, explain the difference between a debit and a credit and explain what the normal balance of the six account types is.

Quick Check Answers

1. *a* 2. *d* 3. *b* 4. *b* 5. *b* 6. *d* 7. *c* 8. *b* 9. *a* 10. *d*

For online homework, exercises, and problems that provide you immediate feedback, please visit myaccountinglab.com.

3

The Adjusting Process

Are these balances correctly showing everything the company OWNS?

Are these balances correctly showing everything the company OWES?

SMART TOUCH LEARNING
Balance Sheet
May 31, 2013

Assets				Liabilities	
Current assets:				Current liabilities:	
Cash		$ 4,800		Accounts payable	$ 48,700
Accounts receivable		2,600		Salary payable	900
Inventory		30,500		Interest payable	100
Supplies		600		Unearned service revenue	400
Prepaid rent		2,000		Total current liabilities	50,100
Total current assets			$ 40,500	Long-term liabilities:	
Plant assets:				Notes payable	20,000
Furniture	$18,000			Total liabilities	70,100
Less: Accumulated depreciation—furniture	300	17,700			
Building	48,000				
Less: Accumulated depreciation—building	200	47,800		Owner's Equity	
Total plant assets			65,500	Bright, capital	35,900
Total assets			$106,000	Total liabilities and owner's equity	$106,000

Learning Objectives

1. Differentiate between accrual and cash-basis accounting

2. Define and apply the accounting period concept, revenue recognition and matching principles, and time period concept

3. Explain why adjusting entries are needed

4. Journalize and post adjusting entries

5. Explain the purpose of and prepare an adjusted trial balance

6. Prepare the financial statements from the adjusted trial balance

7. Understand the alternate treatment of unearned revenues and prepaid expenses (see Appendix 3A, located at myaccountinglab.com)

If you're a business owner, manager, shareholder, or even an employee paid on commissions, you're anxious to see the final results of the period for your company. What is the company's net income or loss?

Chapter 1 introduced you to the accounting equation and the financial statements. In Chapter 2 you learned about T-accounts, debits, credits, and the trial balance. But have you captured all the transactions for a particular period? Not yet.

● ● ●

In this chapter, we'll continue our exploration of the accounting cycle by learning how to update the accounts at the end of the period. This process is called *adjusting the books*, and it requires special journal entries called *adjusting journal entries*. For example, you'll see how at the end of a particular period, you must determine how many supplies you have used and how much you owe your employees and make adjusting entries to account for these amounts. These are just some of the adjusting entries you need to make before you can see the complete picture of how well your company performed—and determine commissions for salespeople and drawings for the owner.

We'll apply these principles to Smart Touch Learning for the month of May in this chapter, but these principles apply to giant companies such as **eBay** and **ExxonMobil** as well. They also apply to the business you may own or operate some day. Let's get started by comparing the accrual basis and cash basis of accounting.

Accrual Accounting Versus Cash-Basis Accounting

There are two ways to do accounting:

①　Differentiate between accrual and cash-basis accounting

- **Accrual accounting** records the effect of each transaction as it occurs—that is, revenues are recorded when earned and expenses are recorded when incurred. Most businesses use the accrual basis as covered in this book.
- **Cash-basis accounting** records only cash receipts and cash payments. It ignores receivables, payables, and depreciation. Only very small businesses use the cash basis of accounting.

Suppose Smart Touch purchased $200 of office supplies on account on May 15, 2013, and paid the account in full on June 3, 2013. On the accrual basis, the business records this transaction as follows:

May 15	Office supplies (A+)	200	
	Accounts payable (L+)		200
	Purchased supplies on account.		
Jun 3	Accounts payable (L–)	200	
	Cash (A–)		200
	Paid on account.		

In contrast, cash-basis accounting ignores this transaction on May 15 because the business paid no cash. The cash basis records only cash receipts and cash payments. *In the cash basis*,

- cash receipts are treated as revenues.
- cash payments are treated as expenses.

Under the cash basis, Smart Touch would record each cash payment as an expense. So for our office supplies example, the company would recognize the cash basis expense on June 3, 2013, because that is the date that cash was paid. This is faulty accounting because the business acquired supplies, which are assets.

Now let's see how differently the accrual basis and the cash basis account for a revenue. Suppose Smart Touch performed service and earned revenue on May 20, 2013, but did not collect cash until June 5, 2013. Under the accrual basis, the business records $1,000 of revenue on account on May 20 as follows:

	May 20	Accounts receivable (A+)		1,000	
		Service revenue (R+)			1,000
		Earned revenue on account.			
	Jun 5	Cash (A+)		1,000	
		Accounts receivable (A−)			1,000
		Received cash on account.			

Under the cash basis, the business would record no revenue until the cash receipt, which in this case would be on June 5. As a result, cash-basis accounting never reports accounts receivable from customers. In this case, cash-basis accounting actually shows the revenue in the wrong accounting period (June). Revenue should be recorded when it is earned (May), and that is how the accrual basis operates.

Exhibit 3-1 illustrates the difference between the accrual basis and the cash basis for a florist. Keep in mind that the accrual basis is the preferred way to do accounting—and it's required by GAAP.

EXHIBIT 3-1 | **Accrual Accounting Versus Cash-Basis Accounting**

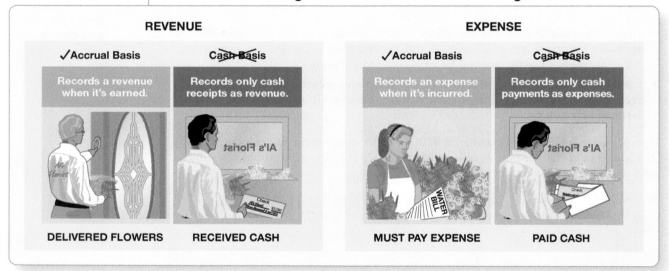

Key Takeaway
Cash-basis accounting and accrual accounting are different. Accrual accounting records revenues and expenses when they are EARNED/INCURRED. Cash-basis accounting records revenues and expenses when cash is RECEIVED or PAID.

Stop & Think...

Most of us think in terms of cash. Did our bank balance go up or down? This is in essence what the cash basis measures—changes in the cash balance. But consider your job. When do you actually earn your salary— when you go to work or when you get paid? When you go to work, you earn. That is when you accrue revenue under the accrual basis—not when you get paid by your employer.

Other Accounting Principles

 Define and apply the accounting period concept, revenue recognition and matching principles, and time period concept

We learned about some key accounting concepts in previous chapters. Now let's look at some additional accounting principles.

The Accounting Period Concept

Smart Touch will know with 100% certainty how well it has operated only if the company sells its assets, pays its liabilities, and gives any leftover cash to its owner(s). This process of going out of business is called **liquidation.** For obvious reasons, it is not practical to measure income this way. Because businesses need periodic reports on their affairs, accountants slice time into small segments and prepare financial statements for specific periods, such as a month, quarter, or year.

The basic accounting period is one year, and most businesses prepare annual financial statements. For most companies, the annual accounting period is the calendar year, from January 1 through December 31. Other companies use a *fiscal year*, which ends on a date other than December 31. The year-end date is usually the low point in business activity for the year. Retailers are a notable example. For instance, **Walmart** and **JCPenney** use a fiscal year that ends on January 31 because their business activity low point comes about a month after the holidays.

The Revenue Recognition Principle

The **revenue recognition principle** tells accountants

- *when* to record revenue—that is, when to make a journal entry for a revenue.
- the *amount* of revenue to record.

"Recording" something in accounting means making an entry in the journal. That is where the process starts.

When to Record Revenue

The revenue recognition principle says to record revenue when it has been earned—but not before. Revenue has been earned when the business has delivered a good or service to the customer. The company has done everything required by the sale agreement—that is, the earnings process is complete. **For you, revenue is earned when you go to work every day—not on the date you get paid.**

Exhibit 3-2 shows two situations that provide guidance on when to record revenue for Smart Touch. The first situation illustrates when *not* to record revenue—because the client merely states his plan. Situation 2 illustrates when revenue *should* be recorded—after the e-learning agency has performed a service for the client.

EXHIBIT 3-2 | **Recording Revenue: The Revenue Recognition Principle**

The Amount of Revenue to Record

Record revenue for the actual value of the item or service transferred to the customer. Suppose that in order to obtain a new client, Sheena Bright performs e-learning services for the cut-rate price of $100. Ordinarily, the business would have charged $200 for this service. How much revenue should the business record? Sheena Bright did not charge $200, so that is not the amount of revenue. Smart Touch charged only $100, so the business records $100 of revenue.

The Matching Principle

The **matching principle** guides accounting for expenses. Recall that expenses—such as salaries, rent, utilities, and advertising—are assets used up and liabilities incurred in order to earn revenue. The matching principle

1. measures all the expenses incurred during the period, and

2. matches the expenses against the revenues of the period.

To match expenses against revenues means to subtract expenses incurred during one month from revenues earned during that same month. The goal is to compute net income or net loss. Exhibit 3-3 illustrates the matching principle.

EXHIBIT 3-3 | **Recording Expenses: The Matching Principle**

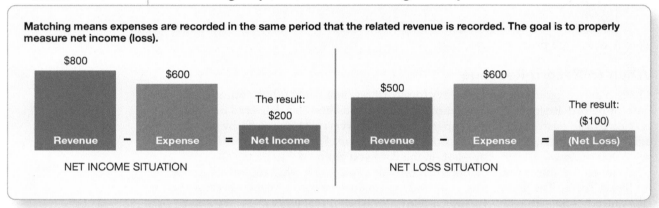

There is a natural link between some expenses and revenues. For example, Smart Touch pays a commission to the employee who sells the e-learning agency's services. Other expenses are not so easy to link to revenues. For example, Smart Touch Learning's monthly rent expense occurs regardless of the revenues earned that month. The matching principle tells us to identify those expenses with a particular period, such as a month or a year when the related revenue occurred. The business will record rent expense each month based on the rental agreement. Smart Touch also pays a monthly salary to its employee.

How does Smart Touch bring its accounts up-to-date for the financial statements? To address this question, accountants use the time-period concept.

The Time-Period Concept

Owners need periodic reports on their businesses. The **time-period concept** requires that information is reported at least annually. Often, companies report more than just annually. To measure income, companies update their accounts at the end of each period, usually monthly.

Let's look at Smart Touch for an example of an accrued expense. On May 31, the business recorded salary expense of $900 that it owed the employee at the end of the month. Smart Touch's accrual entry was as follows:

May 31	Salary expense	(E+)	900	
	Salary payable	(L+)		900
	Accrued salary expense.			

This entry assigns the salary expense to May because that was the month when the employee worked for the company. Without this entry, $900 of May's salary expense would be reported in the wrong period—June. May's expenses would also be understated, and May's net income would be overstated. The accrual entry also records the liability owed at May 31. Without this entry, total liabilities would be understated. The remainder of the chapter shows how to adjust the accounts and bring the books up-to-date.

Why We Adjust the Accounts

At the end of the period, the accountant prepares the financial statements. The end-of-period process begins with the trial balance, which you learned how to prepare in the previous chapter. Exhibit 3-4 is the trial balance of Smart Touch at May 31, 2013.

3 Explain why adjusting entries are needed

EXHIBIT 3-4 | **Unadjusted Trial Balance**

SMART TOUCH LEARNING Unadjusted Trial Balance May 31, 2013		
Account	**Debit**	**Credit**
Cash	$ 4,800	
Accounts receivable	2,200	
Supplies	700	
Prepaid rent	3,000	
Furniture	18,000	
Building	48,000	
Accounts payable		$18,200
Unearned service revenue		600
Notes payable		20,000
Bright, capital		33,200
Bright, drawing	1,000	
Service revenue		7,000
Salary expense	900	
Utilities expense	400	
Total	$79,000	$79,000

This *unadjusted trial balance* lists the revenues and expenses of the e-learning agency for May. But these amounts are incomplete because they omit various revenue and expense transactions. That is why the trial balance is *unadjusted*. Usually, however, we refer to it simply as the trial balance, without the label "unadjusted."

Accrual accounting requires adjusting entries at the end of the period. We must have correct balances for the financial statements. To see why, consider the Supplies account in Exhibit 3-4.

Smart Touch uses supplies during the month. This reduces the supplies on hand (an asset) and creates an expense (supplies expense). It is a waste of time to record supplies expense every time supplies are used. But by the end of the month, enough of the $700 of Supplies on the unadjusted trial balance (Exhibit 3-4) have probably been used that we need to adjust the Supplies account. This is an example of why we need to adjust some accounts at the end of the period.

Adjusting entries assign revenues to the period when they are earned and expenses to the period when they are incurred. Adjusting entries also update the asset and liability accounts. Adjustments are needed to properly measure two things:

1. net income (loss) on the income statement and

2. assets and liabilities on the balance sheet.

This end-of-period process is called *making the adjustments* or *adjusting the books*. Remember the following three facts about adjusting entries:

1. Adjusting entries never involve the Cash account.

2. Adjusting entries either
   a. increase revenue earned (Revenue credit) or
   b. increase an expense (Expense debit).

3. When information is provided about an adjustment to an account and the information is worded as "accrued" an amount for a particular account, you journalize the stated amount to the stated account in your adjusting entry. (This will be explained further in an example later in the chapter.)

> **Key Takeaway**
>
> We adjust accounts to make sure the balance sheet shows the value of what we own (assets) and what we owe (liabilities) on a specific date. We also adjust to make sure all revenues and expenses are recorded in the period they are earned or incurred. Adjusting journal entries either credit a revenue account or debit an expense account, but they NEVER affect the Cash account.

Two Categories of Adjusting Entries

 Journalize and post adjusting entries

The two basic categories of adjusting entries are *prepaids* and *accruals*. In a **prepaid** adjustment, the cash payment occurs before an expense is recorded or the cash receipt occurs before the revenue is earned. Prepaids are also called **deferrals** because the recognition of revenue or expense is deferred to a date after the cash is received or paid. **Accrual** adjustments are the opposite. An accrual records an expense before the cash payment or it records the revenue before the cash is received.

Adjusting entries fall into five types:

1. Prepaid expenses (prepaid)

2. Depreciation (prepaid)

3. Accrued expenses (accrual)

4. Accrued revenues (accrual)

5. Unearned revenues (prepaid)

The focus of this chapter is on learning how to account for these five types of adjusting entries.

Prepaid Expenses

Prepaid expenses are advance payments of expenses. **Prepaid expenses are always paid for before they are used up.** For example, **McDonald's**, the restaurant chain, makes prepayments for rent, insurance, and supplies. Prepaid expenses are considered assets rather than expenses. When the prepayment is used up, the used portion of the asset becomes an expense via an adjusting journal entry.

Prepaid Rent

Some landlords require tenants to pay rent in advance. This prepayment creates an asset for the renter. Suppose Smart Touch prepays three months' office rent of $3,000 ($1,000 per month × three months) on May 1, 2013. The entry to record the payment is as follows:

May 1	Prepaid rent ($1,000 × 3) (A+)	3,000	
	Cash (A–)		3,000
	Paid rent in advance.		

After posting, Prepaid rent has a $3,000 debit balance.

ASSETS

Prepaid rent

May 1	3,000

The trial balance at May 31, 2013, lists Prepaid rent with a debit balance of $3,000 (Exhibit 3-4). Throughout May, Prepaid rent maintains this balance. But $3,000 is *not* the amount of Prepaid rent for the balance sheet at May 31. Why?

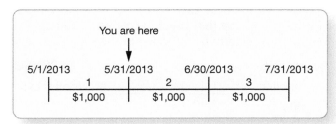

At May 31, Prepaid rent should be decreased for the amount that has been used up. The used-up portion is one month of the three months prepaid, or one-third of the pre-payment. Recall that an asset that has expired is an *expense*. The adjusting entry transfers $1,000 ($3,000 × 1/3) from Prepaid rent to Rent expense. The adjusting entry is as follows:

a.	May 31	Rent expense ($3,000 × 1/3) (E+)	1,000	
		Prepaid rent (A–)		1,000
		To record rent expense.		

After posting, Prepaid rent and Rent expense show correct ending balances:

ASSETS

Prepaid rent

May 1	3,000	May 31	1,000
Bal	2,000		

EXPENSES

Rent expense

May 31	1,000	
Bal	1,000	

Correct asset amount:		Total accounted for:		Correct expense amount:
$2,000	→	$3,000	←	$1,000

The Prepaid rent is an example of an asset that was overstated prior to posting the adjusting entry. Notice that the ending balance in Prepaid rent is now $2,000. Because Prepaid rent is an asset account for Smart Touch, it should contain only two more months of rent on May 31 (for June and July). $1,000 rent per month times two months equals the $2,000 Prepaid rent balance.

The same analysis applies to the prepayment of three months of insurance. The only difference is in the account titles. Prepaid insurance would be used instead of Prepaid rent, and Insurance expense would be used instead of Rent expense. In a computerized system, the adjusting entry can be programmed to recur automatically each accounting period.

Appendix 3A (located at myaccountinglab.com) shows an alternative treatment of prepaid expenses. The end result on the accounts is the same as illustrated here.

Supplies

Supplies are also accounted for as prepaid expenses. Let's look at an example. On May 2, Sheena Bright paid $500 for office supplies. On May 15, she spent another $200 on office supplies.

The May 31 trial balance, therefore, still lists Supplies with a $700 debit balance, as shown in Exhibit 3-4. But Smart Touch's May 31 balance sheet should *not* report supplies of $700. Why not?

During May, the e-learning agency used supplies to conduct business. The cost of the supplies used becomes *supplies expense*. To measure supplies expense, Bright counts the supplies on hand at the end of May. This is the amount of the asset still owned by the business. Assume that supplies costing $600 remain on May 31. Use the Supplies T-account to determine the value of the supplies that were used:

ASSETS			EXPENSES	
Supplies			**Supplies expense**	
May 2	500			
		Supplies		
May 15	200	Used ???	???	
Bal	600		Bal ???	

So, we can solve for the supplies used as follows:

Beginning Supplies + Supplies Purchased − Supplies Used = Ending Supplies
$0 + (500 + 200) − Supplies Used = $600
Supplies Used = $100

The May 31 adjusting entry updates Supplies and records Supplies expense for May as follows:

b.	May 31	Supplies expense ($700 − $600) (E+)	100	
		Supplies (A−)		100
		To record supplies used.		

After posting the adjusting entry, the May 31 balance of Supplies is correctly reflected as $600 and the Supplies expense is correctly reflected as $100.

ASSETS				EXPENSES		
Supplies				**Supplies expense**		
May 2	500					
May 15	200	May 31	100	May 31	100	
Bal	600			Bal	100	

The Supplies account then enters June with a $600 balance, and the adjustment process is repeated each month. Supplies is another example of an asset that was overstated at $700 on the trial balance prior to posting the adjusting entry. The adjusting entry then left the correct balance of Supplies on May 31 of $600.

Depreciation

Plant assets are long-lived tangible assets used in the operation of a business. Examples include land, buildings, equipment, furniture, and automobiles. As a business uses the assets, their value and usefulness decline. The decline in usefulness of a plant asset is an expense, and accountants systematically spread the asset's cost over its useful life. The allocation of a plant asset's cost to expense is called **depreciation**.

You might pay cash for your car the day you buy it, but it's something you own that will last for years, so depreciation allocates the cost spent on the car over the time you use the car. Land is the exception. We record no depreciation for land, as its value typically does not decline with use.

Similarity to Prepaid Expenses

The concept of accounting for plant assets is the same as for a prepaid expense. The major difference is the length of time it takes for the asset to be used up. Prepaid expenses usually expire within a year, but plant assets remain useful for several years. Let's review an example for Smart Touch. On May 3, Smart Touch purchased furniture for $18,000 and made the following journal entry:

May 3	Furniture (A+)		18,000	
	Cash (A−)			18,000
	Purchased furniture.			

After posting, the Furniture account has an $18,000 balance:

ASSETS

Furniture

May 3 18,000	

Sheena Bright believes the furniture will remain useful for five years and then will be worthless. One way to compute depreciation is to divide the cost of the asset ($18,000) by its expected useful life (five years). So, the depreciation for each month is $300 ($18,000/5 years = $3,600/12 months = $300 per month). Depreciation expense for May is recorded by the following adjusting entry:

c.	May 31	Depreciation expense—furniture (E+)	300	
		Accumulated depreciation—furniture (CA+)		300
		To record depreciation on furniture.		

The Accumulated Depreciation Account

Notice that in the above adjusting entry for depreciation we credited Accumulated depreciation—furniture and NOT the asset account Furniture. Why? We need to keep the original cost of the furniture separate from the recovery (depreciation) of that cost because of the historical cost principle. Managers can then refer to the Furniture account to see how much the asset originally cost. This information may help decide how much to pay for new furniture. The **Accumulated depreciation** account is the sum of all the depreciation recorded for the asset, and that total increases (accumulates) over time.

Accumulated depreciation is a contra asset, which means that it is an asset account with a normal credit balance. **Contra means opposite.** A **contra account** has two main characteristics:

- A contra account is paired with and follows its related account.
- A contra account's normal balance (debit or credit) is the opposite of the balance of the related account.

For example, Accumulated depreciation—furniture is the contra account that follows the Furniture account on the balance sheet. The Furniture account has a debit balance, so Accumulated depreciation, a contra asset, has a credit balance.

A business may have a separate Accumulated depreciation account for each depreciable asset. If Smart Touch has both a Building and a Furniture account, it may have these two accounts: Accumulated depreciation—building, and Accumulated depreciation—furniture. However, small companies often have only one Accumulated depreciation account for all their assets.

After posting the depreciation, the accounts appear as follows:

ASSETS			EXPENSES	
NORMAL ASSET	**CONTRA ASSET**			
Furniture	Accumulated depreciation—furniture		Depreciation expense—furniture	
May 3 18,000		May 31 300	May 31 300	
Bal 18,000		Bal 300	Bal 300	

Book Value

The balance sheet reports both Furniture and Accumulated depreciation—furniture. Because it is a contra account, Accumulated depreciation—furniture is subtracted from Furniture. The resulting net amount (cost minus accumulated depreciation) of a plant asset is called its **book value**. For Smart Touch's furniture, the book value is as follows:

Book value of plant assets:	
Furniture	$18,000
Less: Accumulated depreciation—furniture	300
Book value of the furniture	$17,700

The book value represents costs invested in the asset that the business has not yet recovered (expensed).

Suppose the e-learning agency also owns a building that cost $48,000, with monthly depreciation of $200. The following adjusting entry would record depreciation for May:

d.	May 31	Depreciation expense—building (E+)	200	
		Accumulated depreciation—building (CA+)		200
		To record depreciation on building.		

The May 31 balance sheet would report plant assets as shown in Exhibit 3-5.

EXHIBIT 3-5 | **Plant Assets on the Balance Sheet of Smart Touch Learning (May 31)**

Plant Assets		
Furniture	$18,000	
Less: Accumulated depreciation—furniture	300	$17,700
Building	$48,000	
Less: Accumulated depreciation—building	200	47,800
Plant assets, net		$65,500

Accrued Expenses

Businesses often incur expenses before paying for them. The term **accrued expense** refers to an expense of this type. **An accrued expense hasn't been paid for yet.** Consider an employee's salary. The salary expense grows as the employee works, so the expense is said to *accrue*. Another accrued expense is interest expense on a note payable. Interest accrues as time passes on the note. An accrued expense always creates a liability.

Companies do not make weekly journal entries to accrue expenses. Instead, they wait until the end of the period. They make an adjusting entry to bring each expense (and the related liability) up-to-date for the financial statements.

Remember that prepaid expenses and accrued expenses are opposites.

> • A *prepaid expense* is paid first and expensed later.
> • An *accrued expense* is expensed first and paid later.

Next we'll see how to account for accrued expenses.

Accruing Salary Expense

Suppose Smart Touch pays its employee a monthly salary of $1,800—half on the 15th and half on the first day of the next month. Here is a calendar for May and June with the two paydays circled:

May 2013						
Sunday	Monday	Tuesday	Wednesday	Thursday	Friday	Saturday
Apr 28	29	30	May 1	2	3	4
5	6	7	8	9	10	11
12	13	14	15 Pay Day	16	17	18
19	20	21	22	23	24	25
26	27	28	29	30	31	Jun 1 Pay Day

During May, Sheena Bright paid the first half-month salary on Wednesday, May 15, and made this entry:

May 15	Salary expense (E+)	900	
	Cash (A–)		900
	To pay salary.		

After posting, Salary expense shows the following balance:

EXPENSES

Salary expense

May 15	900

The trial balance on May 31 (Exhibit 3-4) includes Salary expense, with a debit balance of $900. This is Smart Touch's salary expense for the first half of May. The second payment of $900 will occur on June 1; however, the expense was incurred in May, so the expense must be recorded in May. On May 31, Smart Touch makes the following adjusting entry:

e.	May 31	Salary expense (E+)	900	
		Salary payable (L+)		900
		To accrue salary expense.		

After posting, both Salary expense and Salary payable are up-to-date:

EXPENSES		LIABILITIES	
Salary expense		**Salary payable**	
May 15	900		
May 31	900	May 31	900
Bal	1,800	Bal	900

Salary expense shows a full month's salary, and Salary payable shows the liability owed at May 31. This is an example of a liability that was understated before the adjusting entry was made. It also is an example of the matching principle: We are recording May's salary expense in May so it will be reported on the same income statement period as May's revenues.

Accruing Interest Expense

Borrowing money creates a liability for a Note payable. If, on May 1, 2013, Smart Touch borrows $20,000 from the bank after signing a one-year note payable, the entry to record the note on May 1, 2013, is as follows:

May 1	Cash (A+)	20,000	
	Note payable (L+)		20,000
	Borrowed money.		

Interest on this note is payable one year later, on May 1, 2014. On May 31, 2013, the company must make an adjusting entry to record the interest expense that has accrued for the month of May. Assume one month's interest expense on this note is $100. The May 31 adjusting entry to accrue interest expense is as follows:

f.	May 31	Interest expense (E+)	100	
		Interest payable (L+)		100
		To accrue interest expense.		

This is another example of a liability that was understated before the adjusting entry was made. After posting, Interest expense and Interest payable have the following balances:

EXPENSES		LIABILITIES	
Interest expense		**Interest payable**	
May 31	100	May 31	100
Bal	100	Bal	100

Accrued Revenues

As we have just seen, expenses can occur before a company makes a cash payment for them, which creates an accrued expense. Similarly, businesses can earn revenue before they receive the cash. This creates an **accrued revenue**, which is a revenue that has been earned but for which the cash has not yet been collected.

Assume that Smart Touch is hired on May 15 to perform e-learning services for the **University of West Florida**. Under this agreement, Smart Touch will earn $800 monthly. During May, Smart Touch will earn half a month's fee, $400, for work May 16 through May 31. On May 31, Smart Touch makes the following adjusting entry to accrue the revenue earned May 16 through May 31:

g.	May 31	Accounts receivable ($800 × 1/2) (A+)	400	
		Service revenue (R+)		400
		To accrue service revenue.		

The unadjusted trial balance in Exhibit 3-4 shows that Accounts receivable has an unadjusted balance of $2,200. Service revenue's unadjusted balance is $7,000 from the day-to-day May transactions recorded in the general journal. (Detailed entries for May transactions are not shown in the Accounts receivable or Service revenue T-accounts. Only adjusting entries are shown.) The adjusting entry updates both accounts.

ASSETS

Accounts receivable

	2,200	
May 31	400	
Bal	2,600	

REVENUES

Service revenue

		7,000
	May 31	400
	Bal	7,400

Without the adjustment, Smart Touch's financial statements would understate both an asset, Accounts receivable, and a revenue, Service revenue.

Now we turn to the final category of adjusting entries.

Unearned Revenues

Some businesses collect cash from customers in advance of performing work. Receiving cash before earning it creates a liability to perform work in the future called **unearned revenue.** The company owes a product or a service to the customer, or it owes the customer his or her money back. Only after completing the job will the business *earn* the revenue. Because of this delay, unearned revenue is also called **deferred revenue. Unearned revenue occurs when the company is paid cash before it does all the work to earn it.**

Suppose, for example, a law firm engages Smart Touch to provide e-learning services, agreeing to pay $600 in advance monthly, beginning immediately. Sheena Bright collects the first amount on May 21. Smart Touch records the cash receipt and a liability as follows:

May 21	Cash (A+)	600	
	Unearned service revenue (L+)		600
	Collected revenue in advance.		

Now the liability account, Unearned service revenue, shows that Smart Touch owes $600 in services.

LIABILITIES

Unearned service revenue

	May 21	600

Unearned service revenue is a liability because the company owes a service to a client in the future.

The May 31 trial balance (Exhibit 3-4) lists Unearned service revenue with a $600 credit balance. During the last 10 days of the month—May 21 through May 31—Smart Touch will *earn* approximately one-third (10 days divided by

Connect To: Ethics

Many unethical schemes that are enacted to artificially inflate earnings or change accounts on the balance sheet are accomplished through adjusting journal entries. Remember that every journal entry will have some document that substantiates why the entry is being made, such as an invoice that supports how many supplies were purchased or a contract with a customer that supports what services are to be provided. "Supporting documents" for unethical entries often don't exist or are modified copies of real documents.

30 days) of the $600, or $200. Therefore, Smart Touch makes the following adjusting entry to record earning $200 of revenue:

h.	May 31	Unearned service revenue ($600 × 1/3) (L–)	200	
		Service revenue (R+)		200
		To record service revenue that was collected in advance.		

This adjusting entry shifts $200 from liability to revenue. Service revenue increases by $200, and Unearned service revenue decreases by $200. Now both accounts are up-to-date at May 31:

LIABILITIES

Unearned service revenue

May 31	200	May 21	600
		Bal	400

REVENUES

Service revenue

		7,000
May 31	400	
May 31	200	
Bal	7,600	

This is an example of a liability that was overstated prior to posting the adjusting journal entry. Remember this key point:

> **An unearned revenue is a liability account, not a revenue account.**

An unearned revenue to one company is a prepaid expense to the company that paid in advance. Consider the law firm in the preceding example. The law firm had prepaid e-learning expense—an asset. Smart Touch had unearned service revenue—a liability.

Exhibit 3-6 summarizes the timing of prepaid and accrual adjustments. Study the exhibit from left to right, and then move down. Appendix 3A (available at myaccountinglab.com) shows an alternative treatment for unearned revenues.

EXHIBIT 3-6	Prepaid and Accrual Adjustments

ORIGINAL ENTRY | **ADJUSTING ENTRY**

PREPAIDS—Cash receipt or Cash payment occurs first.

Prepaid Expenses

Prepaid rent (A+)	XXX	
Cash (A−)		XXX
Pay for rent in advance and record an asset first.		

Rent expense (E+)	XXX	
Prepaid rent (A−)		XXX
Adjust for rent used later.		

Depreciation

Furniture (A+)	XXX	
Cash (A−)		XXX
Pay for furniture in advance and record an asset first.		

Depreciation expense—furniture (E+)	XXX	
Accumulated depreciation—furniture (CA+)		XXX
Adjust for depreciation (use) of asset later.		

Unearned Revenues

Cash (A+)	XXX	
Unearned service revenue (L+)		XXX
Receive cash in advance and reccord a liability first.		

Unearned service revenue (L−)	XXX	
Service revenue (R+)		XXX
Adjust for revenue earned later.		

ACCRUALS—Cash receipt or payment occurs later.

Accrued Expenses

Salary expense (E+)	XXX	
Salary payable (L+)		XXX
Accrue for expense incurred first.		

Salary payable (L−)	XXX	
Cash (A−)		XXX
Pay cash later.		

Accrued Revenues

Accounts receivable (A+)	XXX	
Service revenue (R+)		XXX
Accrue for revenue earned first.		

Cash (A+)	XXX	
Accounts receivable (A−)		XXX
Receive cash later.		

Source: The authors thank Darrel Davis and Alfonso Oddo for suggesting this exhibit.

Exhibit 3-7 on the following page summarizes the adjusting entries of Smart Touch at May 31. The adjustments are keyed by letter.

- Panel A gives the data for each adjustment.
- Panel B shows the adjusting entries.
- Panel C shows the account balances after posting.

Stop & Think...

Look at the eight adjusting entries in Exhibit 3-7 on the next page. Notice that only the last two adjusting entries, (g) and (h), increased revenues. Six of the eight adjusting entries increased expenses. So, when in doubt about an adjustment, most likely it will be an adjusting entry that increases (debits) an expense account. You can refer to the examples in the text and in the exhibit to confirm your adjusting entry.

EXHIBIT 3-7 | **Journalizing and Posting the Adjusting Entries of Smart Touch Learning, Inc.**

PANEL A—Information for Adjustments at May 31, 2013

a. Prepaid rent expired, $1,000.
b. Supplies used, $100.
c. Depreciation on furniture, $300.
d. Depreciation on building, $200.
e. Accrued salary expense, $900.

f. Accrued interest on note, $100.
g. Accrued service revenue, $400.
h. Service revenue that was collected in advance and now has been earned, $200.

PANEL B—Adjusting Entries

	2013	Accounts and Explanations	Debit	Credit
a.	May 31	Rent expense (E+)	1,000	
		Prepaid rent (A–)		1,000
		To record rent expense.		
b.	May 31	Supplies expense (E+)	100	
		Supplies (A–)		100
		To record supplies used.		
c.	May 31	Depreciation expense—furniture (E+)	300	
		Accumulated depreciation—furniture (CA+)		300
		To record depreciation on furniture.		
d.	May 31	Depreciation expense—building (E+)	200	
		Accumulated depreciation—building (CA+)		200
		To record depreciation on building.		
e.	May 31	Salary expense (E+)	900	
		Salary payable (L+)		900
		To accrue salary expense.		
f.	May 31	Interest expense (E+)	100	
		Interest payable (L+)		100
		To accrue interest expense.		
g.	May 31	Accounts receivable (A+)	400	
		Service revenue (R+)		400
		To accrue service revenue.		
h.	May 31	Unearned service revenue (L–)	200	
		Service revenue (R+)		200
		To record service revenue that was collected in advance.		

Handwritten annotations:
- Next to (e): "Act Receivable / Payable"
- Next to (h): "due a Service", "Deferral", "liability"

EXHIBIT 3-7 | **Continued**

PANEL C—Ledger Accounts in T-account form

ASSETS	LIABILITIES	OWNER'S EQUITY	EXPENSES

ASSETS

Cash

Bal	4,800		

Accounts receivable

	2,200		
(g)	400		
Bal	2,600		

Supplies

	700	(b)	100
Bal	600		

Prepaid rent

	3,000	(a)	1,000
Bal	2,000		

Furniture

Bal	18,000		

Building

Bal	48,000		

Accumulated depreciation— furniture

		(c)	300
		Bal	300

Accumulated depreciation— building

		(d)	200

LIABILITIES

Accounts payable

		Bal	18,200

Salary payable

		(e)	900
		Bal	900

Interest payable

		(f)	100
		Bal	100

Unearned service revenue

(h)	200		600
		Bal	400

Notes payable

		Bal	20,000

OWNER'S EQUITY

Bright, capital

		Bal	33,200

Bright, drawing

Bal	1,000		

REVENUE

Service revenue

			7,000
		(g)	400
		(h)	200
		Bal	7,600

EXPENSES

Rent expense

(a)	1,000		
Bal	1,000		

Salary expense

	900		
(e)	900		
Bal	1,800		

Supplies expense

(b)	100		
Bal	100		

Depreciation expense— furniture

(c)	300		
Bal	300		

Depreciation expense— building

(d)	200		
Bal	200		

Interest expense

(f)	100		
Bal	100		

Utilities expense

Bal	400		

The Adjusted Trial Balance

This chapter began with the *unadjusted* trial balance (Exhibit 3-4). After the adjustments, the accounts appear as shown in Exhibit 3-7, Panel C. A useful step in preparing the financial statements is to list the accounts, along with their adjusted balances, on an **adjusted trial balance**. Exhibit 3-8 shows how to prepare the adjusted trial balance.

 5 Explain the purpose of and prepare an adjusted trial balance

EXHIBIT 3-8 | **Preparation of Adjusted Trial Balance**

SMART TOUCH LEARNING
Preparation of Adjusted Trial Balance
May 31, 2013

	Trial Balance		Adjustments		Adjusted Trial Balance		
	Debit	Credit	Debit	Credit	Debit	Credit	
Cash	$ 4,800				$ 4,800		
Accounts receivable	2,200		(g) $ 400		2,600		
Supplies	700			(b) $ 100	600		
Prepaid rent	3,000			(a) 1,000	2,000		
Furniture	18,000				18,000		
Building	48,000				48,000		
Accumulated depreciation—furniture				(c) 300		$ 300	Balance Sheet
Accumulated depreciation—building				(d) 200		200	(Exhibit 3-11)
Accounts payable		$18,200				18,200	
Salary payable				(e) 900		900	
Interest payable				(f) 100		100	
Unearned service revenue		600	(h) 200			400	
Notes payable		20,000				20,000	
Bright, capital		33,200				33,200	Statement of Owner's Equity
Bright, drawing	1,000				1,000		(Exhibit 3-10)
Service revenue		7,000		(g) 400		7,600	
				(h) 200			
Rent expense			(a) 1,000		1,000		
Salary expense	900		(e) 900		1,800		Income Statement
Supplies expense			(b) 100		100		(Exhibit 3-9)
Depreciation expense—furniture			(c) 300		300		
Depreciation expense—building			(d) 200		200		
Interest expense			(f) 100		100		
Utilities expense	400				400		
	$79,000	$79,000	$3,200	$3,200	$80,900	$80,900	

Exhibit 3-8 is also a partial *worksheet*. We will cover the complete worksheet in Chapter 4. For now, simply note how clear this format is. The account titles and the trial balance are copied directly from the trial balance in Exhibit 3-4. The two Adjustments columns show the adjusting journal entries from Exhibit 3-7.

The Adjusted Trial Balance columns give the adjusted account balances. Each amount in these columns is computed by combining the trial balance amounts plus or minus the adjustments. For example, Accounts receivable starts with a debit balance of $2,200. Adding the $400 debit from adjustment (g) gives Accounts receivable an adjusted balance of $2,600. Supplies begins with a debit balance of $700. After the $100 credit adjustment, Supplies has a $600 balance. More than one entry may affect a single account. For example, Service revenue has two adjustments, (g) and (h), and both increased the Service revenue balance.

The Financial Statements

The May 2013 financial statements of Smart Touch are prepared from the adjusted trial balance in Exhibit 3-8. In the right margin of the exhibit, we see how the accounts are distributed to the financial statements. As always,

 Prepare the financial statements from the adjusted trial balance

- the income statement (Exhibit 3-9) reports revenues and expenses.
- the statement of owner's equity (Exhibit 3-10) shows why capital changed during the period.
- the balance sheet (Exhibit 3-11) reports assets, liabilities, and owner's equity.

Preparing the Statements

The financial statements should be prepared in the following order:

1. Income statement—to determine net income or net loss. The income statement should list expenses in descending order by amount, as shown in Exhibit 3-9.

2. Statement of owner's equity—which needs net income or net loss from the income statement for us to compute ending capital.

3. Balance sheet—which needs the amount of ending capital to achieve its balancing feature.

As you will recall from Chapter 1, all financial statements include the following elements:

Heading

- Name of the entity—such as Smart Touch Learning
- Title of the statement—income statement, statement of owner's equity, or balance sheet
- Date, or period, covered by the statement—May 31, 2013, or Month Ended May 31, 2013

Body of the statement

Relationships Among the Financial Statements

The arrows in Exhibits 3-9, 3-10, and 3-11 on the following page show how the financial statements relate to each other.

1. Net income from the income statement increases capital. A net loss decreases capital.

2. Ending capital from the statement of owner's equity goes to the balance sheet and makes total liabilities plus owner's equity equal total assets, satisfying the accounting equation.

    To solidify your understanding of these relationships, trace Net income from the income statement to the statement of owner's equity. Then trace ending Bright, capital to the balance sheet. Note that these are the three main financial statements you learned about in the first chapter. They are always prepared in the order described previously: income statement, then statement of owner's equity, then balance sheet. Recall that we purposely omitted the statement of cash flows, which is covered in detail in a later chapter.

Key Takeaway

The financial statements must be prepared in order: income statement first, statement of owner's equity second, and balance sheet third. It is important for accountants to prepare accurate and complete financial statements because other people rely on the data to make decisions.

EXHIBIT 3-9 | **Preparing the Income Statement from the Adjusted Trial Balance**

SMART TOUCH LEARNING
Income Statement
Month Ended May 31, 2013

Revenue:			
Service revenue			$7,600
Expenses:			
Salary expense		$1,800	
Rent expense		1,000	
Utilities expense		400	
Depreciation expense—furniture		300	
Depreciation expense—building		200	
Interest expense		100	
Supplies expense		100	
Total expenses			3,900
Net income			$3,700

EXHIBIT 3-10 | **Preparing the Statement of Owner's Equity from the Adjusted Trial Balance**

SMART TOUCH LEARNING
Statement of Owner's Equity
Month Ended May 31, 2013

Bright, capital, May 1, 2013	$33,200
Net income	3,700
	36,900
Drawing	(1,000)
Bright, capital, May 31, 2013	$35,900

EXHIBIT 3-11 | **Preparing the Balance Sheet from the Adjusted Trial Balance**

SMART TOUCH LEARNING
Balance Sheet
May 31, 2013

Assets			Liabilities	
Cash		$ 4,800	Accounts payable	$18,200
Accounts receivable		2,600	Salary payable	900
Supplies		600	Interest payable	100
Prepaid rent		2,000	Unearned service revenue	400
Furniture	$18,000		Notes payable	20,000
Less: Accumulated depreciation— furniture	300	17,700	Total liabilities	39,600
Building	48,000			
Less: Accumulated depreciation— building	200	47,800	**Owner's Equity** Bright, capital	35,900
			Total liabilities	
Total assets		$75,500	and owner's equity	$75,500

Ethical Issues in Accrual Accounting

Business transactions or events can pose ethical challenges. Accountants must be honest in their work. Complete and accurate information can help people make wise decisions. Think about the following example.

Smart Touch has done well as a business and wishes to open another office. Assume the company needs to borrow $30,000.

Suppose the e-learning agency understated expenses in order to inflate net income on the income statement. A banker could be tricked into lending the company money. Then if the business could not repay the loan, the bank would lose—all because the banker relied on incorrect accounting information.

Accrual accounting provides opportunities for unethical behavior. For example, a dishonest businessperson could easily overlook depreciation expense at the end of the year. Failing to record depreciation would overstate net income and paint a more favorable picture of the company's financial position.

Decision Guidelines 3-1

ACCOUNTING BASIS AND THE ADJUSTING PROCESS

Take the role of Sheena Bright of Smart Touch Learning. Assume it is now the end of the first year, and Bright wants to know where the business stands financially. The Decision Guidelines give a map of the accounting process to help Bright manage the business.

Decision	Guidelines
• Which basis of accounting better measures business income?	*Accrual basis*, because it provides more complete reports of operating performance and financial position
• How does a company measure revenues?	Revenue recognition principle—Record revenues only after they are earned
• How does a company measure expenses?	Matching principle—Record expenses in the same time period that the related revenues are recorded to more accurately measure net income (loss)
• Where does a company start with the measurement of income at the end of the period?	Preparation of the adjusted trial balance
• How does a company update the accounts for the financial statements?	*Adjusting entries* at the end of the period
• What are the categories of adjusting entries?	Prepaid expenses Accrued revenues Depreciation Unearned revenues Accrued expenses

• How do the adjusting entries differ from other journal entries?	1. Adjusting entries are made only at the end of the period.
	2. Adjusting entries never affect the Cash account.
	3. All adjusting entries debit or credit
	  • at least one *income statement* account (a revenue or an expense), and
	  • at least one *balance sheet* account (an asset or a liability).

• Where are the accounts with their adjusted balances summarized?	*Adjusted trial balance*, which is used to prepare the financial statements

Summary Problem 3-1

The trial balance of Super Employment Services pertains to December 31, 2014, the end of Super's annual accounting period. Data needed for the adjusting entries include the following:

　a. Supplies on hand at year-end, $200.
　b. Depreciation on furniture, $2,000.
　c. Depreciation on building, $1,000.
　d. Salaries owed but not yet paid, $500.
　e. Accrued service revenue, $1,300.
　f. $3,000 of the unearned service revenue has been earned.

Requirements

1. Open the ledger accounts in T-account form with their unadjusted balances as shown for Accounts receivable:

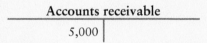

Accounts receivable	
5,000	

2. Journalize Super's adjusting entries at December 31, 2014. Key entries by letter, as in Exhibit 3-7.
3. Post the adjusting entries.
4. Write the trial balance on a worksheet, enter the adjusting entries, and prepare an adjusted trial balance, as shown in Exhibit 3-8.
5. Prepare the income statement, the statement of owner's equity, and the balance sheet. Draw arrows linking the three financial statements.

SUPER EMPLOYMENT SERVICES Trial Balance December 31, 2014		
	Balance	
Account Title	**Debit**	**Credit**
Cash	$ 6,000	
Accounts receivable	5,000	
Supplies	1,000	
Furniture	10,000	
Accumulated depreciation—furniture		$ 4,000
Building	50,000	
Accumulated depreciation—building		30,000
Accounts payable		2,000
Salary payable		
Unearned service revenue		8,000
Mudge, capital		12,000
Mudge, drawing	25,000	
Service revenue		60,000
Salary expense	16,000	
Supplies expense		
Depreciation expense—furniture		
Depreciation expense—building		
Advertising expense	3,000	
Total	$116,000	$116,000

Solution

Requirements 1 and 3

ASSETS

Cash

Bal	6,000

Accounts receivable

	5,000
(e)	1,300
Bal	6,300

Supplies

	1,000	(a)	800
Bal	200		

Furniture

Bal	10,000

Accumulated depreciation—furniture

			4,000
		(b)	2,000
		Bal	6,000

Building

Bal	50,000

Accumulated depreciation—building

			30,000
		(c)	1,000
		Bal	31,000

LIABILITIES

Accounts payable

		Bal	2,000

Salary payable

		(d)	500
		Bal	500

Unearned service revenue

(f)	3,000		8,000
		Bal	5,000

OWNER'S EQUITY

Mudge, capital

		Bal	12,000

Mudge, drawing

Bal	25,000

REVENUE

Service revenue

			60,000
		(e)	1,300
		(f)	3,000
		Bal	64,300

EXPENSES

Salary expense

		16,000
(d)		500
Bal		16,500

Supplies expense

(a)	800
Bal	800

Depreciation expense— furniture

(b)	2,000
Bal	2,000

Depreciation expense— building

(c)	1,000
Bal	1,000

Advertising expense

Bal	3,000

Requirement 2

	2014	Accounts and Explanations	Debit	Credit
a.	Dec 31	Supplies expense ($1,000 – $200) (E+)	800	
		Supplies (A–)		800
		To record supplies used.		
b.	Dec 31	Depreciation expense—furniture (E+)	2,000	
		Accumulated depreciation—furniture (CA+)		2,000
		To record depreciation expense on furniture.		
c.	Dec 31	Depreciation expense—building (E+)	1,000	
		Accumulated depreciation—building (CA+)		1,000
		To record depreciation expense on building.		
d.	Dec 31	Salary expense (E+)	500	
		Salary payable (L+)		500
		To accrue salary expense.		
e.	Dec 31	Accounts receivable (A+)	1,300	
		Service revenue (R+)		1,300
		To accrue service revenue.		
f.	Dec 31	Unearned service revenue (L–)	3,000	
		Service revenue (R+)		3,000
		To record service revenue earned that was collected in advance.		

Requirement 4

SUPER EMPLOYMENT SERVICES
Preparation of Adjusted Trial Balance
December 31, 2014

Account Title	Trial Balance Debit	Trial Balance Credit	Adjustments Debit	Adjustments Credit	Adjusted Trial Balance Debit	Adjusted Trial Balance Credit
Cash	$ 6,000				$ 6,000	
Accounts receivable	5,000		(e) $1,300		6,300	
Supplies	1,000			(a) $ 800	200	
Furniture	10,000				10,000	
Accumulated depreciation—furniture		$ 4,000		(b) 2,000		$ 6,000
Building	50,000				50,000	
Accumulated depreciation—building		30,000		(c) 1,000		31,000
Accounts payable		2,000				2,000
Salary payable				(d) 500		500
Unearned service revenue		8,000	(f) 3,000			5,000
Mudge, capital		12,000				12,000
Mudge, drawing	25,000				25,000	
Service revenue		60,000		(e) 1,300		
				(f) 3,000		64,300
Salary expense	16,000		(d) 500		16,500	
Supplies expense			(a) 800		800	
Depreciation expense—furniture			(b) 2,000		2,000	
Depreciation expense—building			(c) 1,000		1,000	
Advertising expense	3,000				3,000	
Total	$116,000	$116,000	$8,600	$8,600	$120,800	$120,800

Requirement 5

SUPER EMPLOYMENT SERVICES
Income Statement
Year Ended December 31, 2014

Revenue:		
Service revenue		$64,300
Expenses:		
Salary expense	$16,500	
Advertising expense	3,000	
Depreciation expense—furniture	2,000	
Depreciation expense—building	1,000	
Supplies expense	800	
Total expenses		23,300
Net income		$41,000

SUPER EMPLOYMENT SERVICES
Statement of Owner's Equity
Year Ended December 31, 2014

Mudge, capital, January 1, 2014	$ 12,000
Net income	41,000
	53,000
Drawing	(25,000)
Mudge, capital, December 31, 2014	$ 28,000

SUPER EMPLOYMENT SERVICES
Balance Sheet
December 31, 2014

Assets			Liabilities	
Cash		$ 6,000	Accounts payable	$ 2,000
Accounts receivable		6,300	Salary payable	500
Supplies		200	Unearned service revenue	5,000
Furniture	$10,000		Total liabilities	7,500
Less: Accumulated				
depreciation—				
furniture	6,000	4,000		
Building	50,000			
Less: Accumulated			**Owner's Equity**	
depreciation—			Mudge, capital	28,000
building	31,000	19,000	Total liabilities and	
Total assets		$35,500	owner's equity	$35,500

Chapter 3: Demo Doc

Preparation of Adjusting Entries, Adjusted Trial Balance, and Financial Statements

To make sure you understand this material, work through the following demonstration "demo doc" with detailed comments to help you see the concept within the framework of a worked-through problem.

Cloud Break Consulting has the following information at June 30, 2014:

CLOUD BREAK CONSULTING Unadjusted Trial Balance June 30, 2014		
Account Title	**Debit**	**Credit**
Cash	$131,000	
Accounts receivable	104,000	
Supplies	4,000	
Prepaid rent	27,000	
Land	45,000	
Building	300,000	
Accumulated depreciation—building		$155,000
Accounts payable		159,000
Unearned service revenue		40,000
Moe, capital		102,000
Moe, drawing	7,000	
Service revenue		450,000
Salary expense	255,000	
Rent expense	25,000	
Miscellaneous expense	8,000	
Total	$906,000	$906,000

Cloud Break must make adjusting entries for the following items:

a. Supplies on hand at year-end, $1,000.

b. Nine months of rent ($27,000) were paid in advance on April 1, 2014.

c. Depreciation expense on the building of $12,000 has not been recorded.

d. Employees work Monday through Friday. The weekly payroll is $5,000 and is paid every Friday. June 30, 2014, is a Monday.

e. Service revenue of $15,000 must be accrued.

f. Cloud Break received $40,000 in advance for consulting services to be provided evenly from January 1, 2014, through August 31, 2014. None of the revenue from this client has been recorded.

Requirements

1. Open the ledger T-accounts with their unadjusted balances.

2. Journalize Cloud Break's adjusting entries at June 30, 2014, and post the entries to the T-accounts.

3. Total all of the T-accounts in the ledger.

4. Write the trial balance on a worksheet, enter the adjusting entries, and prepare an adjusted trial balance.

5. Prepare the income statement, the statement of owner's equity, and the balance sheet. Draw arrows linking the three financial statements.

Chapter 3: Demo Doc Solution

Requirement 1

Open the ledger T-accounts with their unadjusted balances.

Part 1	Part 2	Part 3	Part 4	Part 5	Demo Doc Complete

Remember from Chapter 2 that opening a T-account means drawing a blank account that looks like a capital "T" and putting the account title across the top. To help find the accounts later, they are usually organized into assets, liabilities, owner's equity, revenue, and expenses (in that order). If the account has a starting balance, it *must* be put in on the correct side.

Remember that debits are always on the left side of the T-account and credits are always on the right side. This is true for *every* account.

The correct side to enter each account's starting balance is the side of *increase* in the account. This is because we expect all accounts to have a *positive* balance (that is, more increases than decreases).

For assets, an increase is a debit, so we would expect all assets to have a debit balance. For liabilities and owner's equity, an increase is a credit, so we would expect all of these accounts to have a credit balance. By the same reasoning, we expect revenues to have credit balances, and expenses and dividends to have debit balances.

The unadjusted balances to be posted into the T-accounts are simply the amounts from the starting trial balance.

ASSETS

Cash
Bal 131,000 |

Accounts receivable
Bal 104,000 |

Supplies
Bal 4,000 |

Prepaid rent
Bal 27,000 |

Land
Bal 45,000 |

Building
Bal 300,000 |

Accumulated depreciation—building
| Bal 155,000

LIABILITIES
Accounts payable
| Bal 159,000

Unearned service revenue
| Bal 40,000

OWNER'S EQUITY

Moe, capital
| Bal 102,000

Moe, drawing
Bal 7,000 |

REVENUE
Service revenue
| Bal 450,000

EXPENSES

Salary expense
Bal 255,000 |

Rent expense
Bal 25,000 |

Miscellaneous expense
Bal 8,000 |

Requirement 2

Journalize Cloud Break's adjusting entries at June 30, 2014, and post the entries to the T-accounts.

Part 1	**Part 2**	Part 3	Part 4	Part 5	Demo Doc Complete

a. **Supplies on hand at year-end, $1,000.**

On June 30, 2014, the unadjusted balance in supplies was $4,000. However, a count shows that only $1,000 of supplies actually remain on hand. The supplies that are no longer there have been used. When assets/benefits are used, an expense is created.

Cloud Break will need to make an adjusting journal entry to reflect the correct amount of supplies on the balance sheet.

Look at the Supplies T-account:

Supplies

Bal	4,000	X
Bal	1,000	

The supplies have decreased because they have been used up. The amount of the decrease is **X**.

$$X = \$4,000 - \$1,000$$
$$X = \$3,000$$

Three thousand dollars of Supplies expense must be recorded to show the value of supplies that have been used.

a.	Jun 30	Supplies expense ($4,000 – $1,000) (E+)	3,000	
		Supplies (A–)		3,000
		To record supplies used.		

After posting, Supplies and Supplies expense hold correct ending balances:

ASSETS

Supplies

Bal	4,000	a.	3,000
Bal	1,000		

EXPENSES

Supplies expense

a.	3,000	
Bal	3,000	

b. **Nine months of rent ($27,000) were paid in advance on April 1, 2014.**

When something is prepaid, such as rent or insurance, it is a *future* benefit (an asset) because the business is now entitled to receive goods or services for the terms of the prepayment. Once those goods or services are received (in this case, once Cloud Break has occupied the building being rented), this becomes a *past* benefit, and therefore an expense.

Cloud Break prepaid $27,000 for nine months of rent on April 1. This means that Cloud Break pays $27,000/9 = $3,000 a month for rent. At June 30, Prepaid rent is adjusted for the amount of the asset that has been used up. Because Cloud Break has occupied the building being rented for three months, three months of the prepayment have been used. The amount of rent used is 3 × $3,000 = $9,000. Because that portion of the past benefit (asset) has expired, it becomes an expense (in this case, the adjusting entry transfers $9,000 from Prepaid rent to Rent expense).

This means that Rent expense must be increased (a debit) and Prepaid rent (an asset) must be decreased (a credit).

b.	Jun 30	Rent expense (E+)		9,000	
		Prepaid rent (A–)			9,000
		To record rent expense.			

	ASSETS			**EXPENSES**	
	Prepaid rent			**Rent expense**	
Bal	27,000		Bal	25,000	
		b. 9,000	b.	9,000	
Bal	18,000		Bal	34,000	

c. **Depreciation expense on the building of $12,000 has not been recorded.**

The cost principle compels us to keep the original cost of a plant asset in that asset account. Because there is $300,000 in the Building account, we know that this is the original cost of the building. We are told in the question that depreciation expense per year is $12,000.

The journal entry to record depreciation expense is *always* the same. It is only the *number* (dollar amount) in the entry that changes. There is always an increase to Depreciation expense (a debit) and an increase to the contra-asset account of Accumulated depreciation (a credit).

c.	Jun 30	Depreciation expense—building (E+)		12,000	
		Accumulated depreciation—building (CA+)			12,000
		To record depreciation on building.			

	ASSETS				**EXPENSES**	
NORMAL ASSET		**CONTRA ASSET**				
Building		**Accumulated depreciation—building**			**Depreciation expense—building**	
Bal	300,000		Bal	155,000		
Bal	300,000		c.	12,000	c.	12,000
			Bal	167,000	Bal	12,000

The book value of the building is its original cost (the amount in the Building T-account) minus the accumulated depreciation on the building.

Book value of plant assets:	
Building	$ 300,000
Less: Accumulated depreciation	167,000
Book value of the building	$ 133,000

d. **Employees work Monday through Friday. The weekly payroll is $5,000 and is paid every Friday. June 30, 2014, is a Monday.**

Salary is an accrued expense. That is, it is a liability that incurs from an *expense* that has not been paid yet. Most employers pay their employees *after* the work has been done, so the work is a past benefit. So this expense (Salary expense, in this case) grows until payday.

Cloud Break's employees are paid $5,000 for five days of work. That means they earn $5,000/5 = $1,000 per day. By the end of the day on Monday, June 30, they have earned $1,000/day $\times$ 1 day = $1,000 of salary.

If the salaries have not been paid, then they are pay*able* (or in other words, they are *owed*) and must be recorded as some kind of payable account. You might be tempted to use accounts payable, but this account is usually reserved for *bills* received. But employees do not typically bill employers for their paychecks, they simply expect to be paid. The appropriate payable account for salaries is Salary payable.

There is an increase to the Salary expense (a debit) and an increase to the liability Salary payable (a credit) of $1,000.

d.	Jun 30	Salary expense (E+)	1,000	
		Salary payable (L+)		1,000
		To accrue salary expense.		

EXPENSES		**LIABILITIES**	
Salary expense		**Salary payable**	
Bal	255,000		d.	1,000
d.	1,000			
Bal	256,000		Bal	1,000

e. **Service revenue of $15,000 must be accrued.**

Accrued revenue is another way of saying "Accounts receivable" (or receipt in the future). When *accrued* revenue is recorded, it means that Accounts receivable is also recorded (that is, customers received goods or services from the business, but the business has not yet received the cash). The business is entitled to these receivables because the revenue has been earned.

Service revenue must be increased by $15,000 (a credit) and the Accounts receivable asset must be increased by $15,000 (a debit).

e.	Jun 30	Accounts receivable (A+)	15,000	
		Service revenue (R+)		15,000
		To accrue service revenue.		

ASSETS		**REVENUES**	
Accounts receivable		**Service revenue**	
	104,000			450,000
e.	15,000		e.	15,000
Bal	119,000		Bal	465,000

f. **Cloud Break received $40,000 in advance for consulting services to be provided evenly from January 1, 2014, through August 31, 2014. None of the revenue from this client has been recorded.**

Cloud Break received cash in advance for work it had not yet performed for the client. By accepting the cash, Cloud Break also accepted the obligation to perform that work (or provide a refund if it did not). In accounting, an obligation is a liability. We call this liability "Unearned revenue" because it *will* be revenue (after the work is performed) but it is not revenue *yet*.

The $40,000 paid in advance is still in the unearned revenue account. However, some of the revenue has been earned as of June 30. Six months of the earnings period have passed (January 1 through June 30), so six months worth of the revenue has been earned.

The entire revenue earnings period is eight months (January 1 through August 31), so the revenue earned per month is $40,000/8 = $5,000. The six months of revenue that have been earned are 6 × $5,000 = $30,000.

So Unearned service revenue, a liability, must be decreased by $30,000 (a debit). Because that portion of the revenue is now earned, it can be recorded as Service revenue. Therefore, Service revenue is increased by $30,000 (a credit).

f.	Jun 30	Unearned service revenue (L–)	30,000	
		Service revenue (R+)		30,000
		To record the earning of service revenue collected in advance.		

The $30,000 has been shifted from "unearned revenue" to "earned" revenue.

LIABILITIES			REVENUES		
Unearned service revenue			Service revenue		
f.	30,000	Bal 40,000		Bal	450,000
				e.	15,000
		Bal 10,000		f.	30,000
				Bal	495,000

Now we will summarize all of the adjusting journal entries:

Ref.	Date	Accounts and Explanation	Debit	Credit
	2014			
a.	Jun 30	Supplies expense ($4,000 – $1,000) (E+)	3,000	
		Supplies (A–)		3,000
		To record supplies used.		
b.	30	Rent expense (E+)	9,000	
		Prepaid rent (A–)		9,000
		To record rent expense.		
c.	30	Depreciation expense—building (E+)	12,000	
		Accumulated depreciation—building (CA+)		12,000
		To record depreciation on building.		
d.	30	Salary expense (E+)	1,000	
		Salary payable (L+)		1,000
		To accrue salary expense.		
e.	30	Accounts receivable (A+)	15,000	
		Service revenue (R+)		15,000
		To accrue service revenue.		
f.	30	Unearned service revenue (L–)	30,000	
		Service revenue (R+)		30,000
		To record the earning of service revenue collected in advance.		

Requirement 3

Total all of the T-accounts in the ledger.

Part 1	Part 2	**Part 3**	Part 4	Part 5	Demo Doc Complete

After posting all of these entries and totaling all of the T-accounts, we have the following:

ASSETS

Cash

Bal 131,000	

Accounts receivable

Bal 104,000	
e. 15,000	
Bal 119,000	

Supplies

Bal 4,000	a. 3,000
Bal 1,000	

Prepaid rent

Bal 27,000	
	b. 9,000
Bal 18,000	

Land

Bal 45,000	

Building

Bal 300,000	

Accumulated depreciation—building

	155,000
c.	12,000
	Bal 167,000

LIABILITIES

Accounts payable

	Bal 159,000

Salary payable

	d. 1,000
	Bal 1,000

Unearned service revenue

f. 30,000	40,000
	Bal 10,000

OWNER'S EQUITY

Moe, capital

	Bal 102,000

Moe, drawing

Bal 7,000	

REVENUE

Service revenue

	450,000
e.	15,000
f.	30,000
	Bal 495,000

EXPENSES

Salary expense

255,000	
d. 1,000	
Bal 256,000	

Supplies expense

a. 3,000	
Bal 3,000	

Rent expense

25,000	
b. 9,000	
Bal 34,000	

Depreciation expense—building

c. 12,000	
Bal 12,000	

Miscellaneous expense

Bal 8,000	

Requirement 4

Write the trial balance on a worksheet, enter the adjusting entries, and prepare an adjusted trial balance.

Part 1	Part 2	Part 3	**Part 4**	Part 5	Demo Doc Complete

First, we must copy the account titles and trial balance amounts directly from the trial balance (shown at the beginning of the question) into the Trial Balance section (columns). Place the amounts in the correct debit or credit column.

Next, we must record the adjusting journal entries in the correct debit or credit columns of the Adjustments section (columns) of the worksheet. Each entry should include a letter identifying the adjusting entry recorded.

Now calculate the new balances for each account by adding the debits and credits across. These should be the same balances that you calculated for the T-accounts in Requirement 3. Place these amounts into the Adjusted Trial Balance columns to give the adjusted account balances.

	CLOUD BREAK CONSULTING Preparation of Adjusted Trial Balance June 30, 2014						
	Trial Balance		Adjustments		Adjusted Trial Balance	
Account Title	Debit	Credit	Debit	Credit	Debit	Credit
Cash	$131,000				$131,000	
Accounts receivable	104,000		(e) $15,000		119,000	
Supplies	4,000			(a) $ 3,000	1,000	
Prepaid rent	27,000			(b) 9,000	18,000	
Land	45,000				45,000	
Building	300,000				300,000	
Accumulated depreciation—building		$155,000		(c) 12,000		$167,000
Accounts payable		159,000				159,000
Salary payable				(d) 1,000		1,000
Unearned service revenue		40,000	(f) 30,000			10,000
Moe, capital		102,000				102,000
Moe, drawing	7,000				7,000	
Service revenue		450,000		(e) 15,000		
				(f) 30,000		495,000
Salary expense	255,000		(d) 1,000		256,000	
Supplies expense			(a) 3,000		3,000	
Rent expense	25,000		(b) 9,000		34,000	
Depreciation expense—building			(c) 12,000		12,000	
Miscellaneous expense	8,000				8,000	
Totals	$906,000	$906,000	$70,000	$70,000	$934,000	$934,000

Be sure that the debit and credit columns equal before moving on to the next section.

Requirement 5

Prepare the income statement, the statement of owner's equity, and the balance sheet. Draw arrows linking the three financial statements.

Part 1	Part 2	Part 3	Part 4	**Part 5**	Demo Doc Complete

The arrows in these statements show how the financial statements relate to each other. Follow the arrow that takes the ending balance of Moe, capital to the balance sheet.

1. Net income from the income statements is reported as an increase to Moe, capital on the statement of owner's equity. A net loss is recorded as a decrease to Moe, capital.

2. Ending Moe, capital from the statement of owner's equity is transferred to the balance sheet. The ending Moe, capital is the final balancing amount for the balance sheet.

CLOUD BREAK CONSULTING
Income Statement
Year Ended June 30, 2014

Revenue:			
	Service revenue		$495,000
Expenses:			
	Salary expense	$256,000	
	Rent expense	34,000	
	Depreciation expense—building	12,000	
	Supplies expense	3,000	
	Miscellaneous expense*	8,000	
	Total expenses		313,000
Net income			$182,000

*Miscellaneous expense is always listed last, even if it is larger than other expenses.

CLOUD BREAK CONSULTING
Statement of Owner's Equity
Year Ended June 30, 2014

Moe, capital, July 1, 2013	$102,000
Net income	182,000
	284,000
Drawing	(7,000)
Moe, capital, June 30, 2014	$277,000

CLOUD BREAK CONSULTING
Balance Sheet
June 30, 2014

Assets			Liabilities	
Cash		$131,000	Accounts payable	$159,000
Accounts receivable		119,000	Salary payable	1,000
Supplies		1,000	Unearned service revenue	10,000
Prepaid rent		18,000	Total liabilities	$170,000
Land		45,000		
Building	$300,000			
Less: Accumulated			**Owner's Equity**	
depreciation	167,000	133,000	Moe, capital	277,000
			Total liabilities and	
Total assets		$447,000	owner's equity	$447,000

Part 1	Part 2	Part 3	Part 4	Part 5	**Demo Doc Complete**

Review *The Adjusting Process*

● Accounting Vocabulary

Accrual (p. 136)
The cash payment occurs after an expense is recorded or the cash is received after the revenue is earned.

Accrual-Basis Accounting (p. 131)
Accounting that records revenues when earned and expenses when incurred.

Accrued Expense (p. 140)
An expense that the business has incurred but not yet paid.

Accrued Revenue (p. 142)
A revenue that has been earned but for which the cash has not been collected yet.

Accumulated Depreciation (p. 139)
The sum of all depreciation expense recorded to date for an asset.

Adjusted Trial Balance (p. 147)
A list of all the accounts with their adjusted balances.

Adjusting Entries (p. 135)
Entries made at the end of the period to assign revenues to the period in which they are earned and expenses to the period in which they are incurred. Adjusting entries help measure the period's income and bring the related asset and liability accounts to correct balances for the financial statements.

Book Value (of a plant asset) (p. 140)
The asset's cost minus accumulated depreciation.

Cash-Basis Accounting (p. 131)
Accounting that records transactions only when cash is received or paid.

Contra Account (p. 139)
An account that always has a companion account and whose normal balance is opposite that of the companion account.

Deferral (p. 136)
The cash payment occurs before an expense is recorded or the cash is received before the revenue is earned. Also called a **prepaid**.

Deferred Revenue (p. 143)
A liability created when a business collects cash from customers in advance of doing work. Also called **unearned revenue**.

Depreciation (p. 138)
The allocation of a plant asset's cost over its useful life.

Liquidation (p. 132)
The process of going out of business by selling all the assets, paying all the liabilities, and giving any leftover cash to the owner(s).

Matching Principle (p. 134)
Guide to accounting for expenses. Identify all expenses incurred during the period, measure the expenses, and match them against the revenues earned during that same time period.

Plant Assets (p. 138)
Long-lived tangible assets—such as land, buildings, and equipment—used in the operation of a business.

Prepaid (p. 136)
The cash payment occurs before an expense is recorded or the cash is received before the revenue is earned. Also called a **deferral**.

Revenue Recognition Principle (p. 133)
The basis for recording revenues: tells accountants when to record revenue and the amount of revenue to record.

Time-Period Concept (p. 134)
Ensures that information is reported at least annually.

Unearned Revenue (p. 143)
A liability created when a business collects cash from customers in advance of doing work. Also called **deferred revenue**.

● Destination: Student Success

Student Success Tips

The following are hints on some common trouble areas for students in this chapter:

- Recall the difference between accrual accounting and cash-basis accounting: Accrual accounting records revenues and expenses when they are EARNED or INCURRED. Cash-basis accounting records revenues and expenses when cash is RECEIVED or PAID.

- Remember that debits = credits for every adjusting journal entry.

- The amount of the adjusting journal entry will ALWAYS affect either a revenue account (credit) or an expense account (debit). The adjustment amount in the adjusting journal entry will equal the additional EARNINGS for a revenue account or the additional INCURRENCE of EXPENSE for an expense account.

- Adjusting entries NEVER affect the Cash account.

- Trial balance amount +/– the Adjustment amount = the Adjusted trial balance amount. Use the rules of debit/credit to determine whether the adjustment is a + or –.

Getting Help

If there's a learning objective from the chapter you aren't confident about, try using one or more of the following resources:

- Practice additional exercises or problems at the end of Chapter 3 that cover the specific learning objective that is challenging you.

- Watch the white board videos for Chapter 3 located at myaccountinglab.com under the Chapter Resources button.

- Review the Chapter 3 Demo Doc located on page 157 of the textbook.

- Go to myaccountinglab.com and select the Study Plan button. Choose Chapter 3 and work the questions covering that specific learning objective until you've mastered it.

- Work the Chapter 3 pre/post tests in myaccountinglab.com.

- Visit the learning resource center on your campus for tutoring.

● Quick Check

1. What are the distinctive features of accrual accounting and cash-basis accounting?
   a. Accrual accounting records only receivables, payables, and depreciation.
   b. Accrual accounting is superior because it provides more information.
   c. Cash-basis accounting records all transactions.
   d. All the above are true.

2. The revenue recognition principle says
   a. divide time into annual periods to measure revenue properly.
   b. record revenue only after you have earned it.
   c. measure revenues and expenses in order to compute net income.
   d. record revenue after you receive cash.

3. Adjusting the accounts is the process of
   a. subtracting expenses from revenues to measure net income.
   b. recording transactions as they occur during the period.
   c. updating the accounts at the end of the period.
   d. zeroing out account balances to prepare for the next period.

4. Which types of adjusting entries are natural opposites?
   a. Net income and net loss
   b. Expenses and revenues
   c. Prepaids and accruals
   d. Prepaids and depreciation

5. Assume that the weekly payroll of In the Woods Camping Supplies is $300. December 31, end of the year, falls on Tuesday, and In the Woods will pay its employee on Friday for the full week. What adjusting entry will In the Woods make on Tuesday, December 31? (Use five days as a full work week.)

   a.
Salary expense	120	
Salary payable		120

   b.
Salary payable	300	
Salary expense		300

   c.
Salary expense	180	
Cash		180

   d. No adjustment is needed because the company will pay the payroll on Friday.

6. Get Fit Now gains a client who prepays $540 for a package of six physical training sessions. Get Fit Now collects the $540 in advance and will provide the training later. After four training sessions, what should Get Fit Now report on its income statement?
   a. Service revenue of $360
   b. Service revenue of $540
   c. Unearned service revenue of $360
   d. Cash of $180

7. Assume you prepay Get Fit Now for a package of six physical training sessions. Which type of account should you have in your records?
   a. Accrued revenue
   b. Accrued expense
   c. Prepaid expense
   d. Unearned revenue

8. Unearned revenue is always
   a. owner's equity because you collected the cash in advance.
   b. revenue.
   c. a liability.
   d. an asset.

Experience the Power of Practice!

As denoted by the logo, all of these questions, as well as additional practice materials, can be found in

MyAccountingLab.

Please visit myaccountinglab.com

9. The adjusted trial balance shows
   a. amounts that may be out of balance.
   b. amounts ready for the financial statements.
   c. assets, liabilities, and owner's equity only.
   d. revenues and expenses only.

10. Accounting data flow from the
    a. income statement to the statement of owner's equity.
    b. statement of owner's equity to the balance sheet.
    c. balance sheet to the income statement.
    d. Both a and b are correct.

Answers are given after Apply Your Knowledge (p. 197).

Assess Your Progress

● Short Exercises

MyAccountingLab **S3-1** ❶ **Comparing accrual and cash-basis accounting [5 min]**
Suppose you work summers house-sitting for people while they are away on vacation. Some of your customers pay you immediately after you finish a job. Some customers ask you to send them a bill. It is now June 30 and you have collected $900 from cash-paying customers. Your remaining customers owe you $1,300.

Requirements

1. How much service revenue would you have under the
   a. cash basis?
   b. accrual basis?

2. Which method of accounting provides more information about your house-sitting business?

S3-2 ❶ **Comparing accrual and cash-basis accounting [5 min]**
The Johnny Flowers Law Firm uses a client database. Suppose Johnny Flowers paid $2,900 for a computer.

Requirements

1. Describe how the business should account for the $2,900 expenditure under
   a. the cash basis.
   b. the accrual basis.

2. State why the accrual basis is more realistic for this situation.

S3-3 ❷ **Applying the revenue recognition principle [5 min]**
Northwest Magazine sells subscriptions for $36 for 12 issues. The company collects cash in advance and then mails out the magazines to subscribers each month.

Requirement

1. Apply the revenue recognition principle to determine
   a. when *Northwest Magazine* should record revenue for this situation.
   b. the amount of revenue *Northwest Magazine* should record for three issues.

S3-4 ❷ **Applying the matching principle [5 min]**
Suppose on January 1 you prepaid apartment rent of $5,700 for the full year.

Requirement

1. At July 31, what are your two account balances for this situation?

S3-5   ❸ **Identifying types of adjusting entries [5 min]**
A select list of transactions for Anuradha's Goals follows:

Apr	1	Paid six months of rent, $4,800.
	10	Received $1,200 from customer for six-month service contract that began April 1.
	15	Purchased computer for $1,000.
	18	Purchased $300 of office supplies on account.
	30	Work performed but not yet billed to customer, $500.
	30	Employees earned $600 in salary that will be paid May 2.

Requirement

1. For each transaction, identify what type of adjusting entry would be needed.

S3-6   ❹ **Journalizing adjusting entries [5 min]**
On April 1 your company prepaid six months of rent, $4,800.

Requirements

1. Prepare the journal entry for the April 1 payment.
2. Prepare the adjusting entry required at April 30.
3. Post to the two accounts involved and show their balances at April 30.

S3-7   ❹ **Posting adjusting entries [5 min]**
On May 1 your company paid cash of $54,000 for computers that are expected to remain useful for three years. At the end of three years, the value of the computers is expected to be zero, so depreciation is $18,000 per year.

Requirements

1. Post the purchase of May 1 and the depreciation on May 31 to T-accounts for the following accounts: Computer equipment, Accumulated depreciation—computer equipment, and Depreciation expense—computer equipment. Show their balances at May 31. (Assume that the journal entries have been completed.)
2. What is the computer equipment's book value on May 31?

S3-8   ❹ **Accruing interest expense and posting to T-accounts [10 min]**
Thompson Travel borrowed $68,000 on October 1, 2012, by signing a one-year note payable to Metro One Bank. Thompson's interest expense for the remainder of the fiscal year (October through December) is $884.

Requirements

1. Make the adjusting entry to accrue interest expense at December 31, 2012. Date the entry and include its explanation.
2. Post to the T-accounts of the two accounts affected by the adjustment.

S3-9   ❹ **Accounting for unearned revenues [5–10 min]**
Metro Magazine collects cash from subscribers in advance and then mails the magazines to subscribers over a one-year period.

Requirements

1. Journalize the entry to record the original receipt of $170,000 cash.
2. Journalize the adjusting entry that *Metro Magazine* makes to record the earning of $12,000 of subscription revenue that was collected in advance. Include an explanation for the entry.

S3-10 ⑤ **Preparing an adjusted trial balance [10 min]**

Famous Cut Hair Stylists has begun the preparation of its adjusted trial balance as follows:

	Trial Balance		Adjustments		Adjusted Trial Balance	
FAMOUS CUT HAIR STYLISTS Preparation of Adjusted Trial Balance December 31, 2012						
Account	Debit	Credit	Debit	Credit	Debit	Credit
Cash	$ 800					
Supplies	900					
Equipment	19,100					
Accumulated depreciation		$ 1,000				
Accounts payable		200				
Interest payable						
Note payable		2,500				
Fabio, capital		7,400				
Service revenue		14,800				
Rent expense	4,500					
Supplies expense						
Depreciation expense						
Interest expense	600					
Total	$25,900	$25,900				

Year-end data include the following:

    a. Supplies on hand, $300.
    b. Depreciation, $1,000.
    c. Accrued interest expense, $600.

Requirement

    1. Complete Famous Cut's adjusted trial balance. Key each adjustment by letter.

Note: Short Exercises 3-11 and 3-12 should be used only after completing Short Exercise 3-10.

S3-11 ⑥ **Preparing an income statement [10–15 min]**

Refer to the data in Short Exercise 3-10.

Requirement

    1. Compute Famous Cut's net income for the year ended December 31, 2012.

S3-12 ⑥ **Preparing a balance sheet [5 min]**

Refer to the data in Short Exercise 3-10.

Requirement

    1. Compute Famous Cut's total assets at December 31, 2012.

● Exercises

E3-13 **①②** **Comparing accrual and cash-basis accounting, and applying the revenue recognition principle [5–10 min]**

MyAccountingLab

Momentous Occasions is a photography business that shoots videos at college parties. The freshman class pays $100 in advance on March 3 just to guarantee your services for its party to be held April 2. The sophomore class promises a minimum of $280 for filming its formal dance, and actually pays cash of $410 on February 28 at the party.

Requirement

1. Answer the following questions about the correct way to account for revenue under the accrual basis.
   a. Considering the $100 paid by the freshman class, on what date was revenue earned? Did the earnings occur on the same date cash was received?
   b. Considering the $410 paid by the sophomore class, on what date was revenue earned? Did the earnings occur on the same date cash was received?

E3-14 **①④⑥** **Comparing accrual and cash-basis accounting, preparing adjusting entries, and preparing income statements [15-25 min]**

Sweet Catering completed the following selected transactions during May, 2012:

May	1	Prepaid rent for three months, $1,500.
	5	Paid electricity expenses, $400.
	9	Received cash for meals served to customers, $2,600.
	14	Paid cash for kitchen equipment, $2,400.
	23	Served a banquet on account, $3,000.
	31	Made the adjusting entry for rent (from May 1).
	31	Accrued salary expense, $1,400.
	31	Recorded depreciation for May on kitchen equipment, $40.

Requirements

1. Prepare journal entries for each transaction.
2. Using the journal entries as a guide, show whether each transaction would be handled as a revenue or an expense using both the cash and accrual basis by completing the following table.

	Amount of Revenue (Expense) for May	
Date	Cash-Basis Amount of Revenue (Expense)	Accrual-Basis Amount of Revenue (Expense)

3. After completing the table, calculate the amount of net income or net loss for Sweet Catering under the accrual and cash basis for May.
4. Considering your results from Requirement 3, which method gives the best picture of the true earnings of Sweet Catering? Why?

E3-15 **②** **Applying the time-period concept [5–10 min]**

Consider the following situations:

a. Business receives $2,000 on January 1 for 10-month service contract for the period January 1 through October 31.
b. Total salary for all employees is $3,000 per month. Employees are paid on the 1st and 15th of the month.
c. Work performed but not yet billed to customers for the month is $900.
d. The company pays interest on its $10,000, 6% note payable of $50 on the first day of each month.

Requirement

1. Assume the company records adjusting entries monthly. Calculate the amount of each adjustment needed, if any, as of February 28.

E3-16 ❷ ❹ **Applying accounting principles and preparing journal entries for prepaid rent [10–15 min]**

Consider the facts presented in the following table for Tropical View:

	Situation			
	A	B	C	D
Beginning Prepaid rent	$ 1,200	$ 900	$ 200	$ 700
Payments for Prepaid rent				
during the year...	1,400	b	1,800	d
Total amount to account for	2,600	1,400	2,000 ?	?
Subtract: Ending Prepaid rent.......................	600	500	c	400
Rent expense	$ a	$ 900	$1,900	$1,100

Requirements

1. Complete the table by filling in the missing values.

2. Prepare one journal entry for each situation, if required, for the missing amounts (a–d). Label the journal entries by letter.

E3-17 ❸ ❹ **Categorizing and journalizing adjusting entries [10–15 min]**

Consider the following independent situations at December 31, 2014.

a. On August 1, a business collected $3,300 rent in advance, debiting Cash and crediting Unearned rent revenue. The tenant was paying one year's rent in advance. At December 31, the business must account for the amount of rent it has earned.

b. Salary expense is $1,700 per day—Monday through Friday—and the business pays employees each Friday. This year December 31 falls on a Thursday.

c. The unadjusted balance of the Supplies account is $3,500. Supplies on hand total $1,700.

d. Equipment depreciation was $300.

e. On March 1, when the business prepaid $600 for a two-year insurance policy, the business debited Prepaid insurance and credited Cash.

Requirements

1. For each situation, indicate which category of adjustment is described.

2. Journalize the adjusting entry needed on December 31 for each situation. Use the letters to label the journal entries.

E3-18 ❹ **Recording adjustments in T-accounts and calculating ending balances [10–20 min]**

The accounting records of Maura Grayson Architect include the following selected, unadjusted balances at March 31: Accounts receivable, $1,400; Supplies, $1,100; Salary payable, $0; Unearned service revenue, $600; Service revenue, $4,200; Salary expense, $1,300; Supplies expense, $0. The data developed for the March 31 adjusting entries are as follows:

a. Service revenue accrued, $900.

b. Unearned service revenue that has been earned, $200.

c. Supplies on hand, $600.

d. Salary owed to employee, $400.

Requirement

1. Open a T-account for each account and record the adjustments directly in the T-accounts, keying each adjustment by letter. Show each account's adjusted balance. Journal entries are not required.

E3-19 ④⑤ **Preparing adjusting entries and preparing an adjusted trial balance [10–15 min]**

First Class Maids Company, the cleaning service, started the preparation of its adjusted trial balance as follows:

		FIRST CLASS MAIDS COMPANY	
		Preparation of Adjusted Trial Balance	
		December 31, 2012	

Account	Trial Balance Debit	Trial Balance Credit
Cash	$ 700	
Supplies	3,000	
Prepaid insurance	800	
Equipment	29,000	
Accumulated depreciation		$ 7,000
Accounts payable		2,800
Salary payable		
Unearned service revenue		500
Molly, capital		7,200
Molly, drawing	3,000	
Service revenue		25,000
Salary expense	6,000	
Supplies expense		
Depreciation expense		
Insurance expense		
Total	$42,500	$42,500

During the 12 months ended December 31, 2012, First Class Maids

    a. used supplies of $1,800.
    b. used up prepaid insurance of $620.
    c. used up $460 of the equipment through depreciation.
    d. accrued salary expense of $310 that First Class Maids hasn't paid yet.
    e. earned $360 of the unearned service revenue.

Requirement

    1. Prepare an adjusted trial balance. Use Exhibit 3-8 as a guide. Key each adjustment by letter.

Note: Exercise 3-20 should be used only in conjunction with Exercise 3-19.

 E3-20 ④⑤ **Using an adjusted trial balance to prepare adjusting journal entries [10 min]**

Refer to the data in Exercise 3-19.

Requirement

    1. Journalize the five adjustments, all dated December 31, 2012. Explanations are not required.

E3-21   **4 5** Using the adjusted trial balance to determine the adjusting journal entries [10–15 min]

The adjusted trial balance of Jobs–4–U Employment Service follows but is incomplete.

	Trial Balance		Adjusted Trial Balance	
Account	Debit	Credit	Debit	Credit
Cash	$ 900		$ 900	
Accounts receivable	4,100		5,600	
Supplies	1,000		500	
Equipment	32,500		32,500	
Accumulated depreciation		$14,400		$15,400
Salary payable				1,200
Yost, capital		23,300		23,300
Yost, drawing	4,800		4,800	
Service revenue		9,100		10,600
Salary expense	2,500		3,700	
Rent expense	1,000		1,000	
Depreciation expense			1,000	
Supplies expense			500	
Total	$46,800	$46,800	$50,500	$50,500

JOBS–4–U EMPLOYMENT SERVICE
Adjusted Trial Balance
April 30, 2012

Requirements

1. Calculate and enter the adjustment amounts directly in the missing Adjustments columns.
2. Prepare each adjusting journal entry calculated in Requirement 1. Date the entries and include explanations.

E3-22   **4 6** Journalizing adjusting entries and analyzing their effect on the income statement [5–10 min]

The following data at January 31, 2013 is given for EBM.

a. Depreciation, $500.
b. Prepaid rent expired, $600.
c. Interest expense accrued, $300.
d. Employee salaries owed for Monday through Thursday of a five-day workweek; weekly payroll, $13,000.
e. Unearned service revenue earned, $1,300.

Requirements

1. Journalize the adjusting entries needed on January 31, 2013.
2. Suppose the adjustments made in Requirement 1 were not made. Compute the overall overstatement or understatement of net income as a result of the omission of these adjustments.

E3-23 **4** **6** **Using adjusting journal entries and computing financial statement amounts [10–20 min]**

The adjusted trial balances of Superior International at August 31, 2012, and August 31, 2011, include the following amounts:

	2012	2011
Supplies	$ 2,400	$ 1,200
Salary payable	2,500	4,100
Unearned service revenue	12,100	17,100

Analysis of the accounts at August 31, 2012, reveals the following transactions for the fiscal year ending in 2012:

Cash payments for supplies	$ 6,100
Cash payments for salaries	47,300
Cash receipts in advance for service revenue	83,200

Requirement

1. Compute the amount of Supplies expense, Salary expense, and Service revenue to report on the Superior International income statement for 2012.

Note: Exercise 3-24 should be used only in conjunction with Exercise 3-19.

E3-24 **5** **6** **Using an adjusted trial balance to prepare financial statements [10 min]**

Refer to the data in Exercise 3-19.

Requirements

1. Compute First Class Maids Company's net income for the period ended December 31, 2012.
2. Compute First Class Maids Company's total assets at December 31, 2012.

Note: Exercise 3-25 should be used only after completing Exercise 3-21.

E3-25 **6** **Preparing the financial statements [20 min]**

Refer to the adjusted trial balance in Exercise 3-21 for the month ended April 30, 2012.

Requirements

1. Prepare the income statement.
2. Prepare the statement of owner's equity.
3. Prepare the balance sheet.

E3-26   ⑥ **Preparing the income statement [15 min]**

The accountant for Reva Stewart, CPA, has posted adjusting entries (a) through (e) to the accounts at December 31, 2012. Selected balance sheet accounts and all the revenues and expenses of the entity follow in T-account form.

Accounts receivable				Supplies		
	22,700			1,200	(a)	600
(e)	800					

Acc. depr.—equipment				Acc. depr.—building		
			5,000			30,000
		(b)	1,900		(c)	5,000

Salary payable				Service revenue		
		(d)	900			105,700
					(e)	800

Salary expense				Supplies expense		
	28,200			(a)	600	
(d)	900					

Depreciation expense—equip.			Depreciation expense—bldg.		
(b)	1,900		(c)	5,000	

Requirements

1. Prepare the income statement of Reva Stewart, CPA, for the year ended December 31, 2012.
2. Were 2012 operations successful?

E3-27   ⑥ **Preparing the statement of owner's equity [10-15 min]**

Rolling Hill Interiors began the year with Hill, capital of $20,000. On July 12, Dana Hill, the owner, invested $14,000 cash. The income statement for the year ended December 31, 2012, reported net income of $63,000. During this fiscal year, Hill withdrew cash of $6,000 each month.

Requirement

1. Prepare Rolling Hill Interiors' statement of owner's equity for the year ended December 31, 2012.

● Problems (Group A)

P3-28A ❶ **Comparing accrual and cash-basis accounting [15–25 min]**

Schaad's Stews completed the following transactions during June, 2012:

Jun	1	Prepaid rent for June through September, $3,600.
	2	Purchased computer for cash, $900.
	3	Performed catering services on account, $2,300.
	5	Paid Internet service provider invoice, $100.
	6	Catered wedding event for customer and received cash, $1,500.
	8	Purchased $150 of supplies on account.
	10	Collected $1,200 on account.
	14	Paid account payable from June 8.
	15	Paid salary expense, $1,200.
	30	Recorded adjusting entry for rent (see June 1).
	30	Recorded $25 depreciation on computer.
	30	There are $40 of supplies still on hand.

Requirement

1. Show whether each transaction would be handled as a revenue or an expense, using both the cash and accrual basis, by completing the following table.

	Amount of Revenue (Expense) for June	
Date	Cash-Basis Amount of Revenue (Expense)	Accrual-Basis Amount of Revenue (Expense)
Jun 1		

P3-29A ❷ **Applying the revenue principle [10–20 min]**

Crum's Cookies uses the accrual method of accounting and properly records transactions on the date they occur. Descriptions of customer transactions follow:

a. Received $3,000 cash from customer for six months of service beginning April 1, 2012.

b. Catered event for customer on April 28. Customer paid Crum's invoice of $600 on May 10.

c. Scheduled catering event to be held June 3. Customer paid Crum's a $500 deposit on May 25.

d. Catered customer's wedding on May 3. Customer paid Crum's an $800 deposit on April 15 and the balance due of $1,000 on May 3.

e. The company provided catering to a local church's annual celebration service on May 15. The church paid the $800 fee to Crum's on the same day.

f. The company provides food to the local homeless shelter two Saturdays each month. The cost of each event to the shelter is $280. The shelter paid Crum $1,120 on May 25 for April and May's events.

g. On April 1, Crum's entered into an annual service contract with an oil company to cater the customer's monthly staff events. The contract's total amount was $4,000, but Crum's offered a 2.5% discount since the customer paid the entire year in advance at the signing of the contract. The first event was held in April.

h. Crum's signed contract for $1,000 on May 5 to cater X-treme sports events to be held June 15, June 27, October 1, and November 15.

Requirement

1. Calculate the amount of revenue earned during May, 2012 for Crum's Cookies for each transaction.

P3-30A ③ **Explain why an adjusting entry is needed and calculate the amount of the adjustment [15–25 min]**

Descriptions of transactions and how they were recorded follow for October, 2012 for Ausley Acoustics.

---

a. Received $1,500 cash from customer for three months of service beginning October 1, 2012, and ending December 31, 2012. The company recorded a $1,500 debit to Cash and a $1,500 credit to Unearned service revenue.

b. Employees are paid $1,000 every Friday for the five-day work week. October 31, 2012, is on Wednesday.

c. The company pays $240 on October 1 for their six-month auto insurance policy. The company recorded a $240 debit to Prepaid insurance and a $240 credit to Cash.

d. The company purchased office furniture for $6,300 on January 2, 2012. The company recorded a $6,300 debit to Office furniture and a $6,300 credit to Accounts payable. Annual depreciation for the furniture is $900.

e. The company began October with $50 of supplies on hand. On October 10, the company purchased supplies on account of $100. The company recorded a $100 debit to Supplies and a $100 credit to Accounts payable. The company used $120 of supplies during October.

f. The company received its electric bill on October 30 for $125 but did not pay it until November 10. On November 10, it recorded a $125 debit to Utilities expense and a $125 credit to Cash.

g. The company paid November's rent on October 30 of $800. On October 30, the company recorded an $800 debit to Rent expense and an $800 credit to Cash.

Requirement

1. Indicate if an adjusting entry is needed for each item on October 31 and why the entry is needed (i.e., an asset or liability account is over/understated). Indicate which specific account on the balance sheet is misstated. Finally, indicate the correct balance that should appear in the balance sheet account after the adjustment is made. Use the following table guide. Item a is completed as an example:

Item	Adjustment needed?	Asset/ Liability	Over-/ Understated?	Balance sheet account	Correct balance on October 31
a.	Yes	Liability	Overstated	Unearned service revenue	$1,000

P3-31A ① ④ ⑥ **Comparing accrual and cash-basis accounting, preparing adjusting entries, and preparing income statements [15–25 min]**

Charlotte's Golf School completed the following transactions during March, 2012:

Mar	1	Prepaid insurance for March through May, $600.
	4	Performed services (gave golf lessons) on account, $2,500.
	5	Purchased equipment on account, $1,600.
	8	Paid property tax expense, $100.
	11	Purchased office equipment for cash, $1,500.
	19	Performed services and received cash, $900.
	24	Collected $400 on account.
	26	Paid account payable from March 5.
	29	Paid salary expense, $1,000.
	31	Recorded adjusting entry for March insurance expense (see March 1).
	31	Debited unearned revenue and credited revenue in an adjusting entry, $1,200.

Requirements

1. Prepare journal entries for each transaction.

2. Using the journal entries as a guide, show whether each transaction would be handled as a revenue or an expense, using both the cash and accrual basis, by completing the following table.

	Amount of Revenue (Expense) for March	
Date	Cash-Basis Amount of Revenue (Expense)	Accrual-Basis Amount of Revenue (Expense)
Mar 1		

3. After completing the table, calculate the amount of net income or net loss for the company under the accrual and cash basis for March.

4. Considering your results from Requirement 3, which method gives the best picture of the true earnings of Charlotte's Golf School? Why?

P3-32A ➍ **Journalizing adjusting entries [15–25 min]**
Laughter Landscaping has the following independent cases at the end of the year on December 31, 2014.

a. Each Friday, Laughter pays employees for the current week's work. The amount of the weekly payroll is $7,000 for a five-day workweek. This year December 31 falls on a Wednesday.

b. Details of Prepaid insurance are shown in the account:

Prepaid insurance

Jan   1 $4,500

Laughter prepays a full year's insurance each year on January 1. Record insurance expense for the year ended December 31.

c. The beginning balance of Supplies was $4,000. During the year, Laughter purchased supplies for $5,200, and at December 31 the supplies on hand total $2,400.

d. Laughter designed a landscape plan, and the client paid Laughter $7,000 at the start of the project. Laughter recorded this amount as Unearned service revenue. The job will take several months to complete, and Laughter estimates that the company has earned 60% of the total revenue during the current year.

e. Depreciation for the current year includes Equipment, $3,700; and Trucks, $1,300. Make a compound entry.

Requirement

1. Journalize the adjusting entry needed on December 31, 2014, for each of the previous items affecting Laughter Landscaping.

P3-33A ④ **Analyzing and journalizing adjustments [15–20 min]**

Galant Theater Production Company's unadjusted and adjusted trial balances at December 31, 2012, follow.

GALANT THEATER PRODUCTION COMPANY					
Adjusted Trial Balance					
December 31, 2012					
	Trial Balance		Adjusted Trial Balance		
Account	Debit	Credit	Debit	Credit	
Cash	$ 3,900		$ 3,900		
Accounts receivable	6,100		6,900		
Supplies	1,700		300		
Prepaid insurance	2,700		2,100		
Equipment	25,000		25,000		
Accumulated depreciation		$ 8,800		$ 13,200	
Accounts payable		4,000		4,000	
Salary payable				300	
Galant, capital		20,300		20,300	
Galant, drawing	30,500		30,500		
Service revenue		71,000		71,800	
Depreciation expense			4,400		
Supplies expense			1,400		
Utilities expense	4,700		4,700		
Salary expense	29,500		29,800		
Insurance expense			600		
Total	$ 104,100	$ 104,100	$ 109,600	$ 109,600	

Requirement

1. Journalize the adjusting entries that account for the differences between the two trial balances.

P3-34A ④⑤ **Journalizing and posting adjustments to the T-accounts and preparing an adjusted trial balance [45–60 min]**

The trial balance of Arlington Air Purification System at December 31, 2012, and the data needed for the month-end adjustments follow.

ARLINGTON AIR PURIFICATION SYSTEM Trial Balance December 31, 2012		
Account	Debit	Credit
Cash	$ 7,700	
Accounts receivable	19,200	
Prepaid rent	2,400	
Supplies	1,300	
Equipment	19,900	
Accumulated depreciation		$ 4,300
Accounts payable		3,600
Salary payable		
Unearned service revenue		2,600
Able, capital		39,500
Able, drawing	9,500	
Service revenue		15,400
Salary expense	3,500	
Rent expense		
Depreciation expense		
Advertising expense	1,900	
Supplies expense		
Total	$ 65,400	$ 65,400

Adjustment data at December 31 follow:

   a. Unearned service revenue still unearned, $1,100.
   b. Prepaid rent still in force, $500.
   c. Supplies used during the month, $600.
   d. Depreciation for the month, $900.
   e. Accrued advertising expense, $900. (Credit Accounts payable)
   f. Accrued salary expense, $1,100.

Requirements

1. Journalize the adjusting entries.
2. The unadjusted balances have been entered for you in the general ledger accounts. Post the adjusting entries to the ledger accounts.
3. Prepare the adjusted trial balance.
4. How will Arlington Air Purification System use the adjusted trial balance?

P3-35A (4)(5)(6) **Preparing and posting adjusting journal entries; preparing an adjusted trial balance and financial statements [45–60 min]**

The trial balance of Lexington Inn Company at December 31, 2012, and the data needed for the month-end adjustments follow.

LEXINGTON INN COMPANY Trial Balance December 31, 2012		
Account	Debit	Credit
Cash	$ 12,100	
Accounts receivable	14,300	
Prepaid insurance	2,300	
Supplies	1,100	
Building	411,000	
Accumulated depreciation		$312,500
Accounts payable		1,950
Salary payable		
Unearned service revenue		2,400
Calvasina, capital		114,740
Calvasina, drawing	2,860	
Service revenue		15,600
Salary expense	2,700	
Insurance expense		
Depreciation expense		
Advertising expense	830	
Supplies expense		
Total	$447,190	$447,190

Adjustment data at December 31 follow:

a. Prepaid insurance still in force, $700.
b. Supplies used during the month, $500.
c. Depreciation for the month, $1,600.
d. Accrued salary expense, $400.
e. Unearned service revenue still unearned, $1,400.

Requirements

1. Journalize the adjusting entries.
2. The unadjusted balances have been entered for you in the general ledger accounts. Post the adjusting entries to the ledger accounts.
3. Prepare the adjusted trial balance.
4. Prepare the income statement, statement of owner's equity, and balance sheet for the business for the month ended December 31, 2012.

P3-36A (5)(6) **Prepare an adjusted trial balance and financial statements. [45–60 min]**

Consider the unadjusted trial balance of Reliable Limo Service Company at June 30, 2012, and the related month-end adjustment data.

	Balance	
RELIABLE LIMO SERVICE COMPANY Trial Balance June 30, 2012		
Account	**Debit**	**Credit**
Cash	$ 6,900	
Accounts receivable	1,100	
Prepaid rent	3,500	
Supplies	1,100	
Automobile	77,000	
Accumulated depreciation		$ 3,400
Accounts payable		3,300
Salary payable		
Wake, capital		80,000
Wake, drawing	4,400	
Service revenue		9,600
Salary expense	1,500	
Rent expense		
Fuel expense	800	
Depreciation expense		
Supplies expense		
Total	$96,300	$96,300

Adjustment data at June 30 follow:

    a. Accrued service revenue at June 30, $1,500.
    b. One-fifth of the prepaid rent expired during the month.
    c. Supplies on hand at June 30, $700.
    d. Depreciation on automobile for the month, $1,400.
    e. Accrued salary expense at June 30 for one day only. The five-day weekly payroll is $1,500.

Requirements

1. Write the trial balance on a worksheet, using Exhibit 3-8 as an example, and prepare the adjusted trial balance of Reliable Limo Service Company at June 30, 2012. Key each adjusting entry by letter.

2. Prepare the income statement and the statement of owner's equity for the month ended June 30, 2012, and the balance sheet at that date.

P3-37A ⑥ **Preparing financial statements from an adjusted trial balance. [20–30 min]**
The adjusted trial balance of Party Piano Tuning Service at fiscal year end May 31, 2012, follows.

PARTY PIANO TUNING SERVICE
Adjusted Trial Balance
May 31, 2012

Account Title	Balance Debit	Balance Credit
Cash	$ 12,600	
Accounts receivable	10,800	
Supplies	1,900	
Equipment	25,900	
Accumulated depreciation		$ 12,500
Accounts payable		3,300
Unearned service revenue		4,700
Salary payable		800
Note payable		14,000
Lindros, capital		13,600
Lindros, drawing	38,000	
Service revenue		65,000
Depreciation expense	5,600	
Salary expense	9,600	
Utilities expense	3,900	
Insurance expense	3,700	
Supplies expense	1,900	
Total	$113,900	$113,900

Requirements

1. Prepare Party's 2012 income statement.
2. Prepare the statement of owner's equity for the year.
3. Prepare the year-end balance sheet.
4. Which financial statement reports Party's results of operations? Were the 2012 operations successful? Cite specifics from the financial statements to support your evaluation.
5. Which statement reports the company's financial position?

● Problems **(Group B)**

P3-38B ❶ **Comparing accrual and cash-basis accounting [15–25 min]**

Smith's Stews completed the following transactions during April 2012:

Apr 1	Prepaid rent for April through July, $4,800.
2	Purchased computer for cash, $3,600.
3	Performed catering services on account, $3,400.
5	Paid Internet service provider invoice, $225.
6	Catered wedding event for customer and received cash, $2,000.
8	Purchased $130 of supplies on account.
10	Collected $1,900 on account.
14	Paid account payable from April 8.
15	Paid salary expense, $1,000.
30	Recorded adjusting entry for rent (see April 1).
30	Recorded $100 depreciation on computer.
30	There are $35 of supplies still on hand.

Requirement

1. Show whether each transaction would be handled as a revenue or an expense, using both the cash and accrual basis, by completing the table.

	Amount of Revenue (Expense) for April	
Date	Cash-Basis Amount of Revenue (Expense)	Accrual-Basis Amount of Revenue (Expense)
Apr 1		

P3-39B ❷ **Applying the revenue principle [10–20 min]**

Nibble's Cookies uses the accrual method of accounting and properly records transactions on the date they occur. Descriptions of customer transactions follows:

a. Received $4,800 cash from customer for six months of service beginning January 1, 2012.

b. Catered event for customer on January 28. Customer paid Nibble's invoice of $800 on February 10.

c. Scheduled catering event to be held June 3. Customer paid Nibble's a $750 deposit on February 25.

d. Catered customer's wedding on February 3. Customer paid Nibble's a $600 deposit on January 15 and the balance due of $1,500 on February 3.

e. The company provided catering to a local church's annual celebration service on February 15. The church paid the $900 fee to Nibble's on the same day.

f. The company provides food to the local homeless shelter two Saturdays each month. The cost of each event to the shelter is $260. The shelter paid Nibble's $1,040 on February 25 for January and February's events.

g. On December 1, 2011, Nibble's entered into an annual service contract with an oil company to cater the customer's monthly staff events. The contract total amount was $8,000, but Nibble's offered a 1% discount since the customer paid the entire year in advance at the signing of the contract. The first event was held in December of last year.

h. Nibble's signed contract for $1,600 on February 5 to cater X-treme sports events to be held June 15, June 27, October 1, and November 15.

Requirement

1. Calculate the amount of revenue earned during February 2012 for Nibble's Cookies for each transaction.

P3-40B ③ **Explain why an adjusting entry is needed and calculate the amount of the adjustment [15–25 min]**

Descriptions of transactions and how they were recorded follows for October 2012 for Ashley Acoustics.

a. Received $3,600 cash from customer for three months of service beginning October 1, 2012 and ending December 31, 2012. The company recorded a $3,600 debit to Cash and a $3,600 credit to Unearned service revenue.

b. Employees are paid $1,500 every Friday for the five-day work week. October 31, 2012 is on Wednesday.

c. The company pays $420 on October 1 for their six-month auto insurance policy. The company recorded a $420 debit to Prepaid insurance and a $420 credit to Cash.

d. The company purchased office furniture for $6,000 on January 2, 2012. The company recorded a $6,000 debit to Office furniture and a $6,000 credit to Accounts payable. Annual depreciation for the furniture is $1,200.

e. The company began October with $55 of supplies on hand. On October 10 the company purchased supplies on account of $115. The company recorded a $115 debit to Supplies and a $115 credit to Accounts payable. The company used $80 of supplies during October.

f. The company received their electric bill on October 30 for $205, but did not pay it until November 10. On November 10 they recorded a $205 debit to Utilities expense and a $205 credit to Cash.

g. The company paid November's rent on October 30 of $550. On October 30 the company recorded a $550 debit to Rent expense and a $550 credit to Cash.

Requirement

1. Indicate if an adjusting entry is needed for each item on October 31 and why the entry is needed (i.e., an asset or liability account is over/understated). Indicate which specific account on the balance sheet is misstated. Finally, indicate the correct balance that should appear in the balance sheet account after the adjustment is made. Use the table guide below. Item a is completed as an example:

Item	Adjustment needed?	Asset/ Liability	Over-/ Understated?	Balance sheet account	Correct balance on October 31
a.	Yes	Liability	Overstated	Unearned service revenue	$2,400

P3-41B ① ④ ⑥ **Comparing accrual and cash-basis accounting, preparing adjusting entries, and preparing income statements [15–25 min]**

Carolina's Golf School completed the following transactions during October 2012:

Oct	1	Prepaid insurance for October through December, $900.
	4	Performed services (gave golf lessons) on account, $2,400.
	5	Purchased equipment on account, $1,500.
	8	Paid property tax expense, $200.
	11	Purchased office equipment for cash, $1,000.
	19	Performed services and received cash, $700.
	24	Collected $500 on account.
	26	Paid account payable from October 5.
	29	Paid salary expense, $1,400.
	31	Recorded adjusting entry for October insurance expense (see October 1).
	31	Debited unearned revenue and credited revenue in an adjusting entry, $1,100.

Requirements

1. Prepare journal entries for each transaction.

2. Using the journal entries as a guide, show whether each transaction would be handled as a revenue or an expense, using both the cash and accrual basis, by completing the following table:

	Amount of Revenue (Expense) for October	
Date	Cash-Basis Amount of Revenue (Expense)	Accrual-Basis Amount of Revenue (Expense)
Oct 1		

3. After completing the table, calculate the amount of net income or net loss for the company under the accrual and cash basis for October.

4. Considering your results from Requirement 3, which method gives the best picture of the true earnings of Carolina's Golf School? Why?

P3-42B ④ **Journalizing adjusting entries [15–25 min]**
Lindsey Landscaping has the following independent cases at the end of the year on December 31, 2014.

a. Each Friday, Lindsey pays employees for the current week's work. The amount of the weekly payroll is $6,500 for a five-day workweek. This year December 31 falls on a Wednesday.

b. Details of Prepaid insurance are shown in the account:

Prepaid insurance		
Jan 1 $5,500		

Lindsey prepays a full year's insurance each year on January 1. Record insurance expense for the year ended December 31.

c. The beginning balance of Supplies was $4,200. During the year, Lindsey purchased supplies for $5,100, and at December 31, the supplies on hand total $2,400.

d. Lindsey designed a landscape plan, and the client paid Lindsey $9,000 at the start of the project. Lindsey recorded this amount as Unearned service revenue. The job will take several months to complete, and Lindsey estimates that the company has earned 70% of the total revenue during the current year.

e. Depreciation for the current year includes Equipment, $3,600; and Trucks, $1,400. Make a compound entry.

Requirement

1. Journalize the adjusting entry needed on December 31, 2014, for each of the previous items affecting Lindsey Landscaping.

P3-43B ④ **Analyzing and journalizing adjustments [15–20 min]**
Showtime Theater Production Company's unadjusted and adjusted trial balances at December 31, 2012, follow.

	SHOWTIME THEATER PRODUCTION COMPANY Adjusted Trial Balance December 31, 2012			
	Trial Balance		Adjusted Trial Balance	
Account	Debit	Credit	Debit	Credit
Cash	$ 3,500		$ 3,500	
Accounts receivable	6,000		6,900	
Supplies	1,300		500	
Prepaid insurance	2,100		1,300	
Equipment	23,000		23,000	
Accumulated depreciation		$ 8,100		$ 11,600
Accounts payable		5,000		5,000
Salary payable				500
Webber, capital		21,100		21,100
Webber, drawing	28,500		28,500	
Service revenue		59,600		60,500
Depreciation expense			3,500	
Supplies expense			800	
Utilities expense	5,400		5,400	
Salary expense	24,000		24,500	
Insurance expense			800	
Total	$ 93,800	$ 93,800	$ 98,700	$ 98,700

Requirement

1. Journalize the adjusting entries that account for the differences between the two trial balances.

P3-44B **4** **5** **Journalizing and posting adjustments to the T-accounts, and preparing an adjusted trial balance [45–60 min]**
The trial balance of Canton Air Purification System at December 31, 2012, and the data needed for the month-end adjustments follow.

CANTON AIR PURIFICATION SYSTEM Trial Balance December 31, 2012		
Account	Debit	Credit
Cash	$ 7,200	
Accounts receivable	19,400	
Prepaid rent	2,200	
Supplies	1,600	
Equipment	20,000	
Accumulated depreciation		$ 3,700
Accounts payable		3,400
Salary payable		
Unearned service revenue		2,600
Canton, capital		39,000
Canton, drawing	9,600	
Service revenue		15,900
Salary expense	3,300	
Rent expense		
Depreciation expense		
Advertising expense	1,300	
Supplies expense		
Total	$ 64,600	$ 64,600

Adjustment data at December 31 follow:

a. Unearned service revenue still unearned, $1,800.
b. Prepaid rent still in force, $600.
c. Supplies used during the month, $400.
d. Depreciation for the month, $700.
e. Accrued advertising expense, $900. (Credit Accounts payable)
f. Accrued salary expense, $800.

Requirements

1. Journalize the adjusting entries.
2. The unadjusted balances have been entered for you in the general ledger accounts. Post the adjusting entries to the ledger accounts.
3. Prepare the adjusted trial balance.
4. How will Canton Air Purification System use the adjusted trial balance?

P3-45B ④⑤⑥ **Preparing and posting adjusting journal entries; preparing an adjusted trial balance and financial statements. [45–60 min]**

The trial balance of Concord Bed and Breakfast Company at December 31, 2012, and the data needed for the month-end adjustments follow.

CONCORD BED AND BREAKFAST COMPANY Trial Balance December 31, 2012		
Account	Debit	Credit
Cash	$ 12,000	
Accounts receivable	14,400	
Prepaid insurance	2,800	
Supplies	1,400	
Building	435,000	
Accumulated depreciation		$310,500
Accounts payable		1,930
Salary payable		
Unearned service revenue		3,000
Wagner, capital		141,060
Wagner, drawing	2,940	
Service revenue		15,700
Salary expense	2,800	
Insurance expense		
Depreciation expense		
Advertising expense	850	
Supplies expense		
Total	$472,190	$472,190

Adjustment data at December 31 follow:

    a. Prepaid insurance still in force, $900.
    b. Supplies used during the month, $500.
    c. Depreciation for the month, $1,000.
    d. Accrued salary expense, $300.
    e. Unearned service revenue still unearned, $1,500.

Requirements

1. Journalize the adjusting entries.
2. The unadjusted balances have been entered for you in the general ledger accounts. Post the adjusting entries to the ledger accounts.
3. Prepare the adjusted trial balance.
4. Prepare the income statement, statement of owner's equity, and balance sheet for the business for the month ended December 31, 2012.

P3-46B   ⑤ ⑥ **Prepare an adjusted trial balance and financial statements [45–60 min]**
Consider the unadjusted trial balance of Star Limo Service Company at September 30, 2012, and the related month-end adjustment data.

STAR LIMO SERVICE COMPANY Trial Balance September 30, 2012		
	Balance	
Account	Debit	Credit
Cash	$ 6,800	
Accounts receivable	1,400	
Prepaid rent	5,000	
Supplies	1,200	
Automobile	72,000	
Accumulated depreciation		$ 3,800
Accounts payable		3,600
Salary payable		
Simmons, capital		75,000
Simmons, drawing	3,700	
Service revenue		9,700
Salary expense	1,400	
Rent expense		
Fuel expense	600	
Depreciation expense		
Supplies expense		
Total	$92,100	$92,100

Adjustment data at September 30 follow:

a. Accrued service revenue at September 30, $1,800.
b. One-fifth of the prepaid rent expired during the month.
c. Supplies on hand at September 30, $800.
d. Depreciation on automobile for the month, $1,000.
e. Accrued salary expense at September 30 for one day only. The five-day weekly payroll is $1,200.

Requirements

1. Write the trial balance on a worksheet, using Exhibit 3-8 as an example, and prepare the adjusted trial balance of Star Limo Service at September 30, 2012. Key each adjusting entry by letter.
2. Prepare the income statement and the statement of owner's equity for the month ended September 30, 2012, and the balance sheet at that date.

P3-47B ⑥ **Preparing financial statements from an adjusted trial balance [20–30 min]**

The adjusted trial balance of A Plus Events Piano Tuning Service at fiscal year end October 31, 2012, follows.

	A PLUS EVENTS PIANO TUNING SERVICE Adjusted Trial Balance October 31, 2012		
		Balance	
Account Title		**Debit**	**Credit**
Cash		$ 12,300	
Accounts receivable		10,700	
Supplies		1,800	
Equipment		25,800	
Accumulated depreciation			$ 12,300
Accounts payable			3,300
Unearned service revenue			4,600
Salary payable			700
Note payable			15,000
Bach, capital			9,000
Bach, drawing		36,000	
Service revenue			66,000
Depreciation expense		5,500	
Salary expense		9,600	
Utilities expense		4,100	
Insurance expense		3,700	
Supplies expense		1,400	
Total		$110,900	$110,900

Requirements

1. Prepare A Plus's 2012 income statement.
2. Prepare the statement of owner's equity for the year.
3. Prepare the year-end balance sheet.
4. Which financial statement reports A Plus's results of operations? Were 2012 operations successful? Cite specifics from the financial statements to support your evaluation.
5. Which statement reports the company's financial position?

● Continuing Exercise

E3-48 ④⑤ **Preparing adjusting entries and preparing an adjusted trial balance [20–30 min]**   *MyAccountingLab*

This exercise continues the Lawlor Lawn Service situation from Exercise 2-61 of Chapter 2. Start from the trial balance and the posted T-accounts that Lawlor Lawn Service prepared at May 31, 2012.

Requirements

1. Open these additional T-accounts: Accumulated depreciation—equipment; Depreciation expense—equipment; Supplies expense.
2. Mindy Lawlor determines there are $40 in Lawn supplies left at May 31, 2012. Depreciation on the equipment was $30 for the month. Journalize any required adjusting journal entries.

3. Post to the T-accounts, keying all items by date.

4. Prepare the adjusted trial balance, as illustrated in Exhibit 3-8.

● Continuing Problem

P3-49 **④ ⑤ ⑥ Preparing adjusting entries; preparing an adjusted trial balance; and preparing financial statements from an adjusted trial balance [40–50 min]**
This problem continues the Draper Consulting situation from Problem 2-62 of Chapter 2. Start from the trial balance and the posted T-accounts that Draper Consulting prepared at December 18, 2012, as follows:

DRAPER CONSULTING Trial Balance December 18, 2012		
	Balance	
Account Title	Debit	Credit
Cash	$ 16,500	
Accounts receivable	1,500	
Supplies	900	
Equipment	1,800	
Accumulated depreciation—equipment		
Furniture	4,200	
Accumulated depreciation—furniture		
Accounts payable		$ 5,100
Salary payable		
Unearned service revenue		
Draper, capital		18,000
Draper, drawing		
Service revenue		2,600
Rent expense	550	
Utilities expense	250	
Salary expense		
Depreciation expense—equipment		
Depreciation expense—furniture		
Supplies expense		
Total	$25,700	$25,700

Later in December, the business completed these transactions, as follows:

Dec 21	Received $1,400 in advance for client service to be performed evenly over the next 30 days.
21	Hired a secretary to be paid $2,055 on the 20th day of each month. The secretary begins work immediately.
26	Paid $450 on account.
28	Collected $300 on account.
30	Draper withdrew cash of $1,400.

Requirements

1. Open these additional T-accounts: Accumulated depreciation—equipment; Accumulated depreciation—furniture; Salary payable; Unearned service revenue; Salary expense; Depreciation expense—equipment; Depreciation expense—furniture; Supplies expense.

2. Journalize the transactions of December 21–30.

3. Post to the T-accounts, keying all items by date.

4. Prepare a trial balance at December 31. Also set up columns for the adjustments and for the adjusted trial balance, as illustrated in Exhibit 3-8.

5. At December 31, the business gathers the following information for the adjusting entries:

   a. Accrued service revenue, $550.
   b. Earned $700 of the service revenue collected in advance on December 21.
   c. Supplies on hand, $200.
   d. Depreciation expense—equipment, $30; furniture, $70.
   e. Accrued $685 expense for secretary's salary.

   On your worksheet, make these adjustments directly in the adjustments columns, and complete the adjusted trial balance at December 31. Throughout the book, to avoid rounding errors, we base adjusting entries on 30-day months and 360-day years.

6. Journalize and post the adjusting entries. In the T-accounts, denote each adjusting amount as *Adj* and an account balance as *Bal.*

7. Prepare the income statement and the statement of owner's equity of Draper Consulting for the month ended December 31, 2012, and prepare the balance sheet at that date.

● Practice Set

④ ⑤ Preparing adjusting entries and preparing an adjusted trial balance [20–30 min]

MyAccountingLab

Using the trial balance prepared in Chapter 2, consider the following adjustment data gathered by Evan:

a. Evan prepared an inventory of supplies and found there were $50 of supplies in the cabinet on November 30.
b. One month's combined depreciation on all assets was estimated to be $170.

Requirements

1. Using the data provided from the trial balance, the previous adjustment information, and the information from Chapter 2, prepare all required adjusting journal entries for November.

2. Prepare an adjusted trial balance as of November 30 for Shine King Cleaning.

Apply Your Knowledge

● Decision Cases

Decision Case 3-1 Lee Nicholas has been the owner and has operated World.com Advertising since its beginning 10 years ago. The company has prospered. Recently, Nicholas mentioned that he would sell the business for the right price.

Assume that you are interested in buying World.com Advertising. You obtain the most recent monthly trial balance, which follows. Revenues and expenses vary little from month to month, and January is a typical month. The trial balance shown is a preliminary or unadjusted trial balance. The controller informs you that the necessary accrual adjustments should include revenues of $3,800 and expenses of $1,100. Also, if you were to buy World.com Advertising, you would hire a manager so you could devote your time to other duties. Assume that this person would require a monthly salary of $5,000.

WORLD.COM ADVERTISING
Trial Balance
January 31, 2015

Account Title	Balance Debit	Balance Credit
Cash	$ 9,700	
Accounts receivable	14,100	
Prepaid expenses	2,600	
Building	221,300	
Accumulated depreciation		$ 68,600
Accounts payable		13,000
Salary payable		
Unearned service revenue		56,700
Nicholas, capital		110,400
Nicholas, drawing	9,000	
Service revenue		12,300
Rent expense		
Salary expense	3,400	
Utilities expense	900	
Depreciation expense		
Supplies expense		
Total	$261,000	$261,000

Requirements

1. Assume that the most you would pay for the business is 20 times the monthly net income *you could expect to earn* from it. Compute this possible price.

2. Nicholas states the least he will take for the business is an amount equal to the business's owner's equity balance on January 31. Compute this amount.

3. Under these conditions, how much should you offer Nicholas? Give your reason.

Decision Case 3-2 One year ago, Tyler Stasney founded Swift Classified Ads. Stasney remembers that you took an accounting course while in college and comes to you for advice. He wishes to know how much net income his business earned during the past year in order to decide whether to keep the company going. His accounting records consist of the T-accounts from his ledger, which were prepared by an accountant who moved to another city. The ledger at December 31 follows. The accounts have *not* been adjusted.

Stasney indicates that at year-end, customers owe him $1,600 for accrued service revenue. These revenues have not been recorded. During the year, Stasney collected $4,000 service revenue in advance from customers, but he earned only $900 of that amount. Rent expense for the year was $2,400, and he used up $1,700 of the supplies. Stasney determines that depreciation on his equipment was $5,000 for the year. At December 31, he owes his employee $1,200 accrued salary.

Cash		Accounts receivable		Prepaid rent		Supplies	
Dec 31 5,800		Dec 31 12,000		Jan 2 2,800		Jan 2 2,600	

Equipment		Accumulated depreciation				Accounts payable	
Jan 2 36,000							Dec 31 21,500

Unearned service revenue		Salary payable	
	Dec 31 4,000		

		Stasney, capital		Stasney, drawing		Service revenue	
			Dec 31 20,000	Dec 31 28,000			Dec 31 59,500

Salary expense		Depreciation expense		Rent expense		Utilities expense	
Dec 31 17,000						Dec 31 800	

Supplies expense	

Requirement

1. Help Stasney compute his net income for the year. Advise him whether to continue operating Swift Classified Ads.

● Ethical Issue 3-1

The net income of Steinbach & Sons, a department store, decreased sharply during 2014. Mort Steinbach, manager of the store, anticipates the need for a bank loan in 2015. Late in 2014, Steinbach instructs the store's accountant to record a $2,000 sale of furniture to the Steinbach family, even though the goods will not be shipped from the manufacturer until January 2015. Steinbach also tells the accountant *not* to make the following December 31, 2014, adjusting entries:

Salaries owed to employees	$900
Prepaid insurance that has expired	400

Requirements

1. Compute the overall effects of these transactions on the store's reported income for 2014.
2. Why is Steinbach taking this action? Is his action ethical? Give your reason, identifying the parties helped and the parties harmed by Steinbach's action. (Challenge)
3. As a personal friend, what advice would you give the accountant? (Challenge)

● Fraud Case 3-1

XM, Ltd., was a small engineering firm that built hi-tech robotic devices for electronics manufacturers. One very complex device was partially completed at the end of 2014. Barb McLauren, head engineer and owner, knew the experimental technology was a failure and XM would not be able to complete the $20,000,000 contract next year. However, she was getting ready to sell the company and retire in January. She told the controller that the device was 80% complete at year-end, and on track for successful completion the following spring; the controller accrued 80% of the contract revenue in December 2014. McLauren sold the company in January 2015 and retired. By mid-year, it became apparent that XM would not be able to complete the project successfully, and the new owner would never recoup his investment.

Requirements

1. For complex, hi-tech contracts, how does a company determine the percentage of completion and the amount of revenue to accrue?

2. What action do you think was taken by XM in 2015 with regard to the revenue that had been accrued the previous year?

● Financial Statement Case 3-1

Amazon.com—like all other businesses—makes adjusting entries prior to year-end in order to measure assets, liabilities, revenues, and expenses properly. Examine **Amazon**'s balance sheet and Note 3. Pay particular attention to Accumulated depreciation.

Requirements

1. Open T-accounts for the following accounts with the balances shown on the annual reports at December 31, 2008 (amounts in millions, as in the **Amazon.com** financial statements):

Accumulated depreciation	$ 555
Accounts payable	3,594
Other assets	720

2. Assume that during 2009 **Amazon.com** completed the following transactions (amounts in millions). Journalize each transaction (explanations are not required).

a. Recorded depreciation expense, $70. (In order to simplify this exercise, the amount shown here is not the same as the actual amount disclosed in Note 3 of the annual report.)

b. Paid the December 31, 2008, balance of accounts payable.

c. Purchased inventory on account, $5,605.

d. Purchased other assets for cash of $754.

3. Post to the three T-accounts. Then the balance of each account should agree with the corresponding amount reported in **Amazon**'s December 31, 2009, balance sheet. Check to make sure they do agree with **Amazon**'s actual balances. You can find Accumulated depreciation in Note 3.

● Team Project 3-1

It's Just Lunch is a nationwide service company that arranges lunch dates for clients. **It's Just Lunch** collects cash up front for a package of dates. Suppose your group is opening an **It's Just Lunch** office in your area. You must make some important decisions—where to locate, how to advertise, and so on—and you must also make some accounting decisions. For example, what will be the end of your business's accounting year? How often will you need financial statements to evaluate operating performance and financial position? Will you use the cash basis or the accrual basis? When will you account for the revenue that the business earns? How will you account for the expenses?

Requirements

Write a report (or prepare an oral presentation, as directed by your professor) to address the following considerations:

1. Will you use the cash basis or the accrual basis of accounting? Give a complete explanation of your reasoning.

2. How often do you want financial statements? Why? Discuss how you will use each financial statement.

3. What kind of revenue will you earn? When will you record it as revenue?

4. Prepare a made-up income statement for **It's Just Lunch** for the year ended December 31, 2015. List all the business's expenses, starting with the most important (largest dollar amount) and working through to the least important (smallest dollar amount). Merely list the accounts. Dollar amounts are not required.

● Communication Activity 3-1

In 25 words or fewer, explain adjusting journal entries.

Quick Check Answers

1. *b* 2. *b* 3. *c* 4. *c* 5. *a* 6. *a* 7. *c* 8. *c* 9. *b* 10. *d*

For online homework, exercises, and problems that provide you immediate feedback, please visit myaccountinglab.com.

4

Completing the Accounting Cycle

> All accounts not on the balance sheet reset to zero at the end of a period, and update the capital balance.

SMART TOUCH LEARNING
Balance Sheet
May 31, 2013

Assets				Liabilities		
Current assets:				Current liabilities:		
Cash		$ 4,800		Accounts payable		$ 48,700
Accounts receivable		2,600		Salary payable		900
Inventory		30,500		Interest payable		100
Supplies		600		Unearned service revenue		400
Prepaid rent		2,000		Total current liabilities		50,100
Total current assets			$ 40,500	Long-term liabilities:		
Plant assets:				Notes payable		20,000
Furniture	$18,000			Total liabilities		70,100
Less: Accumulated depreciation—furniture	300	17,700				
Building	48,000					
Less: Accumulated depreciation—building	200	47,800		**Owner's Equity**		
Total plant assets			65,500	**Bright, capital**		**35,900**
Total assets			$106,000	Total liabilities and owner's equity		$106,000

Learning Objectives

1. Prepare an accounting worksheet
2. Use the worksheet to prepare financial statements
3. Close the revenue, expense, and drawing accounts
4. Prepare the post-closing trial balance
5. Classify assets and liabilities as current or long-term
6. Describe the effect of various transactions on the current ratio and the debt ratio
7. Understand reversing entries (see Appendix 4A, located at myaccountinglab.com)

What do football, baseball, basketball, hockey, soccer, and accounting have in common? They all have a player in each position and each game starts with a score of zero.

Sheena Bright and Greg Moore have operated Smart Touch Learning and Greg's Tunes, respectively, for a month. They took in revenue, incurred expenses, and earned net income during the first month. It is time to look ahead to the next period.

Should Smart Touch or Greg's Tunes start month 2 with the net income that the business earned last month? No, just like a game, both companies must start from zero in order to measure their business performance in the second month. Therefore, they must set their accounting scoreboard back to zero.

This process of getting back to zero is called *closing the books*, and it is the last step in the accounting cycle. The **accounting cycle** is the process by which companies produce their financial statements.

● ● ●

This chapter completes the accounting cycle by showing how to close the books. It begins with the *adjusted trial balance*, which you learned about in Chapter 3. In this chapter we'll learn how to prepare a more complete version of an adjusted trial balance document called the *worksheet*. Worksheets help by summarizing lots of data in one place.

The accounting cycle starts with the beginning asset, liability, and owner's equity account balances left over from the preceding period. Exhibit 4-1 outlines the complete accounting cycle of Smart Touch and every other business. Start with item 1 and move clockwise.

EXHIBIT 4-1 | The Accounting Cycle

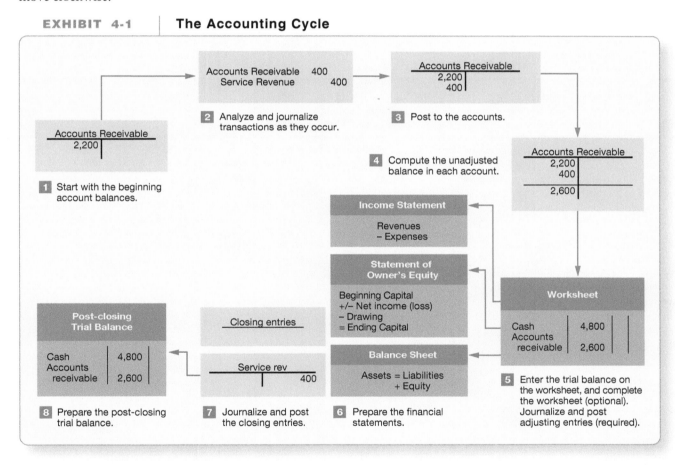

Accounting takes place at two different times:

- During the period—Journalizing transactions, posting to the accounts
- End of the period—Adjusting the accounts, preparing the financial statements, and closing the accounts

The end-of-period work also readies the accounts for the next period. In Chapters 3 and 4, we cover the end-of-period accounting for service businesses such as Greg's Tunes and Smart Touch. Chapter 5 shows how a merchandising entity such as **Walmart** or **Sports Academy** adjusts and closes its books.

The Worksheet

 Prepare an accounting worksheet

Accountants often use a **worksheet**—a document with several columns—to summarize data for the financial statements. The worksheet is not a journal, a ledger, or a financial statement. It is merely a summary device that helps identify the accounts that need adjustment. An Excel spreadsheet works well for preparing a worksheet. Note that the worksheet is an internal document. It is not meant to be given to outsiders.

Exhibits 4-2 though 4-6 illustrate the development of a typical worksheet for Smart Touch. The heading at the top displays the following information:

- Name of the business (Smart Touch Learning)
- Title of the document (Worksheet)
- Period covered by the worksheet (Month Ended May 31, 2013)

A step-by-step description of the worksheet follows, with all amounts given in Exhibits 4-2 though 4-6. Simply turn the acetate pages to follow from exhibit to exhibit.

1. **Enter the account titles and their unadjusted balances in the Trial Balance columns of the worksheet, and total the amounts.** (See Exhibit 4-2.) The data

EXHIBIT 4-2 | **Trial Balance**

SMART TOUCH LEARNING Worksheet Month Ended May 31, 2013											
	Trial Balance		Adjustments		Adj. Trial Balance		Income Statement		Balance Sheet	
	Debit	Credit	Debit	Credit	Debit	Credit	Debit	Credit	Debit	Credit
Cash	$ 4,800									
Accounts receivable	2,200									
Supplies	700									
Prepaid rent	3,000									
Furniture	18,000									
Building	48,000									
Accumulated depreciation—furniture										
Accumulated depreciation—building										
Accounts payable		$18,200								
Salary payable										
Interest payable										
Unearned service revenue		600								
Notes payable		20,000								
Bright, capital		33,200								
Bright, drawing	1,000									
Service revenue		7,000								
Rent expense										
Salary expense	900									
Supplies expense										
Depreciation expense—furniture										
Depreciation expense—building										
Interest expense										
Utilities expense	400									
	$79,000	$79,000								

EXHIBIT 4-3 | **Adjustments**

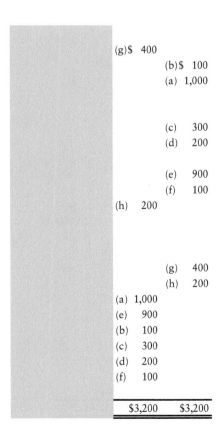

(g)$	400		
		(b)$	100
		(a)	1,000
		(c)	300
		(d)	200
		(e)	900
		(f)	100
(h)	200		
		(g)	400
		(h)	200
(a)	1,000		
(e)	900		
(b)	100		
(c)	300		
(d)	200		
(f)	100		
	$3,200		$3,200

EXHIBIT 4-4 | **Adjusted Trial Balance**

	Debit	Credit
	$ 4,800	
	2,600	
	600	
	2,000	
	18,000	
	48,000	
		$ 300
		200
		18,200
		900
		100
		400
		20,000
		33,200
	1,000	
		7,600
	1,000	
	1,800	
	100	
	300	
	200	
	100	
	400	
	$80,900	$80,900

EXHIBIT 4-5 | **Income Statement and Balance Sheet**

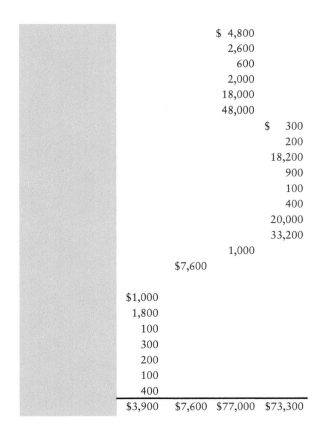

$ 4,800			
2,600			
600			
2,000			
18,000			
48,000			
		$ 300	
		200	
		18,200	
		900	
		100	
		400	
		20,000	
		33,200	
	1,000		
	$7,600		
$1,000			
1,800			
100			
300			
200			
100			
400			
$3,900	$7,600	$77,000	$73,300

EXHIBIT 4-6 | **Computation of Net Income**

Net income	3,700			3,700
	$7,600	$7,600	$77,000	$77,000

come from the ledger accounts before any adjustments. Accounts are listed in proper order (Cash first, Accounts receivable second, and so on). Total debits must equal total credits. Note that these two columns of the worksheet are the same as the trial balance from Chapter 3.

2. **Enter the adjusting entries in the Adjustments columns, and total the amounts.** Exhibit 4-3 includes the May adjusting entries that we made in Chapter 3. The adjusting entries, letters a–h from Exhibit 3-8, are posted into the adjustments column of the worksheet.

3. **Compute each account's adjusted balance by combining the trial balance and adjustment figures. Enter each account's adjusted amount in the Adjusted Trial Balance columns.** Exhibit 4-4 shows the worksheet with the adjusted trial balance completed. For example, Cash is up-to-date, so it receives no adjustment. Accounts receivable's adjusted balance of $2,600 is computed by adding the $400 adjustment to the unadjusted amount of $2,200. For Supplies we subtract the $100 credit adjustment from the unadjusted debit balance of $700. Note that an account may receive more than one adjustment. For example, Service revenue has two adjustments. The adjusted balance of $7,600 is computed by taking the unadjusted balance of $7,000 and adding the adjustment credits of $400 and $200 to arrive at the $7,600 adjusted balance. As on the trial balance, total debits must equal total credits on the adjusted trial balance. Notice how the three completed column sets of Exhibit 4-4 look exactly like Exhibit 3-8.

4. **Draw an imaginary line above the first revenue account (in this case, Service revenue). Every account above that line (assets, liabilities, and equity accounts) is copied from the Adjusted Trial Balance to the Balance Sheet columns. Every account below the line (revenues and expenses) is copied from the Adjusted Trial Balance to the Income Statement columns.** Each account's balance should appear in only one column, as shown in Exhibit 4-5.

First, total the *income statement columns*, as follows:

Income Statement

- Debits (Dr.) ⟶ Total expenses = $3,900 ⎫ Difference = $3,700, a net income
- Credits (Cr.) ⟶ Total revenues = $7,600 ⎭ because total credits (revenues) exceed total debits (expenses)

Then total the *balance sheet* columns:

Balance Sheet

- Debits (Dr.) ⟶ Total assets and drawing = $77,000 ⎫ Difference = $3,700,
- Credits (Cr.) ⟶ Total liabilities, owner's equity, ⎬ a net income because
  and accumulated depreciation = $73,300 ⎭ total debits are greater

5. **On the income statement, compute net income or net loss as total revenues minus total expenses. Enter net income (loss) as the balancing amount on the income statement. Also enter net income (loss) as the balancing amount on the balance sheet. Then total the financial statement columns.** Exhibit 4-6 presents the completed worksheet.

Revenue (total **credits** on the income statement).............................	$ 7,600
Expenses (total **debits** on the income statement).............................	(3,900)
Net income...	$ 3,700

Net Income

Net income of $3,700 is entered as the balancing amount in the debit column of the income statement. This brings total debits up to total credits on the income statement. Net income is also entered as the balancing amount in the credit column of the balance sheet. Net income brings the balance sheet into balance. Note that the difference in these columns is the same: Net income.

Net Loss

If expenses exceed revenues, the result is a net loss. In that event, print Net loss on the worksheet next to the result. The net loss amount should be entered in the *credit* column of the income statement (to balance out) and in the *debit* column of the balance sheet (to balance out). After completion, total debits should equal total credits in both the Income Statement columns and in the Balance Sheet columns.

Now practice what you have learned by working Summary Problem 4-1.

Summary Problem 4-1

The trial balance of Super Employment Services, at December 31, 2014, follows.

SUPER EMPLOYMENT SERVICES Trial Balance December 31, 2014		
	Balance	
Account Title	**Debit**	**Credit**
Cash	$ 6,000	
Accounts receivable	5,000	
Supplies	1,000	
Furniture	10,000	
Accumulated depreciation—furniture		$ 4,000
Building	50,000	
Accumulated depreciation—building		30,000
Accounts payable		2,000
Salary payable		
Unearned service revenue		8,000
Mudge, capital		12,000
Mudge, drawing	25,000	
Service revenue		60,000
Salary expense	16,000	
Supplies expense		
Depreciation expense—furniture		
Depreciation expense—building		
Advertising expense	3,000	
Total	$116,000	$116,000

Data needed for the adjusting entries include the following:

  a. Supplies on hand at year-end, $200.
  b. Depreciation on furniture, $2,000.
  c. Depreciation on building, $1,000.
  d. Salaries owed but not yet paid, $500.
  e. Accrued service revenue, $1,300.
  f. $3,000 of the unearned service revenue was earned during 2014.

Requirement

1. Prepare the worksheet of Super Employment Services for the year ended
   December 31, 2014. Key each adjusting entry by the letter corresponding
   to the data given.

Solution

SUPER EMPLOYMENT SERVICES
Worksheet
Year Ended December 31, 2014

Account Title	Trial Balance Dr.	Trial Balance Cr.	Adjustments Dr.	Adjustments Cr.	Adjusted Trial Balance Dr.	Adjusted Trial Balance Cr.	Income Statement Dr.	Income Statement Cr.	Balance Sheet Dr.	Balance Sheet Cr.
Cash	$ 6,000				$ 6,000				$ 6,000	
Accounts receivable	5,000		(e) $1,300		6,300				6,300	
Supplies	1,000			(a) $ 800	200				200	
Furniture	10,000				10,000				10,000	
Accumulated depreciation— furniture		$ 4,000		(b) 2,000		$ 6,000				$ 6,000
Building	50,000				50,000				50,000	
Accumulated depreciation—building		30,000		(c) 1,000		31,000				31,000
Accounts payable		2,000				2,000				2,000
Salary payable				(d) 500		500				500
Unearned service revenue		8,000	(f) 3,000			5,000				5,000
Mudge, capital		12,000				12,000				12,000
Mudge, drawing	25,000				25,000				25,000	
Service revenue		60,000		(e) 1,300						
				(f) 3,000		64,300		$64,300		
Salary expense	16,000		(d) 500		16,500		$16,500			
Supplies expense			(a) 800		800		800			
Depreciation expense—furniture			(b) 2,000		2,000		2,000			
Depreciation expense—building			(c) 1,000		1,000		1,000			
Advertising expense	3,000				3,000		3,000			
	$116,000	$116,000	$8,600	$8,600	$120,800	$120,800	$23,300	$64,300	$97,500	$56,500
Net income							41,000			41,000
							$64,300	$64,300	$97,500	$97,500

Completing the Accounting Cycle

 2 Use the worksheet to prepare financial statements

The worksheet helps accountants make the adjusting entries, prepare the financial statements, and close the accounts. First, let's prepare the financial statements. We'll start by returning to the running example of Smart Touch Learning, whose financial statements are given in Exhibit 4-7 on the following page. Notice that these are identical to the financial statements prepared in Chapter 3 (Exhibits 3-9 though 3-11).

Preparing the Financial Statements from a Worksheet

The worksheet shows the amount of net income or net loss for the period, but it is an internal document. We still must prepare the financial statements for external decision makers. Exhibit 4-7 on the next page shows the May financial statements for Smart Touch (based on data from the worksheet in Exhibit 4-6). We can prepare the business's financial statements immediately after completing the worksheet.

Stop & Think...

Look at the formal financial statements in Exhibit 4-7 and the worksheet financial statement columns in Exhibit 4-6. The income number is the same on both sheets, so why do we need to do both a worksheet and a formal document, such as an income statement? The answer is the worksheet will be used mainly by internal decision makers, whereas the formal financial statements will be used by external decision makers.

Recording the Adjusting Entries from a Worksheet

Adjusting the accounts requires journalizing entries and posting to the accounts. We learned how to prepare adjusting journal entries in Chapter 3. The adjustments that are journalized after they are entered on the worksheet are *exactly* the same adjusting journal entries. Panel A of Exhibit 4-8 on page 206 repeats Smart Touch's adjusting entries that we journalized in Chapter 3. Panel B shows the revenue and the expense accounts after all adjustments have been posted. Only the revenue and expense accounts are presented here to focus on the closing process.

EXHIBIT 4-7 | **Financial Statements**

SMART TOUCH LEARNING
Income Statement
Month Ended May 31, 2013

Revenue:		
Service revenue		$7,600
Expenses:		
Salary expense	$1,800	
Rent expense	1,000	
Utilities expense	400	
Depreciation expense—furniture	300	
Depreciation expense—building	200	
Interest expense	100	
Supplies expense	100	
Total expenses		3,900
Net income		$3,700

SMART TOUCH LEARNING
Statement of Owner's Equity
Month Ended May 31, 2013

Bright, capital, May 1, 2013	$ 33,200
Net income	3,700
	36,900
Drawing	(1,000)
Bright, capital, May 31, 2013	$ 35,900

SMART TOUCH LEARNING
Balance Sheet
May 31, 2013

Assets			Liabilities	
Cash		$ 4,800	Accounts payable	$18,200
Accounts receivable		2,600	Salary payable	900
Supplies		600	Interest payable	100
Prepaid rent		2,000	Unearned service revenue	400
Furniture	$18,000		Notes payable	20,000
Less: Accumulated			Total liabilities	39,600
depreciation—				
furniture	300	17,700		
Building	48,000			
Less: Accumulated				
depreciation—			**Owner's Equity**	
building	200	47,800	Bright, capital	35,900
			Total liabilities	
Total assets		$75,500	and owner's equity	$75,500

EXHIBIT 4-8	**Journalizing and Posting the Adjusting Entries of Smart Touch Learning**

PANEL A—Adjusting Entries

a.	Rent expense (E+)		1,000	
	Prepaid rent (A–)			1,000
	To record rent expense.			
b.	Supplies expense (E+)		100	
	Supplies (A–)			100
	To record supplies used.			
c.	Depreciation expense—furniture (E+)		300	
	Accumulated depreciation—furniture (CA+)			300
	To record depreciation on furniture.			
d.	Depreciation expense—building (E+)		200	
	Accumulated depreciation—building (CA+)			200
	To record depreciation on building.			
e.	Salary expense (E+)		900	
	Salary payable (L+)			900
	To accrue salary expense.			
f.	Interest expense (E+)		100	
	Interest payable (L+)			100
	To accrue interest expense.			
g.	Accounts receivable (A+)		400	
	Service revenue (R+)			400
	To accrue service revenue.			
h.	Unearned service revenue (L–)		200	
	Service revenue (R+)			200
	To record service revenue that was collected in advance.			

PANEL B—Ledger Accounts

REVENUES

Service revenue

			7,000
		(g)	400
		(h)	200
		Bal	7,600

EXPENSES

Rent expense

(a)	1,000		
Bal	1,000		

Salary expense

	900		
(e)	900		
Bal	1,800		

Supplies expense

(b)	100		
Bal	100		

Depreciation expense— furniture

(c)	300		
Bal	300		

Depreciation expense— building

(d)	200		
Bal	200		

Interest expense

(f)	100		
Bal	100		

Utilities expense

Bal	400		

Accountants can use the worksheet to prepare monthly statements (as in Exhibit 4-7) without journalizing and posting the adjusting entries. A big advantage of the worksheet is that a small business can see the complete results of a period on one page. Many small companies journalize and post the adjusting entries only at the end of the year.

Now we are ready to move to the last step—closing the accounts.

Closing the Accounts

Closing the accounts occurs at the end of the period. Closing consists of journalizing and posting the closing entries in order to get the accounts ready for the next period. The closing process zeroes out all the revenues and all the expenses in order to measure each period's net income separately from all other periods. It also updates the Capital account balance. The last step in the closing process zeroes out drawing.

3 Close the revenue, expense, and drawing accounts

Stop & **Think...**

Have you ever closed an account at a bank? How much was left in your account when you closed it? You needed to take all the money out, right? Well it's the same theory behind closing journal entries—after closing, we leave a zero balance in all revenue, expense, and drawing accounts.

Recall that the income statement reports net income for a specific period. For example, the business's net income for 2013 relates exclusively to 2013. At December 31, 2013, Smart Touch closes its revenue and expense accounts for the year. For this reason, revenues and expenses are called **temporary accounts** (also known as **nominal accounts**). For example, Smart Touch's balance of Service revenue at May 31, 2013, is $7,600. This balance relates exclusively to May and must be zeroed out before Smart Touch records revenue for June. Similarly, the various expense account balances are for May only and must also be zeroed out at the end of the month.

The Bright, drawing account is also temporary and must be closed at the end of the period because it measures the owner drawing for only that one period. All temporary accounts (drawing, revenues, and expenses) are closed (zeroed).

By contrast, the **permanent accounts** (also known as **real accounts**)—the assets, liabilities, and capital—are not closed at the end of the period. Another way to remember which accounts are permanent is to recall that all accounts on the balance sheet are permanent accounts because they are part of the accounting equation.

Closing entries transfer the revenue, expense, and drawing balances to the Capital account to ready the company's books for the next period.

As an intermediate step, the revenues and the expenses may be transferred first to an account titled **Income summary**. The Income summary account *summarizes* the net income (or net loss) for the period by collecting the sum of all the expenses (a debit) and the sum of all the revenues (a credit). **The Income summary account is like a temporary "holding tank" that shows the amount of net income or net loss of the current period.** Its balance—net income or net loss—is then transferred (closed) to the Capital account (the final account in the closing process). Exhibit 4-9 summarizes the closing process.

EXHIBIT 4-9 | **The Closing Process**

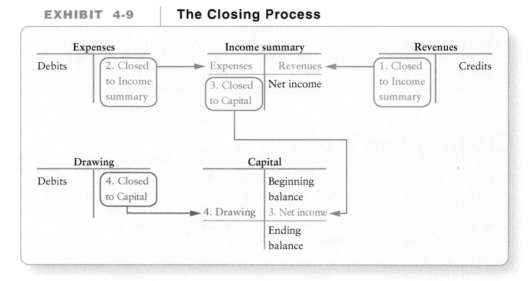

Closing Temporary Accounts

As we stated previously, all temporary accounts are closed (zeroed out) during the closing process. **Temporary accounts are not permanent. Only the accounting equation accounts (the balance sheet accounts) are permanent.** The four steps in closing the books follow (and are illustrated in Exhibit 4-10).

> **STEP 1:** Make the revenue accounts equal zero via the Income summary account. This closing entry transfers total revenues to the *credit* side of the Income summary account.
>
> **STEP 2:** Make expense accounts equal zero via the Income summary account. This closing entry transfers total expenses to the *debit* side of the Income summary account.
>
> The Income summary account now holds the net income or net loss of the period. The Income summary T-account is presented next:

Income summary

Closing Entry 2	Expenses	Closing Entry 1	Revenues
Expenses > Revenues	Net Loss	Revenues > Expenses	Net Income

> **STEP 3:** Make the Income summary account equal zero via the Capital account. This closing entry transfers net income (or net loss) to the Capital account.
>
> **STEP 4:** Make the Drawing account equal zero via the Capital account. This entry transfers the drawing to the *debit* side of the Capital account.

These steps are best illustrated with an example. Suppose Smart Touch closes its books at the end of May. Exhibit 4-10 on the following page shows the complete closing process for Smart Touch's training agency. Panel A gives the closing entries, and Panel B shows the accounts after posting. After the closing entries, Bright, capital ends with a balance of $35,900. Trace this balance to the statement of owner's equity and then to the balance sheet in Exhibit 4-7.

EXHIBIT 4-10 | **Journalizing and Posting the Closing Entries**

PANEL A—Journalizing

Closing Entries

	Date	Accounts	Debit	Credit
1	May 31	Service revenue (R–)	7,600	
		Income summary		7,600
2	31	Income summary	3,900	
		Rent expense (E–)		1,000
		Salary expense (E–)		1,800
		Supplies expense (E–)		100
		Depreciation expense—furniture (E–)		300
		Depreciation expense—building (E–)		200
		Interest expense (E–)		100
		Utilities expense (E–)		400
3	31	Income summary ($7,600 − $3,900)	3,700	
		Bright, capital (Q+)		3,700
4	31	Bright, capital (Q–)	1,000	
		Bright, drawing (D–)		1,000

(handwritten in margin: Temporary)

PANEL B—Posting

Rent expense

Adj	1,000		
Bal	1,000	Clo 2	1,000
Bal	0		

Salary expense

	900		
Adj	900		
Bal	1,800	Clo 2	1,800
Bal	0		

Supplies expense

Adj	100		
Bal	100	Clo 2	100
Bal	0		

Depreciation expense—furniture

Adj	300		
Bal	300	Clo 2	300
Bal	0		

Depreciation expense—building

Adj	200		
Bal	200	Clo 2	200
Bal	0		

Interest expense

Adj	100		
Bal	100	Clo 2	100
Bal	0		

Utilities expense

Bal	400	Clo 2	400
Bal	0		

Income summary

Clo 2	3,900	Clo 1	7,600
Clo 3	3,700	Bal	3,700
		Bal	0

Service revenue

			7,000
		Adj	400
		Adj	200
Clo 1	7,600	Bal	7,600
		Bal	0

Bright, drawing

Bal	1,000	Clo 4	1,000
Bal	0		

Bright, capital

Clo 4	1,000		33,200
		Clo 3	3,700
		Bal	35,900

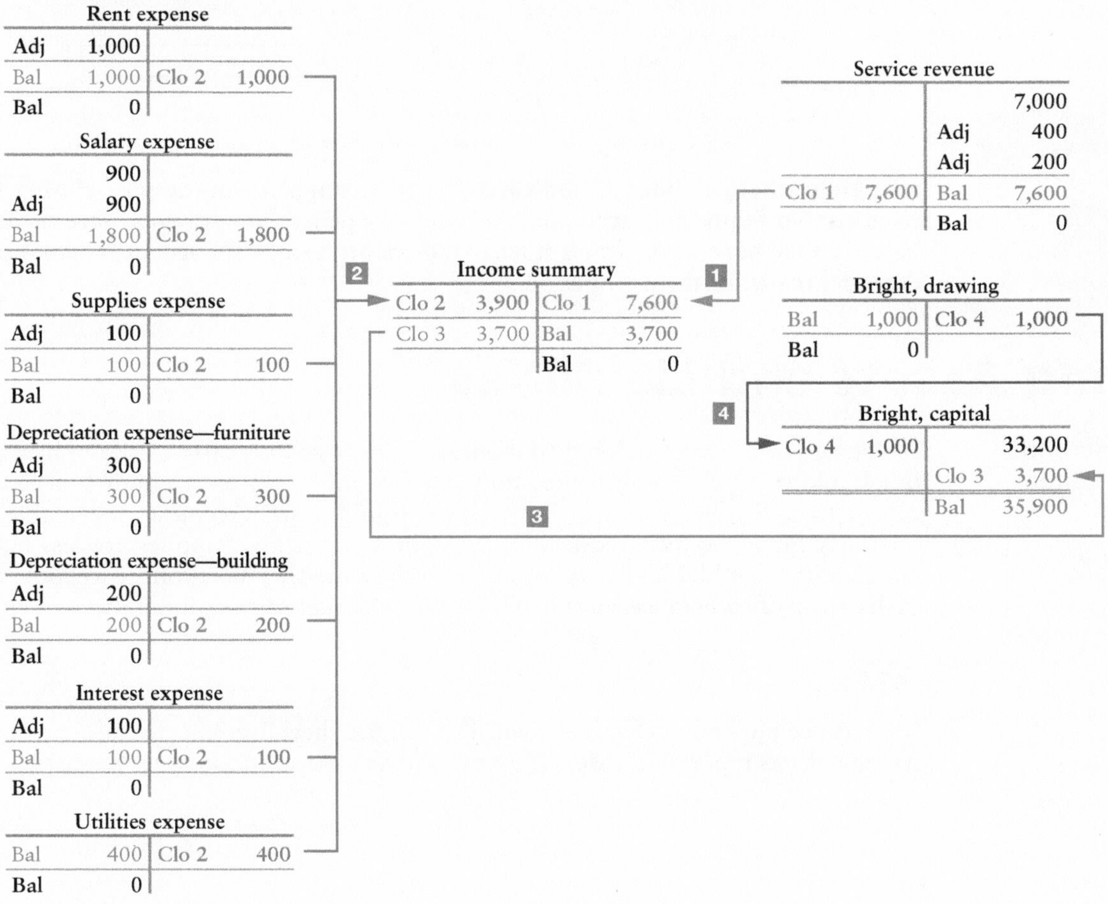

Adj = Amount posted from an adjusting entry
Clo = Amount posted from a closing entry
Bal = Balance

Post-Closing Trial Balance

 4   Prepare the post-closing trial balance

The accounting cycle can end with a **post-closing trial balance** (see Exhibit 4-11). This optional step lists the accounts and their adjusted balances after closing.

EXHIBIT 4-11 | **Post-Closing Trial Balance**

SMART TOUCH LEARNING Post-Closing Trial Balance May 31, 2013	Debit	Credit
Cash	$ 4,800	
Accounts receivable	2,600	
Supplies	600	
Prepaid rent	2,000	
Furniture	18,000	
Building	48,000	
Accumulated depreciation—furniture		$ 300
Accumulated depreciation—building		200
Accounts payable		18,200
Salary payable		900
Interest payable		100
Unearned service revenue		400
Notes payable		20,000
Bright, capital		35,900
Total	$ 76,000	$ 76,000

Key Takeaway

In summary, the post-closing trial balance contains the same accounts that the balance sheet contains—assets, liabilities, and capital.

Only assets, liabilities, and capital accounts appear on the post-closing trial balance. No temporary accounts—revenues, expenses, or drawing—are included because they have been closed (their balances are zero). The ledger is now up-to-date and ready for the next period.

Classifying Assets and Liabilities

5   Classify assets and liabilities as current or long-term

Assets and liabilities are classified as either *current* or *long-term* to show their relative liquidity. **Liquidity** measures how quickly and easily an account can be converted to cash, because cash is the most liquid asset. Accounts receivable are relatively liquid because receivables are collected quickly. Supplies are less liquid, and furniture and buildings are even less so because they take longer to convert to cash. A classified balance sheet lists assets in the order of their liquidity.

Assets

Owners need to know what they own. The balance sheet lists assets in liquidity order. Balance sheets report two asset categories: *current assets* and *long-term assets*.

Current Assets

Current assets will be converted to cash, sold, or used up during the next 12 months, or within the business's operating cycle if the cycle is longer than a year. Current assets are items that will be used up in a year, like your notebook paper for this class or the change in your pocket. The **operating cycle** is the time span when

1. cash is used to acquire goods and services,

2. these goods and services are sold to customers, and

3. the business collects cash from customers.

For most businesses, the operating cycle is a few months. Cash, Accounts receivable, Supplies, and Prepaid expenses are current assets. Merchandising entities such as **Lowes** and **Coca-Cola** have another current asset: inventory. Inventory shows the cost of the goods the company holds for sale to customers, like tools at **Lowes** or cans of soda for **Coca-Cola**.

Long-Term Assets

Long-term assets are all the assets that will not be converted to cash within the business's operating cycle. Long-term assets can be used for more than a year, like your car or computer. One category of long-term assets is plant assets (also called fixed assets or property, plant, and equipment). Land, Buildings, Furniture, and Equipment are plant assets. Of these, Smart Touch has Furniture and a Building.

Other categories of long-term assets include Long-Term Investments and Other Assets (a catchall category). We will discuss these categories in later chapters.

Liabilities

Owners need to know when they must pay each liability. The balance sheet lists liabilities in the order in which they must be paid. Balance sheets report two liability categories: *current liabilities* and *long-term liabilities*.

Current Liabilities

Current liabilities must be paid either with cash or with goods and services within one year, or within the entity's operating cycle if the cycle is longer than a year. Your cell phone bill is a current liability because you have to pay it every month. Accounts payable, Notes payable due within one year, Salary payable, Interest payable, and Unearned revenue are all current liabilities.

Long-Term Liabilities

All liabilities that do not need to be paid within the entity's operating cycle are classified as **long-term liabilities**. When you buy a car, you often sign up for several years of car payments, making it a long-term liability. Many notes payable are long-term, such as a mortgage on a building.

The Classified Balance Sheet

So far we have presented the *unclassified* balance sheet of Smart Touch. We are now ready for the balance sheet that is actually used in practice—called a **classified balance sheet**. Exhibit 4-12 presents Smart Touch's classified balance sheet using the data from Exhibit 4-7 on page 205.

Smart Touch classifies each asset and each liability as either current or long-term. Notice that the Total assets of $75,500 is the same as the Total assets on the unclassified balance sheet in Exhibit 4-7.

Connect To: Ethics

The classification of assets and liabilities as current or long-term affects many key ratios that outsiders use to evaluate the financial health of a company. Many times, the classification of a particular account is very clear—for example, a building is normally a long-term asset. But what if the company must demolish the existing building within six months due to some structural default? It would not be ethical to still show the building as a long-term asset.

EXHIBIT 4-12 | **Classified Balance Sheet in Account Form**

SMART TOUCH LEARNING
Balance Sheet
May 31, 2013

Assets				Liabilities	
Current assets:				Current liabilities:	
Cash		$ 4,800		Accounts payable	$18,200
Accounts receivable		2,600		Salary payable	900
Supplies		600		Interest payable	100
Prepaid rent		2,000		Unearned service revenue	400
Total current assets			$10,000	Total current liabilities	19,600
Plant assets:				Long-term liabilities:	
Furniture	$18,000			Notes payable	20,000
Less: Accumulated depreciation—furniture	300	17,700		Total liabilities	39,600
Building	48,000				
Less: Accumulated depreciation—building	200	47,800		**Owner's Equity**	
Total plant assets			65,500	Bright, capital	35,900
Total assets			$75,500	Total liabilities and owner's equity	$75,500

Balance Sheet Forms

Smart Touch's balance sheet in Exhibit 4-12 lists the assets on the left and the liabilities and the equity on the right in an arrangement known as the *account form*. The balance sheet of Smart Touch in Exhibit 4-13 lists the assets at the top and the liabilities and owner's equity below in an arrangement known as the *report form*. Although either form is acceptable, the report form is more popular.

EXHIBIT 4-13	**Classified Balance Sheet in Report Form**

SMART TOUCH LEARNING
Balance Sheet
May 31, 2013

Assets			
Current assets:			
Cash		$ 4,800	
Accounts receivable		2,600	
Supplies		600	
Prepaid rent		2,000	
Total current assets			$10,000
Plant assets:			
Furniture	$18,000		
Less: Accumulated depreciation—furniture	300	17,700	
Building	48,000		
Less: Accumulated depreciation—building	200	47,800	
Total plant assets			65,500
Total assets			$75,500
Liabilities			
Current liabilities:			
Accounts payable			$18,200
Salary payable			900
Interest payable			100
Unearned service revenue			400
Total current liabilities			19,600
Long-term liabilities			
Notes payable			20,000
Total liabilities			39,600
Owner's Equity			
Bright, capital			35,900
Total owner's equity			35,900
Total liabilities and owner's equity			$75,500

Accounting Ratios

Accounting is designed to provide information that business owners, managers, and lenders then use to make decisions. A bank considering lending money to a business must predict whether that business can repay the loan. If Smart Touch already has a lot of debt, repayment is less certain than if it does not owe much money. To measure the business's financial position, decision makers use financial ratios that they compute from the company's financial statements. Two of the most widely used decision aids in business are the current ratio and the debt ratio.

 6 Describe the effect of various transactions on the current ratio and the debt ratio

Current Ratio

The **current ratio** measures a company's ability to pay its current liabilities with its current assets. This ratio is computed as follows:

$$\text{Current ratio} = \frac{\text{Total current assets}}{\text{Total current liabilities}}$$

A company prefers to have a high current ratio because that means it has plenty of current assets to pay its current liabilities. A current ratio that has increased from the prior period indicates improvement in a company's ability to pay its current debts. A current ratio that has decreased from the prior period signals deterioration in the company's ability to pay its current liabilities. **Your personal current ratio is your checking account balance (your current assets) divided by your monthly bills (your current liabilities).**

A Rule of Thumb: A strong current ratio is 1.50, which indicates that the company has $1.50 in current assets for every $1.00 in current liabilities. A current ratio of 1.00 is considered low and somewhat risky.

Debt Ratio

The **debt ratio** measures an organization's overall ability to pay its total liabilities (debt). The debt ratio is computed as follows:

$$\text{Debt ratio} = \frac{\text{Total liabilities}}{\text{Total assets}}$$

Key Takeaway

The current ratio measures liquidity within one year by comparing current assets to current liabilities. The debt ratio measures the ability to pay liabilities in the long term by comparing all liabilities to all assets. The different ratios give different views of a company's financial health.

The debt ratio indicates the proportion of a company's assets that are financed with debt. A *low* debt ratio is safer than a high debt ratio. Why? Because a company with low liabilities usually has low required payments and is less likely to get into financial difficulty. **Your personal debt ratio is everything you owe divided by everything you own.**

A Rule of Thumb: A debt ratio below 0.60, or 60%, is considered safe for most businesses, as it indicates that the company owes only $0.60 for every $1.00 in total assets. A debt ratio above 0.80, or 80%, borders on high risk.

Now study the Decision Guidelines feature, which summarizes what you have learned in this chapter.

Current Assets – Current Liabilities =
CA – CL = Working Capital

Decision Guidelines 4-1

COMPLETING THE ACCOUNTING CYCLE

Suppose you own Greg's Tunes or Smart Touch Learning. How can you measure the success of your business? The Decision Guidelines describe the accounting process you will use to provide the information for any accounting decisions you need to make.

Decision	Guidelines
• What document summarizes the effects of all the entity's transactions and adjustments throughout the period?	The *worksheet* with columns for • Trial balance • Adjustments • Adjusted trial balance • Income statement • Balance sheet
• What is the last *major* step in the accounting cycle?	*Closing entries for the temporary accounts:* • Revenues • Expenses } Income statement accounts • Drawing
• Why close out the revenues, expenses, and drawing accounts?	Because these *temporary accounts* have balances that relate only to one accounting period and *do not* carry over to the next period
• Which accounts do *not* get closed out?	*Permanent (balance sheet) accounts:* • Assets • Liabilities • Capital The balances of these accounts *do* carry over to the next period.
• How do businesses classify their assets and liabilities for reporting on the balance sheet?	*Current* (within one year, or the entity's operating cycle if longer than a year), or *Long-term* (not current)
• How do Greg Moore and Sheena Bright evaluate their companies?	There are many ways, such as the company's net income (or net loss) on the income statement and the trend of net income from year to year. Another way to evaluate a company is based on the company's *financial ratios*. Two key ratios are the current ratio and the debt ratio:

$$\text{Current ratio} = \frac{\text{Total current assets}}{\text{Total current liabilities}}$$

The *current ratio* measures the company's ability to pay current liabilities with current assets.

$$\text{Debt ratio} = \frac{\text{Total liabilities}}{\text{Total assets}}$$

The *debt ratio* measures the company's overall ability to pay liabilities. The debt ratio shows the proportion of the company's assets that are financed with debt.

Summary Problem 4-2

Refer to the data in Summary Problem 4-1 (Super Employment Services).

Requirements

1. Journalize and post the adjusting entries. (Before posting to the accounts, enter into each account its balance as shown in the trial balance. For example, enter the $5,000 balance in the Accounts receivable account before posting its adjusting entry.) Key adjusting entries by *letter*, as shown in the worksheet solution to Summary Problem 4-1. You can take the adjusting entries straight from the worksheet in the chapter.

2. Journalize and post the closing entries. (Each account should carry its balance as shown in the adjusted trial balance.) To distinguish closing entries from adjusting entries, key the closing entries by *number*. Draw arrows to illustrate the flow of data, as shown in Exhibit 4-10. Indicate the balance of the Mudge, capital account after the closing entries are posted.

3. Prepare the income statement for the year ended December 31, 2014.

4. Prepare the statement of owner's equity for the year ended December 31, 2014. Draw an arrow linking the income statement to the statement of owner's equity.

5. Prepare the classified balance sheet at December 31, 2014. Use the account form. All liabilities are current. Draw an arrow linking the statement of owner's equity to the balance sheet.

Solution

Requirement 1

		Adjusting Entries		
a.	Dec 31	Supplies expense (E+)	800	
		Supplies (A–)		800
b.	31	Depreciation expense—furniture (E+)	2,000	
		Accumulated depreciation—furniture (CA+)		2,000
c.	31	Depreciation expense—building (E+)	1,000	
		Accumulated depreciation—building (CA+)		1,000
d.	31	Salary expense (E+)	500	
		Salary payable (L+)		500
e.	31	Accounts receivable (A+)	1,300	
		Service revenue (R+)		1,300
f.	31	Unearned service revenue (L–)	3,000	
		Service revenue (R+)		3,000

Accounts receivable

	5,000	
(e)	1,300	
Bal	6,300	

Supplies

	1,000	(a)	800	
Bal	200			

Accumulated depreciation—furniture

		4,000	
	(b)	2,000	
	Bal	6,000	

Accumulated depreciation—building

		30,000	
	(c)	1,000	
	Bal	31,000	

Salary payable

	(d)	500	
	Bal	500	

Unearned service revenue

(f)	3,000	8,000	
		Bal	5,000

Service revenue

		60,000	
	(e)	1,300	
	(f)	3,000	
	Bal	64,300	

Salary expense

	16,000	
(d)	500	
Bal	16,500	

Supplies expense

(a)	800	
Bal	800	

Depreciation expense—furniture

(b)	2,000	
Bal	2,000	

Depreciation expense—building

(c)	1,000	
Bal	1,000	

Requirement 2

		Closing Entries			
1.	Dec 31	Service revenue	(R–)	64,300	
		Income summary			64,300
2.	31	Income summary		23,300	
		Salary expense	(E–)		16,500
		Supplies expense	(E–)		800
		Depreciation expense—furniture	(E–)		2,000
		Depreciation expense—building	(E–)		1,000
		Advertising expense	(E–)		3,000
3.	31	Income summary ($64,300 – $23,300)		41,000	
		Mudge, capital	(Q+)		41,000
4.	31	Mudge, capital	(Q–)	25,000	
		Mudge, drawing	(D–)		25,000

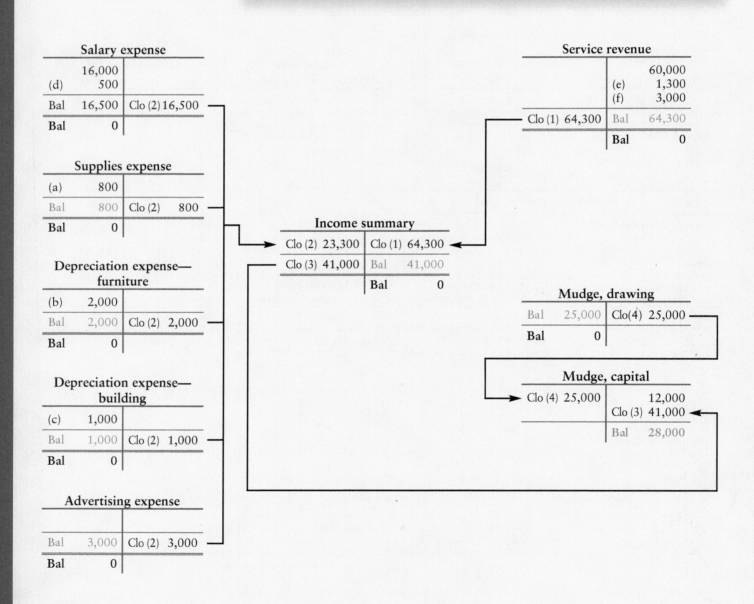

Requirement 3

SUPER EMPLOYMENT SERVICES
Income Statement
Year Ended December 31, 2014

Revenue:		
Service revenue		$64,300
Expenses:		
Salary expense	$16,500	
Advertising expense	3,000	
Depreciation expense—furniture	2,000	
Depreciation expense—building	1,000	
Supplies expense	800	
Total expenses		23,300
Net income		$41,000

Requirement 4

SUPER EMPLOYMENT SERVICES
Statement of Owner's Equity
Year Ended December 31, 2014

Mudge, capital, January 1, 2014	$ 12,000
Net income	41,000
	53,000
Drawing	(25,000)
Mudge, capital, December 31, 2014	$ 28,000

Requirement 5

SUPER EMPLOYMENT SERVICES
Balance Sheet
December 31, 2014

Assets			Liabilities	
Current assets:			Current liabilities:	
Cash		$ 6,000	Accounts payable	$ 2,000
Accounts receivable		6,300	Salary payable	500
Supplies		200	Unearned service	
Total current assets		12,500	revenue	5,000
Long-term assets:			Total current liabilities	7,500
Furniture	$10,000			
Less: Accumulated depreciation—furniture	6,000	4,000		
Building	50,000		**Owner's Equity**	
Less: Accumulated depreciation—building	31,000	19,000	Mudge, capital	28,000
Total assets		$35,500	Total liabilities and owner's equity	$35,500

Chapter 4: Demo Doc

Accounting Worksheets and Closing Entries

To make sure you understand this material, work through the following demonstration "demo doc" with detailed comments to help you see the concept within the framework of a worked-through problem.

This question continues on from the Cloud Break Consulting Demo Doc in Chapter 3.

Use the data from the adjusted trial balance of Cloud Break Consulting at June 30, 2014:

CLOUD BREAK CONSULTING Adjusted Trial Balance June 30, 2014		
Account Title	**Debit**	**Credit**
Cash	$131,000	
Accounts receivable	119,000	
Supplies	1,000	
Prepaid rent	18,000	
Land	45,000	
Building	300,000	
Accumulated depreciation—building		$167,000
Accounts payable		159,000
Salary payable		1,000
Unearned service revenue		10,000
Moe, capital		102,000
Moe, drawing	7,000	
Service revenue		495,000
Salary expense	256,000	
Supplies expense	3,000	
Rent expense	34,000	
Depreciation expense—building	12,000	
Miscellaneous expense	8,000	
Totals	$934,000	$934,000

Requirements

1. Prepare Cloud Break's accounting worksheet showing the adjusted trial balance, the income statement accounts, and the balance sheet accounts.
2. Journalize and post Cloud Break's closing entries.

Chapter 4: Demo Doc Solution

Requirement 1

Prepare Cloud Break's accounting worksheet showing the adjusted trial balance, the income statement accounts, and the balance sheet accounts.

Part 1	Part 2	Part 3	Part 4	Part 5	Demo Doc Complete

   The accounting worksheet is very similar to the adjusted trial balance; however, the worksheet has additional debit and credit columns for the income statement and balance sheet.

CLOUD BREAK CONSULTING Worksheet Month Ended June 30, 2014						
	Adjusted Trial Balance		**Income Statement**		**Balance Sheet**	
Account Title	Debit	Credit	Debit	Credit	Debit	Credit
Cash	$131,000					
Accounts receivable	119,000					
Supplies	1,000					
Prepaid rent	18,000					
Land	45,000					
Building	300,000					
Accumulated depreciation—building		$167,000				
Accounts payable		159,000				
Salary payable		1,000				
Unearned service revenue		10,000				
Moe, capital		102,000				
Moe, drawing	7,000					
Service revenue		495,000				
Salary expense	256,000					
Supplies expense	3,000					
Rent expense	34,000					
Depreciation expense—building	12,000					
Miscellaneous expense	8,000					
	$934,000	$934,000				

   The accounts that belong on the income statement are put into the income statement columns and all other accounts are put into the balance sheet columns.

The income statement lists revenues and expenses. So Cloud Break's revenues (Service revenue) and expenses (Salary expense, Supplies expense, Rent expense, Depreciation expense—building, and Miscellaneous expense) are copied over to the income statement columns.

CLOUD BREAK CONSULTING
Worksheet
Month Ended June 30, 2014

Account Title	Adjusted Trial Balance Debit	Adjusted Trial Balance Credit	Income Statement Debit	Income Statement Credit	Balance Sheet Debit	Balance Sheet Credit
Cash	$131,000					
Accounts receivable	119,000					
Supplies	1,000					
Prepaid rent	18,000					
Land	45,000					
Building	300,000					
Accumulated depreciation—building		$167,000				
Accounts payable		159,000				
Salary payable		1,000				
Unearned service revenue		10,000				
Moe, capital		102,000				
Moe, drawing	7,000					
Service revenue		495,000		$495,000		
Salary expense	256,000		$256,000			
Supplies expense	3,000		3,000			
Rent expense	34,000		34,000			
Depreciation expense—building	12,000		12,000			
Miscellaneous expense	8,000		8,000			
	$934,000	$934,000	$313,000	$495,000		
Net income			182,000			
			$495,000	$495,000		

Net income is calculated by subtracting the expenses from the revenues, $495,000 – $313,000 = $182,000. Notice that this is the same as net income from the income statement prepared in the Chapter 3 Demo Doc.

The other accounts (assets, liabilities, equity, and drawing) are now copied over to the balance sheet columns.

CLOUD BREAK CONSULTING
Worksheet
Month Ended June 30, 2014

Account Title	Adjusted Trial Balance Debit	Credit	Income Statement Debit	Credit	Balance Sheet Debit	Credit
Cash	$131,000				$131,000	
Accounts receivable	119,000				119,000	
Supplies	1,000				1,000	
Prepaid rent	18,000				18,000	
Land	45,000				45,000	
Building	300,000				300,000	
Accumulated depreciation—building		$167,000				$167,000
Accounts payable		159,000				159,000
Salary payable		1,000				1,000
Unearned service revenue		10,000				10,000
Moe, capital		102,000				102,000
Moe, drawing	7,000				7,000	
Service revenue		495,000		$495,000		
Salary expense	256,000		$256,000			
Supplies expense	3,000		3,000			
Rent expense	34,000		34,000			
Depreciation expense—building	12,000		12,000			
Miscellaneous expense	8,000		8,000			
	$934,000	$934,000	$313,000	$495,000	$621,000	$439,000
Net income			182,000			182,000
			$495,000	$495,000	$621,000	$621,000

Net income is added to the credit side of the balance sheet to make total credits equal total debits. This is because net income increases Moe, capital (and therefore equity) as seen in Requirement 2 of this Demo Doc (where the closing entries are journalized).

Requirement 2

Journalize and post Cloud Break's closing entries.

Part 1	**Part 2**	Part 3	Part 4	Part 5	Demo Doc Complete

We prepare closing entries to (1) clear out the revenue, expense, and drawing accounts to a zero balance in order to get them ready for the next period—that is, they must begin the next period empty so that we can evaluate each period's earnings separately from other periods. We also need to (2) update the Moe, capital account by transferring net income (or net loss) and drawing into it.

The Capital balance is calculated each year using the following formula:

> Beginning capital
> + Net income (or – Net loss)
> – Drawing
> = Ending capital

You can see this in the Capital T-account as well:

Capital	
	Beginning capital
	Net income
Drawing	
	Ending capital

This formula is the key to preparing the closing entries. We will use this formula, but we will do it *inside* the Capital T-account.

From the adjusted trial balance, we know that beginning Moe, capital is $102,000. The first component of the formula is already in the T-account.

The next component is net income, which is *not* yet in the Moe, capital account. There is no T-account with net income in it, but we can *create* one.

We will create a new T-account called *Income summary*. We will place in the Income summary account all the components of net income and come out with the net income number at the bottom. Remember:

> Revenues – Expenses = Net income (or Net loss)

This means that we need to get all of the revenues and expenses into the Income summary account.

Look at the Service revenue T-account:

Service revenue	
	Bal 495,000

In order to clear out all the income statement accounts so that they are empty to begin the next year, the first step is to debit each revenue account for the amount of its credit balance. Service revenue has a *credit* balance of $495,000, so to bring that to zero, we need to *debit* Service revenue for $495,000.

This means that we have part of our first closing entry:

1.	Service revenue (R–)	495,000	
	???		495,000

What is the credit side of this entry? The reason we were looking at Service revenue to begin with was to help calculate net income using the Income summary account. So the other side of the entry must go to the Income summary account:

1.	Service revenue	(R–)	495,000	
	Income summary			495,000

Part 1	Part 2	**Part 3**	Part 4	Part 5	Demo Doc Complete

The second step is to *credit* each expense account for the amount of its *debit* balance to bring each expense account to zero. In this case, we have five different expenses:

Salary expense	
Bal 256,000	

Supplies expense	
Bal 3,000	

Rent expense	
Bal 34,000	

Depreciation expense—building	
Bal 12,000	

Miscellaneous expense	
Bal 8,000	

The sum of all the expenses will go to the debit side of the Income summary account:

2.	Income summary		313,000	
	Salary expense	(E–)		256,000
	Supplies expense	(E–)		3,000
	Rent expense	(E–)		34,000
	Depreciation expense—building	(E–)		12,000
	Miscellaneous expense	(E–)		8,000

Part 1	Part 2	Part 3	**Part 4**	Part 5	Demo Doc Complete

Now look at the Income summary account:

Income summary	
	1. 495,000
2. 313,000	
	Bal 182,000

Remember that the credit of $495,000 is from the first closing entry prepared at the beginning of this requirement.

The purpose of creating the Income summary was to get the net income number into a single account. Notice that the Income summary balance is the same net income number that appears on the income statement and in the accounting worksheet in Requirement 1.

Income summary now has a *credit* balance of $182,000. The third step in the closing process is to transfer net income to the Moe, capital account. To zero out the Income summary account, we must *debit* the Income summary for $182,000:

3.	Income summary	182,000	
	???		182,000

What is the credit side of this entry? It is the Moe, capital account. The reason we created the (temporary) Income summary account was to help calculate the net income or net loss for the Moe, capital account. So the credit side of the entry must go to Moe, capital:

3.	Income summary	182,000	
	Moe, capital (Q+)		182,000

This entry adds the net income to Moe, capital. Notice that it also brings the Income summary account to a zero balance.

Part 1	Part 2	Part 3	Part 4	**Part 5**	Demo Doc Complete

The last component of the capital formula is drawing. There is already a Moe, drawing account:

Moe, drawing

Bal 7,000	

The final step in the closing process is to transfer Moe, drawing to the debit side of the Moe, capital account. The Moe, drawing account has a *debit* balance of $7,000, so to bring that to zero, we need to *credit* Moe, drawing by $7,000. The balancing debit will go to Moe, capital:

4.	Moe, capital (Q–)	7,000	
	Moe, drawing (D–)		7,000

This entry subtracts Moe, drawing from the Moe, capital account.
Moe, capital now holds the following data:

Moe, capital

		102,000	Beginning capital
	3.	182,000	Net income
Drawing 4. 7,000			
	Bal 277,000		Ending capital

The formula to update Moe, capital has now been re-created inside the Moe, capital T-account.

The following accounts are included in the closing process:

Service revenue				Income summary		
		495,000			**1.**	495,000
1.	495,000		**2.**	313,000		
	Bal	0			Bal	182,000
			3.	182,000		
Salary expense					Bal	0
256,000						
	2.	256,000		Moe, drawing		
Bal	0			7,000		
					4.	7,000
Supplies expense				Bal	0	
3,000						
	2.	3,000		Moe, capital		
Bal	0					102,000
					3.	182,000
Rent expense			**4.**	7,000		
34,000					Bal	277,000
	2.	34,000				
Bal	0					

Depreciation expense—building		
12,000		
	2.	12,000
Bal	0	

Miscellaneous expense		
8,000		
	2.	8,000
Bal	0	

Notice that all the temporary accounts (the revenues, the expenses, Drawing, and Income summary) now have a zero balance.

Part 1	Part 2	Part 3	Part 4	Part 5	**Demo Doc Complete**

Review *Completing the Accounting Cycle*

● Accounting Vocabulary

Accounting Cycle (p. 199)
Process by which companies produce their financial statements for a specific period.

Classified Balance Sheet (p. 211)
A balance sheet that classifies each asset and each liability as either current or long-term.

Closing the Accounts (p. 207)
Step in the accounting cycle at the end of the period. Closing the accounts consists of journalizing and posting the closing entries to set the balances of the revenue, expense, and drawing accounts to zero for the next period.

Closing Entries (p. 207)
Entries that transfer the revenue, expense, and drawing balances to the Capital account.

Current Assets (p. 211)
Assets that are expected to be converted to cash, sold, or used up during the next 12 months, or within the business's normal operating cycle if the cycle is longer than a year.

Current Liabilities (p. 211)
Debts due to be paid with cash or with goods and services within one year, or within the entity's operating cycle if the cycle is longer than a year.

Current Ratio (p. 214)
Current assets divided by current liabilities. This ratio measures the company's ability to pay current liabilities from current assets.

Debt Ratio (p. 214)
Total liabilities divided by total assets. This ratio reveals the proportion of a company's assets that it has financed with debt.

Income Summary (p. 207)
A temporary "holding tank" account into which revenues and expenses are transferred prior to their final transfer to the Capital account.

Liquidity (p. 210)
Measure of how quickly an item can be converted to cash.

Long-Term Assets (p. 211)
Any assets that will NOT be converted to cash or used up within the business's operating cycle, or one year, whichever is greater.

Long-Term Liabilities (p. 211)
Liabilities that are not current.

Nominal Accounts (p. 207)
The revenue and expense accounts that relate to a particular accounting period and are closed at the end of that period. For a company, the Drawing account is also temporary. Also called **temporary accounts**.

Operating Cycle (p. 211)
Time span during which cash is paid for goods and services, which are then sold to customers from whom the business collects cash.

Permanent Accounts (p. 207)
Accounts that are *not* closed at the end of the period—the asset, liability, and capital accounts. Also called **real accounts**.

Post-Closing Trial Balance (p. 210)
List of the accounts and their balances at the end of the period after journalizing and posting the closing entries. This last step of the accounting cycle ensures that the ledger is in balance to start the next accounting period. It should include only balance sheet accounts.

Real Accounts (p. 207)
Accounts that are not closed at the end of the period—the assets, liabilities, and capital accounts. Also called **permanent accounts**.

Reversing Entries (online Appendix 4A)
Special journal entries that ease the burden of accounting for transactions in the next period.

Temporary Accounts (p. 207)
The revenue and expense accounts that relate to a particular accounting period and are closed at the end of that period. For a company, the Drawing account is also temporary. Also called **nominal accounts**.

Worksheet (p. 200)
An internal columnar document designed to help move data from the trial balance to their financial statements.

● Destination: Student Success

Student Success Tips

The following are hints on some common trouble areas for students in this chapter:

● Be sure you remember the four closing entries, paying special attention to which accounts are closed. (TIP: Make temporary accounts = zero.)

● Practice the 5-column worksheets. Remember that debits = credits in the first 3 columns. Debits from columns 4 and 5 (Income Statement and Balance Sheet) do not equal credits until you post the net income or net loss for the period. (TIP: Total Debits from Column 3 = Column 4 Debits + Column 5 Debits.)

● Recall the classification difference between current (normally, 1 year or less) and long term (more than a year). (TIP: If it lasts more than a year, it's long term.)

Getting Help

If there's a learning objective from the chapter you aren't confident about, try using one or more of the following resources:

● Practice additional exercises or problems at the end of Chapter 4 that cover the specific learning objective that is challenging you.

● Watch the white board tips and/or videos for Chapter 4 located at myaccountinglab.com under the Chapter Resources button.

● Review the Chapter 4 Demo Doc located on page 220 of the textbook.

● Go to myaccountinglab.com and select the Study Plan button. Choose Chapter 4 and work the questions covering that specific learning objective until you've mastered it.

● Destination: Student Success (Continued)

Student Success Tips

- Remember the formulas for the current ratio and debt ratio. (TIP: The current ratio usually should be greater than 1; the debt ratio should be less than 1.)

Getting Help

- Work the Chapter 4 pre/post tests in myaccountinglab.com.
- Consult the Check Figures for End of Chapter starters, exercises, and problems—located at myaccountinglab.com.
- Visit the learning resource center on your campus for tutoring.

● Quick Check

1. Consider the steps in the accounting cycle in Exhibit 4-1. Which part of the accounting cycle provides information to help a business decide whether to expand its operations?
   - a. Post-closing trial balance
   - b. Adjusting entries
   - c. Closing entries
   - d. Financial statements

2. Which columns of the accounting worksheet show unadjusted amounts?
   - a. Adjustments
   - b. Trial Balance
   - c. Income Statement
   - d. Balance Sheet

3. Which of the following accounts may appear on a post-closing trial balance?
   - a. Cash, Salary payable, and Capital
   - b. Cash, Salary payable, and Service revenue
   - c. Cash, Service revenue, and Salary expense
   - d. Cash, Salary payable, and Salary expense

4. Which situation indicates a net loss within the Income Statement columns of the worksheet?
   - a. Total credits exceed total debits
   - b. Total debits exceed total credits
   - c. Total debits equal total credits
   - d. None of the above

5. Supplies has a $10,000 unadjusted balance on your trial balance. At year-end you count supplies of $6,000. What adjustment will appear on your worksheet?

   a.
Supplies	4,000	
Supplies expense		4,000

   b.
Supplies expense	6,000	
Supplies		6,000

   c.
Supplies expense	4,000	
Supplies		4,000

   d. No adjustment is needed because the Supplies account already has a correct balance.

6. Which of the following accounts is *not* closed?
   - a. Depreciation expense
   - b. Drawing
   - c. Service revenue
   - d. Accumulated depreciation

7. What do closing entries accomplish?
   - a. Zero out the revenues, expenses, and drawing
   - b. Transfer revenues, expenses, and drawing to the Capital account
   - c. Bring the Capital account to its correct ending balance
   - d. All of the above

Experience the Power of Practice!

As denoted by the logo, all of these questions, as well as additional practice materials, can be found in

MyAccountingLab.

Please visit myaccountinglab.com

8. Which of the following is *not* a closing entry?

a.

Capital	XXX	
Drawing		XXX

b.

Service revenue	XXX	
Income summary		XXX

c.

Salary payable	XXX	
Income summary		XXX

d.

Income summary	XXX	
Rent expense		XXX

9. Assets and liabilities are listed on the balance sheet in order of their

a. purchase date.   c. liquidity.

b. adjustments.   d. balance.

10. Clean Water Softener Systems has cash of $600, receivables of $900, and supplies of $400. Clean owes $500 on accounts payable and salary payable of $200. Clean's current ratio is

a. 2.71   c. 0.63

b. 2.50   d. 0.37

Answers are given after Apply Your Knowledge (p. 253).

Assess Your Progress

● Short Exercises

MyAccountingLab   **S4-1**   ❶ **Explaining worksheet items [10 min]**

Link Back to Chapter 3 (Adjusting Entries). Consider the following adjusting entries:

			Journal Entry		
	Date		Accounts and Explanations	Debit	Credit
a.	Apr	30	Rent expense	900	
			Prepaid rent		900
b.		30	Unearned service revenue	350	
			Service revenue		350
c.		30	Supplies expense	200	
			Supplies		200
d.		30	Salary expense	850	
			Salary payable		850
e.		30	Depreciation expense—furniture	450	
			Accumulated depreciation—furniture		450

Requirement

1. State one reason why each of the previous adjusting entries were made.

   Example: The explanation for journal entry a could be some of the Prepaid rent has expired. Another correct explanation would be the asset account Prepaid rent was overstated. A third correct explanation would be that Rent expense incurred was understated.

S4-2   ① **Explaining worksheet items [10–15 min]**
Link Back to Chapters 2 and 3 (Definitions of Accounts). Consider the following list of accounts:

a. Accounts receivable   f. Accounts payable

b. Supplies   g. Unearned service revenue

c. Prepaid rent   h. Service revenue

d. Furniture   i. Rent expense

e. Accumulated depreciation—
   furniture

Requirement

1. Explain what a normal balance in each account means. For example, if the account is "Cash," the explanation would be "the balance of cash on a specific date."

S4-3   ② **Using the worksheet to prepare financial statements [5–10 min]**
Answer the following questions:

Requirements

1. What type of normal balance does the Capital account have—debit or credit?

2. Which type of income statement account has the same type of balance as the Capital account?

3. Which type of income statement account has the opposite type of balance as the Capital account?

4. What do we call the difference between total debits and total credits on the income statement? Into what account is the difference figure closed at the end of the period?

S4-4   ③ **Journalizing closing entries [10–15 min]**
It is December 31 and time for you to close the books for Brett Tilman Enterprises.

Requirement

1. Journalize the closing entries for Brett Tilman Enterprises:

a. Service revenue, $20,600.
b. Make a single closing entry for all the expenses: Salary, $7,200; Rent, $4,500; Advertising, $3,400.
c. Income summary.
d. Drawing, $3,800.

S4-5   ③ **Posting closing entries directly to T-accounts [5 min]**
It is December 31 and time for your business to close the books. The following balances appear on the books of Sarah Simon Enterprises:

   a. Drawing, $8,500.
   b. Service revenue, $23,700.
   c. Expense account balances: Salary, $6,100; Rent, $4,000; Advertising, $3,300.

Requirements

1. Set up each T-account given and insert its adjusted balance as given (denote as *Bal*) at December 31. Also set up a T-account for Simon, capital, $26,100, and for Income summary.

2. Post the closing entries to the accounts, denoting posted amounts as *Clo*.

3. Compute the ending balance of Simon, capital.

S4-6   ③ **Making closing entries [5 min]**
Brown Insurance Agency reported the following items at November 30, 2012:

Sales and marketing expense	$2,100	Cash	$1,100
Other assets	700	Service revenue	5,500
Depreciation expense	800	Accounts payable	500
Long-term liabilities	600	Accounts receivable	900

Requirement

1. Journalize Brown's closing entries, as needed for these accounts.

S4-7   ③ **Posting closing entries [5 min]**
Patel Insurance Agency reported the following items at September 30:

Sales and marketing expense	$1,600	Cash	$1,300
Other assets	700	Service revenue	4,000
Depreciation expense	900	Patel, capital	500
Long-term liabilities	600	Accounts receivable	900

Requirement

1. Prepare T-accounts for Patel Insurance Agency. Insert the account balances prior to closing. Post the closing entries to the affected T-accounts, and show each account's ending balance after closing. Also show the Income summary T-account. Denote a balance as *Bal* and a closing entry amount as *Clo*.

S4-8   ④ **Preparing a post-closing trial balance [10 min]**
After closing its accounts at July 31, 2012, Goodrow Electric Company had the following account balances:

Long-term liabilities	$ 800	Equipment	$ 4,500
Land	1,200	Cash	100
Accounts receivable	1,600	Service revenue	0
Total expenses	0	Goodrow, capital	3,000
Accounts payable	1,100	Supplies	200
Unearned service revenue	1,400	Accumulated depreciation	1,300
Goodrow, drawing	0		

Requirement

1. Prepare Goodrow's post-closing trial balance at July 31, 2012.

S4-9   ⑤ **Classifying assets and liabilities as current or long-term [5 min]**
Jet Fast Printing reported the following:

Buildings	$4,200	Service revenue	$1,115
Accounts payable	600	Cash	400
Total expenses	1,200	Receivables	700
Accumulated depreciation	3,000	Interest expense	110
Accrued liabilities (such as Salary payable)	400	Equipment	1,100
Prepaid expenses	300		

Requirements

1. Identify the assets (including contra assets) and liabilities.
2. Classify each asset and each liability as current or long-term.

S4-10   ⑤ **Classifying assets and liabilities as current or long-term [10 min]**
Link Back to Chapter 3 (Book Value). Examine Jet Fast Printing's account balances in Short Exercise 4-9.

Requirement

1. Identify or compute the following amounts for Jet Fast Printing:
   a. Total current assets
   b. Total current liabilities
   c. Book value of plant assets
   d. Total long-term liabilities

S4-11   ⑥ **Computing the current and debt ratios [10–15 min]**
Heart of Texas Telecom has these account balances at December 31, 2012:

Note payable, long-term	$ 7,800	Accounts payable	$ 3,700
Prepaid rent	2,300	Accounts receivable	5,700
Salary payable	3,000	Cash	3,500
Service revenue	29,400	Depreciation expense	6,000
Supplies	500	Equipment	15,000

Requirements

1. Compute Heart of Texas Telecom's current ratio and debt ratio.
2. How much in *current* assets does Heart of Texas Telecom have for every dollar of *current* liabilities that it owes?

● Exercises

E4-12   ① **Preparing a worksheet [30–40 min]**
Data for the unadjusted trial balance of Mexican Riviera Tanning Salon at March 31, 2012, follow.

Cash	$ 13,000	Service revenue	$ 89,900
Equipment	66,500	Salary expense	42,200
Accumulated depreciation	18,500	Depreciation expense	
Accounts payable	3,200	Supplies expense	
Supplies	1,400	Neeland, drawing	
Neeland, capital	11,500		

Adjusting data for March 2012 are:

a. Accrued service revenue, $2,600.   c. Accrued salary expense, $1,700.
b. Supplies used in operations, $400.   d. Depreciation expense, $4,100.

Les Neeland, the owner, has received an offer to sell the company. He needs to know the net income for the month covered by these data.

Requirements

1. Prepare the worksheet for Mexican Riviera Tanning Salon.
2. How much was the net income/net loss for March?

E4-13 ❶ **Preparing a worksheet and using it to calculate net income [20–30 min]**
The trial balance of Telegraphic Link at November 30, follows:

	TELEGRAPHIC LINK Trial Balance November 30, 2012		
		Balance	
Account		Debit	Credit
Cash		$ 4,000	
Accounts receivable		3,200	
Prepaid rent		1,900	
Supplies		3,000	
Equipment		34,800	
Accumulated depreciation			$ 1,600
Accounts payable			5,400
Salary payable			
Thomas, capital			35,700
Thomas, drawing		2,100	
Service revenue			8,600
Depreciation expense			
Salary expense		1,700	
Rent expense			
Utilities expense		600	
Supplies expense			
Total		$51,300	$51,300

Additional information at November 30, 2012:

a. Accrued service revenue, $600.
b. Depreciation, $300.
c. Accrued salary expense, $800.
d. Prepaid rent expired, $500.
e. Supplies used, $100.

Requirements

1. Complete Telegraphic Link's worksheet for the month ended November 30, 2012.
2. How much was net income for November?

Note: Exercise 4-14 should be used only after completing Exercise 4-13.

E4-14 ❷ **Preparing financial statements from the completed worksheet [15–20 min]**
Use your answer from E4-13.

Requirement

1. Prepare Telegraphic Link's balance sheet as of November 30, 2012.

Note: Exercise 4-15 should be used only after completing Exercise 4-13.

E4-15 ❸ **Journalizing adjusting and closing entries [15–20 min]**
Use your answer from E4-13.

Requirement

1. Journalize Telegraphic Link's adjusting and closing entries at November 30, 2012.

Note: Exercise 4-16 should be used only after completing Exercise 4-13 and 4-15.

E4-16   ❸ **Using the worksheet, and posting adjusting and closing entries [20–30 min]**
Consider the entries prepared in Exercise 4-15.

Requirements

1. Set up T-accounts for those accounts affected by the adjusting and closing entries in Exercise 4-15.

2. Post the adjusting and closing entries to the accounts; denote adjustment amounts by *Adj*, closing amounts by *Clo*, and balances by *Bal*. Double underline the accounts with zero balances after you close them, and show the ending balance in each account.

E4-17   ❸ **Preparing adjusting and closing entries [20 min]**
Link Back to Chapter 3 (Adjusting Entries). Todd McKinney Magic Show's accounting records include the following account balances as of December 31:

	2011	2012
Prepaid rent	$ 200	$ 3,100
Unearned service revenue	1,000	500

During 2012, the business recorded the following:

a. Prepaid annual rent of $8,000.
b. Made the year-end adjustment to record rent expense of $5,100 for the year.
c. Collected $4,400 cash in advance for service revenue to be earned later.
d. Made the year-end adjustment to record the earning of $4,900 service revenue that had been collected in advance.

Requirements

1. Set up T-accounts for Prepaid rent, Rent expense, Unearned service revenue, and Service revenue. Insert beginning and ending balances for Prepaid rent and Unearned service revenue.

2. Journalize the adjusting entries a–d, and post to the accounts. Explanations are not required.

3. What is the balance in Service revenue after adjusting?

4. What is the balance in Rent expense after adjusting?

5. Journalize any required closing entries.

E4-18 ❸ **Preparing closing entries from a partial worksheet [15–25 min]**

The adjusted trial balance from the January worksheet of Silver Sign Company follows:

SILVER SIGN COMPANY		
Partial Worksheet		
Month Ended January 31, 2012		

	Adjusted Trial Balance	
Account	Debit	Credit
Cash	$14,300	
Supplies	2,400	
Prepaid rent	1,400	
Equipment	45,000	
Accumulated depreciation		$ 6,100
Accounts payable		4,500
Salary payable		300
Unearned service revenue		4,500
Note payable, long-term		5,300
Silver, capital		32,600
Silver, drawing	800	
Service revenue		16,800
Salary expense	3,600	
Rent expense	1,400	
Depreciation expense	400	
Supplies expense	200	
Utilities expense	600	
Total	$70,100	$70,100

Requirements

1. Journalize Silver's closing entries at January 31.

2. How much net income or net loss did Silver earn for January? How can you tell?

E4-19 ❸ **Preparing a statement of owner's equity [5–10 min]**

Selected accounts of Guitars by Peter for the year ended December 31, 2012, follow:

Peter, capital			Peter, drawing				Income summary			
Clo	31,000	Jan 1 152,000	Mar 31 10,000				Clo	100,000	Clo	220,000
		Clo 120,000	Jun 30 7,000				Clo	120,000	Bal	120,000
		Bal 241,000	Sep 30 8,000							
			Dec 31 6,000							
			Bal 31,000	Clo	31,000					

Requirement

1. Prepare the company's statement of owner's equity for the year.

E4-20   **3** **Identifying and journalizing closing entries [15 min]**

Gunther recorded the following transactions and year-end adjustments during 2012:

Journal Entry		
Accounts and Explanations	Debit	Credit
Prepaid rent	8,000	
Cash		8,000
Prepaid the annual rent.		
Rent expense	5,100	
Prepaid rent		5,100
Adjustment to record rent expense for the year.		
Cash	4,200	
Unearned service revenue		4,200
Collected cash in advance of service revenue to be earned.		
Unearned service revenue	4,700	
Service revenue		4,700
Adjustment to record revenue earned.		

Requirements

1. Assuming that there were no other service revenue and rent expense transactions during 2012, journalize Gunther's closing entries at the end of 2012.

2. Open T-accounts for Service revenue and Rent expense. Post the closing entries to these accounts. What are their balances after closing?

E4-21   **3** **Identifying and journalizing closing entries [10–15 min]**

The accountant for Klein Photography has posted adjusting entries (a)–(e) to the following selected accounts at December 31, 2012.

Accounts receivable				Supplies		
	46,000				5,000	(b) 2,400
(a)	2,000					

Accumulated depr.—furniture			Accumulated depr.—building		
		8,000			30,000
	(c)	800		(d)	6,200

Salary payable			Klein, capital		
	(e)	700			47,000

Klein, drawing			Service revenue		
	57,000				108,000
				(a)	2,000

Salary expense			Supplies expense		
	25,400		(b)	2,400	
(e)	700				

Depreciation expense—furniture			Depreciation expense—building		
(c)	800		(d)	6,200	

Requirements

1. Journalize Klein Photography's closing entries at December 31, 2012.
2. Determine Klein Photography's ending Klein, capital balance at December 31, 2012.

Note: Exercise 4-22 should be prepared only after completing Exercises 4-13 through 4-16.

 4 Preparing a post-closing trial balance [10–15 min]
Review your answers from Exercises 4-13 through 4-16.

Requirement

1. Prepare the post-closing trial balance of Telegraphic Link at November 30, 2012.

E4-23 **5 6 Preparing a classified balance sheet, and calculating the current and debt ratios [15–20 min]**
The adjusted trial balance amounts from the August worksheet of Brian O'Brion Dance Studio Company follow:

BRIAN O'BRION DANCE STUDIO COMPANY Partial Worksheet Month Ended August 31, 2012		
	Adjusted Trial Balance	
Account	Debit	Credit
Cash	$15,800	
Supplies	2,000	
Prepaid rent	900	
Equipment	49,000	
Accumulated depreciation		$ 5,500
Accounts payable		4,500
Salary payable		500
Unearned service revenue		5,100
Long-term note payable		4,400
O'Brion, capital		36,500
O'Brion, drawing	1,100	
Service revenue		18,100
Salary expense	3,000	
Rent expense	1,500	
Depreciation expense	300	
Supplies expense	400	
Utilities expense	600	
Total	$74,600	$74,600

Requirements

1. Prepare the classified balance sheet of Brian O'Brion Dance Studio Company at August 31, 2012. Use the report form. You must compute the ending balance of O'Brion, capital.
2. Compute O'Brion's current ratio and debt ratio at August 31, 2012. One year ago, the current ratio was 1.49 and the debt ratio was 0.29. Indicate whether O'Brion's ability to pay current and total debts has improved, deteriorated, or remained the same during the current year.

Problems (Group A)

P4-24A   **1 2** **Preparing a worksheet and the financial statements [40–50 min]**   *MyAccountingLab*

The trial balance and adjustment data of Myla's Motors at November 30, 2012, follow:

Account	Debit	Credit
MYLA'S MOTORS Trial Balance November 30, 2012		
	Balance	
Account	Debit	Credit
Cash	$ 4,300	
Accounts receivable	26,600	
Supplies	500	
Prepaid insurance	1,700	
Equipment	53,500	
Accumulated depreciation		$36,400
Accounts payable		13,400
Wages payable		
Unearned service revenue		8,000
Myla, capital		19,700
Myla, drawing	3,800	
Service revenue		16,000
Depreciation expense		
Wage expense	1,600	
Insurance expense		
Utilities expense	1,500	
Supplies expense		
Total	$93,500	$93,500

Additional data at November 30, 2012:

 a. Depreciation on equipment, $1,100.
 b. Accrued wage expense, $600.
 c. Supplies on hand, $200.
 d. Prepaid insurance expired during November, $200.
 e. Unearned service revenue earned during November, $4,000.
 f. Accrued service revenue, $800.

Requirements

1. Complete Myla's worksheet for November. Key adjusting entries by letter.
2. Prepare the income statement, the statement of owner's equity, and the classified balance sheet in account form for the month ended November 30, 2012.

P4-25A ① ② ③ **Preparing a worksheet, financial statements, and closing entries [50–60 min]**

The trial balance of Fugazy Investment Advisers at December 31, 2012, follows:

	Balance	
FUGAZY INVESTMENT ADVISERS Trial Balance December 31, 2012		
Account	**Debit**	**Credit**
Cash	$ 32,000	
Accounts receivable	46,000	
Supplies	3,000	
Equipment	25,000	
Accumulated depreciation		$ 11,000
Accounts payable		15,000
Salary payable		
Unearned service revenue		2,000
Note payable, long-term		39,000
Fugazy, capital		38,000
Fugazy, drawing	50,000	
Service revenue		97,000
Salary expense	32,000	
Supplies expense		
Depreciation expense		
Interest expense	3,000	
Rent expense	9,000	
Insurance expense	2,000	
Total	$202,000	$202,000

Adjustment data at December 31, 2012:

a. Unearned service revenue earned during the year, $500.
b. Supplies on hand, $1,000.
c. Depreciation for the year, $6,000.
d. Accrued salary expense, $1,000.
e. Accrued service revenue, $4,000.

Requirements

1. Enter the account data in the Trial Balance columns of a worksheet, and complete the worksheet through the Adjusted Trial Balance. Key each adjusting entry by the letter corresponding to the data given. Leave a blank line under Service revenue.

2. Prepare the income statement, the statement of owner's equity, and the classified balance sheet in account format.

3. Prepare closing journal entries from the worksheet.

4. Did the company have a good or a bad year during 2012? Give the reason for your answer.

P4-26A ① ② ③ ④ ⑤ ⑥ **Completing the accounting cycle [120–150 min]**

The trial balance of Wolfe Anvils at October 31, 2012, and the data for the month-end adjustments follow:

	WOLFE ANVILS		
	Trial Balance		
	October 31, 2012		
		Balance	
Account	Debit	Credit	
Cash	$ 4,300		
Accounts receivable	15,000		
Prepaid rent	2,700		
Supplies	1,600		
Equipment	31,200		
Accumulated depreciation		$ 3,000	
Accounts payable		6,900	
Salary payable			
Unearned service revenue		5,400	
Wolfe, capital		26,600	
Wolfe, drawing	3,500		
Service revenue		18,900	
Salary expense	2,500		
Rent expense			
Depreciation expense			
Supplies expense			
Total	$60,800	$60,800	

Adjustment data:

a. Unearned service revenue still unearned at October 31, $1,200.
b. Prepaid rent still in force at October 31, $2,500.
c. Supplies used during the month, $1,000.
d. Depreciation for the month, $300.
e. Accrued salary expense at October 31, $200.

Requirements

1. Prepare adjusting journal entries.
2. Enter the trial balance on a worksheet and complete the worksheet through the Adjusted Trial Balance of Wolfe Anvils for the month ended October 31, 2012.
3. Prepare the income statement, the statement of owner's equity, and the classified balance sheet in report form.
4. Using the worksheet data that you prepared, journalize the closing entries and post the adjusting and closing entries to T-accounts. Use dates and show the ending balance of each account.
5. Prepare a post-closing trial balance.
6. Calculate the current and debt ratios for the company.

P4-27A ①②③④⑤⑥ **Completing the accounting cycle [120–150 min]**
The trial balance of Racer Internet at March 31, 2012, follows:

	RACER INTERNET		
	Trial Balance		
	March 31, 2012		
		Bal	ance
Account	Debit	Credit
Cash	$ 4,300	
Accounts receivable	15,100	
Prepaid rent	2,300	
Supplies	1,000	
Equipment	30,600	
Accumulated depreciation		$ 3,900
Accounts payable		6,400
Salary payable		
Unearned service revenue		9,800
Racer, capital		23,000
Racer, drawing	4,100	
Service revenue		17,300
Salary expense	3,000	
Rent expense		
Depreciation expense		
Supplies expense		
Total	$60,400	$60,400

Adjusting data at March 31, 2012:

    a. Unearned service revenue still unearned, $500.
    b. Prepaid rent still in force, $2,000.
    c. Supplies used during the month, $800.
    d. Depreciation for the month, $400.
    e. Accrued salary expense, $600.

Requirements

1. Journalize adjusting journal entries.
2. Enter the trial balance on a worksheet and complete the worksheet of Racer Internet.
3. Prepare the income statement, statement of owner's equity, and classified balance sheet in report form.
4. Using the worksheet data that you prepared, journalize the closing entries, and post the adjusting and closing entries to T-accounts. Use dates and show the ending balance of each account.
5. Prepare a post-closing trial balance.
6. Calculate the current and debt ratios for the company.

P4-28A ❸ **Journalizing adjusting and closing entries [45–60 min]**

The *unadjusted* trial balance and adjustment data of Elias Real Estate Appraisal Company at June 30, 2012, follow:

ELIAS REAL ESTATE APPRAISAL COMPANY Unadjusted Trial Balance June 30, 2012		
Account Title	Debit	Credit
Cash	$ 4,900	
Accounts receivable	4,000	
Supplies	3,000	
Prepaid insurance	2,200	
Building	74,400	
Accumulated depreciation		$ 18,800
Land	13,600	
Accounts payable		19,500
Interest payable		8,800
Salary payable		1,300
Elias, capital		30,800
Elias, drawing	27,900	
Service revenue		97,900
Salary expense	32,400	
Depreciation expense	0	
Insurance expense	4,200	
Utilities expense	4,000	
Supplies expense	6,500	
Total	$ 177,100	$ 177,100

Adjustment data at June 30, 2012:

    a. Prepaid insurance expired, $300.
    b. Accrued service revenue, $1,300.
    c. Accrued salary expense, $900.
    d. Depreciation for the year, $8,500.
    e. Supplies used during the year, $600.

Requirements

1. Open T-accounts for Elias, capital and all the accounts that follow on the trial balance. Insert their unadjusted balances. Also open a T-account for Income summary, which has a zero balance.

2. Journalize the adjusting entries and post to the accounts that you opened. Show the balance of each revenue account and each expense account.

3. Journalize the closing entries and post to the accounts that you opened. Draw double underlines under each account balance that you close to zero.

4. Compute the ending balance of Elias, capital.

P4-29A ⑤⑥ **Preparing a classified balance sheet in report form, and using the current and debt ratios to evaluate a company [30–40 min]**

Selected accounts of Blume Irrigation System at December 31, 2012, follow:

Insurance expense	$ 900	Accounts payable	$24,700
Note payable, long-term	2,800	Accounts receivable	43,100
Other assets	2,200	Accumulated depreciation—building	24,000
Building	55,800	Blume, capital, December 31, 2011	52,000
Prepaid insurance	4,000	Accumulated depreciation—equipment	7,900
Salary expense	16,300	Cash	11,000
Salary payable	3,900	Interest payable	400
Service revenue	74,800	Blume, drawing	2,000
Supplies	3,300	Equipment	23,000
Unearned service revenue	1,600	Depreciation expense	30,500

Requirements

1. Prepare the company's classified balance sheet in report form at December 31, 2012.
2. Compute the company's current ratio and debt ratio at December 31, 2012. At December 31, 2011, the current ratio was 1.81 and the debt ratio was 0.34. Did the company's ability to pay debts improve or deteriorate, or did it remain the same during 2012?

● Problems (Group B)

MyAccountingLab

P4-30B ①② **Preparing a worksheet and the financial statements [40–50 min]**

The trial balance and adjustment data of Brooke's Motors at September 30, 2012, follow:

BROOKE'S MOTORS
Trial Balance
September 30, 2012

Account	Debit	Credit
		Balance
Cash	$ 4,200	
Accounts receivable	26,500	
Supplies	800	
Prepaid insurance	1,800	
Equipment	53,500	
Accumulated depreciation		$36,300
Accounts payable		13,300
Wages payable		
Unearned service revenue		8,500
Brooke, capital		19,000
Brooke, drawing	3,500	
Service revenue		16,500
Depreciation expense		
Wage expense	2,100	
Insurance expense		
Utilities expense	1,200	
Supplies expense		
Total	$93,600	$93,600

Additional data at September 30, 2012:

    a. Depreciation on equipment, $1,100.
    b. Accrued wage expense, $500.
    c. Supplies on hand, $700.
    d. Prepaid insurance expired during September, $200.
    e. Unearned service revenue earned during September, $4,500.
    f. Accrued service revenue, $900.

Requirements

1. Complete Brooke's worksheet for September. Key adjusting entries by letter.
2. Prepare the income statement, the statement of owner's equity, and the classified balance sheet in account form for the month ended September 30, 2012.

P4-31B ❶❷❸ **Preparing a worksheet, financial statements, and closing entries [50–60 min]**
The trial balance of Giambi Investment Advisers at December 31, 2012, follows:

GIAMBI INVESTMENT ADVISERS		
Trial Balance		
December 31, 2012		

	Balance	
Account	**Debit**	**Credit**
Cash	$ 28,000	
Accounts receivable	50,000	
Supplies	8,000	
Equipment	26,000	
Accumulated depreciation		$ 16,000
Accounts payable		14,000
Salary payable		
Unearned service revenue		1,000
Note payable, long-term		44,000
Giambi, capital		40,000
Giambi, drawing	50,000	
Service revenue		97,000
Salary expense	32,000	
Supplies expense		
Depreciation expense		
Interest expense	7,000	
Rent expense	7,000	
Insurance expense	4,000	
Total	$212,000	$212,000

Adjustment data at December 31, 2012:

    a. Unearned service revenue earned during the year, $500.
    b. Supplies on hand, $5,000.
    c. Depreciation for the year, $8,000.
    d. Accrued salary expense, $1,000.
    e. Accrued service revenue, $3,000.

Requirements

1. Enter the account data in the Trial Balance columns of a worksheet, and complete the worksheet through the Adjusted Trial Balance. Key each adjusting entry by the letter corresponding to the data given. Leave a blank line under Service revenue.
2. Prepare the income statement, the statement of owner's equity, and the classified balance sheet in account format.
3. Prepare closing journal entries from the worksheet.
4. Did the company have a good or a bad year during 2012? Give the reason for your answer.

P4-32B ① ② ③ ④ ⑤ ⑥ **Completing the accounting cycle [120–150 min]**
The trial balance of Leopard Anvils at January 31, 2012, and the data for the month-end adjustments follow:

	LEOPARD ANVILS Trial Balance January 31, 2012		
		Balance	
Account	Debit	Credit
Cash	$ 4,400	
Accounts receivable	14,800	
Prepaid rent	2,300	
Supplies	1,200	
Equipment	30,100	
Accumulated depreciation		$ 4,600
Accounts payable		7,500
Salary payable		
Unearned service revenue		4,900
Leopard, capital		25,700
Leopard, drawing	4,800	
Service revenue		17,400
Salary expense	2,500	
Rent expense		
Depreciation expense		
Supplies expense		
Total	$60,100	$60,100

Adjustment data:

a. Unearned service revenue still unearned at January 31, $400.
b. Prepaid rent still in force at January 31, $1,800.
c. Supplies used during the month, $1,100.
d. Depreciation for the month, $400.
e. Accrued salary expense at January 31, $500.

Requirements

1. Prepare adjusting journal entries.
2. Enter the trial balance on a worksheet and complete the worksheet through the Adjusted Trial Balance of Leopard Anvils for the month ended January 31, 2012.
3. Prepare the income statement, the statement of owner's equity, and the classified balance sheet in report form.

4. Using the worksheet data that you prepared, journalize and post the adjusting and closing entries to T-accounts. Use dates and show the ending balance of each account.

5. Prepare a post-closing trial balance.

6. Calculate the current and debt ratios for the company.

P4-33B ① ② ③ ④ ⑤ ⑥ **Completing the accounting cycle [120–150 min]**
The trial balance of Road Runner Internet at July 31, 2012, follows:

ROAD RUNNER INTERNET Trial Balance July 31, 2012		
	Balance	
Account	Debit	Credit
Cash	$ 4,200	
Accounts receivable	14,600	
Prepaid rent	2,000	
Supplies	1,600	
Equipment	30,900	
Accumulated depreciation		$ 3,900
Accounts payable		6,700
Salary payable		
Unearned service revenue		5,400
Runner, capital		25,800
Runner, drawing	3,200	
Service revenue		17,700
Salary expense	3,000	
Rent expense		
Depreciation expense		
Supplies expense		
Total	$59,500	$59,500

Adjusting data at July 31, 2012:

a. Unearned service revenue still unearned, $1,200.
b. Prepaid rent still in force at July 31, $1,900.
c. Supplies used during the month, $800.
d. Depreciation for the month, $300.
e. Accrued salary expense at July 31, $500.

Requirements

1. Journalize adjusting journal entries.
2. Enter the trial balance on a worksheet and complete the worksheet for Road Runner Internet.
3. Prepare the income statement, statement of owner's equity, and classified balance sheet in report form.
4. Using the worksheet data that you prepared, journalize the closing entries and post the adjusting and closing entries to T-accounts. Use dates and show the ending balance of each account.
5. Prepare a post-closing trial balance.
6. Calculate the current and debt ratios for the company.

P4-34B ❸ **Journalizing adjusting and closing entries [45–60 min]**

The *unadjusted* trial balance and adjustment data of Smith Real Estate Appraisal Company at June 30, 2012, follow:

SMITH REAL ESTATE APPRAISAL COMPANY Unadjusted Trial Balance June 30, 2012		
Account Title	**Debit**	**Credit**
Cash	$ 4,600	
Accounts receivable	3,500	
Supplies	3,000	
Prepaid insurance	2,100	
Building	74,700	
Accumulated depreciation		$ 18,600
Land	14,000	
Accounts payable		18,900
Interest payable		8,000
Salary payable		600
Smith, capital		33,000
Smith, drawing	27,000	
Service revenue		97,500
Salary expense	32,100	
Depreciation expense	0	
Insurance expense	5,100	
Utilities expense	3,600	
Supplies expense	6,900	
Total	$ 176,600	$ 176,600

Adjustment data at June 30, 2012:

    a. Prepaid insurance expired, $400.
    b. Accrued service revenue, $1,100.
    c. Accrued salary expense, $700.
    d. Depreciation for the year, $8,500.
    e. Supplies used during the year, $100.

Requirements

1. Open T-accounts for Smith, capital and all the accounts that follow on the trial balance. Insert their unadjusted balances. Also open a T-account for Income summary, which has a zero balance.

2. Journalize the adjusting entries and post to the accounts that you opened. Show the balance of each revenue account and each expense account.

3. Journalize the closing entries and post to the accounts that you opened. Draw double underlines under each account balance that you close to zero.

4. Compute the ending balance of Smith, capital.

P4-35B ⑤ ⑥ **Preparing a classified balance sheet in report form, and using the current and debt ratios to evaluate a company [30–40 min]**

Selected accounts of Browne Irrigation Systems at December 31, 2012, follow:

Insurance expense	$ 500	Accounts payable	$22,300
Note payable, long-term	4,200	Accounts receivable	43,600
Other assets	2,000	Accumulated depreciation—building	24,200
Building	58,200	Browne, capital, December 31, 2011	54,000
Prepaid insurance	4,800	Accumulated depreciation—equipment	6,900
Salary expense	17,700	Cash	6,500
Salary payable	2,800	Interest payable	400
Service revenue	73,000	Browne, drawing	5,000
Supplies	3,300	Equipment	23,000
Unearned service revenue	1,800	Depreciation expense	25,000

Requirements

1. Prepare the company's classified balance sheet in report form at December 31, 2012.
2. Compute the company's current ratio and debt ratio at December 31, 2012. At December 31, 2011, the current ratio was 1.83 and the debt ratio was 0.39. Did the company's ability to pay debts improve or deteriorate, or did it remain the same during 2012?

● Continuing Exercise

E4-36   This exercise continues the Lawlor Lawn Service situation from Exercise 3-48 of Chapter 3. Start from the posted T-accounts and the *adjusted* trial balance for Lawlor Lawn Service prepared for the company at May 31, 2012:

MyAccountingLab

Requirements

1. Complete the accounting worksheet at May 31, 2012.
2. Journalize and post the closing entries at May 31, 2012. Denote each closing amount as *Clo* and an account balance as *Bal*.

Continuing Problem

This problem continues the Draper Consulting situation from Problem 3-49 of Chapter 3.

P4-37   Start from the posted T-accounts and the *adjusted* trial balance that Draper Consulting prepared for the company at December 31:

		DRAPER CONSULTING **Adjusted Trial Balance** December 31, 2012		
			Balance	
		Account Title	Debit	Credit
		Cash	$16,350	
		Accounts receivable	1,750	
		Supplies	200	
		Equipment	1,800	
		Accumulated depreciation—equipment		$ 30
		Furniture	4,200	
		Accumulated depreciation—furniture		70
		Accounts payable		4,650
		Salary payable		685
		Unearned service revenue		700
		Draper, capital		18,000
		Draper, drawing	1,400	
		Service revenue		3,850
		Rent expense	550	
		Utilities expense	250	
		Salary expense	685	
		Depreciation expense—equipment	30	
		Depreciation expense—furniture	70	
		Supplies expense	700	
		Total	$27,985	$27,985

Requirements

1. Complete the accounting worksheet at December 31.
2. Journalize and post the closing entries at December 31. Denote each closing amount as *Clo* and an account balance as *Bal.*
3. Prepare a classified balance sheet at December 31.

Practice Set

Refer to the Practice Set data provided in Chapters 1, 2, and 3.

Requirements

1. Prepare an accounting worksheet.
2. Prepare an income statement, statement of owner's equity, and balance sheet using the report format.
3. Prepare closing entries for the month.
4. Prepare a post-closing trial balance.

Apply Your Knowledge

● Decision Case 4-1

One year ago, Ralph Collins founded Collins Consignment Sales Company, and the business has prospered. Collins comes to you for advice. He wishes to know how much net income the business earned during the past year. The accounting records consist of the T-accounts in the ledger, which were prepared by an accountant who has moved. The accounts at December 31 follow:

Cash	Accounts receivable	Prepaid rent	Supplies
Dec 31 Bal 5,800	Dec 31 Bal 12,300	Jan 2 2,800	Jan 2 2,600

Equipment	Accumulated depreciation		Accounts payable
Jan 2 52,000			Dec 31 Bal 18,500

Salary payable	Unearned service revenue	Collins, capital	Collins, drawing
	Dec 31 Bal 4,100	Jan 2 40,000	Dec 31 Bal 50,000

Service revenue		Salary expense	Depreciation expense
Dec 31 Bal 80,700		Dec 31 Bal 17,000	

Advertising expense	Utilities expense	Supplies expense	
	Dec 31 Bal 800		

Collins indicates that, at year-end, customers owe him $1,000 accrued service revenue, which he expects to collect early next year. These revenues have not been recorded. During the year, he collected $4,100 service revenue in advance from customers, but the business has earned only $800 of that amount. During the year he has incurred $2,400 of advertising expense, but he has not yet paid for it. In addition, he has used up $2,100 of the supplies. Collins determines that depreciation on equipment was $7,000 for the year. At December 31, he owes his employee $1,200 accrued salary. The owner made no capital investments during the year.

Collins expresses concern that drawing during the year might have exceeded the business's net income. To get a loan to expand the business, Collins must show the bank that the business's owner's equity has grown from its original $40,000 balance. Has it? You and Collins agree that you will meet again in one week.

Requirement

1. Prepare the financial statement that helps address the first issue concerning Collins. Can he expect to get the loan? Give your reason(s).

● Ethical Issue 4-1

Link Back to Chapter 3 (Revenue Principle). Grant Film Productions wishes to expand and has borrowed $100,000. As a condition for making this loan, the bank requires that the business maintain a current ratio of at least 1.50.

Business has been good but not great. Expansion costs have brought the current ratio down to 1.40 on December 15. Rita Grant, owner of the business, is considering what might happen if she reports a current ratio of 1.40 to the bank. One course of action for Grant is to record in December $10,000 of revenue that the business will earn in January of next year. The contract for this job has been signed.

Requirements

1. Journalize the revenue transaction, and indicate how recording this revenue in December would affect the current ratio.

2. Discuss whether it is ethical to record the revenue transaction in December. Identify the accounting principle relevant to this situation, and give the reasons underlying your conclusion.

● Fraud Case 4-1

Arthur Chen, a newly minted CPA, was on his second audit job in the Midwest with a new client called Parson Farm Products. He was looking through the last four years of financials, and doing a few ratios, when he noticed something odd. The current ratio went from 1.9 in 2007 down to 0.3 in 2008, despite the fact that 2008 had record income. He decided to sample a few transactions from December 2008. He found that many of Parson's customers had returned products to the company because of substandard quality. Chen discovered that the company was clearing the receivables (i.e., crediting accounts receivable) but "stashing" the debits in an obscure long-term asset account called "grain reserves" to keep the company's income "in the black" (i.e., positive income).

Requirements

1. How did the fraudulent accounting just described affect the current ratio? (Hint: Think about Cash.)

2. Can you think of any reasons why someone in the company would want to take this kind of action?

● Financial Statement Case 4-1

This case, based on the balance sheet of **Amazon.com** in Appendix A at the end of the book, will familiarize you with some of the assets and liabilities of that company. Use the **Amazon.com** balance sheet to answer the following questions.

Requirements

1. Which balance sheet format does **Amazon.com** use?

2. Name the company's largest current asset and largest current liability at December 31, 2009.

3. Compute **Amazon**'s current ratios at December 31, 2009 and 2008. Did the current ratio improve, worsen, or hold steady during 2009?

4. Under what category does **Amazon** report furniture, fixtures, and equipment?

5. What was the cost of the company's fixed assets at December 31, 2009? What was the amount of accumulated depreciation? What was the book value of the fixed assets? See Note 3 for the data.

● Team Project 4-1

Kathy Wintz formed a lawn service business as a summer job. To start the business on May 1, she deposited $1,000 in a new bank account in the name of the business. The $1,000 consisted of a $600 loan from Bank One to her company, Wintz Lawn Service, and $400 of her own money. The company gave $400 of capital to Wintz. Wintz rented lawn equipment, purchased supplies, and hired other students to mow and trim customers' lawns.

At the end of each month, Wintz mailed bills to the customers. On August 31, she was ready to dissolve the business and return to college. Because she was so busy, she kept few records other than the checkbook and a list of receivables from customers.

At August 31, the business's checkbook shows a balance of $2,000, and customers still owe $750. During the summer, the business collected $5,500 from customers. The business checkbook lists payments for supplies totaling $400, and it still has gasoline, weed eater cord, and other supplies that cost a total of $50. The business paid employees $1,800 and still owes them $300 for the final week of the summer.

Wintz rented some equipment from Ludwig's Machine Shop. On May 1, the business signed a six-month rental agreement on mowers and paid $600 for the full rental period in advance. Ludwig's will refund the unused portion of the prepayment if the equipment is returned in good shape. In order to get the refund, Wintz has kept the mowers in excellent condition. In fact, the business had to pay $300 to repair a mower.

To transport employees and equipment to jobs, Wintz used a trailer that the business bought for $300. The business estimates that the summer's work used up one-third of the trailer's service potential. The business checkbook lists a payment of $500 for cash withdrawals during the summer. The business paid the loan back during August. (For simplicity, ignore any interest expense associated with the loan.)

Requirements

1. Prepare the income statement and the statement of owner's equity of Wintz Lawn Service for the four months May through August.

2. Prepare the classified balance sheet of Wintz Lawn Service at August 31.

3. Was Wintz's summer work successful? Give the reason for your answer.

● Communication Activity 4-1

In 25 words or fewer, explain the rationale for closing the temporary accounts.

Quick Check Answers

1. *d* 2. *b* 3. *a* 4. *b* 5. *c* 6. *d* 7. *d* 8. *c* 9. *c* 10. *a*

For online homework, exercises, and problems that provide you immediate feedback, please visit myaccountinglab.com.

Comprehensive Problem for Chapters 1–4

Journalizing, Posting, Worksheet, Adjusting, Closing, and the Financial Statements

Matthews Delivery Service completed the following transactions during its first month of operations for January 2012:

a. Matthews Delivery Service began operations by receiving $6,000 cash and a truck valued at $11,000. The business gave Matthews capital to aquire these assets.

b. Paid $300 cash for supplies.

c. Prepaid insurance, $700.

d. Performed delivery services for a customer and received $800 cash.

e. Completed a large delivery job, billed the customer $1,500, and received a promise to collect the $1,500 within one week.

f. Paid employee salary, $700.

g. Received $12,000 cash for performing delivery services.

h. Collected $600 in advance for delivery service to be performed later.

i. Collected $1,500 cash from a customer on account.

j. Purchased fuel for the truck, paying $200 with a company credit card. (Credit Accounts payable)

k. Performed delivery services on account, $900.

l. Paid office rent, $600. This rent is not paid in advance.

m. Paid $200 on account.

n. Owner withdrew cash of $2,100.

Requirements

1. Record each transaction in the journal. Key each transaction by its letter. Explanations are not required.

2. Post the transactions that you recorded in Requirement 1 in the T-accounts.

Cash	Service revenue
Accounts receivable	Salary expense
Supplies	Depreciation expense
Prepaid insurance	Insurance expense
Delivery truck	Fuel expense
Accumulated depreciation	Rent expense
Accounts payable	Supplies expense
Salary payable	
Unearned service revenue	
Matthews, capital	
Matthews, drawing	
Income summary	

3. Enter the trial balance in the worksheet for the month ended January 31, 2012. Complete the worksheet using the adjustment data given at January 31.
    a. Accrued salary expense, $700.
    b. Depreciation expense, $60.
    c. Prepaid insurance expired, $250.
    d. Supplies on hand, $200.
    e. Unearned service revenue earned during January, $500.

4. Prepare Matthews Delivery Service's income statement and statement of owner's equity for the month ended January 31, 2012, and the classified balance sheet on that date. On the income statement, list expenses in decreasing order by amount—that is, the largest expense first, the smallest expense last.

5. Journalize and post the adjusting entries beginning with a.

6. Journalize and post the closing entries.

7. Prepare a post-closing trial balance at January 31, 2012.

5

Merchandising Operations

Does the company update inventory perpetually or only at the end of a period?

SMART TOUCH LEARNING
Balance Sheet
May 31, 2013

Assets				Liabilities	
Current assets:				Current liabilities:	
Cash		$ 4,800		Accounts payable	$ 48,700
Accounts receivable		2,600		Salary payable	900
Inventory		**30,500**		Interest payable	100
Supplies		600		Unearned service revenue	400
Prepaid rent		2,000		Total current liabilities	50,100
Total current assets			$ 40,500	Long-term liabilities:	
Plant assets:				Notes payable	20,000
Furniture	$18,000			Total liabilities	70,100
Less: Accumulated depreciation—furniture	300	17,700			
Building	48,000				
Less: Accumulated depreciation—building	200	47,800		**Owner's Equity**	
Total plant assets			65,500	Bright, capital	35,900
Total assets			$106,000	Total liabilities and owner's equity	$106,000

Learning Objectives

1. Describe and illustrate merchandising operations and the two types of inventory systems

2. Account for the purchase of inventory using a perpetual system

3. Account for the sale of inventory using a perpetual system

4. Adjust and close the accounts of a merchandising business

5. Prepare a merchandiser's financial statements

6. Use gross profit percentage, inventory turnover, and days in inventory to evaluate a business

7. Account for the sale of inventory using a periodic system (Appendix 5A)

8. Prepare worksheets for a merchandiser (see Appendix 5B, located at myaccountinglab.com)

So what kind of business do you think you want to own, manage, or invest in? A business that offers a service or a business that sells a product?

Chapters 1–4 discussed Smart Touch Learning and Greg's Tunes. Smart Touch and Greg's Tunes are similar. Both are proprietorships, and they follow similar accounting procedures. However, Greg Moore's music business differs from Sheena Bright's e-learning service in one important way: Bright provides a service for customers, whereas Moore sells both services and products—event music services and CDs. Businesses that sell a product are called **merchandisers** because they sell merchandise, or goods, to customers.

● ● ●

In this chapter, we'll introduce accounting for merchandisers, showing how to account for the purchase and sale of inventory, the additional current asset that merchandisers have. **Inventory** is defined as the merchandise that a company holds for sale to customers. For example, Greg's Tunes must hold some CD inventory in order to operate. **Walmart** carries food inventory in addition to clothing, housewares, and school supplies. A **Honda** dealer holds inventories of automobiles and auto parts.

In this chapter, Smart Touch has decided to discontinue its service business and instead plans to sell tutorial CDs and DVDs that it purchases from a vendor. With its change in business strategy, Smart Touch is now considered a merchandiser. By continuing the same company with a different business strategy in the examples, we will give you a basis for comparison between service and merchandising businesses. We'll also cover examples using Greg's Tunes. Let's get started by looking at some basics of merchandising operations.

What Are Merchandising Operations?

1 Describe and illustrate merchandising operations and the two types of inventory systems

Merchandising consists of buying and selling products rather than services. Exhibit 5-1 shows how a service entity's financial statements (on the left) differ from a merchandiser's financial statements (on the right). As you can see, merchandisers have some new balance sheet and income statement items.

EXHIBIT 5-1 | **Financial Statements of a Service Company and a Merchandising Company**

SERVICE CO.* Balance Sheet—Partial June 30, 2013		MERCHANDISING CO.** Balance Sheet—Partial June 30, 2013	
Assets		**Assets**	
Current assets:		Current assets:	
Cash	$X	Cash	$X
Short-term investments	X	Short-term investments	X
Accounts receivable, net	X	Accounts receivable, net	X
Prepaid insurance	X	Inventory	X
		Prepaid insurance	X

*Such as Smart Touch before it changed to a merchandising operation.

**Such as Greg's Tunes

SERVICE CO. Income Statement Year Ended June 30, 2013		MERCHANDISING CO. Income Statement Year Ended June 30, 2013	
Service revenue	$XXX	Sales revenue	$X,XXX
Operating expenses:		Cost of goods sold	X
Salary expense	X	Gross profit	$ XXX
Depreciation expense	X	Operating expenses:	
Rent expense	X	Salary expense	X
Net income	$ X	Depreciation expense	X
		Rent expense	X
		Net income	$ X

Balance Sheet:
- Inventory, an asset

Income Statement:
- Sales revenue (or simply, Sales)
- Cost of goods sold, an expense

We'll define these new items later in the chapter. Notice we now show the expenses heading as Operating expenses. These are the same expenses you've been learning about in previous chapters. The heading just categorizes the expenses as operating rather than *all* expenses. For now, let's examine the operating cycle of a merchandising business.

The Operating Cycle of a Merchandising Business

The operating cycle of a merchandiser is as follows (see Exhibit 5-2):

1. It begins when the company purchases inventory from a **vendor.**

2. The company then sells the inventory to a **customer.**

3. Finally, the company collects cash from customers.

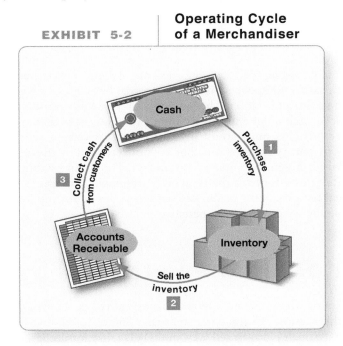

EXHIBIT 5-2 | **Operating Cycle of a Merchandiser**

Now let's see how companies account for their inventory. We begin with journal entries. Then we post to the ledger accounts and, finally, prepare the financial statements.

Inventory Systems: Perpetual and Periodic

There are two main types of inventory accounting systems:

- Periodic system
- Perpetual system

The **periodic inventory system** is normally used for relatively inexpensive goods. A small, local store without optical-scanning cash registers does not keep a running record of every loaf of bread and every key chain that it sells. Instead, the business physically counts its inventory periodically to determine the quantities on hand.

Restaurants and small retail stores often use the periodic system. Appendix 5A covers the periodic system, which is becoming less and less popular with the use of computers.

The **perpetual inventory system** keeps a running *computerized* record of inventory—that is, the number of inventory units and the dollar amounts are perpetually (constantly) updated. This system achieves better control over the inventory. A modern perpetual inventory system records the following:

- Units purchased and cost amount
- Units sold and sales and cost amounts
- The quantity of inventory on hand and its cost

In this system, inventory and purchasing systems are integrated with accounts receivable and sales. For example, **Target**'s computers use bar codes to keep up-to-the-minute records and show the current inventory at any time.

Bar code

In a perpetual system, the "cash register" at a **Target** store is a computer terminal that records sales and updates inventory records. Bar codes such as the one illustrated here are scanned by a laser. The bar coding represents inventory and cost data that keep track of each unique inventory item. However, note that even in a perpetual system, the business must count inventory at least once a year. The physical count captures inventory transactions that are not recorded by the electronic system (such as misplaced, stolen, or damaged inventory). The count establishes the correct amount of ending inventory for the financial statements and also serves as a check on the perpetual records. Most businesses use bar codes and computerized cash registers, which is why we cover the perpetual system.

Accounting for Inventory in the Perpetual System

 Account for the purchase of inventory using a perpetual system

As noted previously, the cycle of a merchandising entity begins with the purchase of inventory. In this section, we trace the steps that Smart Touch takes to account for inventory. Smart Touch plans to sell CDs and DVDs that it purchases from **RCA**.

1. **RCA**, the vendor, ships the CD and DVD inventory to Smart Touch and sends an invoice the same day. The **invoice** is the seller's (**RCA**'s) request for payment from the buyer (Smart Touch). An invoice is also called a *bill*. Exhibit 5-3 is the bill that Smart Touch receives from **RCA**.

2. After the inventory is received, Smart Touch pays **RCA**.

Purchase of Inventory

Here we use the actual invoice in Exhibit 5-3 to illustrate the purchasing process. Suppose Smart Touch receives the goods on June 3, 2013. Smart Touch records this purchase on account as follows:

Jun 3	Inventory (A+)	700	
	Accounts payable (L+)		700
	Purchased inventory on account.		

The Inventory account, an asset, is used only for goods purchased that Smart Touch owns and intends to resell to customers. Supplies, equipment, and other assets are recorded in their own accounts. Recall that Inventory is an asset until it is sold. We record the Inventory at its *gross value* (total invoice amount before discount) using the *gross method*. An alternative method, the *net method*, will be discussed in future accounting courses.

Purchase Discounts

Many businesses offer customers a discount for early payment. This is called a **purchase discount**. RCA's **credit terms** of "3/15, NET 30 DAYS" mean that Smart Touch can deduct 3% from the total bill (excluding freight charges, if any) if the company pays within 15 days of the invoice date. Otherwise, the full amount—NET—is due in 30 days. These credit terms can also be expressed as "3/15, n/30."

EXHIBIT 5-3 | **Purchase Invoice**

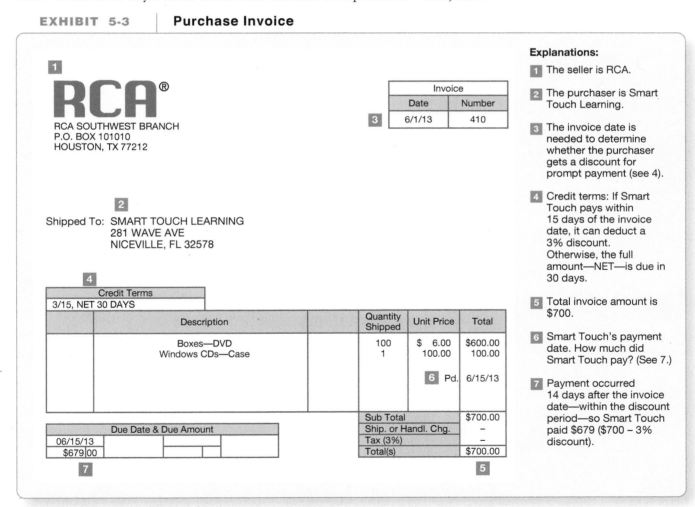

Terms of "n/30" mean that no discount is offered and payment is due 30 days after the invoice date. Most credit terms express the discount, the discount time period, and the final due date. Occasionally, the credit terms are expressed as *eom*, which means payment is due at the end of the current month.

If Smart Touch pays within the discount period, the cash payment entry would be as follows:

Jun 15	Accounts payable (L–)	700	
	Cash ($700 × 0.97) (A–)		679
	Inventory ($700 × 0.03) (A–)		21
	Paid within discount period.		

The discount is credited to Inventory because the discount for early payment decreases the actual cost paid for Inventory, as shown in the T-account:

Inventory

Jun 3	700	Jun 15	21
Bal	679		

Notice that the balance in the Inventory account, $679, is exactly what was paid for the Inventory on June 15, 2013.

What if Smart Touch pays this invoice after the discount period on June 24, 2013? Smart Touch must pay the full $700. In that case, the payment entry is as follows:

Jun 24	Accounts payable (L–)	700	
	Cash (A–)		700
	Paid after discount period.		

Purchase Returns and Allowances

Businesses allow customers to return merchandise that is defective, damaged, or otherwise unsuitable. This is called a **purchase return**. Alternately, the seller may deduct an allowance from the amount the buyer owes. **Purchase allowances** are granted to the purchaser as an incentive to keep goods that are not "as ordered." Together, **purchase returns and allowances** decrease the buyer's cost of the inventory.

Assume that Smart Touch has not yet paid the original **RCA** bill of June 3. Suppose a case of CDs purchased on that invoice (Exhibit 5-3) was damaged in shipment. Smart Touch returns the goods (CDs, in this case) to **RCA** and records the purchase return as follows:

Jun 4	Accounts payable (L–)	100	
	Inventory (A–)		100
	Returned inventory to seller (vendor).		

The exact same entry is made for a purchase allowance granted to the buyer from the seller (vendor). The only difference between a purchase return and a purchase allowance is that, in the case of the allowance, Smart Touch keeps the inventory. See Exhibit 5-4 on the next page for a copy of the purchase allowance granted.

Transportation Costs

Someone must pay the transportation cost of shipping inventory from seller (vendor) to buyer. The purchase agreement specifies FOB (**free on board**) terms to determine when title to the good transfers to the purchaser and who pays the freight. Exhibit 5-5 shows that

- **FOB shipping point** means the buyer takes ownership (title) to the goods at the shipping point. In this case, the buyer (owner of the goods at the shipping point) also pays the freight.

- **FOB destination** means the buyer takes ownership (title) to the goods at the delivery destination point. In this case, the seller (owner of the goods while in transit) usually pays the freight.

  Freight costs are either freight in or freight out.

- **Freight in** is the transportation cost to ship goods INTO the purchaser's warehouse; thus, it is freight on *purchased goods.*
- **Freight out** is the transportation cost to ship goods OUT of the warehouse and to the customer; thus, it is freight on *goods sold.*

EXHIBIT 5-4 | **Purchase Allowance**

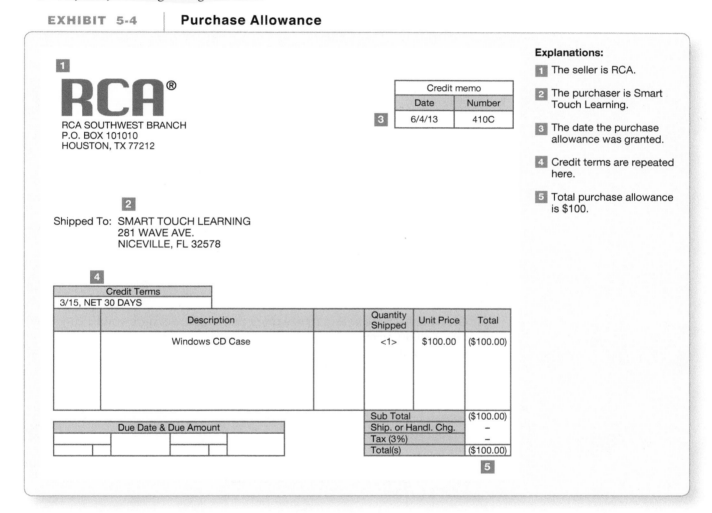

Explanations:

1 The seller is RCA.

2 The purchaser is Smart Touch Learning.

3 The date the purchase allowance was granted.

4 Credit terms are repeated here.

5 Total purchase allowance is $100.

EXHIBIT 5-5 | **FOB Terms Determine Who Pays the Freight**

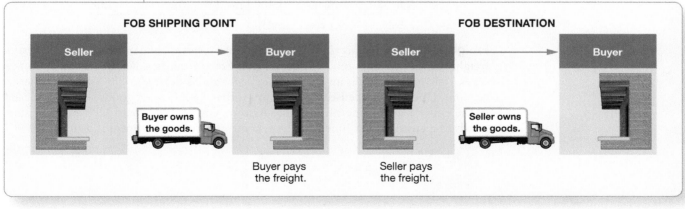

Freight In   FOB shipping point is most common. The buyer owns the goods while they are in transit, so the buyer pays the freight. Because paying the freight is a cost that must be paid to acquire the inventory, freight in becomes part of the cost of inventory. As a result, freight in costs are debited to the Inventory account. Suppose Smart Touch pays a $60 freight charge on June 3 and makes the following entry:

Jun 3	Inventory (A+)	60	
	Cash (A–)		60
	Paid a freight bill.		

The freight charge increases the net cost of the inventory to $660, as follows:

Inventory

Jun 3	Purchase	700	Jun 4	Return	100
Jun 3	Freight in	60			
Bal	Net cost	660			

Discounts are computed only on the merchandise purchased from the seller, in this case $600. Discounts are not computed on the transportation costs, because there is no discount on freight.

Under FOB shipping point, the seller sometimes prepays the transportation cost as a convenience and lists this cost on the invoice. Assume, for example, Greg's Tunes makes a $5,000 purchase of goods, coupled with a related freight charge of $400, on June 20 on terms of 3/5, n/30. The purchase would be recorded as follows:

Jun 20	Inventory ($5,000 + $400) (A+)	5,400	
	Accounts payable (L+)		5,400
	Purchased inventory on account, including freight.		

If Greg's Tunes pays within the discount period, the discount will be computed only on the $5,000 merchandise cost, not on the total invoice of $5,400. The $400 freight is not eligible for the discount. So, the 3% discount would be $150 ($5,000 × 0.03). The entry to record the early payment on June 25 follows:

Jun 25	Accounts payable (L–)	5,400	
	Inventory ($5,000 × 0.03) (A–)		150
	Cash (A–)		5,250

After posting both entries to Greg's Tunes' Inventory T-account below, you can see that the cost Greg's Tunes has invested in this Inventory purchase is equal to the cost paid of $5,250:

Inventory

Jun 20	Purchase	5,400	Jun 25	Discount	150
Bal	Net cost	5,250			

Freight Out   As noted previously, a freight out expense is one in which the seller pays freight charges to ship goods to customers. Freight out is a delivery expense to the seller. Delivery expense is an operating expense and is debited to the Delivery expense account. **Operating expenses** are expenses (other than Cost of goods sold) that occur in the entity's major line of business. Assume Greg's Tunes paid **UPS** $100 to ship goods to a customer on June 23. The entry to record that payment is as follows:

Jun 23	Delivery expense (E+)	100	
	Cash (A–)		100

Summary of Purchase Returns and Allowances, Discounts, and Transportation Costs

Suppose Smart Touch buys $35,000 of inventory, returns $700 of the goods, and takes a 2% early payment discount. Smart Touch also pays $2,100 of freight in. The following summary shows Smart Touch's net cost of this inventory. All amounts are assumed for this illustration.

Purchases of inventory										Net cost of inventory
Inventory	–	Purchase returns and allowances	–	Purchase discounts*	+	Freight in	=			Inventory
$35,000	–	$700	–	$686	+	$2,100	=			$35,714

*Purchase discount of $686 = [Purchases $35,000 – Purchase returns $700] × 0.02 discount]

Inventory			
Purchases of inventory	35,000	Purchase returns & allow.	700
Freight in	2,100	Purchase discount	686*
Bal	35,714		

> **Key Takeaway**
>
> All purchase transactions are between the company and a vendor. In a perpetual system, every transaction that affects the quantity or price of inventory is either debited or credited to the asset, Inventory, based on the rules of debit and credit. Increases debit Inventory (increase in quantity or cost per unit). Decreases credit Inventory (decrease in quantity or cost per unit).

Sale of Inventory

After a company buys inventory, the next step is to sell the goods. We shift now to the selling side and follow Smart Touch through a sequence of selling transactions.

The amount a business earns from selling merchandise inventory is called **Sales revenue (Sales)**. At the time of the sale, two entries must be recorded in the perpetual system: One entry records the sale and the cash (or receivable) at the time of the sale. The second entry records Cost of goods sold (debit the expense) and reduces the Inventory (credit the asset). **Cost of goods sold (COGS)** is the cost of inventory that has been sold to customers. Cost of goods sold (also known as **Cost of sales** or COS) is the merchandiser's major expense.

After making a sale on account, Smart Touch may experience any of the following:

- *A sales return:* The customer may return goods to Smart Touch, asking for a refund or credit to the customer's account.
- *A sales allowance:* Smart Touch may grant a sales allowance to entice the customer to accept non-standard goods. This allowance will reduce the future cash collected from the customer.
- *A sales discount:* If the customer pays within the discount period—under terms such as 2/10, n/30—Smart Touch collects the discounted amount.
- *Freight out:* Smart Touch may have to pay delivery expense to transport the goods to the buyer.

Let's begin with a cash sale.

3 Account for the sale of inventory using a perpetual system

Cash Sale

Sales of retailers, such as Smart Touch and Greg's Tunes, are often made for cash. Suppose Smart Touch made a $3,000 cash sale on June 9, 2013, to a customer and issued the sales invoice in Exhibit 5-6. To the seller, a sales invoice is a bill showing what amount the customer must pay.

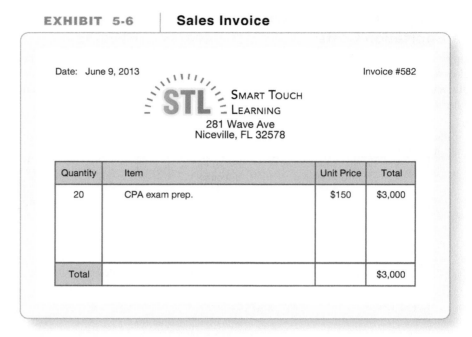

EXHIBIT 5-6 | **Sales Invoice**

Cash sales of $3,000 are recorded by debiting Cash and crediting Sales revenue as follows:

1	Jun 9	Cash (A+)		3,000	
		Sales revenue (R+)			3,000
		Cash sale.			

Smart Touch sold goods. Therefore, a second journal entry must also be made to decrease the Inventory balance. Suppose these goods cost Smart Touch $1,900. The second journal entry will transfer the $1,900 from the Inventory account to the Cost of goods sold account, as follows:

2	Jun 9	Cost of goods sold (E+)		1,900	
		Inventory (A–)			1,900
		Recorded the cost of goods sold.			

The Cost of goods sold account keeps a current balance throughout the period in a perpetual inventory system. In this example, Cost of goods sold is $1,900 (the cost to Smart Touch) rather than $3,000, the selling price (retail) of the goods. **Cost of goods sold is always based on the company's cost, not the retail price.**

	Inventory			Cost of goods sold	
Bal	35,714	2 Cost of sales 1,900 ◄——► 2 Jun 9	1,900		

The computer automatically records the Cost of goods sold entry in a perpetual inventory system. The cashier scans the bar code on the product and the computer performs this task.

Sale on Account

Most sales in the United States are made on account (on credit). Now let's assume that Smart Touch made a $5,000 sale on account on terms of n/10 (no discount offered) for goods that cost $2,900. The entries to record the sale and cost of goods sold follow:

1	Jun 11	Accounts receivable (A+)	5,000	
		Sales revenue (R+)		5,000
		Sale on account.		

2	Jun 11	Cost of goods sold (E+)	2,900	
		Inventory (A–)		2,900
		Recorded the cost of goods sold.		

When Smart Touch receives the cash, it records the cash receipt on account as follows:

	Jun 19	Cash (A+)	5,000	
		Accounts receivable (A–)		5,000
		Collection on account.		

Sales Discounts and Sales Returns and Allowances

We saw that purchase returns and allowances and purchase discounts decrease the cost of inventory purchases. In the same way, **sales returns and allowances** and **sales discounts** decrease the net amount of revenue earned on sales. Sales returns and allowances and Sales discounts are contra accounts to Sales revenue. Recall that a contra account has the opposite normal balance of its companion account. So, Sales returns and allowances and Sales discounts both are contra revenue accounts and have normal debit balances.

Companies maintain separate accounts for Sales discounts and Sales returns and allowances so they can track these items separately. **Net sales revenue** is calculated as Net sales revenue = Sales revenue – Sales returns and allowances – Sales discounts. **Sales made to customers – Sales returned by customers (or allowances granted to customers) – Discounts given to customers who paid early = Net sales.**

$$\begin{array}{c} \text{Sales} \\ \text{revenue} \end{array} - \begin{array}{c} \text{Sales returns} \\ \text{and allowances} \end{array} - \begin{array}{c} \text{Sales} \\ \text{discounts} \end{array} = \begin{array}{c} \text{Net sales} \\ \text{revenue}[1] \end{array}$$

Now let's examine a sequence of Greg's Tunes sale transactions. Assume Greg's Tunes is selling to a customer. On July 7, 2014, Greg's Tunes sells CDs for $7,200 on credit terms of 2/10, n/30. These goods cost Greg's Tunes $4,700. Greg's Tunes' entries to record this credit sale and the related cost of goods sold follow:

1	Jul 7	Accounts receivable (A+)	7,200	
		Sales revenue (R+)		7,200
		Sale on account.		

2	7	Cost of goods sold (E+)	4,700	
		Inventory (A–)		4,700
		Recorded cost of goods sold.		

---

[1]Often abbreviated as Net sales.

Sales Returns Assume that on July 12, 2014, the customer returns $600 of the goods. Greg's Tunes, the seller, records the sales return as follows:

1	Jul 12	Sales returns and allowances	(CR+)		600	
		Accounts receivable	(A–)			600
		Received returned goods.				

Accounts receivable decreases because Greg's Tunes will not collect cash for the returned goods.

Greg's Tunes receives the returned merchandise and updates its inventory records. Greg's Tunes must also decrease Cost of goods sold as follows (the returned goods cost $400):

2	Jul 12	Inventory	(A+)		400	
		Cost of goods sold	(E–)			400
		Placed goods back in inventory.				

Sales Allowances Suppose on July 15 Greg's Tunes grants a $100 sales allowance for goods damaged in transit. A sales allowance is recorded as follows:

1	Jul 15	Sales returns and allowances	(CR+)		100	
		Accounts receivable	(A–)			100
		Granted a sales allowance for damaged goods.				

There is no second entry to adjust inventory for a sales allowance because the seller receives no returned goods from the customer.

After these entries are posted, Accounts receivable has a $6,500 debit balance, as follows:

		Accounts receivable				
Jul 7	Sale	7,200	Jul 12	Return	600	
			15	Allowance	100	
Bal		6,500				

Sales Discounts On July 17, the last day of the discount period, Greg's Tunes collects this receivable. Assuming no freight is included in the invoice, the company's cash receipt is $6,370 [$6,500 – ($6,500 × 0.02)], and the collection entry is as follows:

	Jul 17	Cash	(A+)		6,370	
		Sales discounts ($6,500 × 0.02)	(CR+)		130	
		Accounts receivable	(A–)			6,500
		Cash collection within the discount period.				

Now, Greg's Tunes' Accounts receivable balance is zero:

		Accounts receivable				
Jul 7	Sale	7,200	Jul 12	Return	600	
			15	Allowance	100	
			17	Collection	6,500	
Bal		0				

Notice that all selling transactions utilize accounts beginning with "S," such as Sales revenue, Sales returns and allowances, and Sales discounts.

Net Sales Revenue, Cost of Goods Sold, and Gross Profit

Net sales revenue, cost of goods sold, and gross profit are key elements of profitability. Net sales revenue minus Cost of goods sold is called **Gross profit**, or **Gross margin**. You can also think of gross profit as the mark-up on the inventory.

Gross profit is the extra amount the company received from the customer over what the company paid to the vendor.

$$\text{Net sales revenue} - \text{Cost of goods sold} = \text{Gross profit}$$

Gross profit, along with net income, is a measure of business success. A sufficiently high gross profit is vital to a merchandiser.

The following example will clarify the nature of gross profit. Suppose Greg's Tunes' cost to purchase a CD is $15 and it sells the same CD for $20. Greg's Tunes' gross profit for each CD is $5, computed as follows:

Sales revenue earned by selling one CD	$ 20
Cost of goods sold for the CD (what the CD cost)	15
Gross profit on the sale of one CD	$ 5

The gross profit reported on Greg's Tunes' income statement is the sum of the gross profits on the CDs and all the other products the company sold during the year. The gross profit must cover the company's operating expenses for the company to survive.

Summary Problem 5-1 puts into practice what you have learned in the first half of this chapter.

Summary Problem 5-1

Suppose Heat Miser Air Conditioner Company engaged in the following transactions during June of the current year:

Jun	3	Purchased inventory on credit terms of 1/10 net eom (end of month), $1,600.
	9	Returned 40% of the inventory purchased on June 3. It was defective.
	12	Sold goods for cash, $920 (cost, $550).
	15	Purchased goods for $5,000. Credit terms were 3/15, net 30.
	16	Paid a $260 freight bill on goods purchased.
	18	Sold inventory for $2,000 on credit terms of 2/10, n/30 (cost, $1,180).
	22	Received returned goods from the customer of the June 18 sale, $800 (cost, $480).
	24	Borrowed money from the bank to take advantage of the discount offered on the June 15 purchase. Signed a note payable to the bank for the net amount, $4,850.
	24	Paid supplier for goods purchased on June 15.
	28	Received cash in full settlement of the account from the customer who purchased inventory on June 18.
	29	Paid the amount owed on account from the purchase of June 3.

Requirements

1. Journalize the preceding transactions. Explanations are not required.
2. Set up T-accounts and post the journal entries to show the ending balances in the Inventory and the Cost of goods sold accounts only.

3. Assume that the note payable signed on June 24 requires the payment of $90 interest expense. Was borrowing funds to take the cash discount a wise or unwise decision? What was the net savings or cost of the decision?

Solution

Requirement 1

Jun 3	Inventory (A+)	1,600	
	Accounts payable (L+)		1,600
9	Accounts payable ($1,600 × 0.40) (L–)	640	
	Inventory (A–)		640
12	Cash (A+)	920	
	Sales revenue (R+)		920
12	Cost of goods sold (E+)	550	
	Inventory (A–)		550
15	Inventory (A+)	5,000	
	Accounts payable (L+)		5,000
16	Inventory (A+)	260	
	Cash (A–)		260
18	Accounts receivable (A+)	2,000	
	Sales revenue (R+)		2,000
18	Cost of goods sold (E+)	1,180	
	Inventory (A–)		1,180
22	Sales returns and allowances (CR+)	800	
	Accounts receivable (A–)		800
22	Inventory (A+)	480	
	Cost of goods sold (E–)		480
24	Cash (A+)	4,850	
	Note payable (L+)		4,850
24	Accounts payable (L–)	5,000	
	Inventory ($5,000 × 0.03) (A–)		150
	Cash ($5,000 × 0.97) (A–)		4,850
28	Cash [($2,000 – $800) × 0.98] (A+)	1,176	
	Sales discounts [($2,000 – $800) × 0.02] (CR+)	24	
	Accounts receivable ($2,000 – $800) (A–)		1,200
29	Accounts payable ($1,600 – $640) (L–)	960	
	Cash (A–)		960

Requirement 2

Inventory					Cost of goods sold			
Jun 3	1,600	Jun 9	640		Jun 12	550	Jun 22	480
15	5,000	12	550		18	1,180		
16	260	18	1,180					
22	480	24	150		Bal	1,250		
Bal	4,820							

Requirement 3

Heat Miser's decision to borrow funds was wise because the $150 discount received exceeded the interest paid of $90. Thus, Heat Miser Air Conditioner Company was $60 better off.

Adjusting and Closing the Accounts of a Merchandiser

A merchandiser adjusts and closes accounts the same way a service entity does. If a worksheet is used, the trial balance is entered, and the worksheet is completed to determine net income or net loss.

 Adjust and close the accounts of a merchandising business

Adjusting Inventory Based on a Physical Count

The Inventory account should stay current at all times in a perpetual inventory system. However, the actual amount of inventory on hand may differ from what the books show. Theft, damage, and errors occur. For this reason, businesses take a physical count of inventory *at least* once a year. The most common time to count inventory is at the end of the fiscal year. The business then adjusts the Inventory account based on the physical count.

Greg's Tunes' Inventory account shows an unadjusted balance of $40,500.

	Inventory	
	{	
Dec 31	40,500	

With no shrinkage—due to theft or error—the business should have inventory costing $40,500. But on December 31, Greg's Tunes counts the inventory on hand, and the total cost comes to only $40,200.

Inventory balance before adjustment	−	Actual inventory on hand	=	Adjusting entry to inventory
$40,500	−	$40,200	=	Credit of $300

Greg's Tunes records this adjusting entry for inventory shrinkage:

Dec 31	Cost of goods sold (E+)		300	
	Inventory ($40,500 − $40,200) (A−)			300
	Adjustment for inventory shrinkage.			

This entry brings Inventory to its correct balance.

	Inventory		
	{		
Dec 31 Bal	40,500	Dec 31 Adj	300
Dec 31 Adj Bal	40,200		

Other adjustments, plus a complete merchandising worksheet, are covered in Appendix 5B, located at myaccountinglab.com.

Stop & Think...

Consider the amount of goods a company has available for sale. At the end of the period, the total spent for those items can only appear in two accounts: Inventory (asset) or Cost of goods sold (expense). So what happens to the goods that are missing or damaged? This is considered a cost of doing business and those values are "buried" in the Cost of goods sold amount, rather than shown in a separate account in the ledger.

Closing the Accounts of a Merchandiser

Exhibit 5-7 presents Greg's Tunes' closing entries for December, which are similar to those you learned in Chapter 4, except for the new accounts (highlighted in color). **Closing still means to zero out all accounts that aren't on the balance sheet.** *All amounts are assumed* for this illustration.

EXHIBIT 5-7 | **Closing Entries for a Merchandiser—Amounts Assumed**

Journal

Closing Entries

	Date	Accounts	Debit	Credit
1.	Dec 31	Sales revenue (R–)	169,300	
		Sales discounts (CR–)		1,400
		Sales returns and allowances (CR–)		2,000
		Income summary		165,900
2.	31	Income summary	112,800	
		Cost of goods sold (E–)		90,800
		Wage expense (E–)		10,200
		Rent expense (E–)		8,400
		Depreciation expense (E–)		600
		Insurance expense (E–)		1,000
		Supplies expense (E–)		500
		Interest expense (E–)		1,300
3.	31	Income summary ($165,900 – $112,800)	53,100	
		Moore, capital (Q+)		53,100
4.	31	Moore, capital (Q–)	54,100	
		Moore, drawing (D–)		54,100

Income summary

Clo 2	112,800	Clo 1	165,900
		Bal	53,100
Clo 3	53,100		
		Bal	0

Moore, capital

Clo 4	54,100	Bal	25,900
		Clo 3	53,100
		Bal	24,900

Dividends

Bal	54,100		
		Clo 4	54,100
Bal	0		

The four-step closing process for a merchandising company follows:

STEP 1: Make the revenue and contra revenue accounts equal zero via the Income summary account. This closing entry transfers the difference of total revenues ($169,300) and contra revenues ($1,400 + $2,000) to the *credit* side of the Income summary account, $165,900.

STEP 2: Make expense accounts equal zero via the Income summary account. This closing entry transfers total expenses to the *debit* side of the Income summary account, $112,800.

The Income summary account now holds the net income or net loss of the period. See the following Income summary T-account to illustrate.

Income summary

Closing entry 2	Expenses	Closing entry 1	Revenues
Net loss if Debit balance		Net income if Credit balance	

STEP 3: Make the Income summary account equal zero via the Capital account. This closing entry transfers net income (or net loss) to Capital.

STEP 4: Make the Drawing account equal zero via the Capital account. This entry transfers the drawing to the *debit* side of Capital.

> **Key Takeaway**
>
> Closing entries are made at the end of a period to all accounts that are temporary (not on the balance sheet). To close an account means to make the balance zero.

Preparing a Merchandiser's Financial Statements

Exhibit 5-8 on the next page shows Greg's Tunes' financial statements for 2014.

5 Prepare a merchandiser's financial statements

Income Statement   The income statement begins with Sales, Cost of goods sold, and Gross profit. Then come the operating expenses, which are those expenses other than Cost of goods sold. **Operating expenses are all the normal expenses incurred to run the business other than COGS.**

Both merchandisers and service companies report operating expenses in two categories:

- **Selling expenses** are expenses related to marketing and selling the company's products. These include sales salaries, sales commissions, advertising, depreciation, store rent, utilities on store buildings, property taxes on store buildings, and delivery expense.

- **General expenses** include expenses *not* related to marketing the company's products. These include office expenses, such as the salaries of the executives and office employees; depreciation; rent, other than on stores (for example, rent on the administrative office); utilities, other than on stores (for example, utilities on the administrative office); and property taxes on the administrative office building.

Gross profit minus Operating expenses equals **Operating income** or **Income from operations. Operating income measures the results of the entity's major ongoing activities (normal operations).**

The last section of Greg's Tunes' income statement is **Other revenue and expense.** This category reports revenues and expenses that fall outside Greg's Tunes' main, day-to day, regular operations. Examples include interest revenue, interest expense, and gains and losses on the sale of plant assets. These examples have nothing to do with Greg's Tunes' "normal" business of selling CDs. As a result, they are classified as "other" items.

The bottom line of the income statement is net income:

> **Net income = Total revenues and gains − Total expenses and losses**

We often hear the term *bottom line* to refer to a final result. The bottom line is net income on the income statement.

Statement of Owner's Equity   A merchandiser's statement of owner's equity looks exactly like that of a service business.

EXHIBIT 5-8 | **Financial Statements—Amounts Assumed**

GREG'S TUNES
Income Statement
Year Ended December 31, 2014

Sales revenue		$169,300
Less: Sales returns and allowances	$2,000	
Sales discounts	1,400	3,400
Net sales revenue		$165,900
Cost of goods sold		90,800
Gross profit		$ 75,100
Operating expenses:		
Selling expenses:		
Wage expense	$10,200	
General expenses:		
Rent expense	8,400	
Insurance expense	1,000	
Depreciation expense	600	
Supplies expense	500	20,700
Operating income		$ 54,400
Other revenue and (expense):		
Interest expense		(1,300)
Net income		$ 53,100

GREG'S TUNES
Statement of Owner's Equity
Year Ended December 31, 2014

Moore, capital, Dec 31, 2013	$ 25,900
Net income	53,100
	79,000
Drawing	(54,100)
Moore, capital, Dec 31, 2014	$ 24,900

GREG'S TUNES
Balance Sheet
December 31, 2014

Assets			Liabilities	
Current assets:			Current liabilities:	
Cash		$ 2,800	Accounts payable	$39,500
Accounts receivable		4,600	Unearned sales revenue	700
Inventory		40,200	Wages payable	400
Prepaid insurance		200	Total current liabilities	40,600
Supplies		100	Long-term liabilities:	
Total current assets		47,900	Note payable	12,600
Plant assets:			Total liabilities	53,200
Furniture	$33,200		**Owner's Equity**	
Less: Accumulated			Moore, capital	24,900
depreciation	3,000	30,200	Total liabilities and	
Total assets		$78,100	owner's equity	$78,100

Balance Sheet   For a merchandiser, the balance sheet is the same as for a service business, except merchandisers have an additional current asset, Inventory. Service businesses have no inventory.

Income Statement Formats: Multi-Step and Single-Step

As we saw in Chapter 4, the balance sheet appears in two formats:

- The report format (assets at top, owner's equity at bottom)
- The account format (assets at left, liabilities and owner's equity at right)

There are also two formats for the income statement:

- The multi-step format
- The single-step format

A **multi-step income statement** lists several important subtotals. In addition to net income (the bottom line), it also reports subtotals for gross profit and income from operations. The income statements presented thus far in this chapter have been multi-step, and multi-step format is more popular. The multi-step income statement for Greg's Tunes appears in Exhibit 5-8 (on the previous page).

The **single-step income statement** is the income statement format you first learned about in Chapter 1. It groups all revenues together and all expenses together without calculating other subtotals. Many companies use this format. The single-step format clearly distinguishes revenues from expenses and works well for service entities because they have no gross profit to report. Exhibit 5-9 shows a single-step income statement for Greg's Tunes.

> **Key Takeaway**
>
> The form of the income statement can give users more information for decisions. The multi-step income statement, with more subtotals, has more value than the single-step income statement. REGARDLESS of the form, bottom line net income or loss is the same amount. The preparation of the statement of owner's equity and the balance sheet are the same for merchandising as for service companies. The only difference is the addition of the asset account, Inventory, on the balance sheet.

EXHIBIT 5-9 | **Single-Step Income Statement**

GREG'S TUNES Income Statement Year Ended December 31, 2014		
Revenues:		
Sales revenue		$169,300
Less: Sales returns and allowances	$ 2,000	
Less: Sales discounts	1,400	3,400
Net sales revenue		$165,900
Expenses:		
Cost of goods sold	$90,800	
Wage expense	10,200	
Rent expense	8,400	
Interest expense	1,300	
Insurance expense	1,000	
Depreciation expense	600	
Supplies expenses	500	
Total expenses		$112,800
Net income		$ 53,100

Three Ratios for Decision Making

 Use gross profit percentage, inventory turnover, and days in inventory to evaluate a business

Inventory is the most important asset for a merchandiser. Merchandisers use several ratios to evaluate their operations, among them the *gross profit percentage*, the *rate of inventory turnover*, and *days in inventory*.

The Gross Profit Percentage

Gross profit (gross margin) is net sales minus the cost of goods sold. Merchandisers strive to increase the **gross profit percentage** (also called the **gross margin percentage**), which is computed as follows:

> **For Greg's Tunes**
> **(Values from Exhibit 5-8)**
>
> $$\text{Gross profit percentage} = \frac{\text{Gross profit}}{\text{Net sales revenue}}$$
>
> $$= \frac{\$75,100}{\$165,900} = 0.453 = 45.3\%$$

The gross profit percentage is one of the most carefully watched measures of profitability. A small increase from last year to this year may signal an important rise in income. Conversely, a small decrease from last year to this year may signal trouble.

The Rate of Inventory Turnover

Owners and managers strive to sell inventory quickly because the inventory generates no profit until it is sold. Further, fast-selling inventory is less likely to become obsolete (worthless). The faster the inventory sells, the larger the income. Additionally, larger inventories mean more storage costs, more risk of loss, and higher insurance premiums. Therefore, companies try to manage their inventory levels such that they have just enough inventory to meet customer demand without investing large amounts of money in inventory sitting on the shelves gathering dust. **Inventory turnover** measures how rapidly inventory is sold. It is computed as follows:

> **For Greg's Tunes**
> **(Values from Exhibit 5-8)**
>
> $$\frac{\text{Inventory}}{\text{turnover}} = \frac{\text{Cost of goods sold}}{\text{Average inventory}} = \frac{\text{Cost of goods sold}}{(\text{Beginning inventory*} + \text{Ending inventory})/2}$$
>
> $$= \frac{\$90,800}{(\$38,600\text{*} + \$40,200)/2} = 2.3 \text{ times per year}$$

*Ending inventory from the preceding period. Amount assumed for this illustration.

A high turnover rate is desirable, and an increase in the turnover rate usually means higher profits.

Days in Inventory

Another key measure is the **number of days in inventory** ratio. This measures the average number of days inventory is held by the company and is calculated as follows:

$$\text{Days in inventory} = \frac{365 \text{ days}}{\text{Inventory turnover ratio}}$$

$$= \frac{365 \text{ days}}{2.3 \text{ times}}$$

$$= 159 \text{ days (rounded)}$$

As stated earlier, companies try to manage their inventory levels such that they have just enough inventory to meet customer demand without investing large amounts of money in inventory. It appears Greg's Tunes has nearly a five-month supply of inventory, which seems excessive. More investigation is needed, but it is likely Greg's could reduce its inventory investment and still serve its customers well.

Key Takeaway

Ratios serve as an alternate way to measure how well a company is managing its various assets.

Decision Guidelines 5-1

MERCHANDISING OPERATIONS AND THE ACCOUNTING CYCLE

Merchandising companies like **Walmart** are very different than service companies, like the international CPA firm **Ernst & Young**. How do these two types of businesses differ? How are they similar? The Decision Guidelines answer these questions.

Decision	Guidelines
• How do merchandisers differ from service entities?	• Merchandisers buy and sell *merchandise inventory*. • Service entities perform a *service*.

• How do a merchandiser's financial statements differ from the statements of a service business?

Balance Sheet:

Merchandiser has *Inventory*, an asset.	Service business has *no* inventory.

Income Statement:

Merchandiser

Sales revenue	$XXX
– Cost of goods sold	X
= Gross profit	XX
– Operating expenses	X
= Net income	$ X

Service Business

Service revenue	$XX
– Operating expenses	X
= Net income	$ X

Statement of Owner's Equity: No difference

Decision	Guidelines
• What are the different inventory systems used?	• The *periodic inventory system* shows the correct balances of inventory and cost of goods sold only after a physical count of the inventory has taken place, which occurs at least once each year. • The *perpetual inventory system* is a computerized inventory system that perpetually shows the amount of inventory on hand (the asset) and the cost of goods sold (the expense).

• What are the options for formatting the merchandiser's income statement?

Single-Step Format

Revenues: Sales revenue		$ XXX
Other revenues		X
Total revenues		$XXXX
Expenses: Cost of goods sold		X
Operating expenses		X
Other expenses		X
Total expenses		$ XXX
Net income		$ X

Decision	Guidelines
	Multi-Step Format

Sales revenue............................	\$XXX
– Cost of goods sold................	X
= Gross profit............................	\$ XX
– Operating expenses	X
= Operating income.................	\$ X
+ Other revenues......................	X
– Other expenses......................	(X)
= Net income............................	\$ X

• How can merchandisers evaluate their business operations?

Three key ratios

Gross profit percentage

$$\text{Gross profit percentage} = \frac{\text{Gross profit}}{\text{Net sales revenue}}$$

$$\text{Inventory} - \frac{\text{Purchase returns}}{\text{and allowances}} - \frac{\text{Purchase}}{\text{discounts}} = \frac{\text{Net}}{\text{inventory}}$$

$$\text{Inventory turnover*} = \frac{\text{Cost of goods sold}}{\text{Average inventory}}$$

*In most cases—the higher, the better.

$$\text{Days in inventory} = \frac{365 \text{ days}}{\text{Inventory turnover ratio}}$$

Summary Problem 5-2

The adjusted trial balance of King Cornelius Company follows:

KING CORNELIUS COMPANY Adjusted Trial Balance December 31, 2014		
Account	**Debit**	**Credit**
Cash	$ 5,600	
Accounts receivable	37,100	
Inventory	25,800	
Supplies	1,300	
Prepaid rent	1,000	
Furniture	26,500	
Accumulated depreciation		$ 23,800
Accounts payable		6,300
Salary payable		2,000
Interest payable		600
Unearned sales revenue		2,400
Note payable, long-term		35,000
Cornelius, capital		22,200
Cornelius, drawing	48,000	
Sales revenue		244,000
Interest revenue		2,000
Sales discounts	10,000	
Sales returns and allowances	8,000	
Cost of goods sold	81,000	
Salary expense	72,700	
Rent expense	7,700	
Depreciation expense	2,700	
Utilities expense	5,800	
Supplies expense	2,200	
Interest expense	2,900	
Total	$338,300	$338,300

Requirements

1. Journalize the closing entries at December 31. Post to the Income summary account as an accuracy check on net income. Recall that the credit balance closed out of Income summary should equal net income as computed on the income statement. Also post to Cornelius, capital, whose balance should agree with the amount reported on the balance sheet.
2. Prepare the company's multi-step income statement, statement of owner's equity, and balance sheet in account form. Draw arrows linking the statements. Note: King Cornelius doesn't separate its operating expenses as either selling or general.
3. Compute the inventory turnover and days in inventory for 2014. Inventory at December 31, 2013, was $21,000. Turnover for 2013 was 3.0 times. Would you expect King Cornelius Company to be more profitable or less profitable in 2014 than in 2013? Why?

Requirement 1

Closing Entries

	Date	Accounts	Debit	Credit
	2014			
1	Dec 31	Sales revenue (R–)	244,000	
		Interest revenue (R–)	2,000	
		Sales returns and allowances (CR–)		8,000
		Income summary		228,000
		Sales discounts (CR–)		10,000
2	Dec 31	Income summary	175,000	
		Cost of goods sold (E–)		81,000
		Salary expense (E–)		72,700
		Rent expense (E–)		7,700
		Depreciation expense (E–)		2,700
		Utilities expense (E–)		5,800
		Supplies expense (E–)		2,200
		Interest expense (E–)		2,900
3	Dec 31	Income summary ($228,000 – $175,000)	53,000	
		Cornelius, capital (Q+)		53,000
4	Dec 31	Cornelius, capital (Q–)	48,000	
		Cornelius, drawing (D–)		48,000

Income summary					
Clo 2	175,000	Clo 1	228,000		
Clo 3	53,000	Bal	53,000		
		Bal	0		

Cornelius, capital			
			22,200
Clo 4	48,000	Clo 3	53,000
		Bal	27,200

Requirement 2

KING CORNELIUS COMPANY
Income Statement
Year Ended December 31, 2014

Sales revenue:		$244,000
Less: Sales discounts	$10,000	
Sales returns and allowances	8,000	18,000
Net sales revenue		$226,000
Cost of goods sold		81,000
Gross profit		$145,000
Operating expenses:		
Salary expense	$72,700	
Rent expense	7,700	
Utilities expense	5,800	
Interest expense	2,900	
Depreciation expense	2,700	
Supplies expense	2,200	94,000
Operating income		$ 51,000
Other revenue and (expense):		
Interest revenue		2,000
Net income		$ 53,000

KING CORNELIUS COMPANY
Statement of Owner's Equity
Year Ended December 31, 2014

Cornelius, capital, Dec 31, 2013	$ 22,200
Net income	53,000
	75,200
Drawing	(48,000)
Cornelius, capital, Dec 31, 2014	$ 27,200

KING CORNELIUS COMPANY
Balance Sheet
December 31, 2014

Assets			Liabilities	
Current:			Current:	
Cash		$ 5,600	Accounts payable	$ 6,300
Accounts receivable		37,100	Salary payable	2,000
Inventory		25,800	Interest payable	600
Supplies		1,300	Unearned sales revenue	2,400
Prepaid rent		1,000	Total current liabilities	11,300
Total current assets		70,800	Long-term:	
Plant:			Note payable	35,000
Furniture	$26,500		Total liabilities	46,300
Less: Accumulated			**Owner's Equity**	
depreciation	23,800	2,700	Cornelius, capital	27,200
			Total liabilities and	
Total assets		$73,500	owner's equity	$73,500

Requirement 3

$$\text{Inventory turnover} = \frac{\text{Cost of goods sold}}{\text{Average inventory}}$$

$$= \frac{\$81,000}{(\$21,000 + \$25,800)/2} = 3.5 \text{ times (rounded)}$$

The increase in the rate of inventory turnover from 3.0 to 3.5 suggests higher profits.

$$\text{Days in inventory} = \frac{365 \text{ days}}{\text{Inventory turnover ratio}}$$

$$= \frac{365 \text{ days}}{3.5}$$

$$= 105 \text{ days (rounded)}$$

The days in inventory turnover of 105 suggests the company has almost three and a half months inventory on hand. The company should investigate further to determine if it can reduce the amount of inventory on hand and still supply its customers well.

Review *Merchandising Operations*

● Accounting Vocabulary

Cost of Goods Sold (COGS) (p. 263)
The cost of the inventory that the business has sold to customers. Also called **cost of sales**.

Cost of Sales (p. 263)
The cost of the inventory that the business has sold to customers. Also called **cost of goods sold**.

Credit Terms (p. 259)
The terms of purchase or sale as stated on the invoice. A common example is 2/10, n/30.

Customer (p. 257)
The individual or business that buys goods from a seller.

Free On Board (FOB) (p. 260)
The purchase agreement specifies FOB terms to indicate who pays the freight. FOB terms also determine when title to the goods transfer to the purchaser.

FOB Destination (p. 261)
Situation in which the buyer takes ownership (title) at the delivery destination point and the seller pays the freight.

FOB Shipping Point (p. 260)
Situation in which the buyer takes ownership (title) to the goods at the shipping point and the buyer pays the freight.

Freight In (p. 261)
The transportation cost to ship goods INTO the warehouse; therefore, it is freight on purchased goods.

Freight Out (p. 261)
The transportation cost to ship goods OUT of the warehouse; therefore, it is freight on goods sold to a customer.

General Expenses (p. 271)
Expenses incurred that are not related to marketing the company's products.

Gross Margin (p. 266)
Excess of net sales revenue over cost of goods sold. Also called **gross profit**.

Gross Margin Percentage (p. 274)
Gross profit divided by net sales revenue. A measure of profitability. Also called **gross profit percentage**.

Gross Profit (p. 266)
Excess of net sales revenue over cost of goods sold. Also called **gross margin**.

Gross Profit Percentage (p. 274)
Gross profit divided by net sales revenue. A measure of profitability. Also called **gross margin percentage**.

Income from Operations (p. 271)
Gross profit minus operating expenses. Also called **operating income**.

Inventory (p. 256)
All the goods that the company owns and expects to sell to customers in the normal course of operations.

Inventory Turnover (p. 274)
Ratio of cost of goods sold divided by average inventory. Measures the number of times a company sells its average level of inventory during a period.

Invoice (p. 258)
A seller's request for cash from the purchaser.

Merchandisers (p. 256)
Businesses that sell merchandise, or goods, to customers.

Merchandising (p. 256)
Consists of buying and selling products rather than services.

Multi-Step Income Statement (p. 273)
Format that contains subtotals to highlight significant relationships. In addition to net income, it reports gross profit and operating income.

Net Purchases (p. 304)
Purchases less purchase discounts and purchase returns and allowances.

Net Sales Revenue (p. 265)
Sales revenue less sales discounts and sales returns and allowances.

Number of Days in Inventory (p. 275)
Ratio that measures the average number of days that inventory is held by a company.

Operating Expenses (p. 262)
Expenses, other than cost of goods sold, that are incurred in the entity's major line of business. Examples include rent, depreciation, salaries, wages, utilities, and supplies expense.

Operating Income (p. 271)
Gross profit minus operating expenses. Also called **income from operations**.

Other Revenue and Expense (p. 271)
Revenue or expense that is outside the normal day-to-day operations of a business, such as a gain or loss on the sale of plant assets.

Periodic Inventory System (p. 257)
A system in which the business does not keep a continuous record of inventory on hand. At the end of the period, the business takes a physical count of on-hand inventory and uses this information to prepare the financial statements.

Perpetual Inventory System (p. 258)
The computerized accounting inventory system in which the business keeps a constant/running record of inventory and cost of goods sold.

Purchase Allowances (p. 260)
An amount granted to the purchaser as an incentive to keep goods that are not "as ordered."

Purchase Discount (p. 259)
A discount that businesses offer to purchasers as an incentive for early payment.

Purchase Returns (p. 260)
A situation in which businesses allow purchasers to return merchandise that is defective, damaged, or otherwise unsuitable.

Sales (p. 263)
The amount that a merchandiser earns from selling its inventory. Short name for **Sales revenue**.

Sales Discount (p. 265)
Reduction in the amount of cash received from a customer for early payment. Offered by the seller as an incentive for the purchasers to pay early. A contra account to Sales revenue.

Sales Returns and Allowances (p. 265)
Decreases in the seller's receivable from a customer's return of merchandise or from granting the customer an allowance from the amount owed to the seller. A contra account to Sales revenue.

Sales Revenue (p. 263)
The amount that a merchandiser earns from selling its inventory. Also called **Sales**.

Selling Expenses (p. 271)
Expenses related to marketing and selling the company's products.

Single-Step Income Statement (p. 273)
Format that groups all revenues together and then lists and deducts all expenses together without calculating any subtotals.

Vendor (p. 257)
The individual or business from whom a company purchases goods. A merchandising company mainly purchases inventory from vendors.

Looking for the Demo Docs for Chapter 5? You can find them online at myaccountinglab.com or in the Study Guide.

● Destination: Student Success

Student Success Tips

The following are hints on some common trouble areas for students in this chapter:

- Remember that transactions with customers use selling accounts (Sales, Sales discounts, Sales returns and allowances).

- Perpetual inventory purchasing transactions with vendors use the Inventory account, whether its quantity or cost per unit is increasing or decreasing.

- The four closing entries you learned in Chapter 4 are the same for a merchandiser, you just have more accounts to close. (TIP: Make temporary accounts = zero).

- Discounts, whether sales or purchases, are calculated for early payment ONLY on the cost of goods. No discount is given for freight charges.

- Remember that bottom line net income (loss) is the same whether you prepare a multi-step or a single-step income statement. The difference is that there are more subtotals on the multi-step statement.

- Remember the formulas for gross profit percentage, inventory turnover, and days in inventory. (TIP: Gross profit is a % of net sales; inventory turnover is how many TIMES the average inventory was sold during the year, and the days in inventory ratio represents how many days of inventory you have in the warehouse to meet future sales needs.)

Getting Help

If there's a learning objective from the chapter you aren't confident about, try using one or more of the following resources:

- Practice additional exercises or problems at the end of Chapter 5 that cover the specific learning objective that is challenging you.

- Watch the white board videos for Chapter 5, located at myaccountinglab.com under the Chapter Resources button.

- Go to myaccountinglab.com and select the Study Plan button. Choose Chapter 5 and work the questions covering that specific learning objective until you've mastered it.

- Work the Chapter 5 pre/post tests in myaccountinglab.com.

- Visit the learning resource center on your campus for tutoring.

● Quick Check

Experience the Power of Practice!

As denoted by the logo, all of these questions, as well as additional practice materials, can be found in *MyAccountingLab*.

Please visit myaccountinglab.com

1. Which account does a merchandiser use that a service company does not use?
   a. Cost of goods sold
   b. Inventory
   c. Sales revenue
   d. All of the above

2. The two main inventory accounting systems are the
   a. perpetual and periodic.
   b. purchase and sale.
   c. returns and allowances.
   d. cash and accrual.

3. The journal entry for the purchase of inventory on account is

   a.
Inventory...............................	XXX	
Accounts receivable		XXX

   b.
Accounts payable	XXX	
Inventory...................................		XXX

   c.
Inventory...............................	XXX	
Accounts payable......................		XXX

   d.
Inventory...............................	XXX	
Cash		XXX

4. JC Manufacturing purchased inventory for $5,300 and also paid a $260 freight bill. JC Manufacturing returned 45% of the goods to the seller and later took a 2% purchase discount. What is JC Manufacturing's final cost of the inventory that it kept? (Round your answer to the nearest whole number.)

   a. $2,997

   b. $2,337

   c. $3,117

   d. $2,857

5. Suppose Austin Sound had sales of $300,000 and sales returns of $45,000. Cost of goods sold was $152,000. How much gross profit did Austin Sound report?

   a. $148,000

   b. $103,000

   c. $255,000

   d. $88,000

6. Suppose Dave's Discount's Inventory account showed a balance of $8,000 before the year-end adjustments. The physical count of goods on hand totaled $7,400. To adjust the accounts, Dave Marshall would make the following entry:

   a.
Cost of goods sold...........................	600	
Inventory...................................		600

   b.
Inventory..	600	
Accounts receivable		600

   c.
Accounts payable	600	
Inventory...................................		600

   d.
Inventory..	600	
Cost of goods sold		600

7. Which account in question 6 would Dave Marshall close at the end of the year?

   a. Cost of goods sold

   b. Inventory

   c. Accounts receivable

   d. Accounts payable

8. The final closing entry for a proprietorship is

   a.
Sales revenue...................................	XXX	
Income summary		XXX

   b.
Capital..	XXX	
Drawing..		XXX

   c.
Drawing..	XXX	
Capital..		XXX

   d.
Income summary.............................	XXX	
Expenses.....................................		XXX

9. Which subtotals appear on a multi-step income statement but do not appear on a single-step income statement?

   a. Gross profit and Income from operations

   b. Operating expenses and Net income

   c. Cost of goods sold and Net income

   d. Net sales and Cost of goods sold

10. Assume Juniper Natural Dyes made net Sales of $90,000, and Cost of goods sold totaled $58,000. Average inventory was $17,000. What was Juniper Natural Dyes' gross profit percentage for this period? (Round your answer to the nearest whole percent.)

    a. 36%   c. 64%

    b. 3.4 times   d. 17%

Answers are given after Apply Your Knowledge (page 302).

Assess Your Progress

● Short Exercises

MyAccountingLab **S5-1**   **❶ Comparing periodic and perpetual inventory systems [10 min]**
You may have shopped at a Billy's store. Suppose Billy's purchased T-shirts on January 1 on account for $15,900. Credit terms are 2/15, n/30. Billy's paid within the discount period on January 8. Billy's sold the goods on February 5.

Requirements

1. If Billy's uses a periodic inventory system, in which month will the purchase of inventory be recorded as an expense? How much will the net expense be?

2. If Billy's uses the perpetual inventory system, in which month will the purchase of inventory be recorded as an expense? How much will the net expense be?

S5-2   **❷ Analyzing purchase transactions—perpetual inventory [5–10 min]**
Suppose KC Toys buys $185,800 worth of MegoBlock toys on credit terms of 2/10, n/30. Some of the goods are damaged in shipment, so KC Toys returns $18,530 of the merchandise to MegoBlock.

Requirement

1. How much must KC Toys pay MegoBlock
   a. after the discount period?
   b. within the discount period?

Note: Short Exercise 5-3 should be used only after completing Short Exercise 5-2.

S5-3　**②** **Journalizing purchase transactions—perpetual inventory [10 min]**
Refer to the KC Toys facts in Short Exercise 5-2.

Requirements

1. Journalize the following transactions. Explanations are not required.
   a. Purchase of the goods on July 8, 2012.
   b. Return of the damaged goods on July 12, 2012.
   c. Payment on July 15, 2012.
2. In the final analysis, how much did the inventory cost KC Toys?

S5-4　**②** **Journalizing purchase transactions—perpetual inventory [5–10 min]**
Suppose a Bubba store purchases $61,000 of women's sportswear on account from Tomas on July 1, 2012. Credit terms are 2/10, net 45. Bubba pays electronically, and Tomas receives the money on July 10, 2012.

Requirements

1. Journalize Bubba's transactions for July 1, 2012, and July 10, 2012.
2. What was Bubba's net cost of this inventory?

Note: Short Exercise 5-5 covers this same situation for the seller.

S5-5　**③** **Journalizing sales transactions—perpetual inventory [10 min]**
Consider the facts in the Short Exercise 5-4 as they apply to the seller, Tomas. The goods cost Tomas $32,000.

Requirement

1. Journalize Tomas's transactions for July 1, 2012, and July 10, 2012.

S5-6　**③** **Journalizing sales transactions—perpetual inventory [10 min]**
Suppose Piranha.com sells 2,500 books on account for $15 each (cost of these books is $22,500) on October 10, 2012. One hundred of these books (cost $900) were damaged in shipment, so Piranha.com later received the damaged goods as sales returns on October 13, 2012. Then the customer paid the balance on October 22, 2012. Credit terms offered to the customer were 2/15, net 60.

Requirement

1. Journalize Piranha.com's October 2012 transactions.

Note: Short Exercise 5-7 should be used only after completing Short Exercise 5-6.

S5-7　**③** **Calculating net sales and gross profit—perpetual inventory [5 min]**
Use the data in Short Exercise 5-6 for Piranha.com.

Requirements

1. Calculate net sales revenue for October 2012.
2. Calculate gross profit for October 2012.

S5-8　**④** **Adjusting inventory for shrinkage [5 min]**
Rich's Furniture's Inventory account at year-end appeared as follows:

Inventory	
Unadjusted balance　63,000	

The physical count of inventory came up with a total of $61,900.

Requirement

1. Journalize the adjusting entry.

S5-9   ④ **Journalizing closing entries—perpetual inventory [5–10 min]**

Rockwell RV Center's accounting records include the following accounts at December 31, 2012:

Cost of goods sold	$385,000	Accumulated depreciation	$ 39,000
Accounts payable	17,000	Cash	43,000
Rent expense	21,000	Sales revenue	696,000
Building	108,000	Depreciation expense	12,000
Rockwell, capital	208,800	Rockwell, drawing	61,000
Inventory	261,000	Sales discounts	9,000

Requirement

1. Journalize the required closing entries for Rockwell RV Center for December 31, 2012.

S5-10   ⑤ **Preparing a merchandiser's income statement [5–10 min]**

Carolina Communications reported the following figures in its financial statements:

Cash	$ 3,800	Cost of goods sold	$ 18,000
Total operating expenses	3,500	Equipment, net	10,200
Accounts payable	4,100	Accrued liabilities	1,700
Total owner's equity	4,200	Net sales revenue	28,000
Long–term notes payable	700	Accounts receivable	2,700
Inventory	500		

Requirement

1. Prepare the business's multi-step income statement for the year ended July 31, 2012.

Note: Short Exercise 5-11 should be used only after completing Short Exercise 5-10.

S5-11   ⑤ **Preparing a merchandiser's balance sheet [10 min]**

Review the data in Short Exercise 5-10.

Requirement

1. Prepare Carolina Communications' classified balance sheet at July 31, 2012. Use the report format.

Note: Short Exercise 5-12 should be used only after completing Short Exercises 5-10 and 5-11.

S5-12   ⑥ **Computing the gross profit percentage, the rate of inventory turnover, and days in inventory [10 min]**

Refer to the Carolina Communications data in Short Exercises 5-10 and 5-11.

Requirement

1. Calculate the gross profit percentage, rate of inventory turnover, and days in inventory ratios for 2012. One year earlier, at July 31, 2011, Carolina's inventory balance was $425.

● Exercises

E5-13   **1** **Describing periodic and perpetual inventory systems [10–15 min]**
The following characteristics may be related to either periodic inventory or perpetual
inventory systems or both.

A.	Purchases of inventory are journalized to an asset account at the time of purchase.
B.	Purchases of inventory are journalized to an expense account at the time of purchase.
C.	Inventory records are constantly updated.
D.	Sales made require a second entry to be journalized to record cost of goods sold.
E.	Bar code scanners that record sales transactions are most often associated with this inventory system.
F.	A physical count of goods on hand at year end is required.

Requirement

1. Identify each characteristic as one of the following:
   a. Periodic inventory
   b. Perpetual inventory
   c. Both periodic and perpetual inventory
   d. Neither periodic nor perpetual inventory

E5-14   **2** **Journalizing purchase transactions from an invoice—perpetual inventory
[10–15 min]**
As the proprietor of Kingston Tires, you received the following invoice from a
supplier:

FIELDS DISTRIBUTION, INC.
7290 S. Prospect Street
Ravenna, OH 44266

Invoice date: September 23, 2012

Sold to: Kingston Tires   **Payment terms:** 1/10, n/30
6678 Diamond Avenue
Ravenna, OH 44266

Description	Quantity Shipped	Price	Amount
D39–X4 Radials....................................	4	$38.12	$152.48
M223 Belted-bias.................................	10	42.84	428.40
Q92 Truck tires......................................	6	58.12	348.72
Total..			$929.60

Due date:	Amount:
October 3, 2012	$920.30
October 4 through October 22, 2012	$929.60

Requirements

1. Journalize the transaction required on September 23, 2012.
2. Journalize the return on September 28, 2012, of the D39–X4 Radials, which
   were ordered by mistake.
3. Journalize the payment on October 1, 2012, to Fields Distribution, Inc.

E5-15 ❷ **Journalizing purchase transactions—perpetual system [10–15 min]**

On June 30, 2012, Hayes Jewelers purchased inventory of $5,800 on account from Slater Diamonds, a jewelry importer. Terms were 3/15, net 45. The same day Hayes paid freight charges of $400. Upon receiving the goods, Hayes checked the order and found $800 of unsuitable merchandise, which was returned to Slater on July 4. Then, on July 14, Hayes paid the invoice.

Requirement

1. Journalize all necessary transactions for Hayes Jewelers. Explanations are not required.

E5-16 ❷ ❸ **Computing inventory and cost of goods sold amounts [10–15 min]**

Consider the following incomplete table of merchandiser's profit data:

	Sales		Sales Discounts		Net Sales		Cost of Goods Sold		Gross Profit
$	89,500	$	1,560	$	87,940	$	60,200		(a)
	103,600		4380 (b)		99,220		(c)	$	34,020
	66,200		2,000	64,200	(d)		40,500		(e)
	(f)		2,980		(g)		75,800		36,720

Requirement

1. Calculate the missing table values to complete the table.

E5-17 ❷ ❸ **Journalizing purchase and sales transactions—perpetual system [15–20 min]**

The following transactions occurred during February 2012, for Soul Art Gift Shop:

Feb 3	Purchased $2,700 of inventory on account under terms of 4/10, n/eom (end of month) and FOB shipping point.
7	Returned $400 of defective merchandise purchased on February 3.
9	Paid freight bill of $110 on February 3 purchase.
10	Sold inventory on account for $4,350. Payment terms were 2/15, n/30. These goods cost the company $2,300.
12	Paid amount owed on credit purchase of February 3, less the return and the discount.
16	Granted a sales allowance of $500 on the February 10 sale.
23	Received cash from February 10 customer in full settlement of her debt, less the allowance and the discount.

Requirement

1. Journalize the February transactions for Soul Art Gift Shop. No explanations are required.

E5-18 ❸ **Journalizing sales transactions—perpetual system [10–15 min]**

Refer to the facts presented in Exercise 5-15.

Requirement

1. Journalize the transactions of the seller, Slater Diamonds. Slater's cost of goods sold was 45% of the sales price. Explanations are not required.

E5-19 ❹ **Journalizing adjusting and closing entries, and computing gross profit [10–15 min]**

Emerson St. Paul Book Shop's accounts at June 30, 2012, included the following unadjusted balances:

Inventory	$ 5,400
Cost of goods sold	40,300
Sales revenue	85,300
Sales discounts	1,400
Sales returns and allowances	2,000

The physical count of inventory on hand on June 30, 2012, was $5,000.

Requirements

1. Journalize the adjustment for inventory shrinkage.
2. Journalize the closing entries for June 2012.
3. Compute the gross profit.

E5-20   ❹ **Making closing entries [15–20 min]**

Howe Audio Equipment's accounting records carried the following selected accounts at April 30, 2012:

Inventory	$ 5,900	Selling expense	$ 7,300
Interest revenue	40	Sales revenue	38,400
Accounts payable	1,000	Interest expense	30
Cost of goods sold	26,900	Accounts receivable	600
Other expense	1,700	General and administrative expense	900
Howe, drawing	300	Howe, capital	8,730

Requirements

1. Journalize the closing entries at April 30, 2012.
2. Set up T-accounts for Income summary and Howe, capital. Post the closing entries to the T-accounts and calculate their ending balances.

E5-21   ❹ **Journalizing closing entries [10–15 min]**

The trial balance and adjustments columns of the worksheet of Budget Business Systems at March 31, 2012, follow:

	BUDGET BUSINESS SYSTEMS Worksheet Year Ended March 31, 2012			
	Trial Balance		Adjustments	
Account	Debit	Credit	Debit	Credit
Cash	$ 2,400			
Accounts receivable	8,900		(a)$ 2,500	
Inventory	36,500			(b)$ 4,800
Supplies	13,700			(c) 7,300
Equipment	42,500			
Accumulated depreciation		$ 11,600		(d) 2,300
Accounts payable		9,200		
Salary payable				(e) 1,000
Note payable, long-term		7,900		
Bitzes, capital		34,000		
Bitzes, drawing	43,000			
Sales revenue		232,000		(a) 2,500
Sales discounts	2,500			
Cost of goods sold	111,500		(b) 4,800	
Selling expense	21,100		(c) 5,100	
			(e) 1,000	
General expense	10,300		(c) 2,200	
			(d) 2,300	
Interest expense	2,300			
Total	$294,700	$294,700	$17,900	$17,900

Requirements

1. Compute the adjusted balance for each account that must be closed.
2. Journalize the required closing entries at March 31, 2012.
3. How much was Budget's net income or net loss?

E5-22 **4** **5** **Preparing a merchandiser's multi-step income statement to evaluate the business [10–15 min]**

Review the data in Exercise 5-21.

Requirement

1. Prepare Budget's *multi-step* income statement.

E5-23 **5** **Preparing a single-step income statement. [10–15 min]**

Review the data given in Exercise 5-21.

Requirement

1. Prepare Budget's *single-step* income statement.

E5-24 **6** **Calculating inventory turnover and the gross profit percentage to evaluate the business [10–15 min]**

Review the data in Exercise 5-21.

Requirements

1. Compute the rate of inventory turnover for the fiscal year ended March 31, 2012, assuming $22,000 in average inventory.
2. The inventory turnover rate for the fiscal year ended March 31, 2011, was 3.8 times. Did the inventory turnover rate improve or deteriorate from 2011 to 2012?
3. Calculate the gross profit percentage.
4. The gross profit percentage for the fiscal year ended March 31, 2011, was 62%. Did the gross profit percentage improve or deteriorate during the fiscal year ended March 31, 2012?

E5-25 **6** **Calculating gross profit percentage and inventory turnover to evaluate a business [10 min]**

LanWan Software earned sales revenue of $65,000,000 in 2012. Cost of goods sold was $39,000,000, and net income reached $9,000,000, the company's highest ever. Total current assets included inventory of $3,000,000 at December 31, 2012. Inventory was $5,000,000 on December 31, 2011.

Requirement

1. Compute the company's gross profit percentage and rate of inventory turnover for 2012.

● Problems (Group A)

MyAccountingLab   **P5-26A** **1** **2** **3** **Journalizing purchase and sale transactions [10–15 min]**

Consider the following transactions that occurred in May 2012 for High Roller.

May 1	Purchased $3,000 of inventory from P&M, terms 1/10, n/20.
3	Sold $3,500 of goods to Frames R Us, Inc., terms 2/10, n/eom. *(Cost $2,240).
5	Frames R Us, returned $300 of goods (Cost $198).
11	Paid P&M.
13	Received payment from Frames R Us.

Requirements

1. What type of inventory system is High Roller using—periodic or perpetual?
2. Which transaction date helped you decide?
3. Journalize May transactions for High Roller. No explanations are required.

P5-27A ② ③ **Journalizing purchase and sale transactions—perpetual inventory [20–25 min]**

Consider the following transactions that occurred in September 2012 for Aquamarines.

Sep 3	Purchased inventory on terms 1/15, n/eom, $5,000.
4	Purchased inventory for cash of $1,700.
6	Returned $500 of inventory from September 4 purchase.
8	Sold goods on terms of 2/15, n/35 of $6,000 that cost $2,640.
10	Paid for goods purchased September 3.
12	Received goods from September 8 sale of $400 that cost $160.
23	Received payment from September 8 customer.
25	Sold goods to Smithsons for $1,100 that cost $400. Terms of n/30 were offered. As a courtesy to Smithsons, $75 of freight was added to the invoice for which cash was paid directly to UPS by Aquamarines.
29	Received payment from Smithsons.

Requirement

1. Journalize September transactions for Aquamarines. No explanations are required.

P5-28A ② ③ **Journalizing purchase and sale transactions—perpetual system [15–20 min]**

The following transactions occurred between Belvidere Pharmaceuticals and D & S, the pharmacy chain, during July of the current year:

Jul 6	D & S purchased $12,000 of merchandise from Belvidere on credit terms of 3/10, n/30, FOB shipping point. Separately, D & S paid a $200 bill for freight in. These goods cost Belvidere $3,600.
10	D & S returned $3,000 of the merchandise purchased on July 6. Belvidere accounted for the sales return and placed the goods back in inventory (Belvidere's cost, $1,200).
15	D & S paid $6,000 of the invoice amount owed to Belvidere for the July 6 purchase, less the discount.
27	D & S paid the remaining amount owed to Belvidere for the July 6 purchase.

Requirements

1. Journalize these transactions on the books of D & S.
2. Journalize these transactions on the books of Belvidere Pharmaceuticals.

P5-29A ② ③ **Journalizing purchase and sale transactions—perpetual inventory [20–25 min]**

Thelma's Amusements completed the following transactions during November 2012:

Nov	1	Purchased supplies for cash, $700.
	4	Purchased inventory on credit terms of 3/10, n/eom, $9,600.
	8	Returned half the inventory purchased on November 4. It was not the inventory ordered.
	10	Sold goods for cash, $1,200 (cost, $700).
	13	Sold inventory on credit terms of 2/15, n/45, $9,900 (cost, $5,300).
	14	Paid the amount owed on account from November 4, less the return (November 8) and the discount.
	17	Received defective inventory as a sales return from the November 13 sale, $600. Thelma's cost of the inventory received was $450.
	18	Purchased inventory of $4,100 on account. Payment terms were 2/10, net 30.
	26	Paid the net amount owed for the November 18 purchase.
	28	Received cash in full settlement of the account from the customer who purchased inventory on November 13, less the return and the discount.
	29	Purchased inventory for cash, $12,000, plus freight charges of $200.

Requirement

1. Journalize the transactions on the books of Thelma's Amusements.

P5-30A ④ ⑤ **Preparing financial statements and preparing closing entries [35–45 min]**

Alto Publishers Company's selected accounts as of November 30, 2012, follow:

Selling expenses	$ 18,100	Inventory	$	44,000
Furniture	37,300	Cash		36,100
Sales returns and allowances	3,000	Note payable		21,700
Salary payable	1,400	Accumulated depreciation		23,100
Alto, capital	29,400	Cost of goods sold		53,000
Sales revenue	114,200	Sales discounts		2,400
Accounts payable	13,400	General expenses		9,300

Requirements

1. Prepare the multi-step income statement, statement of owner's equity, and balance sheet for the first year of operations.
2. Prepare closing entries for the first year of operations.

P5-31A ④⑤⑥ **Making closing entries, preparing financial statements, and computing gross profit percentage, inventory turnover, and days in inventory [20–30 min]**

The adjusted trial balance of Big Papi Music Company at June 30, 2012, follows:

BIG PAPI MUSIC COMPANY Adjusted Trial Balance June 30, 2012		
Account	Debit	Credit
Cash	$ 3,600	
Accounts receivable	38,800	
Inventory	17,200	
Supplies	200	
Furniture	40,000	
Accumulated depreciation		$ 8,400
Accounts payable		13,300
Salary payable		1,200
Unearned sales revenue		6,700
Note payable, long–term		15,000
Papi, capital		36,000
Papi, drawing	40,500	
Sales revenue		180,000
Sales returns	5,000	
Cost of goods sold	82,500	
Selling expense	19,200	
General expense	12,000	
Interest expense	1,600	
Total	$ 260,600	$ 260,600

Requirements

1. Journalize Big Papi's closing entries.
2. Prepare Big Papi's single-step income statement for the year.
3. Compute the gross profit percentage, the rate of inventory turnover, and the days in inventory for the fiscal year ending June 30, 2012. Inventory on hand one year ago, at June 30, 2011, was $12,200.
4. For the year ended June 30, 2011, Big Papi's gross profit percentage was 50%, and inventory turnover was 4.9 times. Did the results for the year ended June 30, 2012, suggest improvement or deterioration in profitability over last year?

P5-32A ⑤ **Preparing a multi-step income statement and a classified balance sheet [30–40 min]**

← *Link Back to Chapter 4 (Classified Balance Sheet).* The accounts of Taylor Electronics Company are listed along with their balances before closing for the month ended March 31, 2012.

Interest revenue	$ 200	Accounts payable	$ 16,700
Inventory	45,100	Accounts receivable	33,600
Note payable, long–term	46,000	Accumulated depreciation	37,700
Salary payable	2,700	Taylor, capital, Feb 29	54,100
Sales discounts	2,900	Taylor, drawing	20,000
Sales returns and allowances	7,500	Cash	8,000
Sales revenue	297,000	Cost of goods sold	162,300
Selling expense	38,200	Equipment	129,100
Supplies	6,000	General expenses	16,700
Unearned sales revenue	13,800	Interest payable	1,200

Requirements

1. Prepare Taylor Electronics' *multi-step* income statement.
2. Prepare Taylor Electronics' statement of owner's equity.
3. Prepare Taylor Electronics' classified balance sheet in *report form*.

P5-33A ⑤ ⑥ **Preparing a multi-step income statement and calculating gross profit percentage [15–25 min]**

The records of Grade A Steak Company list the following selected accounts for the quarter ended April 30, 2012:

Interest revenue	$ 800	Accounts payable	$ 17,000
Inventory	45,100	Accounts receivable	33,500
Note payable, long–term	47,000	Accumulated depreciation	37,600
Salary payable	2,400	Angus, capital, Jan 31	53,300
Sales discounts	2,000	Angus, drawing	20,000
Sales returns and allowances	7,500	Cash	7,600
Sales revenue	296,100	Cost of goods sold	162,100
Selling expense	38,300	Equipment	130,600
Supplies	5,700	General expenses	16,300
Unearned sales revenue	13,300	Interest payable	1,200

Requirements

1. Prepare a multi-step income statement.
2. M. Davidson, manager of the company, strives to earn gross profit percentage of at least 50% and net income percentage of 20%. Did Grade A achieve these goals? Show your calculations.

● Problems (Group B)

MyAccountingLab   **P5-34B** ① ② ③ **Journalizing purchase and sale transactions [10–15 min]**

Consider the following transactions that occurred in January 2012 for 5th Grader.

Jan 1	Purchased $5,000 of inventory from M&P, terms 1/10, n/20.
3	Sold $1,000 of goods to Display Town, Inc., terms 2/10, n/eom *(Cost $700).
5	Display Town, Inc., returned $300 of goods (Cost $183).
11	Paid M&P.
13	Received payment from Display Town, Inc.

Requirements

1. What type of inventory system is 5th Grader using—periodic or perpetual?
2. Which transaction date helped you decide?
3. Journalize January transactions for 5th Grader. No explanations are required.

P5-35B ② ③ **Journalizing purchase and sale transactions—perpetual inventory [20–25 min]**

Consider the following transactions that occurred in February 2012 for Gems.

Feb	3	Purchased inventory on terms 1/5, n/eom, $2,000.
	4	Purchased inventory for cash of $1,600.
	6	Returned $600 of inventory from February 4 purchase.
	8	Sold goods on terms of 2/15, n/35 of $7,000 that cost $3,500.
	10	Paid for goods purchased on February 3.
	12	Received goods from February 8 sale of $500 that cost $190.
	23	Received payment from February 8 customer.
	25	Sold goods to Farms for $900 that cost $350. Terms of n/30 were offered. As a courtesy to Farms, $75 of freight was added to the invoice for which cash was paid directly to **UPS** by Gems.
	29	Received payment from Farms.

Requirement

1. Journalize February transactions for Gems. No explanations are required.

P5-36B ② ③ **Journalizing purchase and sale transactions—perpetual system [15–20 min]**

The following transactions occurred between East Pharmaceuticals and E & M, the pharmacy chain, during August of the current year:

Aug	6	E & M purchased $11,000 of merchandise from East on credit terms of 3/10, n/30, FOB shipping point. Separately, E & M paid a $250 bill for freight in. These goods cost East $3,300.
	10	E & M returned $2,750 of the merchandise purchased on August 6. East accounted for the sales return and placed the goods back in inventory (East's cost, $1,100).
	15	E & M paid $5,500 of the invoice amount owed to East for the August 6 purchase less the discount.
	27	E & M paid the remaining amount owed to East for the August 6 purchase.

Requirements

1. Journalize these transactions on the books of E & M.
2. Journalize these transactions on the books of East Pharmaceuticals.

P5-37B ② ③ **Journalizing purchase and sale transactions—perpetual inventory [20–25 min]**

Trisha's Amusements completed the following transactions during January 2012:

Jan	1	Purchased supplies for cash, $740.
	4	Purchased inventory on credit terms of 3/10, n/eom, $9,400.
	8	Returned half the inventory purchased on January 4. It was not the inventory ordered.
	10	Sold goods for cash, $1,700 (cost, $1,200).
	13	Sold inventory on credit terms of 2/15, n/45, $9,300 (cost, $4,700).
	14	Paid the amount owed on account from January 4, less the return (January 8) and the discount.
	17	Received defective inventory as a sales return from the January 13 sale, $700. Trisha's cost of the inventory received was $550.
	18	Purchased inventory of $3,300 on account. Payment terms were 2/10, net 30.
	26	Paid the net amount owed for the January 18 purchase.
	28	Received cash in full settlement of the account from the customer who purchased inventory on January 13, less the return and the discount.
	29	Purchased inventory for cash, $13,000, plus freight charges of $200.

Requirement

1. Journalize the transactions on the books of Trisha's Amusements.

P5-38B ④ ⑤ **Preparing financial statements and preparing closing entries [35–45 min]**
Aspen Publishers Company's selected accounts as of November 30, 2012, follow:

Selling expenses	$ 18,900	Inventory	$ 42,000
Furniture	36,900	Cash	36,200
Sales returns and allowances	2,600	Note payable	21,800
Salary payable	1,100	Accumulated depreciation	22,800
Aspen, capital	27,800	Cost of goods sold	54,000
Sales revenue	114,300	Sales discounts	1,800
Accounts payable	13,600	General expenses	9,000

Requirements

1. Prepare the multi-step income statement, statement of owner's equity, and balance sheet for its first year of operations.
2. Prepare closing entries for the first year of operations.

P5-39B ④ ⑤ ⑥ **Making closing entries, preparing financial statements, and computing gross profit percentage, inventory turnover, and days in inventory [20–30 min]**
The adjusted trial balance of Daddy's Music Company at April 30, 2012, follows:

DADDY'S MUSIC COMPANY Adjusted Trial Balance April 30, 2012		
Account	Debit	Credit
Cash	$ 4,300	
Accounts receivable	38,200	
Inventory	17,800	
Supplies	600	
Furniture	39,400	
Accumulated depreciation		$ 9,000
Accounts payable		13,600
Salary payable		1,200
Unearned sales revenue		6,600
Note payable, long–term		14,000
Otousan, capital		40,100
Otousan, drawing	40,000	
Sales revenue		180,000
Sales returns	8,000	
Cost of goods sold	81,800	
Selling expense	19,200	
General expense	14,000	
Interest expense	1,200	
Total	$ 264,500	$ 264,500

Requirements

1. Journalize Daddy's closing entries.
2. Prepare Daddy's single-step income statement for the year.
3. Compute the gross profit percentage, the rate of inventory turnover, and the days in inventory for the fiscal year ending April 30, 2012. Inventory on hand one year ago, at April 30, 2011, was $13,000.

4. For the year ended April 30, 2011, Daddy's gross profit percentage was 50%, and inventory turnover was 4.9 times. Did the results for the year ended April 30, 2012, suggest improvement or deterioration in profitability over last year?

P5-40B ⑤ **Preparing a multi-step income statement and a classified balance sheet [30–40 min]**

← *Link Back to Chapter 4 (Classified Balance Sheet).* The accounts of Smith Electronics Company are listed along with their balances before closing for the month ended October 31, 2012.

Interest revenue	$ 500	Accounts payable	$ 16,900
Inventory	45,400	Accounts receivable	33,900
Note payable, long–term	47,000	Accumulated depreciation	38,100
Salary payable	3,400	Smith, capital, Sep 30	52,500
Sales discounts	2,700	Smith, drawing	19,000
Sales returns and allowances	8,100	Cash	7,600
Sales revenue	296,500	Cost of goods sold	162,100
Selling expense	37,500	Equipment	130,900
Supplies	6,300	General expenses	16,200
Unearned sales revenue	13,800	Interest payable	1,000

Requirements

1. Prepare Smith Electronics' *multi-step* income statement.
2. Prepare Smith Electronics' statement of owner's equity.
3. Prepare Smith Electronics' classified balance sheet in *report form.*

P5-41B ⑤ ⑥ **Preparing a multi-step income statement and calculating gross profit percentage [15–25 min]**

The records of Hill Tower Steak Company list the following selected accounts for the quarter ended September 30, 2012:

Interest revenue	$ 400	Accounts payable	$ 16,500
Inventory	45,700	Accounts receivable	33,900
Note payable, long–term	42,000	Accumulated depreciation	37,500
Salary payable	3,400	Holstein, capital, Jun 30	52,900
Sales discounts	2,200	Holstein, drawing	18,500
Sales returns and allowances	8,400	Cash	8,100
Sales revenue	296,700	Cost of goods sold	162,400
Selling expense	37,500	Equipment	125,000
Supplies	6,000	General expenses	16,100
Unearned sales revenue	13,200	Interest payable	1,200

Requirements

1. Prepare a multi-step income statement.
2. M. Davidson, manager of the company, strives to earn gross profit percentage of at least 50% and net income percentage of 20%. Did Hill Tower achieve these goals? Show your calculations.

● Continuing Exercise

E5-42 ② ③ ④ ⑤ **Journalizing purchase and sale transactions—perpetual inventory; making closing entries, and preparing financial statements [30–40 min]**

This exercise continues the Lawlor Lawn Service situation from Exercise 4-36 of Chapter 4. Lawlor Lawn Service has also begun selling plants that it purchases from a wholesaler. During June, Lawlor Lawn Service completed the following transactions:

Jun	2	Completed lawn service and received cash of $800.
	5	Purchased 110 plants on account for inventory, $304, plus freight in of $15.
	15	Sold 60 plants on account, $600 (cost $174).
	17	Consulted with a client on landscaping design for a fee of $250 on account.
	20	Purchased 120 plants on account for inventory, $384.
	21	Paid on account, $400.
	25	Sold 110 plants for cash, $990 (cost $337).
	30	Recorded the following adjusting entries:
		Depreciation $30
		Physical count of plant inventory, 30 plants (cost $96)

Requirements

1. Open the following selected T-accounts in the ledger: Cash; Accounts receivable; Lawn supplies; Plant inventory; Equipment; Accumulated depreciation—equipment; Accounts payable; Salary payable; Lawlor, capital; Lawlor, drawing; Income summary; Service revenue; Sales revenue; Cost of goods sold; Salary expense; Rent expense; Utilities expense; Depreciation expense—equipment; and Supplies expense.

2. Journalize and post the June transactions. Key all items by date. Compute each account balance, and denote the balance as *Bal*.

3. Journalize and post the closing entries. Denote each closing amount as *Clo*. After posting all closing entries, prove the equality of debits and credits in the ledger.

4. Prepare the June income statement of Lawlor Lawn Service. Use the single-step format.

● Continuing Problem

P5-43 ② ③ ④ ⑤ **Journalizing purchase and sale transactions—perpetual inventory; making closing entries, and preparing financial statements [30–40 min]**

This problem continues the Draper Consulting situation from Problem 4-37 of Chapter 4. Draper performs systems consulting. Draper has also begun selling accounting software. During January, Draper Consulting completed the following transactions:

Jan	2	Completed a consulting engagement and received cash of $7,800.
	2	Prepaid three months office rent, $1,650.
	7	Purchased 80 units software inventory on account, $1,680, plus freight in, $80.
	18	Sold 40 software units on account, $3,500 (cost $880).
	19	Consulted with a client for a fee of $1,000 on account.
	20	Paid employee salary, $2,055.
	21	Paid on account, $1,760.
	22	Purchased 240 units software inventory on account, $6,240.
	24	Paid utilities, $250.
	28	Sold 120 units software for cash, $4,680 (cost $2,960).
	31	Recorded the following adjusting entries:
		Accrued salary expense, $685
		Depreciation, $100 (Equipment, $30; Furniture, $70)
		Expiration of prepaid rent, $550
		Physical count of inventory, 145 units, $3,770

Requirements

1. Open the following selected T-accounts in the ledger: Cash; Accounts receivable; Software inventory; Prepaid rent; Accumulated depreciation—equipment; Accumulated depreciation—furniture; Accounts payable; Salary payable; Draper, capital; Draper, drawing; Income summary, Service revenue; Sales revenue; Cost of goods sold; Salary expense; Rent expense; Utilities expense; Depreciation expense—equipment; and Depreciation expense—furniture.

2. Journalize and post the January transactions. Key all items by date. Compute each account balance, and denote the balance as *Bal.*

3. Journalize and post the closing entries. Denote each closing amount as *Clo.* After posting all closing entries, prove the equality of debits and credits in the ledger.

4. Prepare the January income statement of Draper Consulting. Use the single-step format.

● Practice Set

This problem continues the Shine King Cleaning practice set begun in Chapter 1 and continued through Chapters 2, 3, and 4.

MyAccountingLab

P5-44 ②③④⑤ **Journalizing purchase and sale transactions—perpetual inventory; making closing entries, and preparing financial statements [30–40 min]**

Shine King Cleaning has decided that, in addition to providing cleaning services, it will sell cleaning products. During December 2012, Shine King completed the following transactions:

Dec	2	Purchased 600 units of inventory for $3,600 from Sparkle, Co., on terms, 3/10, n/20.
	5	Purchased 400 units of inventory from Borax on terms 4/5, n/30. The total invoice was for $3,200, which included a $200 freight charge.
	7	Returned 100 units of inventory to Sparkle from the December 2 purchase (cost $600).
	9	Paid Borax.
	11	Sold 350 units of goods to Happy Maids for $4,900 on terms 5/10, n/30. Shine King's cost of the goods was $2,100.
	12	Paid Sparkle.
	15	Received 30 units with a retail price of $420 of goods back from customer Happy Maids. The goods cost Shine King $180.
	21	Received payment from Happy Maids, settling the amount due in full.
	28	Sold 200 units of goods to Bridget, Inc., for cash of $3,000 (cost $1,144).
	29	Paid cash for Utilities of $350.
	30	Paid cash for Sales commission expense of $225.
	31	Recorded the following adjusting entries: Physical count of Inventory on December 31 showed 330 units of goods on hand, $2,541 Depreciation, $170 Accrued salary expense of $700 Prepared all other adjustments necessary for December

Requirements

1. Add any needed accounts to Shine King's existing chart of accounts.

2. Journalize and post the December transactions. Key all items by date. Compute each account balance, and denote the balance as *Bal.*

3. Journalize and post the adjusting entries. Denote each adjusting amount as *Adj.* After posting all adjusting entries, prove the equality of debits and credits in the ledger.

4. Prepare the December multi-step income statement, statement of owner's equity, and balance sheet for the company.

5. Journalize the December closing entries for the company.

Apply Your Knowledge

• Decision Cases

Decision Case 5-1 ← *Link Back to Chapter 4* (*Classified Balance Sheet, Current Ratio, and Debt Ratio*). Jan Lorange is the owner of Poppa Rollo's Pizza, which has prospered during its second year of operation. In order to help her decide whether to open another pizzeria, Lorange has prepared the current income statement of the business. Lorange read in an industry trade journal that a successful two-year-old pizzeria meets the following criteria:

a. Gross profit percentage is at least 60%.

b. Net income is at least $90,000.

Lorange believes the business meets both criteria. She intends to go ahead with the expansion plan and asks your advice on preparing the income statement in accordance with generally accepted accounting principles. When you point out that the statement includes errors, Lorange assures you that all amounts are correct. But some items are listed in the wrong place.

Requirement

1. Prepare a multi-step income statement and make a recommendation about whether Lorange should undertake the expansion.

POPPA ROLLO'S PIZZA
Income Statement
Year Ended December 31, 2014

Sales revenue	$195,000
Gain on sale of land	24,600
Total revenue	219,600
Cost of goods sold	85,200
Gross profit	134,400
Operating expenses:	
Salary expense	35,600
Interest expense	6,000
Depreciation expense	4,800
Utilities expense	3,700
Total operating expense	50,100
Income from operations	84,300
Other revenue:	
Sales returns	10,700
Net income	$ 95,000

Decision Case 5-2 Bill Hildebrand opened Party-Time T-Shirts to sell T-shirts for parties at his college. The company completed the first year of operations, and the owner is generally pleased with operating results as shown by the following income statement:

PARTY-TIME T-SHIRTS
Income Statement
Year Ended December 31, 2011

Net sales revenue	$350,000
Cost of goods sold	210,000
Gross margin	$140,000
Operating expenses:	
Selling expense	40,000
General expense	25,000
Net income	$ 75,000

Hildebrand is considering how to expand the business. He proposes two ways to increase profits to $100,000 during 2012.

a. Hildebrand believes he should advertise more heavily. He believes additional advertising costing $20,000 will increase net sales by 30% and leave general expense unchanged. Assume that Cost of goods sold will remain at the same percentage of net sales as in 2011, so if net sales increases in 2012, Cost of goods sold will increase proportionately.

b. Hildebrand proposes selling higher-margin merchandise, such as party dresses, in addition to the existing product line. An importer can supply a minimum of 1,000 dresses for $40 each; Party-Time can mark these dresses up 100% and sell them for $80. Hildebrand realizes he will have to advertise the new merchandise, and this advertising will cost $5,000. Party-Time can expect to sell only 80% of these dresses during the coming year.

Requirement

1. Help Hildebrand determine which plan to pursue. Prepare a single-step income statement for 2012 to show the expected net income under each plan.

● Ethical Issue 5-1

Dobbs Wholesale Antiques makes all sales under terms of FOB shipping point. The company usually ships inventory to customers approximately one week after receiving the order. For orders received late in December, Kathy Dobbs, the owner, decides when to ship the goods. If profits are already at an acceptable level, Dobbs delays shipment until January. If profits for the current year are lagging behind expectations, Dobbs ships the goods during December.

Requirements

1. Under Dobbs' FOB policy, when should the company record a sale?
2. Do you approve or disapprove of Dobbs' manner of deciding when to ship goods to customers and record the sales revenue? If you approve, give your reason. If you disapprove, identify a better way to decide when to ship goods. (There is no accounting rule against Dobbs' practice.)

● Fraud Case 5-1

Rae Philippe was a warehouse manager for Atkins Oilfield Supply, a business that operated across eight Western states. She was an old pro and had known most of the other warehouse managers for many years. Around December each year, auditors would come to do a physical count of the inventory at each warehouse. Recently, Rae's brother started his own drilling company, and persuaded Rae to "loan" him 80 joints of 5-inch drill pipe to use for his first well. He promised to have it back to Rae by December, but the well encountered problems and the pipe was still in the ground. Rae knew the auditors were on the way, so she called her friend Andy, who ran another Atkins warehouse. "Send me over 80 joints of 5-inch pipe tomorrow and I'll get them back to you ASAP" said Rae. When the auditors came, all the pipe on the books was accounted for, and they filed a "no-exception" report.

Requirements

1. Is there anything the company or the auditors could do in future to detect this kind of fraudulent practice?
2. How would this kind of action impact the financial performance of the company?

● Financial Statement Case 5-1

This case uses both the income statement (statement of operations) and the balance sheet of **Amazon.com** in Appendix A at the end of the book. It will help you understand the closing process of a business.

Requirements

1. Journalize **Amazon.com**'s closing entries for the revenues and expenses of 2009. Show all amounts in millions as in the **Amazon** financial statements. You may be unfamiliar with certain revenues and expenses, but treat each item on the income statement as either a revenue or an expense. For example, Net sales is the first revenue item. Other items you may be unfamiliar with are as follows: "Other operating expense (income), net" is shown in parentheses, so it should be treated as revenue. "Interest Income" should be treated as revenue. Although the amount shown for "Interest expense" is in parentheses, you may ignore those parentheses for this purpose and treat it similar to other expenses. "Other income (expense), net" is shown as a positive number, so it should be treated as revenue. The "provision for income taxes" should be treated as an expense. "Equity method investment activity, net of tax" is shown in parentheses, so it should be shown as an expense. In your closing entries, ignore all subtotals such as Gross profit, Total operating expenses, Income from operations, Total non-operating income (expense), and Net income (loss).

2. Create a T-account for the Income summary, post to that account, and then close the Income summary. (Note: Use the Retained earnings account to replace the Capital account in your entries.) How much was closed to Retained earnings? How is the amount that was closed to Retained earnings labeled on the income statement?

● Team Project 5-1

With a small team of classmates, visit one or more merchandising businesses in your area. Interview a responsible manager of the company to learn about its inventory policies and accounting system. Obtain answers to the following questions, write a report, and be prepared to make a presentation to the class if your instructor so directs.

Requirements

1. What merchandise inventory does the business sell?

2. From whom does the business buy its inventory? Is the relationship with the supplier new or longstanding?

3. What are the FOB terms on inventory purchases? Who pays the freight, the buyer or the seller? Is freight a significant amount? What percentage of total inventory cost is the freight?

4. What are the credit terms on inventory purchases—2/10, n/30, or other? Does the business pay early to get purchase discounts? If so, why? If not, why not?

5. How does the business actually pay its suppliers? Does it mail a check or pay electronically? What is the actual payment procedure?

6. Which type of inventory accounting system does the business use—perpetual or periodic? Is this system computerized?

7. How often does the business take a physical count of its inventory? When during the year is the count taken? Describe the count procedures followed by the company.

8. Does the manager use the gross profit percentage and the rate of inventory turnover to evaluate the business? If not, show the manager how to use these ratios in decision making.

9. Ask any other questions your group considers appropriate.

● Communication Activity 5-1

In 30 words or fewer, explain the difference between a sales discount and a purchase discount.

Quick Check Answers

1. *d* 2. *a* 3. *c* 4. *c* 5. *b* 6. *a* 7. *a* 8. *b* 9. *a* 10. *a*

For online homework, exercises, and problems that provide you immediate feedback, please visit myaccountinglab.com.

Accounting for Merchandise in a Periodic Inventory System

Some smaller businesses find it too expensive to invest in a perpetual inventory system. These businesses use a periodic system.

7 Account for the sale of inventory using a periodic system

Recording the Purchase of Inventory

All inventory systems use the Inventory account. But in a periodic system, purchases, purchase discounts, purchase returns and allowances, and transportation costs are recorded in separate accounts. Let's account for Smart Touch's purchase of the **RCA** goods in Exhibit 5A-1.

EXHIBIT 5A-1 | **Purchase Invoice**

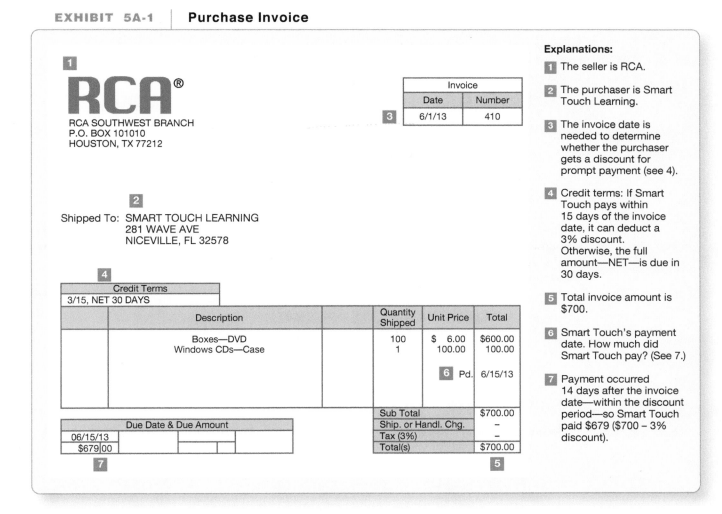

Explanations:

1 The seller is RCA.

2 The purchaser is Smart Touch Learning.

3 The invoice date is needed to determine whether the purchaser gets a discount for prompt payment (see 4).

4 Credit terms: If Smart Touch pays within 15 days of the invoice date, it can deduct a 3% discount. Otherwise, the full amount—NET—is due in 30 days.

5 Total invoice amount is $700.

6 Smart Touch's payment date. How much did Smart Touch pay? (See 7.)

7 Payment occurred 14 days after the invoice date—within the discount period—so Smart Touch paid $679 ($700 – 3% discount).

Recording Purchases and Purchase Discounts

The following entries record the purchase and payment on account within the discount period. Smart Touch received the goods on June 3 and paid within the discount period.

Jun 3	Purchases (E+)	700	
	Accounts payable (L+)		700
	Purchased inventory on account.		
Jun 15	Accounts payable (L−)	700	
	Cash ($700 × 0.97) (A−)		679
	Purchase discounts ($700 × 0.03) (CE+)		21
	Paid within discount period.		

Recording Purchase Returns and Allowances

Suppose that, prior to payment, Smart Touch returned to **RCA** goods costing $100 and also received from **RCA** a purchase allowance of $10. Smart Touch would record these transactions as follows:

Jun 4	Accounts payable (L−)	100	
	Purchase returns and allowances (CE+)		100
	Returned inventory to seller (vendor).		
4	Accounts payable (L−)	10	
	Purchase returns and allowances (CE+)		10
	Received a purchase allowance.		

During the period, the business records the cost of all inventory bought in the Purchases account. The balance of Purchases is a *gross* amount because it does not include subtractions for discounts, returns, or allowances. **Net purchases** is the remainder after subtracting the contra accounts from Purchases:

> Purchases (*debit*)
> − Purchase discounts (*credit*)
> − Purchase returns and allowances (*credit*)
> = Net purchases (a *debit* subtotal, not a separate account)

Recording Transportation Costs

Under the periodic system, costs to transport purchased inventory from seller to buyer are debited to a separate Freight in account, as shown for a $60 freight bill:

Jun 3	Freight in (E+)	60	
	Cash (A−)		60
	Paid a freight bill.		

Recording the Sale of Inventory

Recording sales is streamlined in the periodic system. With no running record of inventory to maintain, we can record a $3,000 sale as follows:

Jun 9	Accounts receivable (A+)	3,000	
	Sales revenue (R+)		3,000
	Sale on account.		

There is no accompanying entry to Inventory and Cost of goods sold in the periodic system.

Accounting for sales discounts and sales returns and allowances is the same as in a perpetual inventory system, except that there are no entries to Inventory or Cost of goods sold.

Cost of goods sold (also called *cost of sales*) is the largest single expense of most businesses that sell merchandise, such as Smart Touch and **Gap, Inc.** It is the cost of the inventory the business has sold to customers. In a periodic system, cost of goods sold must be computed as shown in Exhibit 5A-2.

Cost of Goods Sold in a Periodic Inventory System

The amount of cost of goods sold is the same regardless of the inventory system—perpetual or periodic. As we have seen under the perpetual system, cost of goods sold is simply the sum of the amounts posted to that account.

Cost of goods sold is computed differently under the periodic system. At the end of each period, the company combines a number of accounts to compute cost of goods sold for the period. Exhibit 5A-2 shows how to make the computation.

EXHIBIT 5A-2	**Measuring Cost of Goods Sold in the Periodic Inventory System**

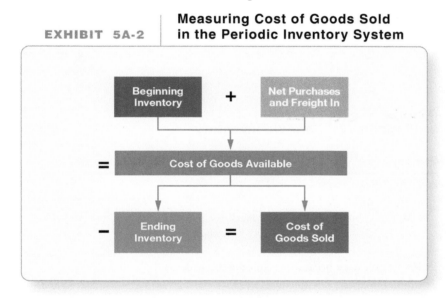

Here is Greg's Tunes' computation of cost of goods sold for 2014:

Cost of goods sold:		
Beginning inventory		$ 38,600
Purchases	$91,400	
Less: Purchase discounts	3,000	
Purchase returns and allowances	1,200	
Net purchases		87,200
Freight in		5,200
Cost of goods available		131,000
Less: Ending inventory		40,200
Cost of goods sold		$ 90,800

Cost of goods sold is reported as the first expense on the merchandiser's income statement, immediately following net sales on a multi-step statement.

Exhibit 5A-3 summarizes this appendix by showing Greg's Tunes' net sales revenue, cost of goods sold, and gross profit on the income statement for the periodic system. (All amounts are assumed.)

Exhibit 5A-4 on page 306 is intended to provide a side-by-side comparison of periodic and perpetual inventory journal entries for the same company's transactions.

EXHIBIT 5A-3 | Partial Income Statement Periodic Inventory System

GREG'S TUNES
Income Statement
Year Ended December 31, 2014

Sales revenue				$169,300
Less: Sales returns and allowances				2,000
Sales discounts				1,400
Net sales revenue				$165,900
Cost of goods sold:				
Beginning inventory			$ 38,600	
Purchases		$91,400		
Less: Purchase discounts		3,000		
Purchase returns and allowances		1,200		
Net purchases			87,200	
Freight in			5,200	
Cost of goods available			$131,000	
Less: Ending inventory			40,200	
Cost of goods sold				90,800
Gross profit				$ 75,100

Extra Credit
Essay - Show entries

EXHIBIT 5A-4 | Perpetual vs. Periodic Inventory

PERPETUAL INVENTORY			PERIODIC INVENTORY		
Jan 1: Purchase of Inventory for $500 (Terms: 1/10, n/15)					
	DR	CR		DR	CR
Inventory (A+)	500		Purchases (E+)	500	
Accounts payable (L+)		500	Accounts payable (L+)		500
Jan 4: Purchaser returns $100 of inventory because it is not the size ordered					
	DR	CR		DR	CR
Accounts payable (L–)	100		Accounts payable (L–)	100	
Inventory (A–)		100	Purchase returns & allowances (CE+)		100
Jan 10: Purchaser pays balance taking advantage of terms					
	DR	CR		DR	CR
Accounts payable (L–)	400		Accounts payable (L–)	400	
Inventory (400 × 0.01) (A–)		4	Purchase discounts (CE+)		4
Cash (A–)		396	Cash (A–)		396
Jan 12: Purchaser pays freight bill of $15 to UPS for shipping of Jan 1 purchase					
	DR	CR		DR	CR
Inventory (A+)	15		Freight in (E+)	15	
Cash (A–)		15	Cash (A–)		15

Note that the net COST of all goods acquired is the same.

1) Perpetual: Inventory (500DR – 100CR – 4CR + 15DR = 411)
2) Periodic: Purchases 500DR – Purchase Returns 100CR – Purchase Discounts 4CR + Freight In 15DR = 411

Appendix 5A Assignments

● Short Exercises

S5A-1   **7** **Computing cost of goods sold in a periodic inventory system [5 min]**
G Wholesale Company began the year with inventory of $6,000. During the year, G purchased $97,000 of goods and returned $6,200 due to damage. G also paid freight charges of $1,500 on inventory purchases. At year-end, G's adjusted inventory balance stood at $17,300. G uses the periodic inventory system.

Requirement

1.   Compute G's cost of goods sold for the year.

Experience the Power of Practice!

As denoted by the logo, all of these questions, as well as additional practice materials, can be found in

MyAccountingLab .

Please visit myaccountinglab.com

● Exercises

MyAccountingLab

E5A-2   **7** **Journalizing periodic transactions [10–15 min]**
On April 30, Fire & Ice Jewelers purchased inventory of $7,200 on account from Ruby Jewels, a jewelry importer. Terms were 3/15, net 45. On receiving the goods, Fire & Ice checked the order and found $600 of unsuitable merchandise. Therefore, Fire & Ice returned $600 of merchandise to Ruby on May 4.
    On May 14, Fire & Ice paid the net amount owed from April 30, less the return.

Requirement

1.   Journalize indicated transactions of Ruby Jewels. Use the periodic inventory system. Explanations are not required.

E5A-3   **7** **Journalizing periodic transactions [10–15 min]**
Refer to the business situation in Exercise 5A-2.

Requirement

1.   Journalize the transactions of Fire & Ice Jewelers. Use the periodic inventory system. Explanations are not required.

E5A-4   **7** **Cost of goods sold in a periodic system [10–15 min]**
Delta Electric uses the periodic inventory system. Delta reported the following selected amounts at May 31, 2012:

Inventory, May 31, 2011	$ 16,000	Freight in	$ 4,000
Inventory, May 31, 2012	23,000	Sales revenue	174,000
Purchases (of inventory)	84,000	Sales discounts	6,000
Purchase discounts	3,000	Sales returns	17,000
Purchase returns	9,000	Owner's equity	47,000

Requirement

1.   Compute Delta's

a.   Net sales revenue.
b.   Cost of goods sold.
c.   Gross profit.

● Problem (Group A)

MyAccountingLab **P5A-5A** ⑦ **Journalizing periodic transactions [10–15 min]**

Assume that the following transactions occurred between Brighton Medical Supply and a Best drug store during April of the current year.

Apr	6	Best purchased $5,800 of merchandise from Brighton Medical Supply on credit terms of 2/10, n/30, FOB shipping point. Separately, Best paid freight in of $150.
	10	Best returned $900 of the merchandise to Brighton.
	15	Best paid $2,900 of the invoice amount owed to Brighton for the April 6 purchase, less the discount.
	27	Best paid the remaining amount owed to Brighton for the April 6 purchase.

Requirement

1. Journalize these transactions, first on the books of the Best drug store and second on the books of Brighton Medical Supply. Use the periodic inventory system.

● Problem (Group B)

MyAccountingLab **P5A-6B** ⑦ **Journalizing periodic transactions [10–15 min]**

Assume that the following transactions occurred between Springfield Medical Supply and a Brookston drug store during September of the current year.

Sep	6	Brookston purchased $6,300 of merchandise from Springfield Medical Supply on credit terms of 2/10, n/30, FOB shipping point. Separately, Brookston paid freight in of $500.
	10	Brookston returned $700 of the merchandise to Springfield.
	15	Brookston paid $3,150 of the invoice amount owed to Springfield for the September 6 purchase, less the discount.
	27	Brookston paid the remaining amount owed to Springfield for the September 6 purchase.

Requirement

1. Journalize these transactions, first on the books of the Brookston drug store and second on the books of Springfield Medical Supply. Use the periodic inventory system.

Comprehensive Problem for Chapters 1–5

Completing a Merchandiser's Accounting Cycle

The end-of-month trial balance of St. Paul Technology at January 31, 2012, follows:

		Account	Debit	Credit
		ST. PAUL TECHNOLOGY Trial Balance January 31, 2012		
		Cash	$ 16,260	
		Accounts receivable	18,930	
		Inventory	65,000	
		Supplies	2,580	
		Building	188,090	
		Accumulated depreciation—building		$ 35,300
		Furniture	44,800	
		Accumulated depreciation—furniture		5,500
		Accounts payable		27,900
		Salary payable		
		Unearned sales revenue		6,480
		Note payable, long-term		85,000
		Tarsus, capital		152,190
		Tarsus, drawing	9,100	
		Sales revenue		179,930
		Sales discounts	7,100	
		Sales returns and allowances	8,080	
		Cost of goods sold	101,900	
		Selling expense	21,380	
		General expense	9,080	
		Total	$492,300	$492,300

Additional data at January 31, 2012:

a. Supplies consumed during the month, $1,400. Half is selling expense, and the other half is general expense.

b. Depreciation for the month: building, $3,800; furniture, $4,600. One-fourth of depreciation is selling expense, and three-fourths is general expense.

c. Unearned sales revenue earned during January, $4,420.

d. Accrued salaries, a general expense, $1,100.

e. Inventory on hand, $63,460. St. Paul uses the perpetual inventory system.

Requirements

1. Using four-column accounts, open the accounts listed on the trial balance, inserting their unadjusted balances. Date the balances of the following accounts January 1: Supplies; Building; Accumulated depreciation—building; Furniture; Accumulated depreciation—furniture; Unearned sales revenue; and Tarsus, capital. Date the balance of Tarsus, drawing, January 31. Also open the Income summary account.

2. Enter the trial balance on a worksheet, and complete the worksheet for the month ended January 31, 2012. St. Paul Technology groups all operating expenses under two accounts, Selling expense and General expense. Leave two blank lines under Selling expense and three blank lines under General expense.

3. Prepare the company's *multi-step* income statement and statement of owner's equity for the month ended January 31, 2012. Also prepare the balance sheet at that date in *report* form.

4. Journalize the adjusting and closing entries at January 31.

5. Post the adjusting and closing entries.

2 0 0 9

P A R T I A L
A N N U A L   R E P O R T

http://media.corporate-ir.net/media_files/irol/97/97664/2007AR.pdf

Report of Ernst & Young LLP, Independent Registered Public Accounting Firm

The Board of Directors and Stockholders
Amazon.com, Inc.

We have audited the accompanying consolidated balance sheets of Amazon.com, Inc. as of December 31, 2009 and 2008, and the related consolidated statements of operations, stockholders' equity, and cash flows for each of the three years in the period ended December 31, 2009. These financial statements are the responsibility of the Company's management. Our responsibility is to express an opinion on these financial statements based on our audits.

We conducted our audits in accordance with the standards of the Public Company Accounting Oversight Board (United States). Those standards require that we plan and perform the audit to obtain reasonable assurance about whether the financial statements are free of material misstatement. An audit includes examining, on a test basis, evidence supporting the amounts and disclosures in the financial statements. An audit also includes assessing the accounting principles used and significant estimates made by management, as well as evaluating the overall financial statement presentation. We believe that our audits provide a reasonable basis for our opinion.

In our opinion, the financial statements referred to above present fairly, in all material respects, the consolidated financial position of Amazon.com, Inc. at December 31, 2009 and 2008, and the consolidated results of its operations and its cash flows for each of the three years in the period ended December 31, 2009, in conformity with U.S. generally accepted accounting principles.

As discussed in Note 1 to the consolidated financial statements, the Company adopted FASB No. 141(R) *Business Combinations*, codified in ASC 805, *Business Combinations*, effective January 1, 2009.

We also have audited, in accordance with the standards of the Public Company Accounting Oversight Board (United States), Amazon.com, Inc.'s internal control over financial reporting as of December 31, 2009, based on criteria established in Internal Control—Integrated Framework issued by the Committee of Sponsoring Organizations of the Treadway Commission and our report dated January 28, 2010 expressed an unqualified opinion thereon.

/s/ Ernst & Young LLP

Seattle, Washington
January 28, 2010

37

AMAZON.COM, INC.

CONSOLIDATED STATEMENTS OF CASH FLOWS
(in millions)

	Year Ended December 31,		
	2009	2008	2007
CASH AND CASH EQUIVALENTS, BEGINNING OF PERIOD	$ 2,769	$ 2,539	$1,022
OPERATING ACTIVITIES:			
Net income	902	645	476
Adjustments to reconcile net income to net cash from operating activities:			
Depreciation of fixed assets, including internal-use software and website development, and other amortization	378	287	246
Stock-based compensation	341	275	185
Other operating expense (income), net	103	(24)	9
Losses (gains) on sales of marketable securities, net	(4)	(2)	1
Other expense (income), net	(15)	(34)	12
Deferred income taxes	81	(5)	(99)
Excess tax benefits from stock-based compensation	(105)	(159)	(257)
Changes in operating assets and liabilities:			
Inventories	(531)	(232)	(303)
Accounts receivable, net and other	(481)	(218)	(255)
Accounts payable	1,859	812	928
Accrued expenses and other	300	247	429
Additions to unearned revenue	1,054	449	244
Amortization of previously unearned revenue	(589)	(344)	(211)
Net cash provided by (used in) operating activities	3,293	1,697	1,405
INVESTING ACTIVITIES:			
Purchases of fixed assets, including internal-use software and website development	(373)	(333)	(224)
Acquisitions, net of cash acquired, and other	(40)	(494)	(75)
Sales and maturities of marketable securities and other investments	1,966	1,305	1,271
Purchases of marketable securities and other investments	(3,890)	(1,677)	(930)
Net cash provided by (used in) investing activities	(2,337)	(1,199)	42
FINANCING ACTIVITIES:			
Excess tax benefits from stock-based compensation	105	159	257
Common stock repurchased		(100)	(248)
Proceeds from long-term debt and other	87	98	115
Repayments of long-term debt and capital lease obligations	(472)	(355)	(74)
Net cash provided by (used in) financing activities	(280)	(198)	50
Foreign-currency effect on cash and cash equivalents	(1)	(70)	20
Net increase in cash and cash equivalents	675	230	1,517
CASH AND CASH EQUIVALENTS, END OF PERIOD	$ 3,444	$ 2,769	$2,539
SUPPLEMENTAL CASH FLOW INFORMATION:			
Cash paid for interest	$ 32	$ 64	$ 67
Cash paid for income taxes	48	53	24
Fixed assets acquired under capital leases and other financing arrangements	147	148	74
Fixed assets acquired under build-to-suit leases	188	72	15
Conversion of debt	—	605	1

See accompanying notes to consolidated financial statements.

38

AMAZON.COM, INC.

CONSOLIDATED STATEMENTS OF OPERATIONS
(in millions, except per share data)

	Year Ended December 31,		
	2009	2008	2007
Net sales	$24,509	$19,166	$14,835
Cost of sales	18,978	14,896	11,482
Gross profit	5,531	4,270	3,353
Operating expenses (1):			
Fulfillment	2,052	1,658	1,292
Marketing	680	482	344
Technology and content	1,240	1,033	818
General and administrative	328	279	235
Other operating expense (income), net	102	(24)	9
Total operating expenses	4,402	3,428	2,698
Income from operations	1,129	842	655
Interest income	37	83	90
Interest expense	(34)	(71)	(77)
Other income (expense), net	29	47	(8)
Total non-operating income (expense)	32	59	5
Income before income taxes	1,161	901	660
Provision for income taxes	(253)	(247)	(184)
Equity-method investment activity, net of tax	(6)	(9)	—
Net income	$ 902	$ 645	$ 476
Basic earnings per share	$ 2.08	$ 1.52	$ 1.15
Diluted earnings per share	$ 2.04	$ 1.49	$ 1.12
Weighted average shares used in computation of earnings per share:			
Basic	433	423	413
Diluted	442	432	424

(1) Includes stock-based compensation as follows:

Fulfillment	$ 79	$ 61	$ 39
Marketing	20	13	8
Technology and content	182	151	103
General and administrative	60	50	35

See accompanying notes to consolidated financial statements.

39

AMAZON.COM, INC.

CONSOLIDATED BALANCE SHEETS
(in millions, except per share data)

	December 31, 2009	December 31, 2008
ASSETS		
Current assets:		
Cash and cash equivalents	$ 3,444	$2,769
Marketable securities	2,922	958
Inventories	2,171	1,399
Accounts receivable, net and other	988	827
Deferred tax assets	272	204
Total current assets	9,797	6,157
Fixed assets, net	1,290	854
Deferred tax assets	18	145
Goodwill	1,234	438
Other assets	1,474	720
Total assets	$13,813	$8,314
LIABILITIES AND STOCKHOLDERS' EQUITY		
Current liabilities:		
Accounts payable	$ 5,605	$3,594
Accrued expenses and other	1,759	1,152
Total current liabilities	7,364	4,746
Long-term debt	109	409
Other long-term liabilities	1,083	487
Commitments and contingencies		
Stockholders' equity:		
Preferred stock, $0.01 par value:		
Authorized shares—500	—	—
Issued and outstanding shares—none		
Common stock, $0.01 par value:		
Authorized shares—5,000		
Issued shares—461 and 445	—	—
Outstanding shares—444 and 428	5	4
Treasury stock, at cost	(600)	(600)
Additional paid-in capital	5,736	4,121
Accumulated other comprehensive income (loss)	(56)	(123)
Retained earnings (accumulated deficit)	172	(730)
Total stockholders' equity	5,257	2,672
Total liabilities and stockholders' equity	$13,813	$8,314

See accompanying notes to consolidated financial statements.

40

AMAZON.COM, INC.

CONSOLIDATED STATEMENTS OF STOCKHOLDERS' EQUITY

(in millions)

	Common Stock		Treasury Stock	Additional Paid-In Capital	Accumulated Other Comprehensive Income (Loss)	Retained Earnings (Accumulated Deficit)	Total Stockholders' Equity
	Shares	Amount					
Balance at December 31, 2006	414	$ 4	$(252)	$2,517	$ (1)	$(1,837)	$ 431
Net income	—	—	—	—	—	476	476
Foreign currency translation losses, net of tax	—	—	—	—	(3)	—	(3)
Change in unrealized losses on available-for-sale securities, net of tax	—	—	—	—	8	—	8
Amortization of unrealized loss on terminated Euro Currency Swap, net of tax	—	—	—	—	1	—	1
Comprehensive income							482
Change in accounting principle	—	—	—	2	—	(14)	(12)
Unrecognized excess tax benefits from stock-based compensation	—	—	—	4	—	—	4
Exercise of common stock options and conversion of debt	8	—	—	92	—	—	92
Repurchase of common stock	(6)	—	(248)	—	—	—	(248)
Excess tax benefits from stock-based compensation	—	—	—	257	—	—	257
Stock-based compensation and issuance of employee benefit plan stock	—	—	—	191	—	—	191
Balance at December 31, 2007	416	4	(500)	3,063	5	(1,375)	1,197
Net income	—	—	—	—	—	645	645
Foreign currency translation losses, net of tax	—	—	—	—	(127)	—	(127)
Change in unrealized losses on available-for-sale securities, net of tax	—	—	—	—	(1)	—	(1)
Comprehensive income							517
Unrecognized excess tax benefits from stock-based compensation	—	—	—	(8)	—	—	(8)
Exercise of common stock options and conversion of debt	14	—	—	624	—	—	624
Repurchase of common stock	(2)	—	(100)	—	—	—	(100)
Excess tax benefits from stock-based compensation	—	—	—	154	—	—	154
Stock-based compensation and issuance of employee benefit plan stock	—	—	—	288	—	—	288
Balance at December 31, 2008	428	4	(600)	4,121	(123)	(730)	2,672
Net income	—	—	—	—	—	902	902
Foreign currency translation gains net of tax	—	—	—	—	62	—	62
Change in unrealized gains on available-for-sale securities, net of tax	—	—	—	—	4	—	4
Amortization of unrealized loss on terminated Euro Currency Swap, net of tax	—	—	—	—	1	—	1
Comprehensive income							969
Exercise of common stock options	7	—	—	19	—	—	19
Issuance of common stock for acquisition activity	9	1	—	1,144	—	—	1,145
Excess tax benefits from stock-based compensation	—	—	—	103	—	—	103
Stock-based compensation and issuance of employee benefit plan stock	—	—	—	349	—	—	349
Balance at December 31, 2009	444	$ 5	$(600)	$5,736	$ (56)	$ 172	$5,257

See accompanying notes to consolidated financial statements.

41

AMAZON.COM, INC.

NOTES TO CONSOLIDATED FINANCIAL STATEMENTS

Note 1—DESCRIPTION OF BUSINESS AND ACCOUNTING POLICIES

Description of Business

Amazon.com opened its virtual doors on the World Wide Web in July 1995 and offers Earth's Biggest Selection. We seek to be Earth's most customer-centric company for three primary customer sets: consumers, sellers, and developers. We serve consumers through our retail websites and focus on selection, price, and convenience. We also manufacture and sell the Kindle e-reader. We offer programs that enable sellers to sell their products on our websites and their own branded websites and to fulfill orders through us. We serve developers through Amazon Web Services, which provides access to technology infrastructure that developers can use to enable virtually any type of business. In addition, we generate revenue through co-branded credit card agreements and other marketing and promotional services, such as online advertising.

We have organized our operations into two principal segments: North America and International. See "Note 11—Segment Information."

Principles of Consolidation

The consolidated financial statements include the accounts of the Company, its wholly-owned subsidiaries, and those entities in which we have a variable interest and are the primary beneficiary. Intercompany balances and transactions have been eliminated.

Use of Estimates

The preparation of financial statements in conformity with U.S. GAAP requires estimates and assumptions that affect the reported amounts of assets and liabilities, revenues and expenses, and related disclosures of contingent liabilities in the consolidated financial statements and accompanying notes. Estimates are used for, but not limited to, valuation of investments, collectability of receivables, sales returns, incentive discount offers, valuation of inventory, depreciable lives of fixed assets and internally-developed software, valuation of acquired intangibles and goodwill, income taxes, stock-based compensation, and contingencies. Actual results could differ materially from those estimates.

Subsequent Events

We have evaluated subsequent events and transactions for potential recognition or disclosure in the financial statements through January 28, 2010, the day the financial statements were issued.

Earnings per Share

Basic earnings per share is calculated using our weighted-average outstanding common shares. Diluted earnings per share is calculated using our weighted-average outstanding common shares including the dilutive effect of stock awards as determined under the treasury stock method.

42

AMAZON.COM, INC.

NOTES TO CONSOLIDATED FINANCIAL STATEMENTS—(Continued)

The following table shows the calculation of diluted shares (in millions):

	Year Ended December 31,		
	2009	2008	2007
Shares used in computation of basic earnings per share	433	423	413
Total dilutive effect of outstanding stock awards (1)	9	9	11
Shares used in computation of diluted earnings per share	442	432	424

(1) Calculated using the treasury stock method, which assumes proceeds are used to reduce the dilutive effect of outstanding stock awards. Assumed proceeds include the unrecognized deferred compensation of stock awards, and assumed tax proceeds from excess stock-based compensation deductions.

Treasury Stock

We account for treasury stock under the cost method and include treasury stock as a component of stockholders' equity.

Cash and Cash Equivalents

We classify all highly liquid instruments, including money market funds that comply with Rule 2a-7 of the Investment Company Act of 1940, with an original maturity of three months or less at the time of purchase as cash equivalents.

Inventories

Inventories, consisting of products available for sale, are accounted for using primarily the FIFO method, and are valued at the lower of cost or market value. This valuation requires us to make judgments, based on currently-available information, about the likely method of disposition, such as through sales to individual customers, returns to product vendors, or liquidations, and expected recoverable values of each disposition category.

We provide fulfillment-related services in connection with certain of our sellers' programs. The third party seller maintains ownership of their inventory, regardless of whether fulfillment is provided by us or the third party seller, and therefore these products are not included in our inventories.

Accounts Receivable, Net, and Other

Included in "Accounts receivable, net, and other" on our consolidated balance sheets are amounts primarily related to vendor and customer receivables. At December 31, 2009 and 2008, vendor receivables, net, were $495 million and $400 million, and customer receivables, net, were $341 million and $311 million.

Allowance for Doubtful Accounts

We estimate losses on receivables based on known troubled accounts and historical experience of losses incurred. The allowance for doubtful customer and vendor receivables was $72 million and $81 million at December 31, 2009 and 2008.

43

Internal-use Software and Website Development

Costs incurred to develop software for internal use and our websites are capitalized and amortized over the estimated useful life of the software. Costs related to design or maintenance of internal-use software and website development are expensed as incurred. For the years ended 2009, 2008, and 2007, we capitalized $187 million (including $35 million of stock-based compensation), $187 million (including $27 million of stock-based compensation), and $129 million (including $21 million of stock-based compensation) of costs associated with internal-use software and website development. Amortization of previously capitalized amounts was $172 million, $143 million, and $116 million for 2009, 2008, and 2007.

Depreciation of Fixed Assets

Fixed assets include assets such as furniture and fixtures, heavy equipment, technology infrastructure, internal-use software and website development. Depreciation is recorded on a straight-line basis over the estimated useful lives of the assets (generally two years for assets such as internal-use software, three years for our technology infrastructure, five years for furniture and fixtures, and ten years for heavy equipment). Depreciation expense is generally classified within the corresponding operating expense categories on our consolidated statements of operations.

Leases and Asset Retirement Obligations

We categorize leases at their inception as either operating or capital leases. On certain of our lease agreements, we may receive rent holidays and other incentives. We recognize lease costs on a straight-line basis without regard to deferred payment terms, such as rent holidays that defer the commencement date of required payments. Additionally, incentives we receive are treated as a reduction of our costs over the term of the agreement. Leasehold improvements are capitalized at cost and amortized over the lesser of their expected useful life or the life of the lease, excluding renewal periods. We establish assets and liabilities for the estimated construction costs incurred under build-to-suit lease arrangements to the extent we are involved in the construction of structural improvements or take some level of construction risk prior to commencement of a lease.

We establish assets and liabilities for the present value of estimated future costs to return certain of our leased facilities to their original condition. Such assets are depreciated over the lease period into operating expense, and the recorded liabilities are accreted to the future value of the estimated restoration costs.

Goodwill

We evaluate goodwill for impairment annually and when an event occurs or circumstances change that indicate that the carrying value may not be recoverable. We test goodwill for impairment by first comparing the book value of net assets to the fair value of the reporting units. If the fair value is determined to be less than the book value, a second step is performed to compute the amount of impairment as the difference between the estimated fair value of goodwill and the carrying value. We estimate the fair value of the reporting units using discounted cash flows. Forecasts of future cash flow are based on our best estimate of future net sales and operating expenses, based primarily on estimated category expansion, pricing, market segment penetration and general economic conditions.

We conduct our annual impairment test as of October 1 of each year, and have determined there to be no impairment for any of the periods presented. There were no events or circumstances from the date of our assessment through December 31, 2009 that would impact this conclusion.

44

See "Note 4—Acquisitions, Goodwill, and Acquired Intangible Assets."

Other Assets

Included in "Other assets" on our consolidated balance sheets are amounts primarily related to marketable securities restricted for longer than one year, the majority of which are attributable to collateralization of bank guarantees and debt related to our international operations; acquired intangible assets, net of amortization; deferred costs; certain equity investments; and intellectual property rights, net of amortization.

Investments

We generally invest our excess cash in investment grade short to intermediate term fixed income securities and AAA-rated money market funds. Such investments are included in "Cash and cash equivalents," or "Marketable securities" on the accompanying consolidated balance sheets, classified as available-for-sale, and reported at fair value with unrealized gains and losses included in "Accumulated other comprehensive income (loss)."

Equity investments are accounted for using the equity method of accounting if the investment gives us the ability to exercise significant influence, but not control, over an investee. The total of these investments in equity-method investees, including identifiable intangible assets, deferred tax liabilities and goodwill, is classified on our consolidated balance sheets as "Other assets." Our share of the investees' earnings or losses and amortization of the related intangible assets, if any, is classified as "Equity-method investment activity, net of tax" on our consolidated statements of operations.

Equity investments without readily determinable fair values for which we do not have the ability to exercise significant influence are accounted for using the cost method of accounting. Under the cost method, investments are carried at cost and are adjusted only for other-than-temporary declines in fair value, distributions of earnings, and additional investments.

Equity investments that have readily determinable fair values are classified as available-for-sale and are recorded at fair value with unrealized gains and losses, net of tax, included in "Accumulated other comprehensive loss."

We periodically evaluate whether declines in fair values of our investments below their cost are other-than-temporary. This evaluation consists of several qualitative and quantitative factors regarding the severity and duration of the unrealized loss as well as our ability and intent to hold the investment until a forecasted recovery occurs. Additionally, we assess whether it is more likely than not we will be required to sell any investment before recovery of its amortized cost basis. Factors considered include quoted market prices; recent financial results and operating trends; other publicly available information; implied values from any recent transactions or offers of investee securities; other conditions that may affect the value of our investments; duration and severity of the decline in value; and our strategy and intentions for holding the investment.

Long-Lived Assets

Long-lived assets, other than goodwill, are reviewed for impairment whenever events or changes in circumstances indicate that the carrying amount of the assets might not be recoverable. Conditions that would necessitate an impairment assessment include a significant decline in the observable market value of an asset, a significant change in the extent or manner in which an asset is used, or any other significant adverse change that would indicate that the carrying amount of an asset or group of assets may not be recoverable.

AMAZON.COM, INC.

NOTES TO CONSOLIDATED FINANCIAL STATEMENTS—(Continued)

For long-lived assets used in operations, impairment losses are only recorded if the asset's carrying amount is not recoverable through its undiscounted, probability-weighted future cash flows. We measure the impairment loss based on the difference between the carrying amount and estimated fair value.

Long-lived assets are considered held for sale when certain criteria are met, including when management has committed to a plan to sell the asset, the asset is available for sale in its immediate condition, and the sale is probable within one year of the reporting date. Assets held for sale are reported at the lower of cost or fair value less costs to sell. Assets held for sale were not significant at December 31, 2009 or 2008.

Accrued Expenses and Other

Included in "Accrued expenses and other" at December 31, 2009 and 2008 were liabilities of $347 million and $270 million for unredeemed gift certificates. We reduce the liability for a gift certificate when it is applied to an order. If a gift certificate is not redeemed, we recognize revenue when it expires or, for a certificate without an expiration date, when the likelihood of its redemption becomes remote, generally two years from date of issuance.

Unearned Revenue

Unearned revenue is recorded when payments are received in advance of performing our service obligations and is recognized over the service period. Current unearned revenue is included in "Accrued expenses and other" and non-current unearned revenue is included in "Other long-term liabilities" on our consolidated balance sheets. Current unearned revenue was $511 million and $191 million at December 31, 2009 and 2008. Non-current unearned revenue was $201 million and $46 million at December 31, 2009 and 2008.

Income Taxes

Income tax expense includes U.S. and international income taxes. Except as required under U.S. tax law, we do not provide for U.S. taxes on our undistributed earnings of foreign subsidiaries that have not been previously taxed since we intend to invest such undistributed earnings indefinitely outside of the U.S. Undistributed earnings of foreign subsidiaries that are indefinitely invested outside of the U.S were $912 million at December 31, 2009. Determination of the unrecognized deferred tax liability that would be incurred if such amounts were repatriated is not practicable.

Deferred income tax balances reflect the effects of temporary differences between the carrying amounts of assets and liabilities and their tax bases and are stated at enacted tax rates expected to be in effect when taxes are actually paid or recovered.

Deferred tax assets are evaluated for future realization and reduced by a valuation allowance to the extent we believe a portion will not be realized. We consider many factors when assessing the likelihood of future realization of our deferred tax assets, including our recent cumulative earnings experience and expectations of future taxable income and capital gains by taxing jurisdiction, the carry-forward periods available to us for tax reporting purposes, and other relevant factors. We allocate our valuation allowance to current and long-term deferred tax assets on a pro-rata basis.

We utilize a two-step approach to recognizing and measuring uncertain tax positions (tax contingencies). The first step is to evaluate the tax position for recognition by determining if the weight of available evidence indicates it is more likely than not that the position will be sustained on audit, including resolution of related

46

appeals or litigation processes. The second step is to measure the tax benefit as the largest amount which is more than 50% likely of being realized upon ultimate settlement. We consider many factors when evaluating and estimating our tax positions and tax benefits, which may require periodic adjustments and which may not accurately forecast actual outcomes. We include interest and penalties related to our tax contingencies in income tax expense.

Fair Value of Financial Instruments

Fair value is defined as the price that would be received to sell an asset or paid to transfer a liability in an orderly transaction between market participants at the measurement date. To increase the comparability of fair value measures, the following hierarchy prioritizes the inputs to valuation methodologies used to measure fair value:

Level 1—Valuations based on quoted prices for identical assets and liabilities in active markets.

Level 2—Valuations based on observable inputs other than quoted prices included in Level 1, such as quoted prices for similar assets and liabilities in active markets, quoted prices for identical or similar assets and liabilities in markets that are not active, or other inputs that are observable or can be corroborated by observable market data.

Level 3—Valuations based on unobservable inputs reflecting our own assumptions, consistent with reasonably available assumptions made by other market participants. These valuations require significant judgment.

We measure the fair value of money market funds based on quoted prices in active markets for identical assets or liabilities. All other financial instruments were valued based on quoted market prices of similar instruments and other significant inputs derived from or corroborated by observable market data.

Revenue

We recognize revenue from product sales or services rendered when the following four revenue recognition criteria are met: persuasive evidence of an arrangement exists, delivery has occurred or services have been rendered, the selling price is fixed or determinable, and collectability is reasonably assured. Revenue arrangements with multiple deliverables are divided into separate units of accounting if the deliverables in the arrangement meet the following criteria: there is standalone value to the delivered item; there is objective and reliable evidence of the fair value of the undelivered items; and delivery of any undelivered item is probable.

We evaluate whether it is appropriate to record the gross amount of product sales and related costs or the net amount earned as commissions. Generally, when we are primarily obligated in a transaction, are subject to inventory risk, have latitude in establishing prices and selecting suppliers, or have several but not all of these indicators, revenue is recorded gross. If we are not primarily obligated and amounts earned are determined using a fixed percentage, a fixed-payment schedule, or a combination of the two, we generally record the net amounts as commissions earned.

Product sales and shipping revenues, net of promotional discounts, rebates, and return allowances, are recorded when the products are shipped and title passes to customers. Retail sales to customers are made pursuant to a sales contract that provides for transfer of both title and risk of loss upon our delivery to the carrier. Return allowances, which reduce product revenue, are estimated using historical experience. Revenue from product sales and services rendered is recorded net of sales and consumption taxes. Amounts received in advance for subscription services, including amounts received for Amazon Prime and other membership programs, are

47

deferred and recognized as revenue over the subscription term. For our products with multiple elements, where objective and reliable evidence of fair value for the undelivered elements cannot be established, we recognize the revenue and related cost over the expected life of the product.

We periodically provide incentive offers to our customers to encourage purchases. Such offers include current discount offers, such as percentage discounts off current purchases, inducement offers, such as offers for future discounts subject to a minimum current purchase, and other similar offers. Current discount offers, when accepted by our customers, are treated as a reduction to the purchase price of the related transaction, while inducement offers, when accepted by our customers, are treated as a reduction to purchase price based on estimated future redemption rates. Redemption rates are estimated using our historical experience for similar inducement offers. Current discount offers and inducement offers are presented as a net amount in "Net sales."

Commissions and per-unit fees received from sellers and similar amounts earned through other seller sites are recognized when the item is sold by seller and our collectability is reasonably assured. We record an allowance for estimated refunds on such commissions using historical experience.

Shipping Activities

Outbound shipping charges to customers are included in "Net sales" and were $924 million, $835 million, and $740 million for 2009, 2008, and 2007. Outbound shipping-related costs are included in "Cost of sales" and totaled $1.8 billion, $1.5 billion, and $1.2 billion for 2009, 2008, and 2007. The net cost to us of shipping activities was $849 million, $630 million, and $434 million for 2009, 2008 and 2007.

Cost of Sales

Cost of sales consists of the purchase price of consumer products and content sold by us, inbound and outbound shipping charges, packaging supplies, and costs incurred in operating and staffing our fulfillment and customer service centers on behalf of other businesses. Shipping charges to receive products from our suppliers are included in our inventory, and recognized as "Cost of sales" upon sale of products to our customers. Payment processing and related transaction costs, including those associated with seller transactions, are classified in "Fulfillment" on our consolidated statements of operations.

Vendor Agreements

We have agreements to receive cash consideration from certain of our vendors, including rebates and cooperative marketing reimbursements. We generally consider amounts received from our vendors as a reduction of the prices we pay for their products and, therefore, we record such amounts as either a reduction of "Cost of sales" on our consolidated statements of operations, or, if the product inventory is still on hand, as a reduction of the carrying value of inventory. Vendor rebates are typically dependent upon reaching minimum purchase thresholds. We evaluate the likelihood of reaching purchase thresholds using past experience and current year forecasts. When volume rebates can be reasonably estimated, we record a portion of the rebate as we make progress towards the purchase threshold.

When we receive direct reimbursements for costs incurred by us in advertising the vendor's product or service, the amount we receive is recorded as an offset to "Marketing" on our consolidated statements of operations.

48

Fulfillment

Fulfillment costs represent those costs incurred in operating and staffing our fulfillment and customer service centers, including costs attributable to buying, receiving, inspecting, and warehousing inventories; picking, packaging, and preparing customer orders for shipment; payment processing and related transaction costs, including costs associated with our guarantee for certain seller transactions; and responding to inquiries from customers. Fulfillment costs also include amounts paid to third parties that assist us in fulfillment and customer service operations. Certain of our fulfillment-related costs that are incurred on behalf of other businesses are classified as cost of sales rather than fulfillment.

Marketing

Marketing costs consist primarily of online advertising, including through our Associates program, sponsored search, portal advertising, and other initiatives. We pay commissions to participants in our Associates program when their customer referrals result in product sales and classify such costs as "Marketing" on our consolidated statements of operations. We also participate in cooperative advertising arrangements with certain of our vendors, and other third parties.

Marketing expenses also consist of public relations expenditures; payroll and related expenses for personnel engaged in marketing, business development, and selling activities; and to a lesser extent, traditional advertising.

Advertising and other promotional costs, which consist primarily of online advertising, are expensed as incurred, and were $593 million, $420 million, and $306 million, in 2009, 2008, and 2007. Prepaid advertising costs were not significant at December 31, 2009 and 2008.

Technology and Content

Technology and content expenses consist principally of payroll and related expenses for employees involved in, application development, category expansion, editorial content, buying, merchandising selection, and systems support, as well as costs associated with the compute, storage and telecommunications infrastructure used internally and supporting Amazon Web Services.

Technology and content costs are expensed as incurred, except for certain costs relating to the development of internal-use software and website development, including software used to upgrade and enhance our websites and processes supporting our business, which are capitalized and amortized over two years.

General and Administrative

General and administrative expenses consist of payroll and related expenses for employees involved in general corporate functions, including accounting, finance, tax, legal, and human relations, among others; costs associated with use by these functions of facilities and equipment, such as depreciation expense and rent; professional fees and litigation costs; and other general corporate costs.

Stock-Based Compensation

Compensation cost for all stock-based awards is measured at fair value on date of grant and recognized over the service period for awards expected to vest. The fair value of restricted stock units is determined based on the number of shares granted and the quoted price of our common stock. Such value is recognized as expense over the service period, net of estimated forfeitures, using the accelerated method. The estimation of stock awards that

49

AMAZON.COM, INC.

NOTES TO CONSOLIDATED FINANCIAL STATEMENTS—(Continued)

will ultimately vest requires judgment, and to the extent actual results or updated estimates differ from our current estimates, such amounts will be recorded as a cumulative adjustment in the period estimates are revised. We consider many factors when estimating expected forfeitures, including types of awards, employee class, and historical experience.

Other Income (Expense), Net

Other income (expense), net, consists primarily of gains and losses on sales of marketable securities, foreign currency transaction gains and losses, and other losses.

Foreign Currency

We have internationally-focused websites for the United Kingdom, Germany, France, Japan, Canada, and China. Net sales generated from internationally-focused websites, as well as most of the related expenses directly incurred from those operations, are denominated in the functional currencies of the resident countries. The functional currency of our subsidiaries that either operate or support these international websites is the same as the local currency. Assets and liabilities of these subsidiaries are translated into U.S. Dollars at period-end exchange rates, and revenues and expenses are translated at average rates prevailing throughout the period. Translation adjustments are included in "Accumulated other comprehensive income (loss)," a separate component of stockholders' equity, and in the "Foreign currency effect on cash and cash equivalents," on our consolidated statements of cash flows. Transaction gains and losses arising from transactions denominated in a currency other than the functional currency of the entity involved are included in "Other income (expense), net" on our consolidated statements of operations.

Gains and losses arising from intercompany foreign currency transactions are included in net income. In connection with the remeasurement of intercompany balances, we recorded gains of $5 million, $23 million and $32 million in 2009, 2008 and 2007.

Recent Accounting Pronouncements

In December 2007, the Financial Accounting Standards Board ("FASB") issued Statements of Financial Accounting Standards ("SFAS") No. 141 (R), *Business Combinations*, codified as Accounting Standards Codification ("ASC") 805, *Business Combinations,* and SFAS No. 160, *Noncontrolling Interests in Consolidated Financial Statements*, codified as ASC 810, *Consolidations.* SFAS No. 141 (R) requires an acquirer to measure the identifiable assets acquired, the liabilities assumed, and any noncontrolling interest in the acquired entity at their fair values on the acquisition date, with goodwill being the excess value over the net identifiable assets acquired. SFAS No. 160 clarifies that a noncontrolling interest in a subsidiary should be reported as equity in the consolidated financial statements. The calculation of earnings per share will continue to be based on income amounts attributable to the parent. SFAS No. 141 (R) impacted acquisitions closed on or after January 1, 2009. Adoption did not have a material impact on our consolidated financial statements on the date of adoption.

In December 2009, the FASB issued Accounting Standards Update ("ASU") 2009-17, which codifies SFAS No. 167, *Amendments to FASB Interpretation No. 46(R)* issued in June 2009. ASU 2009-17 requires a qualitative approach to identifying a controlling financial interest in a variable interest entity ("VIE"), and requires ongoing assessment of whether an entity is a VIE and whether an interest in a VIE makes the holder the primary beneficiary of the VIE. ASU 2009-17 is effective for annual reporting periods beginning after November 15, 2009. We do not expect the adoption of ASU 2009-17 to have a material impact on our consolidated financial statements.

50

AMAZON.COM, INC.

NOTES TO CONSOLIDATED FINANCIAL STATEMENTS—(Continued)

In October 2009, the FASB issued ASU 2009-13, which amends ASC Topic 605, *Revenue Recognition.* Under this standard, management is no longer required to obtain vendor-specific objective evidence or third party evidence of fair value for each deliverable in an arrangement with multiple elements, and where evidence is not available we may now estimate the proportion of the selling price attributable to each deliverable. We have chosen to prospectively adopt this standard as of January 1, 2010.

Sales of our Kindle e-reader are considered arrangements with multiple elements which include the device, wireless access and delivery and software upgrades. The revenue related to the device, which is the substantial portion of the total sale price, and related costs will be recognized at time of delivery. Revenue for the wireless access and delivery and software upgrades will continue to be amortized over the life of the device, which remains estimated at two years.

We cannot reasonably estimate the effect of adopting this standard on future financial periods as the impact will vary based on actual volume of activity under these types of revenue arrangements.

For arrangements entered into prior to the adoption of the new accounting standard and for which revenue had been previously deferred, we will recognize $508 million throughout 2010 and 2011.

In January 2010, the FASB issued ASU 2010-6, *Improving Disclosures About Fair Value Measurements*, which requires reporting entities to make new disclosures about recurring or nonrecurring fair-value measurements including significant transfers into and out of Level 1 and Level 2 fair-value measurements and information on purchases, sales, issuances, and settlements on a gross basis in the reconciliation of Level 3 fair- value measurements. ASU 2010-6 is effective for annual reporting periods beginning after December 15, 2009, except for Level 3 reconciliation disclosures which are effective for annual periods beginning after December 15, 2010. We do not expect the adoption of ASU 2010-6 to have a material impact on our consolidated financial statements.

Note 2—CASH, CASH EQUIVALENTS, AND MARKETABLE SECURITIES

As of December 31, 2009 and 2008 our cash, cash equivalents, and marketable securities primarily consisted of cash, government and government agency securities, AAA-rated money market funds and other investment grade securities. Such amounts are recorded at fair value. The following table summarizes, by major security type, our cash, cash equivalents and marketable securities (in millions):

	December 31, 2009			
	Cost or Amortized Cost	Gross Unrealized Gains	Gross Unrealized Losses	Total Estimated Fair Value
Cash	$ 391	$—	$—	$ 391
Money market funds	2,750	—	—	2,750
Foreign government and agency securities	1,992	7	—	1,999
Corporate debt securities (1)	206	5	—	211
U.S. government and agency securities	1,268	5	(5)	1,268
Asset-backed securities	44	2	—	46
Other fixed income securities	6	—	—	6
Equity securities	2	—	(1)	1
	$6,659	$ 19	$ (6)	$6,672
Less: Long-term marketable securities (2)				(306)
Total cash, cash equivalents, and marketable securities				$6,366

51

NOTES TO CONSOLIDATED FINANCIAL STATEMENTS—(Continued)

	December 31, 2008			
	Cost or Amortized Cost	Gross Unrealized Gains	Gross Unrealized Losses	Total Estimated Fair Value
Cash	$ 355	$—	$—	$ 355
Money market funds	1,682	—	—	1,682
Foreign government and agency securities	1,120	8	—	1,128
Corporate debt securities (1)	194	2	(2)	194
U.S. government and agency securities	589	5	—	594
Asset-backed securities	62	—	(4)	58
Other fixed income securities	23	—	—	23
Equity securities	2	—	(1)	1
	$4,027	$ 15	$ (7)	$4,035
Less: Long-term marketable securities (2)				(308)
Total cash, cash equivalents, and marketable securities				$3,727

(1) Corporate debt securities include investments in financial, insurance, and corporate institutions. No single issuer represents a significant portion of the total corporate debt securities portfolio.

(2) We are required to pledge or otherwise restrict a portion of our marketable securities as collateral for standby letters of credit, guarantees, debt, and real estate lease agreements. We classify cash and marketable securities with use restrictions of twelve months or longer as non-current "Other assets" on our consolidated balance sheets. See "Note 7—Commitments and Contingencies."

The following table summarizes gross gains and gross losses realized on sales of available-for-sale marketable securities (in millions):

	Year Ended December 31,		
	2009	2008	2007
Realized gains	$ 4	$9	$2
Realized losses	—	7	3

The following table summarizes contractual maturities of our cash equivalent and marketable fixed-income securities as of December 31, 2009 (in millions):

	Amortized Cost	Estimated Fair Value
Due within one year	$4,908	$4,909
Due after one year through five years	1,358	1,371
	$6,266	$6,280

52

The following table summarizes, by major security type, our assets that are measured at fair value on a recurring basis and are categorized using the fair value hierarchy (in millions):

		December 31, 2009			
	Cash	Level 1 Estimated Fair Value	Level 2 Estimated Fair Value	Level 3 Estimated Fair Value	Total Estimated Fair Value
Cash	$391	$ —	$ —	$—	$ 391
Money market funds	—	2,750	—	—	2,750
Foreign government and agency securities	—	—	1,999	—	1,999
Corporate debt securities	—	—	211	—	211
U.S. government and agency securities	—	—	1,268	—	1,268
Asset-backed securities	—	—	46	—	46
Other fixed income securities	—	—	6	—	6
Equity securities	—	1	—	—	1
	$391	$2,751	$3,530	$—	$6,672

		December 31, 2008			
	Cash	Level 1 Estimated Fair Value	Level 2 Estimated Fair Value	Level 3 Estimated Fair Value	Total Estimated Fair Value
Cash	$355	$ —	$ —	$—	$ 355
Money market funds	—	1,682	—	—	1,682
Foreign government and agency securities	—	—	1,128	—	1,128
Corporate debt securities	—	—	194	—	194
U.S. government and agency securities	—	—	594	—	594
Asset-backed securities	—	—	58	—	58
Other fixed income securities	—	—	23	—	23
Equity securities	—	1	—	—	1
	$355	$1,683	$1,997	$—	$4,035

53

Note 3—FIXED ASSETS

Fixed assets, at cost, consisted of the following (in millions):

	December 31,	
	2009	2008
Gross Fixed Assets:		
Fulfillment and customer service	$ 551	$ 564
Technology infrastructure	551	348
Internal-use software, content, and website development	398	331
Construction in progress (1)	278	87
Other corporate assets	137	79
Gross fixed assets	1,915	1,409
Accumulated Depreciation:		
Fulfillment and customer service	202	254
Technology infrastructure	178	82
Internal-use software, content, and website development	207	159
Other corporate assets	38	60
Total accumulated depreciation	625	555
Total fixed assets, net	$1,290	$ 854

(1) We capitalize construction in progress and record a corresponding long-term liability for certain lease agreements, including our Seattle, Washington corporate office space subject to leases scheduled to begin upon completion of development between 2010 and 2013. See "Note 6—Other Long-Term Liabilities" and "Note 7—Commitments and Contingencies" for further discussion.

Depreciation expense on fixed assets was $384 million, $311 million, and $258 million, which includes amortization of fixed assets acquired under capital lease obligations of $88 million, $50 million, and $40 million for 2009, 2008, and 2007. Gross assets remaining under capital leases were $430 million and $304 million at December 31, 2009 and 2008. Accumulated depreciation associated with capital leases was $184 million and $116 million at December 31, 2009 and 2008.

Note 4—ACQUISITIONS, GOODWILL, AND ACQUIRED INTANGIBLE ASSETS

2009 Acquisition Activity

On November 1, 2009, we acquired 100% of the outstanding equity of Zappos.com, Inc. ("Zappos"), in exchange for shares of our common stock, to expand our presence in softline retail categories, such as shoes and apparel.

The fair value of Zappos' stock options assumed was determined using the Black-Scholes model. The following table summarizes the consideration paid for Zappos (in millions):

Stock issued	$1,079
Assumed stock options, net	55
	$1,134

54

The purchase price was allocated to the tangible assets and intangible assets acquired and liabilities assumed based on their estimated fair values on the acquisition date, with the remaining unallocated purchase price recorded as goodwill. The fair value assigned to identifiable intangible assets acquired has been determined primarily by using the income approach. Purchased identifiable intangible assets are amortized on a straight-line and accelerated basis over their respective useful lives.

The following summarizes the allocation of the Zappos purchase price (in millions):

Goodwill	$ 778
Other net assets acquired	83
Deferred tax liabilities net	(167)
Intangible assets (1):	
Marketing-related	223
Contract-based	103
Customer-related	114
	$1,134

(1) Acquired intangible assets have estimated useful lives of between 1 and 10 years.

Zappos' financial results have been included in our consolidated statements of income as of November 1, 2009. The following pro forma financial information presents the results as if the Zappos acquisition had occurred at the beginning of each year presented (in millions):

	Year Ended December 31,	
	2009	**2008**
Net sales	$25,064	$19,801
Net income	853	606

We acquired certain additional companies during 2009 for an aggregate purchase price of $26 million, resulting in goodwill of $16 million and acquired intangible assets of $5 million. The results of operations of each of the businesses acquired have been included in our consolidated results from each transactions closing date forward. The effect of these acquisitions on consolidated net sales and operating income during 2009 was not significant.

2008 and 2007 Acquisition Activity

We acquired certain companies during 2008 for an aggregate purchase price of $432 million, resulting in goodwill of $210 million and acquired intangible assets of $162 million.

We acquired certain companies during 2007 for an aggregate purchase price of $33 million, resulting in goodwill of $21 million and acquired intangible assets of $18 million. We also made principal payments of $13 million on acquired debt in connection with one of these acquisitions.

The results of operations of each of the businesses acquired in 2008 and 2007 have been included in our consolidated results from each transaction closing date forward. The effect of these acquisitions on consolidated net sales and operating income during 2008 and 2007 was not significant.

55

NOTES TO CONSOLIDATED FINANCIAL STATEMENTS—(Continued)

Goodwill

The following summarizes our goodwill activity in 2009 (in millions):

Goodwill—January 1, 2009	$ 438
New acquisitions	794
Other adjustments (1)	2
Goodwill—December 31, 2009	$1,234

(1) Primarily includes changes in foreign exchange for goodwill in our International segment.

At December 31, 2009 and December 31, 2008, approximately 9% and 22% of our acquired goodwill related to our International segment.

Intangible Assets

Acquired intangible assets, included within "Other assets" on our consolidated balance sheets, consist of the following:

	December 31,						
	2009				**2008**		
	Weighted Average Life Remaining	Acquired Intangibles, Gross (1)	Accumulated Amortization (1)	Acquired Intangibles, Net	Acquired Intangibles, Gross (1)	Accumulated Amortization (1)	Acquired Intangibles, Net
				(in millions)			
Marketing-related	9.5	$249	$(11)	$238	$ 23	$ (4)	$ 19
Contract-based	3	166	(20)	146	62	(8)	54
Technology and content	3.1	15	(7)	8	10	(5)	5
Customer-related	4.8	215	(40)	175	97	(15)	82
Acquired intangibles (2)	7.3	$645	$(78)	$567	$192	$(32)	$160

(1) Excludes the original cost and accumulated amortization of fully-amortized intangibles.
(2) Intangible assets have estimated useful lives of between 1 and 13 years.

Amortization expense for acquired intangibles was $48 million, $29 million, and $13 million in 2009, 2008, and 2007. Expected future amortization expense of acquired intangible assets as of December 31, 2009 is as follows (in millions):

Year Ended December 31,	
2010	$100
2011	90
2012	74
2013	69
2014	58
Thereafter	176
	$567

56

Note 5—LONG-TERM DEBT

Our long-term debt is summarized as follows:

	December 31,	
	2009	2008
	(in millions)	
6.875% PEACS	$—	$335
Other long-term debt	131	133
	131	468
Less current portion of long-term debt	(22)	(59)
	$109	$409

In February 2008 our Board of Directors authorized a debt repurchase program, replacing our previous debt repurchase authorization in its entirety, and pursuant to which we redeemed for cash the remaining €240 million ($319 million based on the Euro to U.S. Dollar exchange rate on the date of redemption) in principal of our 6.875% PEACS in 2009, and we redeemed the remaining principal amount of $899 million of our outstanding 4.75% Convertible Subordinated Notes in 2008.

Other long-term debt relates to amounts borrowed to fund certain international operations.

Note 6—OTHER LONG-TERM LIABILITIES

Our other long-term liabilities are summarized as follows:

	December 31,	
	2009	2008
	(in millions)	
Tax contingencies	$ 202	$144
Long-term capital lease obligations	143	124
Construction liability	278	87
Other	460	132
	$1,083	$487

Tax Contingencies

As of December 31, 2009 and 2008, we have provided tax reserves for tax contingencies, inclusive of accrued interest and penalties, of approximately $202 million and $144 million for U.S. and foreign income taxes. These contingencies primarily relate to transfer pricing, state income taxes, and research and development credits. See "Note 10—Income Taxes" for discussion of tax contingencies.

AMAZON.COM, INC.

NOTES TO CONSOLIDATED FINANCIAL STATEMENTS—(Continued)

Capital Leases

Certain of our equipment fixed assets, primarily related to technology infrastructure, have been acquired under capital leases. Long-term capital lease obligations are as follows:

	December 31, 2009
	(in millions)
Gross capital lease obligations	$ 276
Less imputed interest	(14)
Present value of net minimum lease payments	262
Less current portion	(119)
Total long-term capital lease obligations	$ 143

Construction Liabilities

We capitalize construction in progress and record a corresponding long-term liability for certain lease agreements, including our Seattle, Washington corporate office space subject to leases scheduled to begin upon completion of development between 2010 and 2013.

For build-to-suit lease arrangements where we are involved in the construction of structural improvements prior to the commencement of the lease or take some level of construction risk, we are considered the owner of the assets during the construction period. Accordingly, as the landlord incurs the construction project costs, the assets and corresponding financial obligation are recorded in "Fixed assets, net" and "Other long-term liabilities" on our consolidated balance sheet. Once the construction is completed, if the lease meets certain "sale-leaseback" criteria, we will remove the asset and related financial obligation from the balance sheet and treat the building lease as an operating lease. If upon completion of construction, the project does not meet the "sale-leaseback" criteria, the leased property will be treated as a capital lease for financial reporting purposes.

The remainder of our other long-term liabilities primarily include deferred tax liabilities, unearned revenue, asset retirement obligations, and deferred rental liabilities.

Note 7—COMMITMENTS AND CONTINGENCIES

Commitments

We lease office, fulfillment center, and data center facilities and fixed assets under non-cancelable operating and capital leases. Rental expense under operating lease agreements was $171 million, $158 million, and $141 million for 2009, 2008, and 2007.

In December 2007, we entered into a series of leases and other agreements for the lease of corporate office space to be developed in Seattle, Washington with initial terms of up to 16 years commencing on completion of development between 2010 and 2013, with options to extend for two five-year periods. We expect to occupy approximately 1.7 million square feet of office space. We also have an option to lease up to an additional approximately 500,000 square feet at rates based on fair market values at the time the option is exercised, subject to certain conditions. In addition, if interest rates exceed a certain threshold, we have the option to provide financing for some of the buildings.

The following summarizes our principal contractual commitments, excluding open orders for inventory purchases that support normal operations, as of December 31, 2009:

	Year Ended December 31,					Thereafter	Total
	2010	2011	2012	2013	2014		
			(in millions)				
Operating and capital commitments:							
Debt principal and interest	$ 31	$ 47	$ 36	$ 36	$—	$ —	$ 150
Capital leases, including interest	130	95	44	8	3	—	280
Operating leases	162	146	130	122	115	317	992
Other commitments (1)(2)	187	101	93	89	88	1,181	1,739
Total commitments	$510	$389	$303	$255	$206	$1,498	$3,161

(1) Includes the estimated timing and amounts of payments for rent, operating expenses, and tenant improvements associated with approximately 1.7 million square feet of corporate office space. The amount of space available and our financial and other obligations under the lease agreements are affected by various factors, including government approvals and permits, interest rates, development costs and other expenses and our exercise of certain rights under the lease agreements.

(2) Excludes $181 million of tax contingencies for which we cannot make a reasonably reliable estimate of the amount and period of payment, if any.

Pledged Securities

We have pledged or otherwise restricted a portion of our cash and marketable securities as collateral for standby letters of credit, guarantees, debt, and real estate leases. We classify cash and marketable securities with use restrictions of twelve months or longer as non-current "Other assets" on our consolidated balance sheets. The amount required to be pledged for certain real estate lease agreements changes over the life of our leases based on our credit rating and changes in our market capitalization. Information about collateral required to be pledged under these agreements is as follows:

	Standby and Trade Letters of Credit and Guarantees	Debt (1)	Real Estate Leases (2)	Total
		(in millions)		
Balance at December 31, 2008	$138	$160	$10	$308
Net change in collateral pledged	4	(3)	(6)	(5)
Balance at December 31, 2009	$142	$157	$ 4	$303

(1) Represents collateral for certain debt related to our international operations.

(2) At December 31, 2009, our market capitalization was $59.8 billion. The required amount of collateral to be pledged will increase by $1.5 million if our market capitalization is equal to or below $40 billion, an additional $5 million if our market capitalization is equal to or below $18 billion, and an additional $6 million if our market capitalization is equal to or below $13 billion.

Legal Proceedings

The Company is involved from time to time in claims, proceedings and litigation, including the following:

In June 2001, Audible, Inc., our subsidiary acquired in March 2008, was named as a defendant in a securities class-action filed in United States District Court for the Southern District of New York related to its

59

initial public offering in July 1999. The lawsuit also named certain of the offering's underwriters, as well as Audible's officers and directors as defendants. Approximately 300 other issuers and their underwriters have had similar suits filed against them, all of which are included in a single coordinated proceeding in the Southern District of New York. The complaints allege that the prospectus and the registration statement for Audible's offering failed to disclose that the underwriters allegedly solicited and received "excessive" commissions from investors and that some investors allegedly agreed with the underwriters to buy additional shares in the aftermarket in order to inflate the price of Audible's stock. Audible and its officers and directors were named in the suits pursuant to Section 11 of the Securities Act of 1933, Section 10(b) of the Securities Exchange Act of 1934, and other related provisions. The complaints seek unspecified damages, attorney and expert fees, and other unspecified litigation costs. In March 2009, all parties, including Audible, reached a settlement of these class actions that would resolve this dispute entirely with no payment required from Audible. The settlement was approved by the Court in October 2009, and that settlement is currently under appeal to the Court of Appeals for the Second Circuit.

Beginning in March 2003, we were served with complaints filed in several different states, including Illinois, by a private litigant, Beeler, Schad & Diamond, P.C., purportedly on behalf of the state governments under various state False Claims Acts. The complaints allege that we (along with other companies with which we have commercial agreements) wrongfully failed to collect and remit sales and use taxes for sales of personal property to customers in those states and knowingly created records and statements falsely stating we were not required to collect or remit such taxes. In December 2006, we learned that one additional complaint was filed in the state of Illinois by a different private litigant, Matthew T. Hurst, alleging similar violations of the Illinois state law. All of the complaints seek injunctive relief, unpaid taxes, interest, attorneys' fees, civil penalties of up to $10,000 per violation, and treble or punitive damages under the various state False Claims Acts. It is possible that we have been or will be named in similar cases in other states as well. We dispute the allegations of wrongdoing in these complaints and intend to vigorously defend ourselves in these matters.

In December 2005, Registrar Systems LLC filed a complaint against us and Target Corporation for patent infringement in the United States District Court for the District of Colorado. The complaint alleges that our website technology, including the method by which Amazon.com enables customers to use Amazon.com account information on websites that Amazon.com operates for third parties, such as Target.com, infringes two patents obtained by Registrar Systems purporting to cover methods and apparatuses for a "World Wide Web Registration Information Processing System" (U.S. Patent Nos. 5,790,785 and 6,823,327) and seeks injunctive relief, monetary damages in an amount no less than a reasonable royalty, prejudgment interest, costs, and attorneys' fees. In September 2006, the Court entered an order staying the lawsuit pending the outcome of the Patent and Trademark Office's re-examination of the patents in suit. We dispute the allegations of wrongdoing in this complaint and intend to vigorously defend ourselves in this matter.

In August 2006, Cordance Corporation filed a complaint against us for patent infringement in the United States District Court for the District of Delaware. The complaint alleges that our website technology, including our 1-Click ordering system, infringes a patent obtained by Cordance purporting to cover an "Object-Based Online Transaction Infrastructure" (U.S. Patent No. 6,757,710) and seeks injunctive relief, monetary damages in an amount no less than a reasonable royalty, treble damages for alleged willful infringement, prejudgment interest, costs, and attorneys' fees. In response, we asserted a declaratory judgment counterclaim in the same action alleging that a service that Cordance has advertised its intent to launch infringes a patent owned by us entitled "Networked Personal Contact Manager" (U.S. Patent No. 6,269,369). In August 2009, the case was tried and the jury ruled that Amazon was not liable on Cordance's claims. An appeal is expected.

In October 2007, Digital Reg of Texas, LLC filed a complaint against our subsidiary, Audible, Inc., and several other defendants in the United States District Court for the Eastern District of Texas. The complaint

60

alleges that Audible's digital rights management technology infringes a patent obtained by Digital Reg purporting to cover a system for "Regulating Access to Digital Content" (U.S. Patent No. 6,389,541) and seeks injunctive relief, monetary damages, enhanced damages for alleged willful infringement, prejudgment and post-judgment interest, costs and attorneys' fees. In November 2009, we obtained a license to the patent in suit and were dismissed from the lawsuit with prejudice.

In January 2009, we learned that the United States Postal Service, including the Postal Service Office of Inspector General, is investigating our compliance with Postal Service rules, and we are cooperating.

In March 2009, Discovery Communications, Inc. filed a complaint against us for patent infringement in the United States District Court for the District of Delaware. The complaint alleges that our Kindle and Kindle 2 wireless reading devices infringe a patent owned by Discovery purporting to cover an "Electronic Book Security and Copyright Protection System" (U.S. Patent No. 7,298,851) and seeks monetary damages, a continuing royalty sufficient to compensate Discovery for any future infringement, treble damages, costs and attorneys fees. In May 2009, we filed counterclaims and an additional lawsuit in the United States District Court for the Western District of Washington against Discovery alleging infringement of several patents owned by Amazon and requesting a declaration that several Discovery patents, including the one listed above, are invalid and unenforceable. We dispute the allegations of wrongdoing and intend to vigorously defend ourselves in this matter.

In March 2009, the Tobin Family Education and Health Foundation filed a complaint against us for patent infringement in the United States District Court for the Middle District of Florida. The complaint alleges, among other things, that the technology underlying the Amazon Associates program infringes a patent owned by Tobin purporting to cover a "Method and System for Customizing Marketing Services on Networks Communication with Hypertext Tagging Conventions" (U.S. Patent No. 7,505,913) and seeks injunctive relief, monetary damages, costs and attorneys fees. We dispute the allegations of wrongdoing and intend to vigorously defend ourselves in this matter.

In April 2009, Parallel Networks, LLC filed a complaint against us for patent infringement in the United States District Court for the Eastern District of Texas. The complaint alleges, among other things, that our website technology infringes a patent owned by Parallel Networks purporting to cover a "Method And Apparatus For Client-Server Communication Using a Limited Capability Client Over A Low-Speed Communications Link" (U.S. Patent No. 6,446,111) and seeks injunctive relief, monetary damages, costs and attorneys fees. We dispute the allegations of wrongdoing and intend to vigorously defend ourselves in this matter.

In May 2009, Big Baboon, Inc. filed a complaint against us for patent infringement in the United States District Court for the Central District of California. The complaint alleges, among other things, that our third-party selling and payments technology infringes a patent owned by Big Baboon, Inc. purporting to cover an "Integrated Business-to-Business Web Commerce and Business Automation System" (U.S. Patent No. 6,115,690) and seeks injunctive relief, monetary damages, treble damages, costs and attorneys fees. We dispute the allegations of wrongdoing and intend to vigorously defend ourselves in this matter.

In June 2009, Bedrock Computer Technologies LLC filed a complaint against us for patent infringement in the United States District Court for the Eastern District of Texas. The complaint alleges, among other things, that our website technology infringes a patent owned by Bedrock purporting to cover a "Method And Apparatus For Information Storage and Retrieval Using a Hashing Technique with External Chaining and On-the-Fly Removal of Expired Data" (U.S. Patent Nos. 5,893,120) and seeks injunctive relief, monetary damages, enhanced damages, a compulsory future royalty, costs and attorneys fees. We dispute the allegations of wrongdoing and intend to vigorously defend ourselves in this matter.

61

AMAZON.COM, INC.

NOTES TO CONSOLIDATED FINANCIAL STATEMENTS—(Continued)

In September 2009, SpeedTrack, Inc. filed a complaint against us for patent infringement in the United States District Court for the Northern District of California. The complaint alleges, among other things, that our website technology infringes a patent owned by SpeedTrack purporting to cover a "Method For Accessing Computer Files and Data, Using Linked Categories Assigned to Each Data File Record on Entry of the Data File Record" (U.S. Patent Nos. 5,544,360) and seeks injunctive relief, monetary damages, enhanced damages, costs and attorneys fees. In November 2009, the Court entered an order staying the lawsuit pending the outcome of the Patent and Trademark Office's re-examination of the patent in suit and the resolution of similar litigation against another party. We dispute the allegations of wrongdoing and intend to vigorously defend ourselves in this matter.

In September 2009, Alcatel-Lucent USA Inc. filed a complaint against us for patent infringement in the United States District Court for the Eastern District of Texas. The complaint alleges that our website technology and digital content distribution systems infringe six of Alcatel-Lucent's patents and seeks injunctive relief, monetary damages, a continuing royalty sufficient to compensate Alcatel-Lucent for any future infringement, treble damages, costs and attorneys fees. In January 2010, we filed counterclaims against Alcatel-Lucent alleging infringement of a patent owned by Amazon and that the patents asserted by Alcatel-Lucent are invalid and unenforceable. We dispute the allegations of wrongdoing and intend to vigorously defend ourselves in this matter.

In October 2009, Eolas Technologies Incorporated filed a complaint against us for patent infringement in the United States District Court for the Eastern District of Texas. The complaint alleges, among other things, that our website technology infringes two patents owned by Eolas purporting to cover "Distributed Hypermedia Method for Automatically Invoking External Application Providing Interaction and Display of Embedded Objects within a Hypermedia Document" (U.S. Patent No. 5,838,906) and "Distributed Hypermedia Method and System for Automatically Invoking External Application Providing Interaction and Display of Embedded Objects within a Hypermedia Document" (U.S. Patent No. 7,599,985) and seeks injunctive relief, monetary damages, costs and attorneys fees. We dispute the allegations of wrongdoing and intend to vigorously defend ourselves in this matter.

In October 2009, Leon Stambler filed a complaint against us for patent infringement in the United States District Court for the Eastern District of Texas. The complaint alleges, among other things, that our use of secure online payments systems and services infringes two patents owned by Stambler purporting to cover a "Method for Securing Information Relevant to a Transaction" (U.S. Patent Nos. 5,793,302 and 5,974,148) and seeks monetary damages, costs and attorneys fees. We dispute the allegations of wrongdoing and intend to vigorously defend ourselves in this matter.

In December 2009, Nazomi Communications, Inc. filed a complaint against us for patent infringement in the United States District Court for the Eastern District of Texas. The complaint alleges, among other things, that the processor core in our Kindle 2 device infringes two patents owned by Nazomi purporting to cover "Java virtual machine hardware for RISC and CISC processors" and "Java hardware accelerator using microcode engine" (U.S. Patent Nos. 7,080,362 and 7,225,436) and seeks monetary damages, injunctive relief, costs and attorneys fees. We dispute the allegations of wrongdoing and intend to vigorously defend ourselves in this matter.

Depending on the amount and the timing, an unfavorable resolution of some or all of these matters could materially affect our business, results of operations, financial position, or cash flows.

See also "Note 10—Income Taxes."

62

AMAZON.COM, INC.

NOTES TO CONSOLIDATED FINANCIAL STATEMENTS—(Continued)

Inventory Suppliers

During 2009, no vendor accounted for 10% or more of our inventory purchases. We generally do not have long-term contracts or arrangements with our vendors to guarantee the availability of merchandise, particular payment terms, or the extension of credit limits.

Note 8—STOCKHOLDERS' EQUITY

Preferred Stock

We have authorized 500 million shares of $0.01 par value Preferred Stock. No preferred stock was outstanding for any period presented.

Common Stock

Common shares outstanding plus shares underlying outstanding stock awards totaled 461 million, 446 million, and 435 million at December 31, 2009, 2008 and 2007. These totals include all stock-based awards outstanding, without regard for estimated forfeitures, consisting of vested and unvested awards. Common shares outstanding increased in 2009 due primarily to issuance of stock to acquire Zappos and vesting of restricted stock units.

Stock Repurchase Activity

We did not repurchase any of our common stock in 2009. We repurchased 2.2 million shares of common stock for $100 million in 2008 under the $1 billion repurchase program authorized by our Board of Directors in February 2008. We repurchased 6.3 million shares of common stock for $248 million in 2007 under the $500 million repurchase program authorized by our Board of Directors in August 2006.

In January 2010, our Board of Directors authorized a program to repurchase up to $2 billion of our common stock which replaces the Board's prior authorization.

Stock Award Plans

Employees vest in restricted stock unit awards over the corresponding service term, generally between two and five years.

Stock Award Activity

We granted restricted stock units representing 6.0 million, 7.3 million, 7.6 million shares of common stock during 2009, 2008, and 2007 with a per share weighted average fair value of $79.24, $72.21, and $47.04.

63

AMAZON.COM, INC.

NOTES TO CONSOLIDATED FINANCIAL STATEMENTS—(Continued)

The following summarizes our restricted stock unit activity (in millions):

	Number of Units
Outstanding at January 1, 2007	14.5
Units granted	7.6
Units vested	(3.3)
Units forfeited	(2.5)
Outstanding at December 31, 2007	16.3
Units granted	7.3
Units vested	(5.5)
Units forfeited	(1.4)
Outstanding at December 31, 2008	16.7
Units granted	6.0
Units vested	(6.0)
Units forfeited	(1.0)
Outstanding at December 31, 2009	15.7

Scheduled vesting for outstanding restricted stock units at December 31, 2009 is as follows (in millions):

	Year Ended December 31,						
	2010	2011	2012	2013	2014	Thereafter	Total
Scheduled vesting—restricted stock units	5.9	5.5	2.6	1.4	0.2	0.1	15.7

As of December 31, 2009, there was $415 million of net unrecognized compensation cost related to unvested stock-based compensation arrangements. This compensation is recognized on an accelerated basis resulting in approximately half of the compensation expected to be expensed in the next twelve months, and has a weighted average recognition period of 1.2 years.

During 2009 and 2008, the fair value of restricted stock units that vested was $551 million and $362 million.

As matching contributions under our 401(k) savings plan, we granted 0.1 million shares of common stock in both 2009 and 2008. Shares granted as matching contributions under our 401(k) plan are included in outstanding common stock when issued.

Common Stock Available for Future Issuance

At December 31, 2009, common stock available for future issuance to employees is 149 million shares.

AMAZON.COM, INC.

NOTES TO CONSOLIDATED FINANCIAL STATEMENTS—(Continued)

Note 9—OTHER COMPREHENSIVE INCOME (LOSS)

The components of other comprehensive income (loss) are as follows:

	Year Ended December 31,		
	2009	2008	2007
	(in millions)		
Net income	$902	$ 645	$476
Net change in unrealized gains/losses on available-for-sale securities:			
Unrealized gains (losses), net of tax of $(2), $0, and $(4)	7	—	8
Reclassification adjustment for losses (gains) included in net income, net of tax effect of $1, $1, and $0	(3)	(1)	—
Net unrealized gains (losses) on available for sale securities	4	(1)	8
Foreign currency translation adjustment, net of tax effect of $0, $3, and $6	62	(127)	(3)
Amortization of net unrealized losses on terminated Euro Currency Swap, net of tax effect of $0, $0, and $0	1	—	1
Other comprehensive income (loss)	67	(128)	6
Comprehensive income	$969	$ 517	$482

Balances within accumulated other comprehensive income (loss) are as follows:

	December 31,	
	2009	2008
	(in millions)	
Net unrealized losses on foreign currency translation, net of tax	$ (66)	$(128)
Net unrealized gains on available-for-sale securities, net of tax	10	6
Net unrealized losses on terminated Euro Currency Swap, net of tax	—	(1)
Total accumulated other comprehensive income (loss)	$ (56)	$(123)

65

Note 10—INCOME TAXES

In 2009, 2008 and 2007 we recorded net tax provisions of $253 million, $247 million, and $184 million. A majority of this provision is non-cash. We have current tax benefits and net operating losses relating to excess stock-based compensation that are being utilized to reduce our U.S. taxable income. As such, cash taxes paid, net of refunds, were $48 million, $53 million, and $24 million for 2009, 2008, and 2007.

The components of the provision for income taxes, net are as follows:

	Year Ended December 31,		
	2009	2008	2007
	(in millions)		
Current taxes:			
U.S. and state	$149	$227	$ 275
International	23	25	8
Current taxes	172	252	283
Deferred taxes:			
U.S. and state	89	3	(109)
International	(8)	(8)	10
Deferred taxes	81	(5)	(99)
Provision for income taxes, net	$253	$247	$ 184

U.S. and international components of income before income taxes are as follows:

	Year Ended December 31,		
	2009	2008	2007
	(in millions)		
U.S.	$ 529	$436	$360
International (1)	632	465	300
Income before income taxes	$1,161	$901	$660

(1) Included in 2008 is the impact of the $53 million non-cash gain associated with the sale of our European DVD rental assets. This gain was taxed at rates substantially below the 35% U.S. federal statutory rate.

The items accounting for differences between income taxes computed at the federal statutory rate and the provision recorded for income taxes are as follows:

	Year Ended December 31,		
	2009	2008	2007
Federal statutory rate	35.0%	35.0%	35.0%
Effect of:			
Impact of foreign tax differential	(16.9)	(13.8)	(11.7)
State taxes, net of federal benefits	1.1	2.8	2.1
Tax credits	(0.4)	(2.2)	(1.1)
Nondeductible stock-based compensation	1.7	1.7	1.4
Valuation allowance	0.4	2.6	(1.2)
Other, net	1.0	1.3	3.4
Total	21.9%	27.4%	27.9%

AMAZON.COM, INC.

NOTES TO CONSOLIDATED FINANCIAL STATEMENTS—(Continued)

The effective tax rate in 2009, 2008, and 2007 was lower than the 35% U.S. federal statutory rate primarily due to earnings of our subsidiaries outside of the U.S. in jurisdictions where our effective tax rate is lower than in the U.S. Included in the total tax provision as a discrete item during 2008 is the impact related to the $53 million noncash gain associated with the sale of our European DVD rental assets. This gain was taxed at rates substantially below the 35% U.S. federal statutory rate.

Deferred income tax assets and liabilities are as follows:

	December 31,	
	2009	**2008**
	(in millions)	
Deferred tax assets:		
Net operating losses—stock-based compensation (1)	$ 120	$ 120
Net operating losses—other	50	31
Net operating losses—obtained through acquisitions (2)	7	14
Stock-based compensation	118	73
Assets held for investment	125	152
Revenue items	58	53
Expense items	172	155
Other items	42	40
Net tax credits (3)	6	2
Total gross deferred tax assets	698	640
Less valuation allowance (4)	(173)	(199)
Deferred tax assets, net of valuation allowance	525	441
Deferred tax liabilities:		
Basis difference in intangible assets	(218)	(80)
Expense items	(168)	(12)
Deferred tax assets, net of valuation allowance and deferred tax liabilities	$ 139	$ 349

---

(1) Excludes unrecognized federal net operating loss carryforward deferred tax assets of $40 million and $73 million at December 31, 2009 and 2008. The total gross deferred tax assets relating to our federal excess stock-based compensation net operating loss carryforwards at December 31, 2009 and 2008 were $160 million and $193 million (relating to approximately $456 million and $550 million of our federal net operating loss carryforwards). The majority of our net operating loss carryforwards begin to expire in 2021 and thereafter.

(2) The utilization of some of these net operating loss carryforwards is subject to an annual limitation under applicable provisions of the Internal Revenue Code.

(3) Presented net of fully reserved deferred tax assets associated with tax credits of $193 million and $130 million at December 31, 2009 and 2008. Total tax credits available to be claimed in future years are approximately $199 million and $171 million as of December 31, 2009 and 2008, and begin to expire in 2017.

(4) Relates primarily to deferred tax assets that would only be realizable upon the generation of future capital gains and net income in certain foreign taxing jurisdictions.

Tax Contingencies

We are subject to income taxes in the U.S. and numerous foreign jurisdictions. Significant judgment is required in evaluating our tax positions and determining our provision for income taxes. During the ordinary

67

AMAZON.COM, INC.

NOTES TO CONSOLIDATED FINANCIAL STATEMENTS—(Continued)

course of business, there are many transactions and calculations for which the ultimate tax determination is uncertain. We establish reserves for tax-related uncertainties based on estimates of whether, and the extent to which, additional taxes will be due. These reserves are established when we believe that certain positions might be challenged despite our belief that our tax return positions are fully supportable. We adjust these reserves in light of changing facts and circumstances, such as the outcome of tax audits. The provision for income taxes includes the impact of reserve provisions and changes to reserves that are considered appropriate.

The reconciliation of our tax contingencies is as follows (in millions):

	December 31,	
	2009	**2008**
	(in millions)	
Gross tax contingencies—January 1, 2009	$166	$112
Gross increases to tax positions in prior periods	15	39
Gross decreases to tax positions in prior periods	—	(4)
Gross increases to current period tax positions	1	22
Audit settlements paid during 2008	—	(3)
Foreign exchange gain (loss) on tax contingencies	(1)	—
Gross tax contingencies—December 31, 2009 (1)	$181	$166

_____

(1) As of December 31, 2009, we had $181 million of tax contingencies of which $180 million, if fully recognized, would decrease our effective tax rate and increase additional paid-in capital by $1 million to reflect the tax benefits of excess stock-based compensation deductions.

Due to the nature of our business operations we expect the total amount of tax contingencies for prior period tax positions will grow in 2010 in comparable amounts to 2009. We do not believe it is reasonably possible that the total amount of unrecognized tax benefits will significantly decrease in 2010. The increase to current period tax positions in 2008 resulted primarily from acquisition-related activity and new regulations.

As of December 31, 2009 and 2008, we had accrued interest and penalties, net of federal income tax benefit, related to tax contingencies of $17 million and $14 million. Interest and penalties, net of federal income tax benefit, recognized for the year ended December 31, 2009 and 2008 was $3 million and $5 million.

We are under examination, or may be subject to examination, by the Internal Revenue Service ("IRS") for calendar years 2005 through 2009. Additionally, any net operating losses that were generated in prior years and utilized in 2005 through 2009 may also be subject to examination by the IRS. We are under examination, or may be subject to examination, in the following major jurisdictions for the years specified: Kentucky for 2005 through 2009, France for 2006 through 2009, Germany for 2003 through 2009, Luxembourg for 2004 through 2009, and the United Kingdom for 2003 through 2009. In addition, in 2007, Japanese tax authorities assessed income tax, including penalties and interest, of approximately $120 million against one of our U.S. subsidiaries for the years 2003 through 2005. We believe that these claims are without merit and are disputing the assessment. Further proceedings on the assessment have been stayed during negotiations between U.S. and Japanese authorities over the double taxation issues the assessment raises, and we have provided bank guarantees to suspend enforcement of the assessment. We also may be subject to income tax examination by Japanese tax authorities for 2006 through 2009.

68

AMAZON.COM, INC.

NOTES TO CONSOLIDATED FINANCIAL STATEMENTS—(Continued)

Note 11—SEGMENT INFORMATION

We have organized our operations into two principal segments: North America and International. We present our segment information along the same lines that our chief executive reviews our operating results in assessing performance and allocating resources.

We allocate to segment results the operating expenses "Fulfillment," "Marketing," "Technology and content," and "General and administrative," but exclude from our allocations the portions of these expense lines attributable to stock-based compensation. We do not allocate the line item "Other operating expense (income), net" to our segment operating results. A significant majority of our costs for "Technology and content" are incurred in the United States and most of these costs are allocated to our North America segment. There are no internal revenue transactions between our reporting segments.

North America

The North America segment consists of amounts earned from retail sales of consumer products (including from sellers) and subscriptions through North America-focused websites such as *www.amazon.com* and *www.amazon.ca*. This segment includes export sales from *www.amazon.com* and *www.amazon.ca*.

International

The International segment consists of amounts earned from retail sales of consumer products (including from sellers) and subscriptions through internationally focused websites such as *www.amazon.co.uk*, *www.amazon.de*, *www.amazon.co.jp*, *www.amazon.fr*, and *www.amazon.cn*. This segment includes export sales from these internationally based sites (including export sales from these sites to customers in the U.S. and Canada), but excludes export sales from *www.amazon.com* and *www.amazon.ca*.

69

NOTES TO CONSOLIDATED FINANCIAL STATEMENTS—(Continued)

Information on reportable segments and reconciliation to consolidated net income is as follows:

	Year Ended December 31,		
	2009	2008	2007
	(in millions)		
North America			
Net sales	$12,828	$10,228	$ 8,095
Cost of sales	9,538	7,733	6,064
Gross profit	3,290	2,495	2,031
Direct segment operating expenses	2,581	2,050	1,631
Segment operating income	$ 709	$ 445	$ 400
International			
Net sales	$11,681	$ 8,938	$ 6,740
Cost of sales	9,440	7,163	5,418
Gross profit	2,241	1,775	1,322
Direct segment operating expenses	1,378	1,127	873
Segment operating income	$ 863	$ 648	$ 449
Consolidated			
Net sales	$24,509	$19,166	$14,835
Cost of sales	18,978	14,896	11,482
Gross profit	5,531	4,270	3,353
Direct segment operating expenses	3,959	3,177	2,504
Segment operating income	1,572	1,093	849
Stock-based compensation	(341)	(275)	(185)
Other operating expense, net	(102)	24	(9)
Income from operations	1,129	842	655
Total non-operating income (expense), net	32	59	5
Provision for income taxes	(253)	(247)	(184)
Equity-method investment activity, net of tax	(6)	(9)	—
Net income	$ 902	$ 645	$ 476

Net sales shipped to customers outside of the U.S. represented approximately half of net sales for 2009, 2008, and 2007. Net sales from *www.amazon.de*, *www.amazon.co.jp*, and *www.amazon.co.uk* each represented 13% to 17% of consolidated net sales in 2009, 2008 and 2007.

Total assets, by segment, reconciled to consolidated amounts were (in millions):

	December 31,	
	2009	2008
North America	$ 9,252	$5,266
International	4,561	3,048
Consolidated	$13,813	$8,314

AMAZON.COM, INC.

NOTES TO CONSOLIDATED FINANCIAL STATEMENTS—(Continued)

Fixed assets, net, by segment, reconciled to consolidated amounts were (in millions):

	December 31,	
	2009	2008
North America	$1,059	$666
International	231	188
Consolidated	$1,290	$854

Depreciation expense, by segment, is as follows (in millions):

	Year Ended December 31,		
	2009	2008	2007
North America	$327	$262	$212
International	57	49	46
Consolidated	$384	$311	$258

Note 12—QUARTERLY RESULTS (UNAUDITED)

The following tables contain selected unaudited statement of operations information for each quarter of 2009 and 2008. The following information reflects all normal recurring adjustments necessary for a fair presentation of the information for the periods presented. The operating results for any quarter are not necessarily indicative of results for any future period. Our business is affected by seasonality, which historically has resulted in higher sales volume during our fourth quarter.

Unaudited quarterly results are as follows (in millions, except per share data):

	Year Ended December 31, 2009 (1)			
	Fourth Quarter	Third Quarter	Second Quarter	First Quarter
Net sales	$9,519	$5,449	$4,651	$4,889
Gross profit	1,976	1,273	1,133	1,148
Income before income taxes	471	262	179	248
Provision for income taxes	85	60	39	69
Net income	384	199	142	177
Basic earnings per share	$ 0.87	$ 0.46	$ 0.33	$ 0.41
Diluted earnings per share	$ 0.85	$ 0.45	$ 0.32	$ 0.41
Shares used in computation of earnings per share:				
Basic	440	432	431	429
Diluted	450	441	440	437

71

AMAZON.COM, INC.

NOTES TO CONSOLIDATED FINANCIAL STATEMENTS—(Continued)

	Year Ended December 31, 2008 (1)			
	Fourth Quarter	**Third Quarter**	**Second Quarter**	**First Quarter**
Net sales (2)	$6,704	$4,264	$4,063	$4,135
Gross profit	1,348	999	967	956
Income before income taxes	302	182	208	207
Provision for income taxes	79	59	46	62
Net income	225	118	158	143
Basic earnings per share	$ 0.52	$ 0.28	$ 0.38	$ 0.34
Diluted earnings per share	$ 0.52	$ 0.27	$ 0.37	$ 0.34
Shares used in computation of earnings per share:				
Basic	428	427	420	417
Diluted	436	436	430	426

(1) The sum of quarterly amounts, including per share amounts, may not equal amounts reported for year-to-date periods. This is due to the effects of rounding and changes in the number of weighted-average shares outstanding for each period.

(2) Our year-over-year revenue growth was 36% for the first three quarters of 2008. For Q4 2008, our quarterly revenue growth rates declined to 18%, driven primarily by decreased consumer demand following disruptions in the global financial markets and changes in foreign exchange rates (excluding the $320 million unfavorable impact from year-over-year changes in foreign exchange rates throughout the fourth quarter, net sales would have grown 24% compared with Q4 2007).

72

Item 9. *Changes in and Disagreements with Accountants On Accounting and Financial Disclosure*

None.

Item 9A. *Controls and Procedures*

Evaluation of Disclosure Controls and Procedures

We carried out an evaluation required by the 1934 Act, under the supervision and with the participation of our principal executive officer and principal financial officer, of the effectiveness of the design and operation of our disclosure controls and procedures, as defined in Rule 13a-15(e) of the 1934 Act, as of December 31, 2009. Based on this evaluation, our principal executive officer and principal financial officer concluded that, as of December 31, 2009, our disclosure controls and procedures were effective to provide reasonable assurance that information required to be disclosed by us in the reports that we file or submit under the 1934 Act is recorded, processed, summarized, and reported within the time periods specified in the SEC's rules and forms and to provide reasonable assurance that such information is accumulated and communicated to our management, including our principal executive officer and principal financial officer, as appropriate to allow timely decisions regarding required disclosures.

Management's Report on Internal Control over Financial Reporting

Management is responsible for establishing and maintaining adequate internal control over financial reporting, as defined in Rule 13a-15(f) of the 1934 Act. Management has assessed the effectiveness of our internal control over financial reporting as of December 31, 2009 based on criteria established in Internal Control—Integrated Framework issued by the Committee of Sponsoring Organizations of the Treadway Commission. As a result of this assessment, management concluded that, as of December 31, 2009, our internal control over financial reporting was effective in providing reasonable assurance regarding the reliability of financial reporting and the preparation of financial statements for external purposes in accordance with generally accepted accounting principles. Ernst & Young has independently assessed the effectiveness of our internal control over financial reporting and its report is included below.

Changes in Internal Control Over Financial Reporting

There were no changes in our internal control over financial reporting during the quarter ended December 31, 2009 that materially affected, or are reasonably likely to materially affect, our internal control over financial reporting.

Limitations on Controls

Our disclosure controls and procedures and internal control over financial reporting are designed to provide reasonable assurance of achieving their objectives as specified above. Management does not expect, however, that our disclosure controls and procedures or our internal control over financial reporting will prevent or detect all error and fraud. Any control system, no matter how well designed and operated, is based upon certain assumptions and can provide only reasonable, not absolute, assurance that its objectives will be met. Further, no evaluation of controls can provide absolute assurance that misstatements due to error or fraud will not occur or that all control issues and instances of fraud, if any, within the Company have been detected.

73

Report of Ernst & Young LLP, Independent Registered Public Accounting Firm

The Board of Directors and Stockholders
Amazon.com, Inc.

We have audited Amazon.com, Inc.'s internal control over financial reporting as of December 31, 2009, based on criteria established in Internal Control—Integrated Framework issued by the Committee of Sponsoring Organizations of the Treadway Commission (the COSO criteria). Amazon.com, Inc.'s management is responsible for maintaining effective internal control over financial reporting and for its assessment of the effectiveness of internal control over financial reporting included in the accompanying Management's Report on Internal Control over Financial Reporting. Our responsibility is to express an opinion on the Company's internal control over financial reporting based on our audit.

We conducted our audit in accordance with the standards of the Public Company Accounting Oversight Board (United States). Those standards require that we plan and perform the audit to obtain reasonable assurance about whether effective internal control over financial reporting was maintained in all material respects. Our audit included obtaining an understanding of internal control over financial reporting, assessing the risk that a material weakness exists, testing and evaluating the design and operating effectiveness of internal control based on the assessed risk, and performing such other procedures as we considered necessary in the circumstances. We believe that our audit provides a reasonable basis for our opinion.

A company's internal control over financial reporting is a process designed to provide reasonable assurance regarding the reliability of financial reporting and the preparation of financial statements for external purposes in accordance with generally accepted accounting principles. A company's internal control over financial reporting includes those policies and procedures that (1) pertain to the maintenance of records that, in reasonable detail, accurately and fairly reflect the transactions and dispositions of the assets of the company; (2) provide reasonable assurance that transactions are recorded as necessary to permit preparation of financial statements in accordance with generally accepted accounting principles, and that receipts and expenditures of the company are being made only in accordance with authorizations of management and directors of the company; and (3) provide reasonable assurance regarding prevention or timely detection of unauthorized acquisition, use, or disposition of the company's assets that could have a material effect on the financial statements.

Because of its inherent limitations, internal control over financial reporting may not prevent or detect misstatements. Also, projections of any evaluation of effectiveness to future periods are subject to the risk that controls may become inadequate because of changes in conditions, or that the degree of compliance with the policies or procedures may deteriorate.

In our opinion, Amazon.com, Inc. maintained, in all material respects, effective internal control over financial reporting as of December 31, 2009, based on the COSO criteria.

We have also audited, in accordance with the standards of the Public Company Accounting Oversight Board (United States), the consolidated balance sheets of Amazon.com, Inc. as of December 31, 2009 and 2008, and the related consolidated statements of operations, stockholders' equity, and cash flows for each of the three years in the period ended December 31, 2009 of Amazon.com, Inc. and our report dated January 28, 2010 expressed an unqualified opinion thereon.

/s/   Ernst & Young LLP

Seattle, Washington
January 28, 2010

74

Item 9B. *Other Information*

None.

PART III

Item 10. *Directors, Executive Officers and Corporate Governance*

Information regarding our Executive Officers required by Item 10 of Part III is set forth in Item 1 of Part I "Business—Executive Officers and Directors." Information required by Item 10 of Part III regarding our Directors and any material changes to the process by which security holders may recommend nominees to the Board of Directors is included in our Proxy Statement relating to our 2010 Annual Meeting of Shareholders, and is incorporated herein by reference. Information relating to our Code of Business Conduct and Ethics and to compliance with Section 16(a) of the 1934 Act is set forth in our Proxy Statement relating to our 2010 Annual Meeting of Shareholders and is incorporated herein by reference. To the extent permissible under Nasdaq rules, we intend to disclose amendments to our Code of Business Conduct and Ethics, as well as waivers of the provisions thereof, on our investor relations website under the heading "Corporate Governance" at www.amazon.com/ir.

Item 11. *Executive Compensation*

Information required by Item 11 of Part III is included in our Proxy Statement relating to our 2010 Annual Meeting of Shareholders and is incorporated herein by reference.

Item 12. *Security Ownership of Certain Beneficial Owners and Management and Related Shareholder Matters*

Information required by Item 12 of Part III is included in our Proxy Statement relating to our 2010 Annual Meeting of Shareholders and is incorporated herein by reference.

Item 13. *Certain Relationships and Related Transactions*

Information required by Item 13 of Part III is included in our Proxy Statement relating to our 2010 Annual Meeting of Shareholders and is incorporated herein by reference.

Item 14. *Principal Accountant Fees and Services*

Information required by Item 14 of Part III is included in our Proxy Statement relating our 2010 Annual Meeting of Shareholders and is incorporated herein by reference.

PART IV

Item 15. *Exhibits, Financial Statement Schedules*

(a) *List of Documents Filed as a Part of This Report:*

(1) *Index to Consolidated Financial Statements:*

Report of Ernst & Young LLP, Independent Registered Public Accounting Firm

Consolidated Statements of Cash Flows for each of the three years ended December 31, 2009

Consolidated Statements of Operations for each of the three years ended December 31, 2009

75

Consolidated Balance Sheets as of December 31, 2009 and 2008

Consolidated Statements of Stockholders' Equity for each of the three years ended December 31, 2009

Notes to Consolidated Financial Statements

Report of Ernst & Young LLP, Independent Registered Public Accounting Firm

(2) *Index to Exhibits*

See exhibits listed under the Exhibit Index below.

SIGNATURES

Pursuant to the requirements of Section 13 or 15(d) of the Securities Exchange Act of 1934, the registrant has duly caused this Report to be signed on its behalf by the undersigned, thereunto duly authorized, as of January 28, 2010.

AMAZON.COM, INC.

By: _____ /S/   JEFFREY P. BEZOS_____

Jeffrey P. Bezos
President, Chief Executive Officer
and Chairman of the Board

Pursuant to the requirements of the Securities Exchange Act of 1934, this Report has been signed below by the following persons on behalf of the registrant and in the capacities indicated as of January 28, 2010.

Signature	Title
/S/ JEFFREY P. BEZOS **Jeffrey P. Bezos**	Chairman of the Board, President and Chief Executive Officer (Principal Executive Officer)
/S/ THOMAS J. SZKUTAK **Thomas J. Szkutak**	Senior Vice President and Chief Financial Officer (Principal Financial Officer)
/S/ SHELLEY REYNOLDS **Shelley Reynolds**	Vice President, Worldwide Controller (Principal Accounting Officer)
/S/ TOM A. ALBERG **Tom A. Alberg**	Director
/S/ JOHN SEELY BROWN **John Seely Brown**	Director
/S/ L. JOHN DOERR **L. John Doerr**	Director
/S/ WILLIAM B. GORDON **William B. Gordon**	Director
/S/ ALAIN MONIÉ **Alain Monié**	Director
/S/ THOMAS O. RYDER **Thomas O. Ryder**	Director
/S/ PATRICIA Q. STONESIFER **Patricia Q. Stonesifer**	Director

77

Glindex

A Combined Glossary/Subject Index

A

Accelerated Depreciation Method. A depreciation method that writes off more of the asset's cost near the start of its useful life than the straight-line method does. 462, 479

Account. The detailed record of all the changes that have occurred in a particular asset, liability, or owner's equity (stockholders' equity) during a period. The basic summary device of accounting. 63, 98
  normal balance of 72
  opening the 69
Account form 212
Account numbers 65

Account Payable. A liability backed by the general reputation and credit standing of the debtor. 15, 36

Account Receivable. The right to receive cash in the future from customers to whom the business has sold goods or for whom the business has performed services. 15, 36

Accounting, and the business environment 1
  accounting vocabulary 2, 36–37
  apply your knowledge
    communication activity 61
    decision cases 58–59
    ethical issues 59
    financial statement case 60
    fraud case 60
    team projects 60–61
  assess your progress
    exercises 39–46, 56
    practice set, 57
    problems 47–55, 56
  business organizations, types of 5–7
  concepts and principles 9–11
  destination: student success 37
  ethics in 5
  governing organizations 4–5
  major business decisions, guidelines for 25
  profession of 4–5
  quick check 38–39
  standards of professional conduct 5
  summary problem 26–27
  transactions in 13–18
    analysis (demo doc) 28–35
    evaluating, user perspective of 18–22
  users of accounting information 2–3

Accounting. The information system that measures business activities, processes that information into reports, and communicates the results to decision makers. 2, 36
  accrual vs. cash-basis 131–32
  financial 2
  managerial 3
  separating from operations 359
Accounting conservatism 313

Accounting Cycle. Process by which companies produce their financial statements for a specific period. 199, 228
  of merchandiser 276
Accounting cycle, completing 199
  accounting ratios 213–214

accounting vocabulary 228
accounting worksheet 200–202
adjusting entries, recording 204–207
apply your knowledge
  communication activity 253
  decision case 251
  ethical issue 251–252
  financial statement case 252
  fraud case 252
  team project 252–253
assess your progress
  exercises 230–238, 249
  practice set 250
  problems 239–249, 250
assets and liabilities, classifying 210–213
balance sheet
  classified 211–212
  forms 212–213
closing the accounts 207–209
decision guidelines 215
demo doc 220–227
destination: student success 228–229
financial statements, preparing 204
post-closing trial balance 210
quick check 229–230
summary problems 202–203, 216–219
Accounting data
  flow of 73

Accounting Equation. The basic tool of accounting, measuring the resources of the business and the claims to those resources: Assets = Liabilities + Equity. 11–13, 36, 63
  assets and liabilities 11
  owner's equity 12
  rules of debit and credit and 68, 71
  transaction analysis using (demo doc) 28–35
Accounting period 132–133
Accounting process
  decision guidelines 152
Accounting profession 4–5
Accounting ratios 213–214
  current ratio 214
  debt ratio 214
Accounting records
  accuracy of 356
Accounting worksheet 200–202
Accounts
  permanent 207
  reasons for adjusting 135–136
  temporary 207, 208
Accounts payable 64, 497
Accounts receivable 63

Accounts Receivable Turnover Ratio. A ratio that measures the number of times the company sells and collects the average receivables balance in a year. To compute accounts receivable turnover, divide net credit sales by average net accounts receivable. 425, 428, 736–737, 749

Accrual. The cash payment occurs after an expense is recorded or the cash is received after the revenue is earned. 136, 162

Accrual-Basis Accounting. Accounting that records revenues when earned and expenses when incurred. 131, 166, 1017
  vs. cash-basis accounting 131–32
  ethical issues in 151

Accrued Expense. An expense that the business has incurred but not yet paid. 136, 140–142, 166
Accrued expenses (accrued liabilities) 499

Accrued Liability. A liability for which the business knows the amount owed but the bill has not been paid. 64, 98

Accrued Revenue. A revenue that has been earned but for which the cash has not been collected yet. 142–143, 166

Accumulated Depreciation. The sum of all depreciation expense recorded to date for an asset. 139, 166

Acid-Test Ratio. Ratio of the sum of cash plus short-term investments plus net current receivables to total current liabilities. Tells whether the entity could pay all its current liabilities if they came due immediately. Also called the quick ratio. 424, 428, 734–735

Acquisitions
  computing 670–671

Activity-Based Costing (ABC). Focuses on activities as the fundamental cost objects. The costs of those activities become the building blocks for allocating the costs of products and services. 882, 902
  accounting vocabulary 902
  activity-based management, using ABC
    for decision making 886–890
    for cost cutting 887–890
    for pricing and product mix decisions 886–887
  apply your knowledge
    communication activity, 923
    decision cases 919–920
    ethical issue 920
    fraud case 920–921
    team project 921–922
  assess your progress
    exercises 904–913, 918
    problems 913–918, 919–920
  decision guidelines 891
  destination: student success 902
  developing system of 883
  refining cost systems 881–886
  quick check 903–904
  summary problems 892–893
  vs. traditional costing systems 883–886

Activity-Based Management (ABM). Using activity-based cost information to make decisions that increase profits while satisfying customers' needs. 886, 902
  cost cutting 887–890
  pricing and product mix decisions 886–887

Additional Paid-In Capital. The paid-in capital in excess of par plus other accounts combined for reporting on the

Mixed Costs. Costs that have both variable and fixed components. 927, 946

Mortgage payable. Long-term debts that are backed with a security interest in specific property. The mortgage will state that the borrower promises to transfer the legal title to specific assets if the mortgage isn't paid on schedule. 532–534, 550

Multi-Step Income Statement. Format that contains subtotals to highlight significant relationships. In addition to net income, it reports gross profit and operating income. 273, 281

Mutual Agency. The ability of partners in a partnership to commit other partners and the business to a contract. 6, 37

N

Natural Resources. Plant assets that come from the earth. Natural resources are like inventories in the ground (oil) or on top of the ground (timber). 453, 472, 479
accounting for 472

Net Book Value. Original cost of the asset less total accumulated depreciation taken on the asset. 466, 479, 1017

Net cash
  on statement of cash flows 706
Net cash inflows 1012, 1013–1015, 1026–1027
Net cash outflows 1012

Net Income. Excess of total revenues over total expenses. Also called net earnings or net profit. 12, 21, 23, 24, 37, 202
on statement of cash flows 666

Net Loss. Excess of total expenses over total revenues. 12, 21, 23, 37, 202

Net (Take-Home) Pay. Gross pay minus all deductions. The amount of compensation that the employee actually takes home. 506, 515

Net Present Value (NPV). The net *difference* between the present value of the investment's net cash inflows and the investment's cost (cash outflows). 1011, 1026–1030, 1037
of project with residual value 1030
with equal periodic net cash inflows 1027–1028
with unequal periodic net cash inflows 1028

Net Purchases. Purchases less purchase discounts and purchase returns and allowances. 281, 304

Net Realizable Value. Net value that a company expects to collect from its receivables. (Accounts receivable − Allowance for uncollectable accounts) 409, 410, 428

Net Sales Revenue. Sales revenue less sales discounts and sales returns and allowances. 265, 281

New-product development time 1158

No Par Stock. No arbitrary amount (par) is assigned by a company to a share of its stock. 585, 603
issuing 587–588

Nominal accounts. The revenue and expense accounts that relate to a particular accounting period and are closed at the end of that period. For a company, the Drawing account is also temporary. Also called temporary accounts. 207, 228

Nominal rate, 536

Noncash activities
  on statement of cash flows 674–675
Noncumulative preferred stock 595–596
Non-like property exchanges 468, 470

Non-Monetary Exchange. Trading an asset for another asset that has similar functionality. The asset received is valued at either 1) fair value of the asset given up or 2) fair value of the asset received plus/minus cash received/paid. Also called a like-kind exchange. 468, 479

Nonsufficient Funds (NSF) Check. A "hot" check; one for which the maker's bank account has insufficient money to pay the check. 365, 381

Normal Balance. The balance that appears on the side of an account—debit or credit—where we record increases. 72, 98

Note Receivable. A written promise for future collection of cash. 64, 98

Note Term. The period of time during which interest is computed. It extends from the original date of the note to the maturity date. Also called the interest period, or simply time period. 418, 428

Notes Payable. Represents debts the business owes because it signed promissory notes to borrow money or to purchase something. 64, 98
computing, on statement of cash flows 671–672

Not-for-profit. Organization that has been approved by the Internal Revenue Service to operate for a religious, charitable, or educational purpose. 6–7, 37

Number of Days in Inventory. Ratio that measures the average number of days that inventory is held by a company. 275, 281
Number of units produced per hour 1158

O

OASDI tax 506

Obsolete. An asset is considered obsolete when a newer asset can perform the job more efficiently than the old. 459, 479
Online banking 368
Opening the account 69

Operating Activities. Activities that create revenue or expense in the entity's major line of business; a section of the statement of cash flows. 663, 681
formats for 664
on statement of cash flows 664, 666–669, 703–704

Operating Budget. Set of budgets that project sales revenue, cost of goods sold, and operating expenses, leading to the budgeted income statement that projects operating income for the period. 1056, 1084
data for 1056–1058
preparing 1058–1060
  inventory, purchases, and cost of goods sold budget 1058–1059
  operating expenses budget 1059
  sales budget 1058

Operating Cycle. Time span during which cash is paid for goods and services, which are then sold to customers from whom the business collects cash. 211, 228
of merchandising business 257

Operating Expenses. Expenses, other than cost of goods sold, that are incurred in the entity's major line of business. Examples include rent, depreciation, salaries, wages, utilities, and supplies expense. 262, 271, 281
Operating expenses budget 1059

Operating Income. Gross profit minus operating expenses. Also called income from operations. 271, 281, 1016
Operational efficiency 356

Opportunity Cost. The benefit forgone by not choosing an alternative course of action. 984, 991
Optional deductions, 506

Ordinary Repairs. Repair work that is debited to an expense account. 457, 479

Other Revenue and Expense. Revenue or expense that is outside the normal day-to-day operations of a business, such as a gain or loss on the sale of plant assets. 271, 281

Outsourcing. The decision to buy or subcontract a component product or service rather than produce it in-house. 814, 964, 991
decisions on 982–987

Outstanding Checks. A check issued by the company and recorded on its books but not yet paid by its bank. 365, 381
Outstanding shares 629

Outstanding Stock. Issued stock in the hands of stockholders. 582, 603

Overallocated (Manufacturing) Overhead. Occurs when the manufacturing overhead allocated to Work in process inventory is more than the amount of manufacturing overhead costs actually incurred. 827, 827
Overhead
  manufacturing 784–789
Overhead Flexible Budget Variance. 1122
Overhead production volume variance 1122
Overtime 505